Members of the Editorial Board for the
75th Anniversary Volume

Speech Communication: Essays to Commemorate the 75th Anniversary of The Speech Communication Association

EDITED BY GERALD M. PHILLIPS AND JULIA T. WOOD

A SPEECH COMMUNICATION ASSOCIATION SPONSORED VOLUME

Southern Illinois University Press
Carbondale and Edwardsville

Library of Congress Cataloging-in-Publication Data

Speech communication : essays to commemorate the 75th anniversary of
    The Speech Communication Association / edited by Gerald M. Phillips
    and Julia T. Wood
        p.   cm.
        "A Speech Communication Association sponsored volume."
        Includes bibliographies.
            1. Oral communication.   2. Speech Communication Association.
    I. Phillips, Gerald M.   II. Wood, Julia T.   III. Speech
    Communication Association.
    P95.S628   1989
    001.54'2—dc19   89-5875
    ISBN 0-8093-1520-3   CIP

The paper used in this publication meets the minimum requirements of
American National Standard for Information Sciences
—Permanence of Paper for Printed Library Materials, ANSI Z39.48-1984. ♾

Contents

Preface

In 1914, seventeen speech teachers formed The National Association of Academic Teachers of Public Speaking to provide academic identity and to promote professional development of members and the discipline. To commemorate its seventy-fifth anniversary, the association authorized this volume of original essays to recognize the achievements of scholarship and to chart an agenda for future inquiry.

In the seven and one-half decades since its founding, the association has evolved in important ways. Notably, the organization is currently called The Speech Communication Association, reflecting enlarged awareness of the complexity and constituents of the communication process. Even as we send this book to press, the membership is facing a vote on another name change that would recognize further expansion of the conceptual boundaries of the field.

Another significant change in the organization has been its growth. No longer a small cadre of teachers of public speaking, the association in 1989 has 7,000 members, whose scholarly and pedagogical interests span the range of human symbolic activities. The increase in membership indicates that contemporary society sufficiently values the study of communication to support more numerous appointments of its scholars in academe as well as a range of communication consultants and trainers in the business sector.

As the discipline has matured, its domain has extended beyond formal speeches to include a broad array of human symbolic activities. While maintaining an abiding interest in public speaking, those engaged in this discipline now focus their professional activities on an expansive set of communication behaviors and relationships, including race and class influences on interaction, nonverbal behavior, linkages between gender and communication, interpersonal interaction, family dynamics, organizational processes, intercultural communication, mass communication, and group discussion as well as on a variety of topics involved in the study of human symbolic activity, such as the rhetoric of protest, freedom of speech, analyses of discursive and nondiscursive symbolic forms, cultural criticism, and interpretive analyses of literature.

vii

It is impressive that in the short span of seventy-five years the field has expanded so significantly in size and intellectual scope and has won recognition and support from both the academic community and the culture in general. The accomplishments that led to this intellectual and demographic growth provided the impetus for this volume of essays.

Purpose of the Volume

Over the years, several scholars have recorded the history and current status of the field: Kibler and Barker (1969), Bitzer and Black (1971), Arnold and Bowers (1984), and Benson (1985). Our goal was not to duplicate these achievements. Instead, we wanted to commemorate the seventy-fifth anniversary of this association with a set of essays that both reflects prior scholarship and redirects the intellectual engagements of the field.

Consisting of competitively selected, original essays, this volume describes contemporary research in the field of speech communication and identifies prospects and challenges for future scholarship. It is not intended to provide a comprehensive survey of the numerous areas currently comprising speech communication. Rather, its goals are to provide a historical and intellectual view of the field and to offer extended explorations of selected aspects of it. As editors, we encouraged expression of new and sometimes controversial ideas about the nature of scholarship. We aimed to provoke the thinking of authors and readers beyond what are and have been the emphases and assumptions characterizing our scholarship.

The authors have engaged in serious reflection about what we currently know, believe, and still need to understand about human symbolic activities. Comprising the book are two chapters that provide broad perspective on the field as a whole and ten that focus on specific topics. Leading off is Professor Dennis Gouran's essay, "Speech Communication after Seventy-five Years: Issues and Prospects." Marking out his purpose as identification of the kinds of questions and answers that have emanated from research conducted by many scholars, Professor Gouran offers an insightful summary of the achievements of scholarship in this field and issues a challenge for future work. In surveying the broad terrain of the discipline, he also provides an overview of many of the areas and issues addressed in detail in chapters that follow.

Following Professor Gouran's foundational essay are ten chapters, each of which focuses on scholarship within a defined area. We will not abstract those here, but we do call readers' attention to the themes that unify the ten chapters. Four questions fundamental to understanding the nature of scholarship and its progress were posed to all authors, and their chapters respond to these:

1. What do we currently know? In addressing this question, chapter authors summarize what they consider proven knowledge or established facts about their topics. In addition to tacitly defining areas, these expositions provide a useful gauge of scholarly progress in particular areas.

2. What do we currently believe? In responding to this question, authors distinguish between that which has been demonstrated to be true by some acceptable contemporary standards of proof and that which we act *as if* is true. All scholars hold assumptions about the nature of what they study and how they study it; inevitably these assumptions bias how scholars define investigatory stances, frame the foci of study, pursue research, and interpret and make sense of the results.

There is, of course, nothing new in noting the inevitable influence of assumptions upon the research process, and certainly there is nothing wrong with their existence and operation. Yet, if unrecognized or unexplicated, assumptions may become confused with demonstrated knowledge. Thus, each chapter attempts to articulate the assumptions, beliefs, and articles of faith that characterize research in defined areas. In doing this, the authors raise the visibility of often unacknowledged assumptions that guide scholarship, thereby encouraging reflection on them and, when appropriate, challenge and reformulation.

3. What are the controversies in the area? Perhaps as certain as death and taxes is disagreement among scholars. Within any area of study there are controversies about issues ranging from definition of what is studied to methods for research. We asked chapter authors to examine their areas and identify the most important controversies, i.e., those issues about which scholars in an area argue. In discussing these, the authors provide insightful accounts of what is contested and the arguments used to support differing positions. In some cases, authors are able to suggest appropriate resolutions of given controversies by appeal to the data supporting a particular position. More often, however, a sound resolution cannot be crafted from existing knowledge. Thus, most authors restrict themselves to identifying disagreements, the reasons undergirding alternative positions, and the implications of the controversy for progress in scholarship. By highlighting significant disagreements and summarizing arguments surrounding them, these chapters offer provocative insights into the intellectual dynamics of scholarship; simultaneously, they invigorate and push forward the discipline by furthering the processes of focused reflection and debate about issues upon which the execution of future research hinges.

4. *What are the urgent questions for scholarship?* Finally, each chapter recommends priorities for future research. Drawing upon what is known, believed, and contested, authors identify what they consider the most pressing issues affecting the progress of scholarship in their areas. Their discussions of this topic reveal serious, creative thought, and we think they will provoke the same in readers.

Although each chapter attends to these four questions, each does so in its own way. We did not restrict authors to linear and discrete discussion of the issues, and they have adopted varied approaches. Using the questions as organizing rubrics for their essays, some authors have written four-section chapters that address them sequentially. Other authors have incorporated the four questions within frameworks chosen to structure their essays. Some authors address each question with a concentrated discussion of it, while others adopt a cyclical approach, in which they return repeatedly to each question, extending prior discussion and weaving that into the overall strands of argument advanced in their essays. Readers will find each of the ten chapters, diversity in form notwithstanding, offers insights about what we know, believe, contest, and need to learn.

Concluding the volume is an essay by Professor Emeritus Carroll C. Arnold. Titled "What Doth the Future Hold?" this chapter begins by reviewing the field's history, noting markers of progress in its emergence as an intellectually mature area of study. The markers he highlights include the qualitative and quantitative record of scholarship, our status and activity in interdisciplinary and international circles, and the kinds of questions we entertain. Upon this background, Professor Arnold then identifies a set of challenges that grow out of increasing disenchantment with linear, mechanical conceptions of human communication, positivism as a philosophy of science, and restrictive definitions of contexts and content of scholarship. He urges members of the discipline to embrace the task of reconceptualizing the communication process in ways responsive to the age in which we live and the concerns that characterize it.

Elaborating this recommendation, Professor Arnold discusses particular issues, problems, and goals for future scholarship.

The authors represented in this volume took seriously the challenges posed by Professors Gouran and Arnold and reinforced by our editorial policies. As editors, we asked authors to go beyond standard treatments of the state of the art and to consider alternatives to what is and has been. We encouraged them not to be bound by conventional frames that have guided research in their areas and, instead, to explore new definitions and directions. The result is a series of essays that is provocative and productive.

Readers will note that the contributors are not unified in their perspectives on scholarship. Rather, they represent divergent views on the nature and goals of research and fundamental differences in theoretical and methodological assumptions. Neither they as authors nor we as editors attempt to reconcile these differing points of view. Instead, we invite readers to evaluate for themselves competing claims, methodological stances, theoretical allegiances, and interpretive practices represented in the chapters that follow. The result, we hope, will be a broadened awareness of possibilities in scholarship and a reinvigoration of discussion about what we seek to know and how we might best conduct our inquiry.

We select three examples to illustrate the provocative and original thinking characteristic of this volume. "Research in Interpretation and Performance Studies," by Mary Strine, Beverly Long, and Mary Frances HopKins, argues that performance is an essentially contested concept. After dislodging the concept from its historical meanings, they proceed to explore the conceptual domain opened by two particular views of performance; they then bring into the foreground the researcher's stance as a constitutive feature of scholarship. In a similar spirit, Sonja Foss problematizes the nature of discourse and criticism of it, a position from which she makes visible the established conceptual framework that informs criticism and promotes thoughtful debate about how alternative understandings of criticism might affect its practice. In a chapter devoted to methodological concerns, H. Lloyd Goodall proposes ethnographic study as an exciting frontier open to communication research. His essay elaborates new understandings of research topics, participants, and presentations that emanate from the practice of ethnography.

These three examples exemplify the heuristic tone of the chapters comprising the volume. Not only providing solid perspective on scholarship as it is and has been, these essays also stake out original positions and trace the implications of those stances for the field's future. Thus, the authors model what they advocate: original thought about the nature and means by which we pursue knowledge.

The Editorial Process and Participants

This volume culminates a year-long process involving a number of individuals and institutions. The project would never have commenced without the active support of the Publication Board of The Speech Communication Association. James Chesbro (Chair), Robert Friedman, and Mary Strine comprised the 1988 Board that authorized the publication of this volume and the funding to defray editorial expenses. The Speech Communication Association provided support and information to us. Also integral to the book's development were the Departments of Speech Communication at the University of North Carolina and The Pennsylvania State University. Both departments supported the editors' involvement in this project and provided essential secretarial assistance. The final institution to which this volume is indebted is the Southern Illinois University Press. From our initial proposal of this project through the final stages of production, we benefitted from the advice and support of Kenney Withers, Director, and from the entire staff, who were consistently helpful, encouraging, and patient.

A number of individuals also made this volume possible. Special thanks for careful, efficient supervision of the logistics of editing are due to Rita Munchinski, Administrative Assistant for the Department of Speech Communication at The Pennsylvania State University. Of course, the authors themselves made major and particularly visible contributions. The high quality of their chapters and the volume as a whole speak for themselves. In addition, they and we owe a debt to people whose contributions are not so visible: the members of the editorial board, whose names appear at the front of this publication. Representing all areas of the discipline, board members provided multiple readings of chapter drafts and offered detailed, consistently thoughtful critiques and recommendations to authors. From our desks we have seen the changes wrought by their efforts as chapters progressed from sometimes foggy and underdeveloped initial form to carefully conceived and argued final versions. The consulting editors' generosity with their time and talents substantially enhanced the quality of this volume.

If these twelve essays are as provocative for readers as they were for us as editors, then the volume will serve a valuable purpose. We hope it stimulates reflection, redirection, and rededication to our individual and collective goals as members of an intellectual community.

It was exciting for us to work with this group of authors who represent the past, present and future of the field. Their work should inform and inspire a generation of scholars to carry us productively to our centennial year.

References

Arnold, C. C., & Bowers, J. W. (Eds.). 1984. Handbook of rhetorical and communication theory. Boston: Allyn & Bacon.

Benson, T. W. (Ed.). 1985. Speech communication in the twentieth century. Carbondale, Il: Southern Illinois University Press.

Bitzer, L. F., & Black, E. (Eds.). 1971. The prospect of rhetoric. Englewood Cliffs, NJ: Prentice Hall.

Kibler, R. J., & Barker, L. L. (Eds.). 1969. Conceptual frontiers in speech-communication. New York: The Speech Association of America.

*Speech Communication:
Essays to Commemorate the
75th Anniversary
of The Speech Communication
Association*

Introduction:
Speech Communication after Seventy-Five Years, Issues and Prospects

DENNIS S. GOURAN

In the seventy-five years since the National Association of Academic Teachers of Public Speaking was established, the study of human communication has been witness to enormous change. What began as a rather limited set of concerns dealing with the improvement of oral communication in the public realm has expanded to include virtually every social context in which communicative behavior occurs. Although many of those investigating communication do so with a view toward producing information to help people become more effective in their interactions with others, the perfection of skills is far less central to the scholarly interest in communication than it once was. Of much greater significance are the discovery and application of principles that help us to understand and account for the ways in which communication functions, or fails to, in its many and varied contexts.

It is not the purpose of this essay, however, to chronicle the study of speech communication as it has evolved since the founding of the professional association we celebrate.[1] Rather, its purpose is to identify

---

1. This type of exploration has been made by several of the contributors to Thomas W. Benson's *Speech Communication in the 20th Century* (1985); the essays by Bochner and Eisenberg, Cohen, and Pearce provide especially good historical overviews. In addition, the essays in Carroll C. Arnold and John W. Bowers's *Handbook of Rhetorical and Communication Theory* (1984) each in one way or another presents information that illuminates the historical evolution of communication inquiry as it has developed in this century. Excellent reviews of the historical perspectives that have been evident in communication related scholarship appear in Ernest G. Bormann's *Communication Theory* (1980) and B. Aubrey Fisher's *Perspectives on Human Communication* (1978).

the sorts of questions that have grown out of efforts to illuminate the processes in which human beings use speech and related forms of expression to relate themselves to others in different social situations. In pursuing that purpose, this chapter will provide an overview of many of the issues addressed in detail by other contributors to this volume.

These issues have to do with various facets of communicative acts, including the selection of symbols that form the messages communicators exchange, the characteristics of those messages, the qualities of interactants that affect the production and reception of messages, the channels through which they are transmitted, and the social contexts in which symbolic exchanges occur. In addition, the chapter introduces many of the issues related to the processes of inquiry evident in scholars' attempts to illuminate our understanding of the nature of human communication, its functions, and its consequences. Finally, the chapter identifies some of the lacunae in current knowledge that offer significant opportunities for future scholarship.

The tone of the chapter is decidedly reflective and tentative. Its intention is to provoke questions about the scholarly study of human communication, and how well it is being done, not to provide definitive judgments about what should be the focus of inquiry or to resolve the attendant methodological and meta-critical issues. If the objectives are achieved, readers should gain a perspective that contributes to their understanding of the remaining chapters and their ability to interpret ongoing scholarship in the field of communication.

Despite its presence in the curriculum of many educational institutions, as an academic field speech communication remains something of an enigma to those not directly associated with it. To some, the name "speech communication" suggests training in the mechanics of speech making, and, perhaps more narrowly, training in certain aspects of the delivery of speeches. Puzzlement often accompanies the discovery that those who teach courses in the area also do research or that a department may offer instruction in such seemingly diverse areas as rhetorical theory; the history and criticism of public address; the oral interpretation of literature; interpersonal, group, and organizational communication; speech pathology and audiology; mass media; cross-cultural studies; and theatre. Upon asking what study in such areas entails, moreover, the inquirer not infrequently is apt to offer an observation about a particular one like, "I thought that's what they do in Business Administration," "How is that different from Philosophy?", "Oh, you mean the kind of thing they are doing in Psychology," or, "But what does that have to do with giving speeches?"

Even those identified with the field are far from consensus about the appropriate domain in which instruction and scholarly inquiry should occur (Gouran, 1979) and, in fact, have been almost from the beginning (Cohen, 1985). The organization of academic departments never seems settled or consistent across educational institutions, and new ways of labeling them continue to surface. Departments emphasizing the study of oral communication are variously called Speech Communication, Speech, Communication, Communication Studies, Rhetoric and Communication Studies, Speech and Theatre, Communication Arts, Communication Arts and Sciences, Speech and Communication Disorders, and the like. In some instances, the name may reflect what a department's faculty considers to be only loosely connected areas of interest. Such departments are often destined for division into separate academic units. In other instances, a department's label may be the result of some administratively created merger that reflects political and economic considerations of the institution.

The history of expansion, splintering, and reorganization of academic departments occurring over the life of what we now call the Speech Communication Association complicates efforts to say very precisely what the field it represents is or what are its main divisions of emphasis. For this reason, I have resisted the temptation that a volume of this type invited, namely, to define speech communication as a particular type of discipline having clearly aligned areas of specialty and relatively fixed boundaries. Its historical fluidity and continually evolving interests militate against one's adequately capturing the field in this way. In addition, such attempts at definition frequently elicit strong disagreements. These result partially from the fact that individuals tend to see disciplines in terms of how they are represented within the organizational structure of the academic institutions with which they happen to be associated or aspire to be like.

More useful to developing a perspective on the body of activity that educational conventions often require us to label is an examination of the matters that scholars concerned with communication must address if scholarly inquiry is to advance knowledge and improve our understanding of human interaction. Such matters are of both a substantive and meta-critical nature and will be reviewed shortly.

This is a book about issues that derive from the work of individuals who have interests that in one way or another relate to processes involving

*symbolic representations of people's cognitive activities and related affective states
and the social consequences of such representations.* (The activities and states
that give rise to symbolic representation are often thought of in such
terms as ideas, impressions, recollections, feelings, reactions, and the
like.) Participants attending a 1968 conference on the future of research
in speech communication described these interests as having to do with
"th ways in which messages link participants during interaction" (Kibler
& Barker, 1969, p. 33). Conferees at yet another important meeting of
similar intent suggested as common to the scholarly interest in communication "any human transaction in which symbols and/or systems influence
attitudes, values, beliefs, and actions" (Bitzer & Black, 1971, p. 214).
Although interest in symbolic processes predates these specific statements, the focus they represent does much to clarify how individuals
investigating various aspects of communication in different social contexts, and reflecting diverse intellectual traditions, can be viewed as
contributing to a larger and transcendent set of concerns.

   A focus on symbolic representations of communicators' cognitive
activities and related affective states and their social consequences, at first
glance, may appear to be narrow and unduly restrictive. Upon more
careful reflection, however, one realizes how broad a range of phenomena
it encompasses. To comprehend the processes in which individuals symbolically relate themselves to one another requires study of innumerable
factors and the complex ways in which they collectively shape the consequences of communicative acts. At a general level, these factors include
the selection and production of symbols, the properties of symbols and
their arrangement, the characteristics of the symbol producer, the attributes of those exposed to them, the media involved in the transmission
of symbols, and the environments or contexts in which symbolic exchanges take place.

   Although we are far from understanding how all of these factors
interrelate, scholarly inquiry has provided indications about many specific
connections and has opened numerous avenues for future inquiry. Such
claims as have been advanced, of course, are open to question and
must be judged within the limitations of the methods of investigation
employed and the world views and scholarly traditions they reflect.[2] Still,

_____

   2. Littlejohn (1989) uses the terms "World View I" and "World View II"
to characterize perspectives reflected in the assumptions and traditions underlying social scientific and humanistic inquiry.

there is an accumulated body of published scholarship that gives insight into the nature of human communication. The knowledge that this scholarship represents provides a basis for responding to two sets of questions. The first deals with the substance of inquiry into communication and the social consequences of symbolic processes. The specific substantive questions of interest are as follows:

1. What factors affect the selection and production of the symbols that comprise communicative acts?
2. How do the properties of symbols and their arrangement in communicative acts contribute to the ways in which they are understood, interpreted, and acted upon?
3. How do the characteristics of message producers affect the perception and interpretation of symbolic behavior?
4. How do characteristics of message recipients influence responses to symbolic behavior?
5. What roles do media play in the process of symbolic exchange?
6. In what ways do the social contexts in which symbolic exchanges occur contribute to the production and reception of communicative acts?

Answers to substantive questions of the kind mentioned above are not likely to gain acceptance simply because we are capable of generating them. Knowledge claims vary in respect to the confidence they both command and deserve. Hence, an equally important set of issues has to do with the "conduct of inquiry"—to use Kaplan's (1964) well-known phrase. The relevant questions include:

1. Have the means of inquiry employed in exploring questions about the processes in which symbolic exchanges occur been appropriate to support the types of claims advanced?
2. What are the assumptions and limitations of the methodological perspectives and modes of inquiry employed?
3. Which methods of inquiry have been most fruitful in producing claims about symbolic representations of cognitive activities and related affective states and their social consequences?
4. What are the pragmatic values of the knowledge derived from scholarly inquiry?
5. What can be done to produce more reliable and useful knowledge about human communication?

It is not my intention to try to answer these questions. Instead, I offer them as a general framework within which the material covered in this book can be explored. None of the individual contributors attempts to answer all of the questions posed. Specialization by its very nature restricts the aspects of a complex phenomenon like communication to which scholarly attention is directed. Neither do the contributors address the questions pertinent to their particular concerns exactly as phrased. This would create too artificial an organizational structure for dealing with substantive and meta-critical issues as they manifest themselves in given areas of study. Nevertheless, when taken in their entirety, the essays comprising this volume provide a basis for understanding what existing scholarship permits us to say about the ways in which symbol users relate themselves to one another and about the consequences of acts involved, as well as how much remains to be determined before the full complexity of human interaction will be illuminated. The remainder of this chapter reflects an attempt to establish the importance of the substantive and meta-critical issues raised and how they may influence future inquiry.

Substantive Issues

What Factors Influence the Selection and Production of the Symbols that Comprise Communicative Acts?

The term *communication* usually conjures up the notion of a message when it is used in ordinary conversation. Messages in this frame of reference are what we communicate. But what is a message? A message is a pattern of thought, configuration of ideas, or other response to internal conditions about which individuals express themselves. The expression is manifest in the symbol or combination of symbols one employs in trying to convey something about the arousing condition to others or in some other sense influence their own internal states. Symbols, then, are a special class of signs by which individuals are purposefully, but with varying degrees of conscious awareness, able to reveal certain aspects of themselves to others (e.g., Langer, 1942; Ogden & Richards, 1923). On that much, there appears to be reasonable agreement, although the specific nature of the inner conditions to which symbols refer has long been a matter of contention.[3]

Since symbols are by definition purposeful representations—that is, they arbitrarily designate something else—some sort of selection mechanism is logically implicit in our view of what it means to engage in a communicative act. The common referents for symbols are thoughts, feelings, memories, cognitions, and other such categories of knowledge the individual possesses and about which he or she has occasion to make revelations to others. Whether or not one accepts these categories, or however else he or she chooses to characterize the cognitive activities and affective states to which symbols refer, it seems clear that arousal of them usually takes some form of expression.

The form of expression involves both selection and production and, consequently, has psychological and physical dimensions. In communication, one chooses with varying degrees of consciousness how to represent an inner state and then physically produces the corresponding symbols and sequences of symbols intended to represent it. Knowledge of how the symbolic sequences we often call messages are selected and produced is crucial to understanding the process of communication in general as well as specific instances of it. At the most fundamental level, success in communication requires an ability on the part of the symbol producer to choose appropriate ways of representing that which he or she wishes others to know, feel, do, or in some way experience. The generation of communicative acts at this level of mental functioning is what rhetoricians typically refer to as *invention.*

The decisional process involved is vitally important, for it facilitates what Pearce (1976) has referred to as "the coordinated management of meaning." It entails not only determining the options available to the symbol producer but some sense of the constraints that are imposed by the receptive capacities, experiences, and abilities of the person or persons with whom one seeks to communicate—a focus well developed in Hart and Burks's (1972) concept of "rhetorical sensitivity." The other party or parties in a symbolic exchange cannot make accurate inferences if the symbol producer represents his or her inner states by means that have no reference in the experience of the other(s). In common parlance, the

---

3. Such terms imply "things" that have material existence. They represent so-called "mental contents." Some scholars prefer to think of inner experiences as neurological and physiological states.

potential for communication breakdown is heightened when symbols and symbolic sequences are alien to the target of communication and idiosyncratic to the producer. The documentation in many computer user manuals written by computer specialists, for instance, appears to assume a knowledge of computer technology far beyond what the average consumer, to whom the material is directed, could reasonably be expected to have accumulated. As a consequence, a novice often finds it necessary to seek the assistance of an experienced user in order to determine what he or she is supposed to do to operate the hardware (machinery) and use the software (programs). As another illustration, a person trying to create public concern about the problem of homelessness is likely to encounter difficulty with those for whom deprivation is not grounded in their own social experience.

Symbols may also be alien because of the producer's lack of familiarity with the codes unique to a given speech community or an inability to produce them in a recognizable form. Whatever the cause, the effect is likely to be a diminished prospect for achieving one's communicative objectives. To the extent that scholarly inquiry improves our understanding of the ways in which symbols are selected and produced for purposeful interaction, we can better account for the frequent lack of success in symbolic exchanges and the lack of correspondence in the meanings the agents involved assign to the symbols employed.

How Do the Properties of Symbols and Their Arrangement in Communicative Acts Contribute to the Ways in Which They Are Understood, Interpreted, and Acted Upon?

As important as the selection and production of symbols are as determinants of responses, these factors only partially explain the consequences of communicative acts. The properties of the symbols themselves are an additional source of influence. As Gregg (1984) points out, symbols induce action and various forms of cognitive activities. Once produced, they have a physical existence and vary in the same respects as other stimuli in a perceptual field. As is the case with physical objects in general, symbols can be misperceived as a result of their intensity, clarity, novelty, duration, and a variety of structural characteristics. With speech, symbols have verbal and nonverbal components, both of which contribute to how they are perceived. In some instances, the properties of a symbol may be such as to render it nearly imperceptible. In such cases, the surrounding symbols may be sufficiently coherent to compensate. One of the contributions of information theory (Shannon & Weaver, 1949) was to demonstrate that considerable redundancy exists in most symbolic strings. Nevertheless, there is a limit on the amount of uncertainty that symbols one receives may possess before they become uninterpretable. Even in situations in which the limit on uncertainty is not exceeded, however, the difficulty one experiences in trying to apprehend particular symbols may divert attention or arouse other responses that interfere with successful communication, or at least with the chances of the symbol producer's being understood in the way he or she has intended. The monotonous speaker is a good example of an individual who, because of the signal properties of his or her message, facilitates inattentiveness, ennui, and even hostility. Any of these conditions is sufficient to interfere with proper reception.

Not only do the properties of individual symbols contribute to the ways in which they are perceived and reacted to, the order within the sequences in which they appear has much to do with how the perceiver will interpret and react to them. Historically, the concept of arrangement in this context has been designated *style*. Properties of symbolic sequences within this frame of reference are considered to vary along such dimensions as simplicity, concreteness, correctness, and appropriateness. Qualities like these relate not only to comprehensibility, but to the aesthetic, attitudinal, and behavioral aspects of responses to communicative acts. Unfamiliar and complex arrangements of symbols increase the likelihood of misunderstanding by those to whom messages are directed. Legal documents often have this quality. Violations of conventional patterns of arrangement (for example, standard grammar and syntax) can have the same consequence, but even if they do not, perceptions of the message producer may be affected and impede his or her achieving desired outcomes.

The arrangement of symbols into larger organizational units or clusters that we ordinarily associate with continuous discourse is also of significance. Some patterns of organization facilitate understanding of what a symbol producer wishes those with whom he or she is interacting to know, feel, or do, and the probability that the person will respond accordingly. A good deal of the pioneering work in the social scientific investigation of persuasion had as a major thrust the relationship of organization to comprehension and attitude change (Hovland, 1957; Hovland, Janis, & Kelley, 1953). However, the notion that the organizational structure of continuous discourse, most notably public speeches, affects reactions to one's utterances dates well into antiquity and was addressed by such philosophers and rhetoricians as Plato (*Phaedrus*), Aristotle (*The Rhetoric*), Cicero (*De Oratore*), and Quintilian (*The Institutes of Oratory*).

Because there are so many potential consequences related to the properties of symbols and the ways in which they are arranged, they constitute an important area of study. To overlook them in efforts to account for the social consequences of symbolic exchange would be an unfortunate omission. The account, at best, would be both inadequate and misleading. In addition, because humans have the ability to make choices about the symbols most appropriate to the representation of their inner states and to the achievement of their communicative goals, the more we can learn about how the properties of symbols relate to others' responses, the better will be the basis for our choices.

How Do the Characteristics of Message Producers Affect the Perception and Interpretation of Symbolic Behavior?

Just as the properties of symbols and the sorts of configurations in which they are manifest influence reception and the subsequent reactions of those to whom communicative acts are directed, so too can the characteristics of the symbol producer have impact on what other parties to an exchange understand or do in response. Personal characteristics both facilitate and inhibit interaction with others. Scholars interested in the concept of source credibility or *ethos*, for instance, have repeatedly produced evidence of a relationship to persuasiveness (e.g., Haiman, 1949; Hovland & Weiss, 1951; J. L. Whitehead, 1971), or what some would refer to as the "perlocutionary force" of a speech act (e.g., Gaines, 1979; Searle, 1969). We know from research on small groups that a participant's status affects the likelihood of other members' responding positively to his or her influence attempts. Those having high status are generally more influential in determining how groups function and in shaping the outcomes they achieve (Shaw, 1981, pp. 271–276). Gender of symbol producers is another factor that appears to have a great deal to do with the ways in which communication is interpreted and responded to

(Bradley, 1980; Phillips & Wood, 1983, pp. 210–269; Spitzak & Carter, 1987). Yet another factor appearing to affect interaction in numerous ways is communicator style (Norton, 1983). Communicator style, the characteristic manner in which a person behaves in interactions with others, can influence their impressions, reactions, and susceptibility to social influence.

Personal attributes also constrain the ways in which symbol producers choose, or even are able, to communicate. Some individuals find the prospect of communication problematic and avoid or limit interaction with others. People having this difficulty are variously described as shy, apprehensive, anxious, reticent, and the like (Phillips, 1981a). Whatever the label, the personal characteristic to which it corresponds reduces the possibilities for one's functioning competently in any number of different social situations. On the other hand, individuals who manifest personal qualities that others value are more easily able to effect desired outcomes in their interactions. The type of communicator Hart and Burks (1972) describe as "rhetorically sensitive" is a case in point. Such individuals exhibit a balance between concern with self and others that those with whom they engage in symbolic exchanges find attractive. As a result, rhetorically sensitive communicators elicit more favorable reactions and greater receptivity to their communicative acts than do individuals lacking this quality.

The relationship between the personal qualities of symbol producers and the responses their utterances evoke is at once subtle and complex. Both the symbol producer and the symbols produced are objects of perception that are difficult to disentangle in the context of ongoing interaction. The effect of this entanglement is that perceptions of a communicative act and, hence, perceivers' responses differ according to who engages in it and the particular set of personal qualities he or she may be perceived to possess. An utterance as simple as "Would you mind holding the door open for me?" could be understood quite differently if made by a person who generally manifests a pleasant manner and by another who is generally unpleasant. In the first instance, the utterance could be regarded as a request; in the latter case, it could be taken as an order or directive.

Asch (1948), in an effort to explain the apparent effect of "prestige suggestion" in messages resulting in changes in attitudes and opinions, came to the conclusion that it is not one's attitude that changes, but rather the attitudinal object. Linking particular ideas to different sources,

in other words, leads to different perceptions of those ideas.[4] This principle would seem to extend beyond the limited phenomenon of prestige
suggestion and apply generally to how the producer/symbol relationship
functions in shaping responses to communicative acts.

Understanding human communication, in no small part, requires
attention to the characteristics of symbol producers. As indicated above,
who is communicating has a great deal to do with what one perceives a
message to be and how he or she thereby is disposed to respond. Inquiry
concerned with those attributes that most directly affect perceptions and
contribute in other ways to interpretations of symbols and how they are
acted upon not only enlarges our understanding of communication,
but also improves the prospects for assisting people to become better
communicators. As least insofar as the personal characteristics over which
individuals have some control are concerned, such knowledge is useful.
Given the large number of personal qualities that we can identify, research
in this area of communication can sustain itself for a long time to come.

*How Do the Characteristics of the Message Recipients Influence Responses on to
Symbolic Behavior?*

How one reacts to the set of symbols that constitutes a communicative act, while influenced by the properties of the symbols themselves
and the characteristics of the symbol producer, still cannot be fully
explained by these factors. The characteristics of the recipient have a
substantial bearing on the responses such acts induce. Those to whom
communicative acts are directed react to symbols on the basis of the
references, or thoughts, they arouse. These references result largely from
the recipient's associations for the symbol producer and the phenomena
to which the symbols refer. As implied in the earlier discussion of symbol
selection, since no two individuals' experiences are identical, seldom if
ever will an interpreter's references correspond perfectly, or even well,
with those of the symbol producer. Theorists concerned with meaning
have argued this point for a long time (e.g., Lee, 1941; Weimer &

---

4. Osgood and Tannenbaum (1955) further refined this notion and demonstrated that the perception of a source and a concept may be altered when linked
by particular types of assertions they classify as "associative" and "disassociative."

Palermo, 1974; Whorf, 1956).[5] This fact alone, however, is insufficient to account for the variance in responses to communicative acts that is attributable to the interpreter.

The interpreter in a communicative exchange possesses the same kinds of personal characteristics as the symbol producer. Indeed, in most interactive contexts, the parties involved are continually switching roles. Some theorists (e.g., Mead, 1934), moreover, see little difference between the roles. To them, the symbol producer is an interpreter whose symbolic choices are a product of communication with oneself. Whether one accepts this conception or not, there are good reasons for believing that the recipient's personal qualities affect perceptions and other aspects of his or her responses to the stimuli that symbols represent. The personal characteristics having the most significance when a communicator is in the interpretive role, of course, may not be the same ones having significance in the selection and production of symbols. It is difficult to tell because researchers have generally not focused on the same qualities in studies of symbol producers and interpreters. This, then, is one of the challenges for future scholarship.

The effects of an interpreter's personal attributes on responses to communicative acts have received continuing emphasis in communication inquiry. Aside from the theoretical value of the knowledge produced, the investigation of such variables is motivated by a desire to determine the sorts of factors about which a symbol producer needs to be conscious if he or she is to maximize the likelihood of producing intended consequences and avoiding unintended ones. (In introductory communication courses, we refer to this as audience analysis.) To this end, communication scholars, in addition to an obvious concern with interpreters' receptive, retrieval, and information processing capacities, have shown an interest in broader aspects of personality. Among the classes of variables examined are self-esteem (e.g., DiVesta & Merwin, 1960), intelligence (e.g., Eagly & Warren, 1976), dogmatism (e.g., Bettinghaus, Steinfatt, & Miller, 1970), ego-involvement (e.g., Sereno & Bodaken, 1972), and, more recently, both gender (e.g., Gilligan, 1982; Rusbult, 1987; Wood, 1986), and cognitive complexity (e.g., Delia, Clark, & Switzer, 1979; Hale, 1980).

---

5. There is a sense, however, in which the exchange of symbols attenuates discrepancies. Interaction itself broadens the base of interactants' experience and, thereby, allows symbolically for greater interpenetration of their inner

The interpreter's role in communicative transactions entails a great deal of inference drawing. The study of personal characteristics helps us to understand how inferences are made and how they, in turn, affect a recipient's reactions in other respects to both the symbol producer and what he or she takes as that person's message. We know, for example, that ego-involvement may contribute to one's seeing another's position on an issue as closer to (assimilation) or further from (contrast) his or her own position than it actually is (Sherif, Sherif, & Nebergall, 1965) and that cognitively simple individuals tend to judge the communicative behavior of others in stereotypic terms (Littlejohn, 1989). We can presume that other personal characteristics have similar distortional effects.

A good illustration of how a personal characteristic can influence responses is suggested by attribution theory. Heider (1958) has pointed out that people vary considerably in their attributional tendencies. There are those who generally see others' behavior as under their conscious control. On the other hand, many people are prone to account for behavior in terms of external influences, or at least, balance their attributions according to the circumstances surrounding the observation of another's behavior. Were a person to say something that proves offensive to the first type of individual, the interpretation of the act as intentional might well produce a defensive reaction and color interpretations of the offending party's subsequent communicative acts.

Difficulties of the type mentioned abound in human communication and are often at the base of misunderstandings, disputes, the dissolution of interpersonal relationships, and various other species of human conflict. When such outcomes occur, moreover, explanations often focus on the symbol producer. The interpreter, however, typically has at least as much to do with the success or failure of communicative acts and the ensuing consequences as the symbol producer. It behooves communication scholars, therefore, to learn as much as possible about the influences that personal attributes have on the reception and interpretation of symbols and the actions that follow from the processes in which they are exchanged.

What Roles Do Media Play in the Process of Symbolic Exchange?

Despite the obvious historical importance of the development of media that have enabled communicators to reach large audiences and to

---

selves. This notion seems to be at the base of Burke's (1966) concepts of identification and consubstantiality.

be linked to others across the boundaries of geography and time, the concept of a medium was not the object of much concern in early descriptions of communication. It was treated in almost obligatory fashion as something writers had to discuss, but either knew little about or were not interested in pursuing. A medium had to do with means of transmission, or conveyances by which symbols are exchanged. Beyond these sorts of minimal characterizations, however, communication scholars had little to say. Even those individuals doing work in the area of mass communication appeared to be concerned primarily with the properties of sources, messages, and message targets. Media, for the most part, represented technological innovations that assisted symbol producers in establishing contact more easily with those they had some desire to reach. The notion that the medium per se made a difference in any other sense was apparently not evident.

The publication of McLuhan's (1964) book *Understanding Media* had considerable impact on the level of importance communication scholars began to attach to the role of media in determining how processes of symbolic exchange function. Although some of McLuhan's claims seemed excessive, even outrageous at times, and his sense of history distorted, the observations he offered suggested to many that the means by which symbols are transmitted and the forms they take influence the recipient's perceptions. In this sense, media bear the same kind of relationship to an interpreter's responses to symbols as the characteristics of the symbol producer. In other words, just as it is difficult to disentangle symbols from the person who produces them, so too does there appear to be an inseparability of the symbol and the medium. As McLuhan put it, "the medium is the message" (p. 23).

Despite burgeoning interest in media, we still know surprisingly little about their effects on the ways in which symbols are perceived and acted upon. *Media* has become a term that refers as much, if not more, to specific contexts of communication and certain kinds of social institutions (DeFleur & Ball-Rokeach, 1989) as it does to the instrumentalities involved in the transmission of symbols. In some instances, scholarly discussion of the concept of a medium leaves one with the impression that it is a thing like a container, within which certain kinds of activities take place. This type of metaphor has served as the basis for the investigation of symbolic processes within media institutions, organizations, and the media themselves (e.g., the critical studies reported in Medhurst & Benson, 1984; Mander, 1983). We attribute great power to the so-called mass media in shaping responses to various kinds of communicative acts, but the paucity of cross-media comparisons renders it next to impossible to make specific claims about their unique influence on the perceptions and resulting responses that exposure to symbols conveyed by a particular medium arouses.

All sorts of effects have been attributed to media use. One topic that has attracted a great deal of attention because of such attributions has to do with the impact that exposure to violent content in television programs and films has on the subsequent occurrence of aggressive and antisocial behavior (e.g., discussions in DeFleur & Ball-Rokeach, 1982; Lowery & DeFleur, 1988; Malamuth & Donnerstein, 1984). Much of the research focusing on media has to do with exposure and its socializing influences. Early researchers were concerned with such phenomena as the effects of reading comic books and going to movies (e.g., Holaday & Stoddard, 1935; Thrasher, 1949). This interest has naturally extended to television (DeFleur & Ball-Rokeach, 1989). However, even with issues such as these that lend themselves to cross-media comparisons, researchers have tended to vary some aspect of message content rather than the medium in, by, or through which the content is manifested.

The fact that scholars have had difficulty isolating the independent effects of the medium in communicative acts does not make this aspect of symbolic exchange any less important. The significance of the medium may be greater now than at any time in the history of the scholarly study of human communication. Most communication still takes place at the interpersonal level and in face-to-face situations. The principal medium of communication remains speech. However, as we move ever further and irreversibly into the Information Age, increasing proportions of communication will involve other media. Electronic media especially have an ever-increasing presence in people's daily lives.[6] Not only is it important, therefore, that scholars continue to study the mass media, but also that they examine how such developments as electronic mail, computer-assisted learning, and computer-mediated communication contribute to symbolic exchange. It seems obvious that such inquiry is necessary if we are to have descriptions of communication that reflect

---

6. So pervasive and influential have electronic media, and mass media in particular, become, in the judgment of some scholars like Meyrowitz (1985), society and the social structures comprising it have undergone fundamental and significant change.

current realities. This is particularly important if communication inquiry is to continue to concern itself with the social consequences of human interaction.

In What Ways Do the Social Contexts in Which Symbolic Exchanges Occur Contribute to the Production and Reception of Communicative Acts?

The term *communication* is often accompanied by a modifier such as *interpersonal, group, organizational,* or *public.* Williams (1989) suggests that these four particular ones indicate the levels of social organization at which communication occurs. Other modifiers distinguish communication according to professional or social use. Hence, one finds such accompanying designations as *legal, religious, medical,* or *business.* We use labels like *mass* and *cross-cultural* to distinguish communication in terms of some audience or participant characteristic, such as size, linguistic background, or ethnic differences. One also finds labels attached to the word *communication* to represent various demographic groups, for instance, *gay, feminist,* and *black.* We further label communication by its functions or purposes with such identifiers as *informational, technical, argumentative,* and *persuasive.*

Although these sorts of labels are typically employed to set apart areas of specialization, to provide titles for courses in communication curricula, and to reflect particular sets of interests various networks of scholars may have, they also implicitly recognize the importance of context in human communication. The situation in which communication takes place has direct relevance for the symbol producer's selection and production of symbols, the medium or media employed in their transmission, and the ways in which the interpreter perceives them as messages and responds. This point was very well articulated in a seminal essay by Bitzer (1968), in which he discussed situational constraints on rhetorical choices. Other scholars have since attempted to demonstrate how such constraints function (e.g., the collection of essays in Campbell & Jamieson, 1978). Similar notions are also evident in work by group and organizational theorists concerned with the communicative choices of leaders and the limits imposed by a group or organization's task and social environments (e.g., Fisher, 1985; Hunt & Larson, 1974).

The argument that contextual factors influence perceptions and responses of recipients in symbolic exchanges was well documented in

Fiedler's continuing program of research on leadership effectiveness
(Fiedler & Garcia, 1987). For this reason, it serves as a useful illustration.
Fiedler repeatedly found that in situations not conducive to effective
group performance, individuals who exhibited controlling, directive
styles of leadership elicited much more favorable reactions than the very
same types of members did under circumstances that were much more
conducive to effective performance. In other words, similar behavior was
perceived differently and effected different outcomes, in part because the
frame of reference in which it was viewed and interpreted varied.

As willing as scholars are to acknowledge the significance contextual
factors have in determining how communication does, or even can,
function, the concept is elusive. Lacking in scholarly literature is substantial evidence of attempts to identify the relevant dimensions of context.
This is not to suggest that potentially important factors have not been
identified, but only that the full range of possibilities has yet to be set
forth. For those who have attempted to assess the effects of situational
influences, the context of communication is restricted to those elements
on which the individual investigator has chosen to focus. Until we have
more precise descriptions of and agreements about the referents for this
concept, its role in communication will likely remain obscure. Thus,
clarifying the dimensions of context and their pragmatic effects is an
important avenue for future research.

Even if the notion of context continues to be elusive and our
knowledge of how it specifically enters into the processes of symbolic
exchanges in which scholars are interested remains limited, it would be
a mistake to discard this concept. Recognizing that what transpires in
any given instance of communication is, in part, a function of influences
lying outside the particular relationship of the parties involved provides
an incentive for trying to develop more complete and useful descriptions
of communication. It may also give the practitioner a greater appreciation
for the fact that he or she is less central to successes and failures in
interactions with others than is commonly presumed. For both of these
reasons, context should continue to be an object of scholarly attention.

Methodological and Meta-Critical Issues

Early conceptions of communication treated the process of symbolic
exchange as linear and static (Berlo, 1960). Success and failure, within

this frame of reference, appear to be largely a matter of whether messages reach their intended destinations, whether message targets are equipped to assign appropriate meanings, and whether they are predisposed to act in accordance with the source's intentions. As the review of substantive issues identified in this chapter indicates, however, the study of human communication has resulted in a considerably more sophisticated conception. That conception reflects recognition of a complex set of interactions among personal, contextual, and symbolic characteristics that determine at any given moment what the parties involved receive, understand, and do in the exchange of symbols they employ to represent various aspects of their inner selves. How well scholars are able to explain this process and to provide information useful for functioning more effectively in it depends on how well they deal with the issues that follow.

Have the Means of Inquiry Employed in Exploring Questions about the Processes in Which Symbolic Exchanges Occur Been Appropriate to Support the Types of Claims Advanced?

The means of inquiry that communication scholars employ to illuminate symbolic processes are important, and people argue about them. Such arguments began almost at the founding of our professional association (Leff & Procario, 1985) and have continued into more recent times (e.g., Miller, 1981; Phillips, 1981b; Wood, 1984). Disputes about means, especially when carried on at an informal level, can easily degenerate into a contest of egos, but more often than not, they reflect serious consideration of the bases on which claims about phenomena like communication rest and the appropriateness of the ways in which relevant information has been produced and assessed.

Communication scholars have utilized many different means to answer questions about the symbolic processes in which they are interested. These can generally be viewed as reflecting either a social science or humanistic orientation. Within each orientation, moreover, published research reveals the application of a variety of methodological tools and approaches to studying communication. Some social scientists rely heavily on experiments and controlled investigations. Others rely on qualitative methods, such as interviews, surveys, interpretive analyses of discourse, and participant observations. Some research necessitates the acquisition of substantial volumes of quantitative data and requires observance of carefully constructed rules of inference for extracting the conclusions the data support, whereas other research reveals a much greater tolerance for more subjective and individualized assessment. Humanistic scholarship is typically more reliant on texts and analytical methods. Conclusions about communication may be drawn from the application of a theory, some aspect of a theory, or a general theoretical perspective that seems to be relevant in the analysis of a text or other relevant artifact of interest. Some scholars are more inductive in their approach, however, and see themselves needing to examine data without preconceived notions of their meanings or what sequence of steps is critical to arriving at conclusions of interest.

Since research findings do not all have the same weight of evidence behind them, one needs to be aware of how they are produced and whether the methods of investigation involved are suitable for the judgments scholars form. A classic study by Bales and Strodtbeck (1951), for instance, has been frequently cited as establishing that problem-solving groups characteristically go through phases of orientation, evaluation, and control. Although that pattern was evident more often than any other, it surfaced in only about one-third of the groups studied. Moreover, all groups were of the zero-history variety. There is no reason to believe that established problem-solving groups exhibit the same pattern. As another illustration, Scheidel (1977) pointed out that the oft-repeated claim that 93 percent of the meaning in communicative transactions is carried by nonverbal elements is based on research involving single words uttered in isolation. When one has this awareness, the claim is far less impressive.

Although specific questions scholars pursue are usually amenable to more than one method or type of inquiry, the avenues open to investigation vary in their appropriateness. For some such avenues, it may even be the case that one is unable to arrive at an intended destination. Unfortunately, references to scholarship in secondary sources (and occasionally primary sources) and in surveys of research frequently treat all findings reported as if the methods by which they were produced are equally sound. As indicated above, often the consumer does not even have a sense of how the information being reported was acquired, processed, and analyzed. One of the purposes of this volume is to overcome that deficiency to some extent by having the individual contributors attend to the means by which scholarship in those areas with which they are concerned has been conducted and to address concerns that relate more generally to what it is that entitles particular claims to knowledge.

What Are the Assumptions and Limitations of the Methodological Perspectives and Modes of Inquiry Employed?

A matter closely related to the appropriateness of the means scholars employ in trying to produce answers to questions about communication has to do with the assumptions that underlie methods of inquiry and the limitations they impose on what one can justifiably conclude about the phenomena under consideration. Ontological and epistemological assumptions affect what scholars choose to study and how they go about studying it. As Littlejohn (1989) notes, some scholars view communicative behavior from a deterministic perspective. They are likely to look for the factors that control, and thereby make predictable, how the parties involved in symbolic exchanges will interact and try to identify relationships among these factors according to established conventions and criteria of inquiry. Others subscribe to a more teleological view and see human actors both as having considerable freedom of choice and as acting within their own volition to achieve particular ends (Bowers & Bradac, 1982). Their methods are apt to be more idiosyncratic and reliant on the scholar's perceptions. Scholars in the first group typically attempt to discover generalizations that apply to communication under all similar circumstances. Those in the other group are more likely to focus on what uniquely contributes to given instances of communication and eschew the notion that similar circumstances necessarily lead to similarities in behavior. For these scholars, in fact, circumstances are largely shaped in the course of interaction.

Assumptions about the ways of knowing and the nature of reality have been the object of philosophical contention and dispute for literally thousands of years. These disputes, moreover, are not likely to be resolved in the foreseeable future. At present, we have no way of establishing in any absolute sense which of the general approaches to communication inquiry is best, although exemplars of particular ones are often disposed to make declarations about such matters. It is possible, however, to assess the legitimacy of claims scholars make within the assumptive system that drives their inquiries and by the acknowledged rules of evidence and inference that apply. It is also possible to note the limitations that certain sets of assumptions and related practices impose on judgment. When viewed in this way, some claims are more permissible than others. A great many are altogether impermissible. These often involve propositions or concepts that cannot be adequately assessed. As an illustration, Shaw and Costanzo (1970) have noted that the psychoanalytic concept of repression has questionable utility because it is not testable in any un-equivocal way. Judgments about the circumstances under which one represses traumatic experiences, therefore, are open to serious reservation. One has similar reservations about the accuracy of judgments about what a person is saying nonverbally that are based on Watzlawick, Beavin, and Jackson's (1967) famous axiom that "one cannot *not* communicate" (p. 49).

In scholarly inquiry, there exists the notion of compelling argument. Briefly stated, such an argument exists when the evidence in support of a given assertion is so overpowering that even those who initially disagree with the claim and who would like to continue disagreeing with it will yield. This assumes, of course, that one is dealing with reasonable people, however skeptical they may be. The claims that derive from scholarly inquiry are in a very real sense arguments, not the revelations of truth that those who produce them often appear to imply. It is an important function of criticism to establish which arguments about communication are more compelling than others. To a substantial degree, the following essays address this issue.

Which Methods of Inquiry Have Been Most Fruitful in Producing Claims about Symbolic Representations of Cognitive Activities and Related Affective States and Their Social Consequences?

Inquiry and the means by which it is conducted in any given area of scholarship may satisfy such criteria as appropriateness, may conform well to the consensual rules of evidence and inference within the assump-tive system that applies, and may still be problematic. When this set of conditions arises, the concern typically focuses on the fruitfulness of research and related theory. Areas of investigation come and go. Scholar-ship often reflects the pursuit of "hot" topics. Lines of research may begin and end with a single individual and consist of a very limited number of studies. Both topics and methods of inquiry become fashionable, only to suffer the same fate as other fashions—nonacceptance or outdatedness. Scholars like to use the phrase *cutting edge* to characterize promising developments. Inquiry that follows, however, may vary considerably in the extent to which the promise is realized.

Although scholarly inquiry is sometimes portrayed as a process in which knowledge advances incrementally and in steady fashion, this view is far from reality. Within given subject areas, critics are quick to point to fragmentation, disjointedness, the lack of agreement about what constitutes the proper objects of study, and the like (e.g., Bormann, 1980; Gouran, 1973; Miller, 1969). What may be true of the area as a whole, however, is not necessarily applicable to inquiry within the specialties and subspecialties of which it is composed. Some lines of work do appear to be more nearly incremental, cumulative, and integratable than others. Typically, this is programmatic research carried out by a group of researchers who share substantive and methodological perspectives.[7] Work that has proved fruitful not only provides insights into the concepts that have been related and the means of investigation employed, but also suggests something about the vision, understanding, and habits of mind of the knowledge producers.

Those areas of inquiry that can be distinguished from others by virtue of their greater yield and overall contribution to the fund of knowledge we have amassed in the study of communication deserve special mention for several reasons. Aside from the obvious fact that they represent the work to which one is most likely to point as evidence of what is known and can be said about processes of symbolic exchange, the contributions may serve as models for inquiry into other aspects of these processes. In addition, they represent a source of attraction to other scholars who, through their combined efforts, can expedite future in-

---

7. Malamuth and Donnerstein (1984) are two such scholars who have worked collaboratively and individually on research aimed at assessing the effects of exposure to pornography on aggressive behavior. Their investigations have moved progressively forward in the conceptualization of what constitutes pornographic material and social aggression as well as in the identification of personal characteristics that mediate observed relationships. Poole and his associates' studies of decision development in group discussion also have this character (e.g., Poole, 1981, 1983a, 1983b; Poole, McPhee, & Seibold, 1982; Poole, Seibold, & McPhee, 1985). Yet another line of research fitting this mold is that of Jackson and Jacobs in the area of argument and argumentative processes (e.g., Jackson, 1982; Jackson & Jacobs, 1980; Jacobs & Jackson, 1983).

quiry. Finally, the recognition of those areas in which scholarly inquiry has proved most fruitful can create a greater awareness of the sorts of phenomena that lend themselves to formal and disciplined study. For these reasons, the other essays, when appropriate, acknowledge bodies of scholarship in which detectable gains in knowledge have been clearly evident and whose viability does not appear to be threatened, or even at issue.

What Are the Pragmatic Values of the Knowledge Derived from Scholarly Inquiry?

The generation of knowledge inevitably carries with it questions about pragmatic value (e.g., Cronkhite, 1969; Gouran, 1979; Nichols, 1977; Wood, 1979, 1984). These are legitimate issues to raise, but sometimes they reduce to an overly simplistic conception of utility. "How will that help me in my job?", "How does that translate into practice?", and "What does that have to do with 'real' communication?" are examples of the kinds of questions asked of scholarship on communication by individuals seeking formulas by which to become more proficient in what they perceive to be a mechanical art. Much, if not most, of the knowledge produced by communication scholars does not have this kind of utility. It was not sought in the interest of reducing communication to simple prescriptions for success. On the other hand, if one takes as an index of utility that knowledge provide a basis for choice, a good deal of what has been learned about symbolic processes can be extended to the practical realm. As Ackoff and Emery (1972) have suggested, the knowledge we acquire from others helps reduce uncertainty concerning how to choose among competing alternatives. To this end, knowledge may have informational, motivational, and instructional value.

Alfred North Whitehead (1929) once characterized the utility of knowledge in the following way: "By utilizing an idea, I mean relating it to that stream, compounded of sense perceptions, feelings, hopes, desires, and of mental activities adjusting to thought, which forms our lives" (p. 15). This conception of utility, or pragmatic value, is one by which communication inquiry can be more appropriately judged. To the extent that scholarship enlarges our understanding in the way Whitehead implies, one can make more intelligent and informed choices. If it reveals how communication functions, what interferes with it, and what facilitates the achievement of communicators' objectives, scholarly inquiry has pragmatic value. In addition, to the extent that scholarship addresses the kinds of problems those involved in processes of symbolic exchange typically face, its direct relevance provides even better bases for choice.

Not all inquiry satisfies the criteria of relevance and providing bases for choice equally well. Some, perhaps far too much, of our research deals with contrived and artificial situations, or ones far removed from the experience of most people. Milgram's (1969) efforts to explain obedience to authority by having naive subjects administer electrical shocks to an experimenter's confederates is a case in point. Still other research strikes one as reflecting highly esoteric sets of interests that, at best, relate only tangentially or very infrequently to processes of symbolic exchange and human interaction. The early work on communication networks had this appearance (e.g., Bavelas, 1948). On the other hand, scholarly work is frequently the target of unwarranted indictments that it lacks apparent utility. In either case, it is important to have some sense of the pragmatic value of the knowledge communication scholars have produced. Human beings are capable of understanding communication more fully and becoming better communicators, but without information that provides a basis for understanding and learning how, they would be just as well off trusting their intuitive impulses—and in some instances possibly better off.

What Can Be Done to Produce More Useful and Reliable Knowledge about Human Communication?

Answers to the question of what can be done to produce more useful and reliable knowledge necessarily vary from one area of inquiry to another and depend on what types of deficiencies are most evident. In some areas, the dominant problems may have to do with the conceptualization of the phenomena that are being studied. In other areas, inquiry may suffer from the absence of appropriate theories with which to relate concepts, provide coherent accounts of observed communicative behavior, or integrate existing facts about such behavior. Study in a given area may be hampered by inadequacies in methods of data gathering and analysis. In still other areas, a major difficulty may be that there are simply too few active scholars at work to advance knowledge appreciably. All areas of communication inquiry undoubtedly suffer from a multiplicity of problems that limit our ability to make meaningful claims about symbolic exchanges and their social consequences, but some are more damaging or critical than others and, therefore, in more urgent need of address. Among these are the imprecision of our definitions of important concepts, the lack of agreed-upon indicators of these concepts, and inadequately developed theories for explaining the complexity of human communication.

A common approach to problem solving in human affairs is to identify the cause(s) of a felt difficulty and to treat or remove it if possible. There is no reason to presume that this approach is inapplicable to the conduct of communication inquiry. The application in this context may be somewhat more complicated than it is in others, however. To recognize, for instance, that an area of study like group communication suffers from a paucity of theories with the corresponding effect that knowledge produced through research remains largely unintegrated provides no assurance that the remedy of generating theories will have the desired consequence. In addition, it is not always clear what constitutes evidence of improvement. Scholars can never be sure that what they do to overcome acknowledged deficiencies is better, as opposed to being merely different.

Despite these difficulties, there is virtually no hope that scholarly inquiry into communication can lead to more useful and reliable knowledge—except perhaps accidentally—unless effort is directed toward identifying the factors that underlie such inadequacies as the evaluation and critique of existing scholarship may establish. To ignore the question would be to reinforce practices of questionable merit. This runs counter to a fundamental assumption that has punctuated significant advances in knowledge and, for that matter, the development of civilization. That assumption is that as a species we are capable of arriving at better understandings of the phenomena we encounter and of devising ever better means by which to achieve such goals.

Prospects

The nature of inquiry poses many problems for scholars, including questions about the value of their work. As the discussion of methodological and meta-critical issues suggests, these focus on matters of appropriateness, ontology and epistemology, fruitfulness, relevance, and utility. Definitive answers to questions are constrained by the limitations of one's world view and methodological perspectives. The value of scholarly inquiry, moreover, is often difficult to establish because of differences in judgment about what constitutes utility. Despite these issues, the prospects for advancing knowledge of communication seem reasonably bright.

The fact that the symbolic processes involved in human communication have captured the attention of so many people of diverse background and differing points of view who seek to understand and illuminate them is encouraging. It suggests a subject posing problems that admit of no easy solution and that are therefore intellectually engaging and conducive to sustained interest. Literally thousands of studies have been published in the pages of journals concerned with communication over the past seventy-five years. The aspects of communication to which scholars attend, moreover, have blossomed into a rich assortment of intriguing questions for which we continue to seek answers. Answers lead to other questions, pose new problems for future inquiry, and attract the attention of new generations of scholars. The evidence of activity indicates a field of study that is very much alive, maturing, open to different styles and methods of inquiry, and accommodating to a mixture of philosophical perspectives and world views.

Its virtues notwithstanding, the study of communication will continue to face the substantive, philosophical, and methodological problems discussed throughout this chapter and the others to follow. Indifference to these difficulties will retard inquiry and limit claims about communication that scholars can credibly and confidently advance. On such matters, not as much progress as some would like has been made. The fact that those in the scholarly community concerned with communication recognize the problems and are willing to debate them, however, is a positive sign and cause for optimism.

We stand at the threshold of the twenty-first century not fully sure of the directions in which scholarly inquiry may lead, but neither have we arrived unprepared to choose. More has been discovered and written about human communication since the founding of the Speech Communication Association than in all of the preceding centuries combined. We have a reasonably good sense of what is known and, hence, what remains to be learned. Past inquiry has provided a foundation on which to build. Considered in the light of these realities, the future of scholarship on human communication looks very promising indeed.

References

Ackoff, R., & Emery, F. (1972). *On purposeful systems.* Chicago: Aldine Press.

Arnold, C. C., & Bowers, J. W. (Eds.). (1984). *Handbook of rhetorical and communication theory.* Boston: Allyn & Bacon.

Asch, S. E. (1948). The doctrine of suggestion, prestige, and imitation in social psychology. *Psychological Review, 55,* 250–276.

Bales, R. F., & Strodtbeck, F. L. (1951). Phases in group problem solving. *Journal of Abnormal and Social Psychology, 46,* 485–495.

Bavelas, A. (1948). A mathematical model for group structures. *Applied Anthropology, 7,* 16–30.

Benson, T. W. (Ed.). (1985). *Speech communication in the 20th century.* Carbondale, IL: Southern Illinois University Press.

Berlo, D. R. (1960). *The process of communication.* New York: Holt, Rinehart and Winston.

Bettinghaus, E. P., Steinfatt, T., & Miller, G. R. (1970). Source evaluation, syllogistic content, and judgments of logical validity by high- and low-dogmatic persons. *Journal of Personality and Social Psychology, 16,* 238–244.

Bitzer, L. F. (1968). The rhetorical situation. *Philosophy & Rhetoric, 1,* 1–14.

Bitzer, L. F., & Black, E. (Eds.). (1971). *The prospect of rhetoric.* Englewood Cliffs, NJ: Prentice-Hall.

Bochner, A. P., & Eisenberg, E. M. (1985). Legitimizing speech communication: An examination of coherence and cohesion in the development of the discipline. In T. W. Benson (Ed.), *Speech communication in the 20th century* (pp. 299–321, 440–444). Carbondale, IL: Southern Illinois University Press.

Bormann, E. G. (1980). *Communication theory.* New York: Holt, Rinehart and Winston.

Bowers, J. W., & Bradac, J. J. (1982). Issues in communication theory: A metatheoretical analysis. In M. Burgoon (Ed.), *Communication yearbook 5* (pp. 1–28). New Brunswick, NJ: Transaction Books.

Bradley, P. H. (1980). Sex, competence, and opinion deviation: An expectations states approach. *Communication Monographs, 47,* 101–110.

Burke, K. (1966). *Language as symbolic interaction.* Berkeley, CA: University of California Press.

Campbell, K. K., & Jamieson, K. H. (Eds.). (1978). *Form and action: Shaping rhetorical action.* Falls Church, VA: Speech Communication Association.

Cohen, H. (1985). The development of research in speech communication: A historical perspective. In T. W. Benson (Ed.), *Speech communication in the 20th century* (pp. 282–298, 436–440). Carbondale, IL: Southern Illinois University Press.

Cronkhite, G. L. (1969). Out of the ivory palaces: A proposal for useful research in communication and decision. In R. J. Kibler & L. L. Barker (Eds.),

Conceptual frontiers in speech-communication (pp. 113–135). New York: Speech Association of America.

DeFleur, M. L., & Ball-Rokeach, S. (1982). *Theories of mass communication* (4th ed.). New York: Longman.

DeFleur, M. L., & Ball-Rokeach, S. (1989). *Theories of mass communication* (5th ed.). New York: Longman.

Delia, J. G., Clark, R. A., & Switzer, D. E. (1979). The content of informal conversations as a function of interactants' interpersonal cognitive complexity. *Communication Monographs, 46*, 274–281.

DiVesta, F. J., & Merwin, J.C. (1960). The effects of need-oriented communication on attitude change. *Journal of Abnormal and Social Psychology, 60*, 80–85.

Eagly, A. H., & Warren, R. (1976). Intelligence, comprehension and opinion change. *Journal of Personality, 44*, 226–242.

Fiedler, F. E., & Garcia, J. E. (1987). *New approaches to effective leadership: Cognitive resources and organizational performance.* New York: Wiley.

Fisher, B. A. (1978). *Perspectives on human communication.* New York: Macmillan.

Fisher, B. A. (1985). Leadership as medium: Treating complexity in group communication research. *Small Group Behavior, 16*, 167–196.

Gaines, R. (1979). Doing by saying: Toward a theory of perlocution. *Quarterly Journal of Speech, 65*, 207–217.

Gilligan, C. (1982). *In a different voice: Psychological theory and women's development.* Cambridge, MA: Harvard University Press.

Gouran, D. S. (1973). Group communication: Perspectives and priorities for future research. *Quarterly Journal of Speech, 59*, 22–29.

Gouran, D. S. (1979). Speech communication: Its conceptual foundation and disciplinary status. *Communication Education, 28*, 1 8.

Gregg, R. B. (1984). *Symbolic inducement and knowing: A study in the foundations of rhetoric.* Columbia, SC: University of South Carolina Press.

Haiman, F. S. (1949). An experimental study of the effects of ethos in public speaking. *Speech Monographs, 16*, 190–202.

Hale, C. (1980). Cognitive complexity-simplicity as a determinant of communication effectiveness. *Communication Monographs, 47*, 304–311.

Hart, R. P., & Burks, D. M. (1972). Rhetorical sensitivity and social interaction. *Speech Monographs, 39*, 75–91.

Heider, F. (1958). *The psychology of interpersonal relations.* New York: Wiley.

Holaday, P. W., & Stoddard, G. D. (1933). *Getting ideas from the movies.* New York: Macmillan.

Hovland, C. I. (Ed.). (1957). *The order of presentation in persuasion.* New Haven, CT: Yale University Press.

Hovland, C. I., Janis, I. L., & Kelley, H. H. (1953). *Communication and persuasion.* New Haven, CT: Yale University Press.

Hovland, C. I., & Weiss, W. (1951). The influence of source credibility on communication effectiveness. *Public Opinion Quarterly, 15,* 636–650.

Hunt, J. G., & Larson, L. L. (Eds.). (1974). *Contingency approaches to leadership.* Carbondale, IL: Southern Illinois University Press.

Jackson, S. (1982). Two models of syllogistic reasoning: An empirical comparison. *Communication Monographs, 49,* 205–213.

Jackson, S., & Jacobs, S. (1980). Structure of conversational argument: Pragmatic bases for the enthymeme. *Quarterly Journal of Speech, 66,* 251–265.

Jacobs, S., & Jackson, S. (1983). Strategy and structure in conversational influence attempts. *Communication Monographs, 50,* 285–304.

Kaplan, A. (1964). *The conduct of inquiry.* San Francisco: Chandler.

Kibler, R. J., & Barker, L. L. (Eds.). (1969). Conceptual frontiers in speech-communication. New York: Speech Association of America.

Langer, S. (1942). *Philosophy in a new key.* Cambridge, MA: Harvard University Press.

Lee, I. J. (1941). *Language habits in human affairs.* New York: Harper & Row.

Leff, M. C., & Procario, M. O. (1985). Rhetorical theory in speech communication. In T. W. Benson (Ed.), *Speech communication in the 20th century* (pp. 3–27, 368–372). Carbondale, IL: Southern Illinois University Press.

Littlejohn, S. W. (1989). *Theories of human communcation* (3rd ed.). Belmont, CA: Wadsworth.

Lowery, S. S., & DeFleur, M. L. (1988). *Milestones in mass communcation research* (2nd ed.). New York: Longman.

Malamuth, N. M., & Donnerstein, E. (Eds.). (1984). *Pornography and sexual aggression.* Orlando, FL: Academic Press.

Mander, M. S. (Ed.). (1983). *Communications in transition.* New York: Praeger.

McLuhan, M. (1964). *Understanding media.* New York: McGraw-Hill.

Mead, G. H. (1934). *Mind, self, and society.* Chicago: University of Chicago Press.

Medhurst, M. J., & Benson, T. W. (Eds.). (1984). *Rhetorical dimensions in media* (rev. ed.). Dubuque, IA: Kendall/Hunt.

Meyrowitz, J. (1985). *No sense of place.* New York: Oxford University Press.

Milgram, S. (1969). *Obedience to authority.* New York: Harper Colophon Books.

Miller, G. R. (1969). Human information processing: Some research guidelines. In R. J. Kibler & L. L. Barker (Eds.), *Conceptual frontiers in speech-communication* (pp. 51–68). New York: Speech Association of America.

Miller, G. R. (1981). " 'Tis the season to be jolly': A yuletide assessment of communication research." *Human Communication Research, 7,* 371–377.

Nichols, M. H. (1977). When you start out for Ithaka . . . . *Central States Speech Journal, 28,* 145–156.

Norton, R. (1983). *Communication style: Theory, applications, and measures.* Beverly Hills, CA: Sage.

Ogden, C. K., & Richards, I. A. (1923). *The meaning of meaning*. London: Kegan, Paul, Trench, Trubner.

Osgood, C., & Tannenbaum, P. H. (1955). The principle of congruity in the prediction of attitude change. *Psychological Review, 62*, 42–55.

Pearce, W. B. (1976). The coordinated management of meaning: A rules based theory of interpersonal communication. In G. R. Miller (Ed.), *Explorations in interpersonal communication* (pp. 17–36). Beverly Hills, CA: Sage.

Pearce, W. B. (1985). Scientific research methods in communication studies and their implications for theory and research. In T. W. Benson (Ed.), *Speech communication in the 20th century* (pp. 255–281, 433–436). Carbondale, IL: Southern Illinois University Press.

Phillips, G. M. (1981a). *Help for shy people*. Englewood Cliffs, NJ: Prentice-Hall.

Phillips, G. M. (1981b). Science and the study of human communication: An inquiry from the other side of the two cultures. *Human Communication Research, 7*, 361–370.

Phillips, G. M., & Wood, J. T. (1983). *Communication and human relationships*. New York: Macmillan.

Poole, M. S. (1981). Decision development in small groups I: A comparison of two models. *Communication Monographs, 48*, 1–24.

Poole, M. S. (1983a). Decision development in small groups II: A study of multiple sequences in decision-making. *Communication Monographs, 50*, 206–233.

Poole, M. S. (1983b). Decision development in small groups III: A multiple sequence model of group decision development. *Communication Monographs, 50*, 321–341.

Poole, M. S., McPhee, R. D., & Seibold, D. R. (1982). A comparison of normative and interactional explanations of group decision-making: Social decision schemes versus valence distributions. *Communication Monographs, 49*, 1–19.

Poole, M. S., Seibold, D. R., & McPhee, R. D. (1985). Group decision-making as a structurational process. *Quarterly Journal of Speech, 71*, 74–102.

Rusbult, C. E. (1987). Responses to dissatisfaction in close relationships: The exit-voice-loyalty-neglect model. In D. Perlman & S. Duck (Eds.). *Intimate relationships: Development, dynamics, and deterioration* (pp. 209–238). London: Sage.

Scheidel, T. M. (1977). Evidence varies with phases of inquiry. *Western Journal of Speech Communication, 41*, 20–31.

Searle, J. (1969). *Speech acts: An essay in the philosophy of language*. Cambridge, Eng.: Cambridge University Press.

Sereno, K. K., & Bodaken, E. M. (1972). Ego involvement and attitude change:

Toward a reconceptualization of persuasive effect. *Speech Monographs, 39,* 151–158.

Shannon, C., & Weaver, W. (1949). *The mathematical theory of communication.* Urbana, IL: University of Illinois Press.

Shaw, M. E. (1981). *Group dynamics: The psychology of small group behavior* (3rd ed.). New York: McGraw-Hill.

Shaw, M. E., & Costanzo, P. R. (1970). *Theories of social psychology.* New York: McGraw-Hill.

Sherif, M., Sherif, C., & Nebergall, R. (1965). *Attitude and attitude change: The social judgment-involvement approach.* Philadelphia: W. B. Saunders.

Spitzak, C., & Carter, K. (1987). Women in communication studies: A typology for revision. *Quarterly Journal of Speech, 73,* 401–423.

Thrasher, F. M. (1949). The comics and delinquency: Cause or scapegoat. *Journal of Educational Sociology, 23,* 195–205.

Watzlawick, P., Beavin, J. H., & Jackson, D. D. (1967). *Pragmatics of human communication.* New York: W. W. Norton.

Weimer, W. B., & Palermo, D. S. (Eds.). (1974). *Cognition and the symbolic process.* Hillsdale, NJ: Lawrence Erlbaum and Associates.

Whitehead, A. N. (1929). *The aims of education.* New York: Macmillan.

Whitehead, J. L. (1971). Effects of authority-based assertion on attitude and credibility. *Speech Monographs, 38,* 311–315.

Whorf, B. L. (1956). *Language, thought, and reality.* New York: Wiley.

Williams, F. (1989). *The new communications* (2nd ed.). Belmont, CA: Wadsworth.

Wood, J. T. (1979). Interpersonal and small group communication research in 1977. *ACA Bulletin,* No. 28, 17–23.

Wood, J. T. (1984). Research and the social world: Honoring the connections. *Communication Quarterly, 32,* 3–8.

Wood, J. T. (1986). Different voices in relationship crises. *American Behavioral Scientist, 24,* 273–303.

Constituted by Agency:
The Discourse and Practice of Rhetorical
Criticism

SONJA K. FOSS

The schemas of perception, assumptions, rationales, definitions, rules, values, and ideological commitments of a discipline are made visible by analysis of the structure for knowledge of that discipline; this structure has been called a variety of names, including *paradigm* (Kuhn, 1970), *discursive formation* (Foucault, 1970, 1972), *world view,* and *conceptual framework.* My goal here is to identify this structure for the discipline of rhetorical criticism—to discover what and how we know about rhetorical criticism through an investigation of its conceptual framework. My purpose is not to demonstrate that our current framework is in error or unproductive but rather to make visible the framework that governs our thought and practice. If we can recognize that this structure is not natural, we may create, if we choose, alternative frameworks.

The text I used in my effort to glean the characteristics of the conceptual framework of rhetorical criticism included major essays and books written about rhetorical criticism since 1915, when the *Quarterly Journal of Speaking* first was published. I relied largely, however, on material appearing in the last twenty or so years, in which the most discourse about the theory and philosophy of rhetorical criticism has been produced.

I did not have to go far to discover a tool to use to unpack our framework for knowledge, for the discipline of rhetorical criticism itself offers critical methods designed to discover a rhetor's world view or how that rhetor structures the world. I chose Kenneth Burke's (1969) pentad, a content-analytic tool designed to discover how a rhetor labels the structure and outstanding ingredients in, and thus names, a situation. Once we are able to see how a rhetor perceives the world, of course, we also are able to see what the appropriate and available actions and practices are from that perspective. Applied to the discourse of rhetorical criticism, a pentadic analysis should suggest, then, how that discourse is structured and how its structure shapes our critical practices.

I plan to proceed in this essay in much the same way that any pentadic analysis is conducted. In describing their situations, rhetors use the five basic elements of a drama—act, agent, agency, purpose, and scene. I will begin by identifying these terms in the discourse of rhetorical criticism. In the second step of a pentadic analysis, the relationships among the five terms are analyzed through an application of ratios. Ratios encourage the critic to look at how one term affects or determines the nature of another term in the pentad, with a goal of discovering the term that seems to control the nature of all or most of the other terms. This featured term constitutes motive for the rhetor's construction of the situation. In the second section of the essay, I will argue that agency is the featured term and will discuss the consequences for rhetorical criticism of viewing this term as the dominant one. Next, I will point to some alternative conceptual frameworks that result from the featuring of terms other than agency. Finally, I will suggest that the issues about which rhetorical critics argue concern which terms ought to be featured and how they ought to be defined in our discourse about criticism.

Terms of the Discourse of Rhetorical Criticism

While different conceptual frameworks have been operative at various times through our history, I see the current framework as being conceptualized in the terms of the pentad in this way:

The *act* is what takes place. In the discourse of rhetorical criticism, the act is the production of a critical essay.

The *agent* is the person who performs the act—the rhetorical critic. The critic produces and brings to fruition the critical essay.

The *agency* is the means or instruments used to perform the act. I have chosen to confine my conception of agency to critical methods or approaches. The agency is the specific tools of inquiry that critics use to analyze their data—the neo-Aristotelian, generic, metaphor, and cluster methods, for example, and the virtually infinite number of methods that critics may invent to answer the questions they ask about their data.

The *purpose* is the reason the agent performs the act. The purpose of rhetorical criticism is to explain how some aspect of rhetoric operates and thus to make a contribution to rhetorical theory. The critic who is attempting to contribute to rhetorical theory does not view an artifact for its own qualities alone but instead moves beyond the particularities of the artifact under study in an effort to discover what that artifact suggests about symbolic processes in general (Becker, 1971, p. 41; Campbell, 1974, pp. 11–14; Croft, 1968, p. 114; Ehninger et al., 1971, p. 208; Gregg, 1985, pp. 42–43).

I acknowledge that my selection of purpose is not consistent with the purpose of a body of rhetorical-critical essays that have focused on the history of rhetorical events in order to improve the historical record. I have chosen not to include this purpose because I have placed my emphasis on current critical practice, which seems to have as purpose, if our journals are an accurate indication, contribution to theory.

The *scene* is the situation or context in which the act occurs. I have defined as the scene for the discourse of rhetorical criticism the academic environment in which the writing, presentation, and dissemination of criticism occurs. Academic journals and conventions are obvious components of our scene, but it also includes the history of rhetorical criticism; the texts of criticism—essays about rhetorical criticism and those in which criticism is practiced; the language of criticism; and the content of the discipline of speech communication, which itself influences the possibilities for the practice of rhetorical criticism (Arnold, 1971, p. 196; Minnick, 1970, p. 109; Said, 1983, pp. 13–14).

Agency as Featured Term

I have described the conceptual framework of rhetorical criticism as one in which the act is the production of a critical essay; the agency is critical methods; the agent is the critic; the purpose is to contribute to rhetorical theory; and the scene is an academic context characterized by a particular body of texts, history, language, and disciplinary content. Not all of these elements receive equal emphasis in the discourse of rhetorical criticism. I believe that what we know in the area of rhetorical criticism has come largely from a featuring of agency or method; our knowledge about criticism and the beliefs we hold about it are methodologically derived. I do not mean that a *particular* method such as genre criticism has organized our thinking but rather that our emphasis on critical procedures of any kind has created a particular conception of criticism for us. In Barnet Baskerville's (1971) words, criticism has been characterized by "our tremendous preoccupation with and proliferation of critical *methods*. Like the old lady who wept with joy every time she heard 'that blessed word "Mesopotamia",' we derive keen sensory pleasure from uttering that blessed word 'methodology' " (p. 116).

Method has been of central concern to rhetorical critics from the beginnings of our discipline, even when we had not yet developed formal methods. Early scholars sought to create a separate field of speech communication by identifying a method or methods for rhetorical criticism; usually, they adopted these methods from disciplines such as English and history. Herbert Wichelns's "The Literary Criticism of Oratory" (1925) had a major influence on the direction of rhetorical criticism largely because it featured a method for critics to use. He listed the topics that should be covered in the analysis of a speech, which then were developed by critics into neo-Aristotelianism and canonized, in particular, in Lester Thonssen and A. Craig Baird's *Speech Criticism* in 1948.

The neo-Aristotelian method came under attack by critics as a "stiff, unimaginative approach" (Sillars, 1964, p. 277) that led to "cookie-cutter" (Brockriede, 1971, p. 129) and "frequently stereotyped, occasionally banal" criticism (Clark, 1957, p. 84). It has been replaced by methodological pluralism, now the norm in our discourse: "The present variety of approaches to critical method demonstrates a healthy liberalism, eclecticism, and sense of experimentation" (Larson, 1976, p. 295). With attacks on neo-Aristotelianism as our primary critical method, we might suppose that agency or method would diminish in importance in the discourse and practice of rhetorical criticism. But a variety of critical approaches has not led to a shift from the discipline's focus on method. An examination of the ratios or relationships among the terms of the discourse about rhetorical criticism suggests that agency continues to be the controlling term for the four other elements.

The *agency-act* ratio, which encourages an examination of how method affects the production of criticism, suggests that a centering of our work on method constrains how we create and present criticism. Jon Ericson (1968) noted this kind of relationship between agency and act when he asserted "that any design for criticism will modify the result of the critical act. That is to say, any critical method may be potentially complex in itself, but it is, nevertheless, a simplification whose very structure influences the critic's end result" (p. 175).

Let me suggest just a few ways in which the critical process has been influenced by a featuring of agency or method. Our criticism tends to be analytic because our methods are ones that disassemble an artifact; we do much less of "returning the addresses to whole experiences" (Thonssen, 1968, p. 186). Our methodological focus has encouraged us to illustrate the forms of our methods rather than to engage in a creative exploration of our data. The result is that after "a while, the strictly rhetorical conclusions of one thesis tend to become remarkably similar to those of another using the same rhetorical categories, no matter how different the speaker or speeches may have been" (Croft, 1968, p. 112). Or, we may be encouraged to spend so much time describing and defending our method that we devote very little attention to an actual analysis of our data. Boring criticism can result, as well, from a featuring of agency or method. The plodding application of the various categories of a method does not always make interesting reading. Certainly, critical essays can be insightful, exciting, and energizing—and many are, despite our discipline's emphasis on agency. I simply am suggesting that insight, excitement, and energy are more difficult to achieve when agency controls the process of criticism.

The featuring of method over other terms in rhetorical criticism has implications not only for act but for purpose—as illustrated in exploration of the *agency-purpose* ratio. Criticism often is not conceptualized or taught as a tool for inquiry that can answer a research question; instead, it is viewed as a method that is itself the end. The natural order of criticism is for the critic to decide what research question is guiding the inquiry and then to select or create a method that, when applied to some data, enables the critic to answer the question. Much of our criticism, however, has been a reversal of this process. The method is selected and the research question—if one is formulated at all—is derived from the method. Even if a contribution to theory is named as a result of the answering of a research question, little is usually done with that contribution, simply because its importance is overshadowed by the emphasis on method.

One consequence of the agency-purpose ratio is labeled "conceptual anomie" by Roderick Hart (1985); it is "the failure to build the necessary bridge between one rhetorical investigation and another" (p. 9). He explains: "Many authors seem incapable of specifying what conceptual move next needs to be made in a chain of research" (p. 10). Again, this seems to be the result of an emphasis on agency at the expense of purpose.

But the most significant result of the emphasis on agency has been the limiting of rhetorical explorations to the confines of existing rhetorical theories. We explicate "existing theories of rhetoric. They become creeds to which the critic renders obedience," as Linnea Ratcliff (1971) describes their effect (p. 133). When method is featured, the theory building that results from a critical study tends to stay confined to the boundaries within which the method was developed and functions. A critic who applies the fantasy-theme method of criticism, for example, is not likely, at the conclusion of the study, to develop a theory that significantly alters or differs from Ernest Bormann's (1972, 1982, 1983, 1985) symbolic-convergence theory, the method's conceptual starting point. Our critical products are an elaboration and extension of our current theories, and we are not likely to develop what Kenneth Gergen (1982) calls *generative theory*, theory that has *"the capacity to challenge the guiding assumptions to foster reconsideration of that which is 'taken for granted,' and thereby to generate fresh alternatives"* (p. 109).

An *agency-agent* ratio suggests that a focus on method has created critics with particular characteristics—some enhance our criticism; others do not. Rewarded are such critical behaviors as coding, classification, illustration, and use of technical jargon rather than the creating of alternative ways to think and talk about constructs or the generation of new starting points for the practice of criticism. I am reminded here of a doctoral student I once advised who loved to play with ideas and who often took them in unlikely directions in his thinking and writing about rhetoric. My colleagues, on the whole, were unappreciative of this proclivity—I suspect for precisely the reason I am describing here. Good critics are those who can adjust their thinking and writing to fit the structure and form required by our methods.

The *agency-scene* ratio suggests that our focus on method confines our criticism to a particular setting or context—in this case, an intellectual, academic one. Technical jargon, the making of minuscule distinctions among categories, and—if it shows off a method—analysis of sometimes trivial topics are made to seem relevant and appropriate by a focus on method. As a result, our criticism is likely to be of interest only to our colleagues in speech communication departments and, even then, only to those who work in our area of specialization.

Featuring of Alternative Terms

While my examples of how agency frames what we know in rhetorical criticism have been more negative than positive, my point is not to argue that agency is not an appropriate term to feature. Any emphasis has both positive and negative consequences for criticism, and I suspect that agency or method serves us no better or worse than other terms we might choose to feature. My goal here is simply to suggest that just as our choice to focus on method develops our criticism in certain directions, our choice to feature a different term would produce a different kind of criticism. In the next section, I will speculate on the nature of the different kinds of criticism that might result were we to feature terms other than agency.

Purpose as Featured Term

Purpose comes the closest to rivaling agency as the featured term in our current discourse about and practice of rhetorical criticism. The call for an emphasis on purpose is exemplified by Baskerville's (1971) suggestion "that we devote some attention to the question of *why* we are doing what we are doing" (p. 123). He elaborates: It "is more important to ask *why* than *how*. Why are we doing what we are doing? What is the *purpose* of all this feverish activity? What is our criticism for? What good is it?" (p. 117). Ralph Eubanks (1970) makes the point, as well: "What's the *ultimate purpose* of rhetorical criticism? Or—put in slightly different terms—What's the *bedrock reason* for having trained rhetorical critics?" (p. 108).

The effect of making purpose the featured term on rhetorical criticism is easily demonstrated in an examination of the purpose-act ratio, suggesting that our critical methods follow our purpose. "Organic or situational" criticism (Campbell, 1972, p. 13) that relies not on predetermined methods but lets the data themselves suggest their "own analytic categories" (Brockriede, 1971, p. 128) is more likely to allow a method to develop that enables the critic to make a contribution to rhetorical theory.

But in some instances, the link between purpose and method can be made even more explicit. When critics sought the relationship between recurring situations and the rhetoric developed in response to them, their purpose suggested the method of generic criticism (Ware & Linkugel, 1973). Feminist criticism developed in much the same way. Its purposes are to re-examine traditional rhetorical theories to discover whether and how they incorporate a consideration of gender and to use that process to improve women's lives. A method of criticism that involves an examination of how gender is conceptualized in a rhetorical act and how it can be changed resulted from these purposes (Foss, 1989, pp. 151–160).

A purpose-agency ratio can continue to alter rhetorical criticism, as well, in that our goal in criticism affects the nature of our critical methods. If we believe that contributing to rhetorical theory means producing understanding of a particular phenomenon (Gronbeck, 1985, p. 11), our methods would be different from those we would use if we see a contribution to rhetorical theory as making generalizations about rhetorical processes (Black, 1978, p. 137). If our contribution is to be a set of "testable hypotheses which, when verified, will have the status of scientific laws" (Bowers, 1968, p. 127) that could be subjected "to experimental verification or rejection" (Hart, 1976, p. 77), our critical methods must allow us to produce such hypotheses. Even with a shared purpose of contribution to rhetorical theory, then, critics can understand such a contribution differently, and different methods may be required to accomplish that contribution.

Criticism today is increasingly guided by a featuring of purpose over agency, then, and critical methods are being developed to fit research questions that are asked in order to make contributions to rhetorical theory. More emphasis on purpose, however, would produce greater changes in our critical practice according to the form we expect a contribution to rhetorical theory to assume.

Agent as Featured Term

The centrality of the critic in the critical process—a featuring of agent—has been recognized, to some extent, in the discourse of rhetorical criticism. Ratcliff (1971), in fact, suggests a shift in focus from agency to agent in her statement urging us to be less concerned with "What method of criticism did the critic use?" and more interested in "Who was the critic?" (p. 134). As Richard Gregg (1985) points out, a view of agent or critic as central is consistent with one of the truisms of our field: "Those of us in communication studies have been saying for some years that meanings are in people, not in messages, though we have not always fully appreciated the implications of the statement" (p. 50). To develop the implications of this statement would affect our criticism in a number of ways.

An agent-agency ratio provides an example. How we conceptualize or define the critic affects the nature of the means we use to practice criticism; new definitions of the critic would require new kinds of agencies for our criticism. The critic has been defined as *"an expert commentator"* with "exceptional understanding" who "makes assertions . . . about 'the way things are' " (Rosenfield, 1968, p. 52). The critic "has earned the right to pass judgment on the productions [of others] . . . . All applicants will not qualify" (Baskerville, 1971, p. 124). The kind of knowledge the critic possesses is not available to everyone, nor is everyone entitled to receive it, as Martin Medhurst (1987) suggests: Critics must "learn the difference between significant works and those of less significance; between authors with something to say and those who merely say something; between audiences who can hear and assimilate the critical lessons and those who having ears, hear not" (pp. 20–21).

In these definitions, the critic is special and in possession of expertise others do not have, expertise derived largely from training in the models and methods of rhetorical criticism. Among the implications of these definitions of the critic is the notion that knowledge of formal rhetorical models is required to produce criticism. Other implications are that certain kinds of knowledge and ways of knowing are superior to others and that experts who have inside knowledge announce it to others.

But an alternative description of the agent would alter radically the agencies or methods of rhetorical criticism that are available. What we study, how we study it, and how we choose to present our findings would be redefined. Our new critic might discover that "insignificant" works are very significant in the lives of the audience for criticism and would choose to study those works as data. Those who do not have "something to say" may be seen simply as those whose critical approaches have not been allowed voice because their approaches differ from the forms and styles used by those who are considered experts. Likewise, audiences who "hear not" the critical lessons of the expert may be those who choose to listen to themselves or to those with qualifications different from those of the expert critic. Critics, in this view, more likely would be students in the process of criticism, along with the so-called nonexperts or nonspe-

cialists in their audiences, learning about and from other ways of conducting criticism. Because these critics would view themselves as experts only
at using one kind of vocabulary and engaging in one way of thinking
about criticism, they would recognize their own blindnesses and make
the effort to investigate and try out diverse critical agencies. Methods
created to deal with judgments from intuition, emotional responses, or
ideological purposes, for example, might be generated.

A featuring of agent in an agent-act ratio in a consideration of
subjectivity suggests another way in which rhetorical criticism would be
reconceptualized. We acknowledge the critic as a subjective human being
whose experiences and values necessarily affect the criticism produced:
"the critic is not an inanimate object, like a prism, with only the capacity
for passive reflection. The critic's humanity is necessarily inherent in his
work. His critical act is constituted of and by his choices and judgments"
(Sloan et al., 1971, p. 224). This subjectivity, we also agree, does not
invalidate our judgments, as Barbara Larson (1976) explains: "[S]ubjec-
tivity and selection is [sic] characteristic of all human perception, analysis,
and judgment, and do not necessarily render illegitimate or invalid
percepts subjectively arrived at" (p. 296).

But the subjectivity of the critic is downplayed in the discourse
about rhetorical criticism because we do not feature the agent or critic
in that discourse. We may not do so because we are uncomfortable with
subjectivity, for how can criticism be rigorous or legitimate or scientific
or any number of good things if it is rooted in individual experience and
bias? We recognize, with Medhurst (1987), that "strict objectivity is a
theoretical impossibility in any language-based discipline" (p. 11), but
we choose not to act on the full implications of that statement. We bring
to the fore terms other than agent in an apparent effort to mitigate the
critic's subjectivity. We choose to feature act, for example, as Medhurst
does when he urges "precision of observation and care of presentation"
(p. 11) or as Thonssen, Baird, and Braden (1970) do when they urge the
critic to display a "dispassionate, objective attitude toward the object of
investigation . . . impersonality of treatment, a detachment, . . ." (p.
22). We may feature agency or method as an antidote to subjectivity,
exemplified in Lawrence Rosenfield's (1968) description of some critical
methods that purport to place "the spectator outside the critical equation"
and "imply that the critic should strive to produce an analysis of the
essential nature of the phenomenon apart from any idiosyncrasies in his
personal responses" (p. 61).

But what if the critic's subjectivity were not seen as dysfunctional and the subjective agent were featured in discourse about rhetorical criticism? Again, we would create a very different kind of rhetorical criticism. Standards of criterial adequacy would deal not with countering the subjectivity and personal bias of the critic but with celebrating, affirming, and fully utilizing them to generate critical insights. The characteristics of the critic—sex, age, status, ethnicity, past experiences, values, and commitments—would be incorporated explicitly in critical products. We would not be disturbed by essays such as Thomas Benson's "Another Shooting in Cowtown" (1981), in which he reported on his involvement in the production of television commercials for a congressional candidate. The essay raised "to the level of textual analysis matters conventionally relegated to personal correspondence or 'corridor talk,' matters such as the ethnographer's own moods and their effects upon the cultural discourse that is 'the text,' . . ." (Mechling & Mechling, 1987, p. 20).

Agent has been downplayed in the discourse and practice of rhetorical criticism. Were it to be featured, we would find various alternative conceptions of rhetorical criticism, including greater diversity in methods, more nearly equal participation by critic and audience in the creation of rhetorical knowledge, and a reconsideration of the role of subjectivity in criticism.

Scene as Featured Term

Selection of scene as the principal stimulus suggests that our critical processes and products are largely dependent for their character on the context or scene in which they are produced. Although some critics use their critical skills to develop speeches and campaigns in various public contexts, the scene is largely the academic environment in which criticism is written and presented. The ratio of scene to purpose, for example, illustrates how criticism changes when scene is the featured term. It encourages us to see our contributions to rhetorical theory as confined by the academic setting and history in which our criticism occurs. If scene is determining, any contribution to rhetorical theory is preselected within the boundaries of that scene or system. The development of radically different theories or major alterations in our theories is difficult or virtually impossible unless we carefully examine our scenic boundaries and deliberately try to escape them. The form and substance of any theory we might develop must accord with the theoretical statements regarded as appropriate in that scene.

The work of Michel Foucault (1970, 1972), among others, suggests yet another effect that a featuring of scene would have on the discourse and practice of rhetorical criticism; in this case, the relationship is captured in a scene-agent ratio. Most of our discourse assumes an autonomous, freely choosing agent at the heart of criticism. The critic—just like the rhetor who is the subject of the study—is seen as having freedom of choice to select from a wide variety of options to develop the critical essay (Foss, 1983, pp. 286–287). A focus on the scene as deterministic, however, suggests that the critic's freedom is sharply curtailed, for the critic's action takes place in a scene of structures and practices in which only certain options are allowed (Mechling & Mechling, 1987, pp. 16–17). Consideration of how the scene determines the nature of the critic would lead us to question not only the notion of freedom of choice but also the related roles of intentionality and subjectivity as they function in rhetorical criticism.

Were we to choose to feature scene in rhetorical criticism, our criticism would be of a different nature. Our theory building would have the potential to expand in very different directions were scenic boundaries questioned, and the freedom of choice we have accorded the critic would become problematic.

Act as Featured Term

A featuring of the act of criticism itself can enable us to envision new directions for rhetorical criticism simply by broadening our range of choices in defining the act. One common way to view the act is as argument. Wayne Brockriede's (1974) statement that "*useful* rhetorical criticism, whatever else it may be, must function as an argument" (p. 165) is representative, as is Rosenfield's (1968) assertion that "criticism is most sensibly conceived of as a special form of reason-giving discourse" (p. 50).

When the critical act is seen as argument, its effects can be seen in a pairing of act with agency; the methods seen as appropriate are agencies that accord with the process of argument. They tend to encourage us, for example, to choose as our data rhetorical phenomena that can be dealt with in the structure of an argument, where our warrants and claims can be labeled and discussed easily. Discursive data such as speeches and essays are clearly appropriate, then, because insights about them can be translated easily into our traditional, verbal argumentative form. Nondiscursive data such as architecture are less appropriate; we are hard put even to identify the claims and warrants that a building makes to a viewer.

But suppose we define the critical act primarily as art, a conception not unfamiliar to the discourse of criticism. Fisher (1969), for example, argues that students "of rhetoric, adopting this view, should not only be able to make their criticisms fine argumentative statements but artistic ones as well" (p. 109). Criticism, he asserts, "assumes an art" (p. 105). Baskerville (1971) also has suggested that a "critic, reflecting upon a work of fine art occasionally manages to create a work of fine art" (p. 123). Works of art are characterized by originality and creativity; a focus on the act as art, then, would suggest methods that highlight these qualities. In Herbert Simons's (1978) terms, we would see methods characterized by greater use of "muddleheaded anecdotalism," where symbols have multiple referents. Other methods and forms of presentation that embody aesthetic and literary principles would be encouraged, including dialogues, narratives with character and plot development, and even visual forms of expression.

Our standards for criterial adequacy for judging critical products also would change if the critical act were defined as art and featured in rhetorical criticism. Works of art are not judged by the standards by which we usually judge rhetorical criticism—how well the critic argues or whether the essay is coherent, for example (Foss, 1983, pp. 288–294). Instead, our standards might include the nature of the insight produced, the emotion generated, the effect on the lives of the people in the audience, or the technical craftsmanship or skill demonstrated in the presentation. Such standards would leave behind many traditional conceptions of what good criticism is, but they also might lead to criticism that functions more as art does—to provoke and stimulate. Not only whether we choose to feature act but also how we define that act, then, has consequences for the discourse and practice of rhetorical criticism.

Controversies over the Conceptual Framework

The issues about which rhetorical critics argue and the most urgent questions confronting us derive, in large part, from how we have chosen to describe rhetorical criticism. A few examples will illustrate that our liveliest controversies are, in fact, clashes over aspects of the conceptual framework of rhetorical criticism.

One kind of issue about which we argue concerns which pentadic term to assign to a given rhetorical construct—act, agency, agent, purpose, or scene. The controversy surrounding the purpose of scholarship in public address is rooted in disagreement about the proper label to assign to the data. Public-address critics and rhetorical historians often believe their task is to describe "specific rhetors addressing specific rhetorical problems in specific rhetorical circumstances" (Hart, 1985, p. 4); theory construction is perceived as having little or no role to play in such studies. Hart summarizes this controversy succinctly:

> All too often one finds specific persons and events occupying the left side of the colon in the titles of public address studies rather than being subsumed (on the right side of the colon) to the intellectual trends for which they stand as evidence. Some among us are still too committed, for example, to writing definitive rhetorical histories of individual presidencies instead of exploring the institutional regularities of the office itself. (p. 5)

The controversy Hart describes concerns the most appropriate pentadic label for an aspect of the critical process. Should the data with which the critic deals—the speeches of a president, for example—be labeled the purpose? In this case, the purpose is to understand that particular rhetoric or to use the rhetoric to improve the historical record. Or should the data be labeled the agency, a view in which the data are seen as the means to achieving the purpose of making a contribution to rhetorical theory?

A second category of issues about which we argue concerns the proper definition of a pentadic element—how best to label the act or the agent, for example. The current discussion about ideological or social criticism illustrates this type of controversy. In social criticism, the critic uses criticism as a vehicle to encourage public discussion about trends in the society, to evaluate a particular way of thinking and acting, or to suggest how society should be (Corcoran, 1984; McGee, 1975, 1978; Wander, 1983, 1984; Wander & Jenkins, 1972). But others argue that societal change is not the most useful definition of purpose in rhetorical criticism because criticism undertaken to comment on a particular issue, situation, or policy tends not to be "enduring; its importance and its functions are immediate and ephemeral" (Campbell, 1974, p. 11). Once the historical situation has been forgotten or the rhetor is no longer the center of the public's attention, social criticism is irrelevant. Those who hold this view then propose a definition of the purpose of criticism as contributing to rhetorical theory.

A third type of issue over which rhetorical critics argue concerns which term should be the controlling one in the discourse about and practice of rhetorical criticism. The controversy over the appropriateness and legitimacy of feminist criticism is an example of this kind of issue. Feminist criticism, in which the conceptualization of gender in an artifact is analyzed in order to de-construct and change conceptions of gender, is often met with hostility, defensiveness, or amusement. It strikes many students, associate editors, and editors as inappropriately political or ideological. They cannot understand how feminist critics can argue that this method of criticism "may be considered as or more central to the analysis of rhetoric than almost any other method of criticism. Its focus is on a fundamental element of human life—gender—and it is dramatically changing the form and content of knowledge about rhetoric" (Foss, 1989, p. 151).

This controversy over feminist criticism can be understood as a conflict about what should be the featured term in the discourse of rhetorical criticism. Feminist critics believe that term should be agent. From their perspective, who the critic is, the sex and gender of that critic, the gender screen through which the critic responds to an artifact, and the critic's personal commitment to creating a better world for women are the most important elements of the critical process; these, of course, are concerns of agent. Those who object to or are suspicious of feminist criticism may choose any of the other terms as controlling; the point is that agent is *not* the term they select as the one that ought to be featured in the discourse about and practice of rhetorical criticism.

These few samples of controversies have illustrated, I hope, how many of the issues about which we argue are rooted in the kind of conceptual framework we see as desirable for rhetorical criticism. These issues should be of concern, for our framework guides all aspects of our critical practice and constrains the insights produced by rhetorical criticism. I deliberately have avoided suggesting the way I believe some of these controversies should be resolved or the term(s) that should control rhetorical criticism because benefits accrue whatever term receives our emphasis. My intent has been simply to make problematic the major elements of our discourse and practice so that we can decide whether that is how we want them to be. As a result of that knowledge, we then can decide thoughtfully and purposefully, that a particular way of describing rhetorical criticism will produce the most insightful criticism or that greater diversity in our conception and practice of criticism is desirable.

References

Arnold, C. C. (1971). Reflections on the Wingspread Conference. In L. F. Bitzer & E. Black (Eds.), *The prospect of rhetoric* (pp. 194 199). Englewood Cliffs, NJ: Prentice-Hall.

Baskerville, B. (1971). Rhetorical criticism, 1971: Retrospect, prospect, introspect. *Southern Speech Communication Journal, 37*, 113–124.

Becker, S. I. (1971). Rhetorical studies for the contemporary world. In L. F. Bitzer & E. Black (Eds.), *The prospect of rhetoric* (pp. 21–43). Englewood Cliffs, NJ: Prentice-Hall.

Benson, T. W. (1981). Another shooting in cowtown. *Quarterly Journal of Speech, 67*, 347–406.

Black, E. (1978). *Rhetorical criticism: A study in method.* Madison, WI: University of Wisconsin Press.

Bormann, E. G. (1972). Fantasy and rhetorical vision: The rhetorical criticism of social reality. *Quarterly Journal of Speech ,58*, 396–407.

Bormann, E. G. (1982). Fantasy and rhetorical vision: Ten years later. *Quarterly Journal of Speech, 68*, 288–305.

Bormann, E. G. (1983). Symbolic convergence: Organizational communication and culture. In L. L. Putnam & M. E. Pacanowsky (Eds.), *Communication and organizations: An interpretive approach* (pp. 99–122). Beverly Hills, CA: Sage.

Bormann, E. G. (1985). Symbolic convergence theory: A communication formulation. *Journal of Communication, 35*, 128–138.

Bowers, J. W. (1968). The pre-scientific function of rhetorical criticism. In T. R. Nilsen (Ed.), *Essays on rhetorical criticism* (pp. 126–145). New York: Random House.

Brockriede, W. (1971). Trends in the study of rhetoric: Toward a blending of criticism and science. In L. F. Bitzer & E. Black (Eds.), *The prospect of rhetoric* (pp. 123–139). Englewood Cliffs, NJ: Prentice-Hall.

Brockriede, W. (1974). Rhetorical criticism as argument. *Quarterly Journal of Speech, 60*, 165–174.

Burke, K. (1969). *A grammar of motives.* Berkeley: University of California Press.

Campbell, K. K. (1972). *Critiques of contemporary rhetoric.* Belmont, CA: Wadsworth.

Campbell, K. K. (1974). Criticism: Ephemeral and enduring. *Speech Teacher, 23*, 9–14.

Clark, R. D. (1957). Lessons from the literary critics. *Western Speech, 21*, 83–89.

Corcoran, F. (1984). The widening gyre: Another look at ideology in Wander and his critics. *Central States Speech Journal, 35*, 54–56.

Croft, A. J. (1968). The functions of rhetorical criticism. In W. A. Linsley (Ed.), *Speech criticism: Methods and materials* (pp. 108–118). Dubuque, IA: Wm. C. Brown.

Ehninger, D., Benson, T. W., Ettlich, E. E., Fisher, W. R., Kerr, H. P.,

Larson, R. L., Nadeau, R. E., & Niles, L. A. (1971). Report of the committee on the scope of rhetoric and the place of rhetorical studies in higher education. In L. F. Bitzer & E. Black (Eds.), *The prospect of rhetoric* (pp. 208–219). Englewood Cliffs, NJ: Prentice-Hall.

Ericson, J. M. (l968). Evaluative and formulative functions in speech criticism. *Western Speech, 32*, 173–176.

Eubanks, R. T. (1970). Rhetorical criticism: Prognoses for the seventies—A symposium: A prognosis by Ralph T. Eubanks. *Southern Speech Journal, 36*, 107–108.

Fisher, W. F. (1969). Method in rhetorical criticism. *Southern Speech Journal, 35*, 101–109.

Foss, S. K. (1983). Criteria for adequacy in rhetorical criticism. *Southern Speech Communication Journal, 49*, 283–295.

Foss, S. K. (1989). *Rhetorical criticism: Exploration and practice.* Prospect Heights, IL: Waveland.

Foucault, M. (1970). *The order of things: An archaeology of the human sciences.* New York: Pantheon.

Foucault, M. (1972). *The archaeology of knowledge* (A. M. S. Smith, Trans.). New York: Pantheon.

Gergen, K. J. (1982). *Toward transformation in social knowledge.* New York: Springer-Verlag.

Gregg, R. B. (1985). The criticism of symbolic inducement: A critical-theoretical connection. In T. L. Benson (Ed.), *Speech communication in the 20th century* (pp. 41–62). Carbondale: Southern Illinois University Press.

Gronbeck, B. E. (1985, November). *The birth, death, and rebirth of public address.* Paper presented at the meeting of the Speech Communication Association, Denver, CO.

Hart, R. P. (1976). Forum: Theory-building and rhetorical criticism: An informal statement of opinion. *Central States Speech Journal, 27*, 70–77.

Hart, R. P. (1985, November). *Public address: Should it be disinterred?* Paper presented at the meeting of the Speech Communication Association, Denver, CO.

Kuhn, T. S. (1970). *The structure of scientific revolutions.* Chicago: University of Chicago Press.

Larson, B. A. (1976). Method in rhetorical criticism: A pedagogical approach and proposal. *Central States Speech Journal, 27*, 295–301.

McGee, M. C. (1975). In search of 'the people': A rhetorical alternative. *Quarterly Journal of Speech, 61*, 235–249.

McGee, M. C. (1978). Not men, but measures: The origins and import of an ideological principle. *Quarterly Journal of Speech, 64*, 141–154.

Mechling, E. W., & Mechling, J. (1987, February). *Post-anthropological reflections on post-rhetorical criticism.* Paper presented at the meeting of the Western Speech Communication Association, Salt Lake City, UT.

Medhurst, M. J. (1987, February). *On freedom, failure, and critical responsibility.* Paper presented at the meeting of the Western Speech Communication Association, Salt Lake City, UT.

Minnick, W. C. (1970). Rhetorical criticism: Prognoses for the Seventies—A symposium: A prognosis by Wayne C. Minnick. *Southern Speech Journal, 36,* 108–110.

Ratcliff, L. (1971). Rhetorical criticism: An alternative perspective. *Southern Speech Communication Journal, 37,* 125–135.

Rosenfield, L. W. (1968). The anatomy of critical discourse. *Speech Monographs, 35,* 50–69.

Said, E. W. (1983). Opponents, audiences, constituencies, and community. In W. J. T. Mitchell (Ed.), *The politics of interpretation* (pp. 7–32). Chicago: University of Chicago Press.

Sillars, M. O. (1964). Rhetoric as act. *Quarterly Journal of Speech, 50,* 277–284.

Simons, H. W. (1978). In praise of muddleheaded anecdotalism. *Western Journal of Speech Communication, 42,* 21–28.

Sloan, T. O., Gregg, R. B., Nilsen, T. R., Rein, I. J., Simons, H. W., Stelzner, H. G., & Zacharias, D. W. (1971). Report of the committee on the advancement and refinement of rhetorical criticism. In L. F. Bitzer & E. Black (Eds.), *The prospect of rhetoric* (pp. 220–227). Englewood Cliffs, NJ: Prentice-Hall.

Thonssen, L. (1968). Random thoughts on the criticism of orators and oratory. *Western Speech, 32,* 185–191.

Thonssen, L., & Baird, A. C. (1948). *Speech criticism.* New York: Ronald.

Thonssen, L., Baird, A. C., & Braden, W. W. (1970). *Speech criticism* (2nd ed.). New York: Ronald.

Wander, P. (1983). The ideological turn in modern criticism. *Central States Speech Journal, 34,* 1–18.

Wander, P. (1984). The third persona: An ideological turn in rhetorical theory. *Central States Speech Journal, 35,* 197–216.

Wander, P., & Jenkins, S. (1972). Rhetoric, society, and the critical response. *Quarterly Journal of Speech, 58,* 441–450.

Ware, B. L., & Linkugel, W. A. (1973). They spoke in defense of themselves: On the generic criticism of apologia. *Quarterly Journal of Speech, 59,* 273–283.

Wichelns, H. A. (1925). The literary criticism of oratory. In A. M. Drummond (Ed.), *Studies in rhetoric and public speaking in honor of James A. Winans* (pp. 181–216). New York: Century.

• 3 •

Contemporary Developments in Rhetorical Criticism: A Consideration of the Effects of Rhetoric

RICHARD A. CHERWITZ
JOHN THEOBALD-OSBORNE

To say that communication has effects is superfluous. Whether the focus of analysis is interpersonal, public, or mass-mediated messages, the underlying pedagogical and scholarly assumption of our discipline is that communication has the power: to arouse emotions; influence the direction, intensity, and salience of beliefs; transform and nurture the development of ideas; and instigate action. Since the rise of early Greek society, practitioners, critics, and theorists have been intrigued by the manner in which communication evokes consequences. The inception of the field of speech communication signaled a renewed interest in the pragmatic (as opposed to literary) characteristics of discourse. Regardless of the types of research we conduct or the kinds of classes we teach, we are at base a community of scholars joined in the assumption that communication can make a difference: we teach and study communication phenomena because we believe that, armed with sufficient and appropriate rhetorical tools, individuals can influence their environment.

Over the past seventy-five years this concern with the consequences of communication has led rhetorical critics to explore at least three broad categories of effect: psychological, philosophical, and political. Critics interested in examining the psychological effects of rhetoric have discerned the influence of communication on the development of self-image and the evocation of states of feeling; they have given attention to the

We would like to thank Professors Kathleen Jamieson and Roderick Hart for their insightful criticisms of earlier drafts of this manuscript.

role played by rhetoric in the maintenance of values, the promotion of ego, and the intensification and amplification of perceptions.

Specifically, researchers dealing with psychological effect contend that there exists an "ego-function of discourse" that explains why a rhetor "may choose to address himself," resulting in a "transaction of self with self" (Gregg, 1971, p. 71). Research shows that a rhetor's force of personality and charisma influence the psychological state of auditors (Boss, 1976). Moreover, criticism focused on effects reveals the importance of biographical-historical data and how they potentially influence a rhetor's "signature" and personality (Hillbruner, 1974). In his call for a neo-Aristotelian approach to criticism, Hill (1972) argues for the importance of analyzing psychological and characterological factors that determine whether an audience is persuaded by the rhetor's case. And Woodward (1979), in his study of presidents and prime ministers, illustrates how "traditional, structural and cultural differences shape public acts" and how such differences may result in an emphasis on "conventional values and unifying themes" (p. 41).

These are only a few representatives of the many studies that examine the psychological influences and effects of rhetoric. While this body of research may have implications for philosophical and political conceptions of effect, it is primarily oriented toward understanding the *psychological* constraints and consequences of communication. Our goal in this chapter is not to treat exhaustively psychological effect studies; in his discussion of "value-affirming" rhetoric, Hart (1984) provides a comprehensive and accessible synthesis of the important contributions to our discipline made by those interested in the psychological consequences of rhetoric.

Critics also have been intrigued by the philosophical effects of communication. Scholars have explored the effects of rhetoric on the development of ideas; the manner in which rhetoric is used to question first premises and alter accepted patterns of intellection is the focus of such criticism. Zyskind (1968), for example, asks whether it is "possible to grasp and formulate how [a rhetor's] mind works—does it indeed have a way of working?" (p. 228) In his case study of Theodore Roosevelt, Zyskind provides an affirmative answer, arguing that philosophically oriented criticism can discover "intelligible structures of thought" existing in the mind of a rhetor and manifested in discourse (p. 252). Similarly, Jamieson (1976) documents how weltanschauung influences and is influenced by rhetoric. She contends that "rhetorical visions develop and decay in response to exigencies perceived through the filter of a worldview"

(p. 4). Conceived in this way, rhetoric can be analyzed for its effect on one's philosophy about the world. Of late, scholars in various academic disciplines have studied the "rhetoric of science" (Overington, 1977; Weimer, 1977) and the "rhetoric of human inquiry" (Gross, 1984; Lyne, 1985; McCloskey, 1985; Nelson & Megill, 1986; Simons, 1985). This research explicates the indispensable role of communication in expanding human knowledge regardless of academic subject matter. These studies remind us that thought and intellection not only are controlled by rhetorical forms, but also may affect rhetoric.

Like psychological effect studies, philosophical approaches may harbor implications for the other consequences of communication. What is important to note, however, is that philosophically inclined critics seem almost exclusively interested in the effect of rhetoric on ideas. Our point is simply that one can choose to examine the effects of rhetoric on either ideas or psychological states without necessarily addressing the larger question of whether or not communication affects policy.

The vast majority of interest in the consequences of communication, however, has focused on political effects: the influence of rhetoric on the allocation of resources by institutions in society. Emphasis has been placed both on the creation and resolution of conflict and on how rhetoric ultimately constrains and influences policy. A discussion of these effects occupies our attention in the remainder of this chapter.

Although the three categories of effect may not be entirely discrete, they seem to provide a useful heuristic for thinking about the different critical frames of reference and points of interest available to rhetorical analysts. To provide a thorough understanding of scholarship within all three categories would be an undertaking beyond the scope of this chapter. Our concern here is the political consequences of rhetoric. Not only is it the case that most effects-oriented research in the past seventy-five years fits within this category, but there exists a need to examine our current state of knowledge regarding political effects. What do we know about such effects?

What are the limits of our research? And what can be done to appreciate fully the political consequences of rhetoric? To help answer these questions, we offer a sociological conception of political effect, suggesting how such an understanding not only allows us to categorize existing scholarship, but offers insight into the kinds of questions that critics should raise in future research.

The preponderance of research treating the political effects of rhetoric has focused on the most obvious, consequential, direct, and empirically instantiated effects attributed to human communication. It is not surprising, therefore, that when we teach our students the art of message production or when we engage in critical analysis, we concern ourselves with such stereotypical and blatant effects as diametrical shifts in beliefs, the emergence of anti- and pro-social behaviors, and the occurrence of overt behaviors. Such gross inspections of communication have led to interesting conclusions: messages have the power to whip up mass hysteria, heighten prejudice, lead nations into war, create protest and revolution, increase violence, promote acquiescence and conformity, and influence elections.[1]

While such conclusions are insightful and attest to the political importance of communication, most discourse probably does not immediately, if ever, produce such extreme consequences. In fact, many of the political effects presupposed by rhetorical analysts as a warrant for critical scrutiny have not been successfully isolated by quantitative researchers.[2] Are we to infer, then, that most messages have no political consequences? Must we conclude that the importance assigned communication rests on the exception rather than the rule or, perhaps, on an erroneous assumption altogether? Moreover, if our messages do not lead immediately to wholesale alterations in beliefs and behaviors, must communication be judged politically ineffectual?

The answer to these questions is no. However, to understand why this is so requires a broadened understanding of political effect. We argue

---

1. In the following section, we shall make specific references to particular studies supporting these conclusions.

2. That quantitative researchers have difficulty in isolating direct effects of communication seems apparent given the trenchant and frequent critiques of effect models (Chaffee & Hochheimer, 1982). Not only have researchers found it difficult to gauge the direct effects of communication, but they have found problematic the use of quantitative instruments to measure cultural and ideological effects. This is because of the tendency to treat messages "as discrete measurable units of information transmitted to receivers" (Fejes, 1984, pp. 219-232). In the pages that follow, we argue that there is value in getting beyond traditional, empirical conceptions of political effect. Our claim, therefore, parallels the recent tendency in mass communication described by Fejes to avoid thinking of effect in strictly quantitative terms. In short, perhaps the reason for our inability to document the political consequences of both public and mass communication may stem from too narrow a conception of effect.

that a theory of communicative effect grounded in the sociological notion of power not only can enrich our awareness of the political consequences of communication, allowing us to see more than the largest, obvious, and empirically discernible results of human message making, but can unite a number of disparate critical methods within one theoretical framework.

The rest of this chapter consists of four sections. In the first, we outline previous patterns of discerning the political effects of communication and explore their underlying assumptions. Arguing that such approaches are not wrong, but merely incomplete, in the second section we underscore the importance of a sociological conception of power to an appreciation of effect; in particular, we examine the theory of power offered by the British sociologist Steven Lukes (1974). In the third section, we delineate a rhetorical analog or counterpart of Lukes's three-dimensional concept of power. Operating with this analog, we present three different yet interrelated types of political effect. Drawing from the ongoing debate about the Strategic Defense Initiative (SDI), we discuss the advantages of criticism stemming from a three-dimensional theory of communicative effect. Finally, we consider implications for rhetoric issuing from such a broadened understanding of political effect.

Traditional Approaches to Studying the Effects of Rhetoric

Traditional approaches to effect have a common thread: all portray effect as a positive, observable consequent of communication that leads to active decision making or attitude change. Effect is conceived as a direct and empirically verifiable product. The traditional, or what we later call "one-dimensional," view of rhetorical effect has its origins in Aristotle's *Rhetoric* (Cooper, 1932). Aristotelian effect is simply communication designed to achieve a specific end: the role of rhetoric is "to be able to discover the means of persuasion in reference to any given subject" (p. 7). The Aristotelian auditor makes active decisions based on the most convincing rhetoric.

The paradigmatic discussion of effect in traditional rhetoric is Wichelns's (1925/1962) "The Literary Criticism of Oratory." "Rhetorical criticism . . . is concerned with effect. It regards speech as a communication to a specific audience" (p. 209). The implication is that effect is unidimensional in its focus on message content and form as persuading specific audiences to accept specific decision making perspectives. Brock and Scott (1980) point to both the complexity and the limitations of this traditional effect standard: "It is an impossible task to be aware of all the possible effects of any complex, human action" (p. 21). Campbell (1972) contends that effects are difficult to gauge because of methodological problems and the inability of analysts to isolate a single speech as the source of effect. Much of the literature in rhetorical criticism conceives of effect at one level—as a phenomenon attesting to direct shifts in people's beliefs, attitudes, and behaviors.

Methodological approaches incorporating the traditional effect standard have produced enlightening rhetorical studies. As early as Thonssen and Baird's (1948) Speech Criticism, critics sought "to establish the direct causal relation between spoken words and subsequent actions" (p. 54). Thonssen and Baird, and those following their lead, saw rhetorical criticism functioning in four ways: to discern social change, to discover surface response, to uncover belief or attitude change, and to highlight long-range effects.

Consistent with these four functions, rhetorical scholars have observed a number of far-reaching political effects of communication. Let us consider a few representative examples. The influence of rhetoric on electoral outcomes has been documented repeatedly by critics (Brock, 1969, Cragen & Shields, 1977; McBath & Fisher, 1969; Simons, Chesbro & Orr, 1973; Swanson, 1977; Trent & Trent, 1974). Similarly, rhetorical analysts have considered the effects of discourse on executive and legislative policy (Bass & Cherwitz, 1978; Cherwitz, 1979; Davis, 1981; Davis & Quimby, 1969; Dedmon, 1966; Hikins, 1983; Hogan, 1986; McKerrow, 1977; Zarefsky, 1986). In addition, critics have ascertained how communication affects social movements (Andrews, 1969; Burgess, 1968; Griffin, 1952, 1964; Hart, 1971: Simons, 1967, 1969, 1970, 1972).

Besides studying specific political consequences, analysts have offered a number of empirical methodologies for documenting effect. Thompson (1945), Brookes (1967), and Brandes (1967), to name just a few, measured audience responses to speeches. In much the same manner, Minnick (1971) combined the neo-Aristotelian approach described by Hill (1972) with empirical measurement techniques to assess the potential effect of speech. As part of his treatment of "language-in-use," Cherwitz (1980) discussed some of the problems with empirical techniques, offering an additional way to document the contributory effects of rhetoric. In the following section we shall comment in greater detail on these methodological difficulties.

Admittedly, this is only a sampling of the voluminous literature treating political effects of communication. In our opinion, little purpose would be served by simply listing and tersely discussing each of these contributions to our understanding of effect. Suffice it to say, the preponderance of research in this area is predicated upon what we described above as the traditional effect standard. We do not wish to imply that these approaches are invalid. Rather, we suggest that they focus on but one dimension of effect. In summarizing traditional assessments, we offer the following generalizations:

1. Political effect is theoretically and methodologically restricted to overt behavioral change and measurable or describable attitudinal change.

2. With the exception of classic discussions by such scholars as Thonssen and Baird (1948), and a handful of contemporary investigations, the concept of political effect is relegated largely to individual case studies. There has been insufficient exploration of the concept theoretically or meta-critically; in short, the concept of political effect has not been informed by nor kept pace with sophisticated advances in other aspects of rhetorical and communication theory.

3. Since prior research assumes that effect is a concept describing human relationships and influence, it is ironic that there is little effort to enrich our theoretical knowledge of political effect through an integration of it with sociological research, specifically, that sociological research dealing with power.

4. Traditional explorations of effect are viewed almost separately and independently from other critical postures. Scholars have proliferated a number of methods for appraising messages, including such approaches as fantasy-theme analysis (Bormann, 1985); dramatism (Burke, 1937); mythic, ideological, and cultural criticism (McGee, 1980; McGuire, 1977); and narration (Fisher, 1987). Each of these modes of criticism—including effect studies themselves—often serves as a unique kind of critical analysis, informed by an accompanying discrete body of literature. At only the most obvious and superficial level has

there been comment on the fact that all of these approaches have in common with traditional effect studies concern for the consequences of communication. To date, therefore, we have not appreciated fully the critical and pedagogical value of viewing all of these perspectives on rhetoric as evolving out of a single, uniform, and consistent theory of communicative effect.

"Power Over" and Political Effect: A Three-Dimensional View

Contemporary theories of power provide a fertile and generally untapped source of thought for the study of the effects of rhetoric. There are many definitions of power, some restrictive, some broad. The common core underlying all definitions of power is the notion that A in some way affects B. Consequently, communicative effect is, at base, a power construct; undergirding the occurrence of communicative effect is the assumption that A's communication in some way affects B. That is to say, if A can affect B, A has power over B.

This commonsensical conclusion is no better seen than in the sociological distinction between "power over" and "power to" (Lukes, 1974, pp. 26–33). Simply put, "power over" is relational and competitive, while "power to" is individual and uncontested. To say that A has power over B requires that a relationship exists between the two parties. Without that relationship there would be no source of power. On the other hand, to claim that A has "power to" underscores the fact that A is in the possession of certain abilities needed to accomplish some act. Because rhetorical communication treats relationships among message, source, and audience, the relational character of "power over" is germane. Moreover, inasmuch as the adherence of an audience to the content of communicator A's message (whether public or mass-mediated) involves the simultaneous rejection of potentially competing contents, communicative effect is inherently conflictual and, thus, an exercise in "power over." It must be understood, however, that the source of A's power over B, while always seen in the context of A's relationship to B, may be attributed partially to certain resources in A's possession. For that reason, the concept of "power to" is relevant to but not sufficient for a complete understanding of communicative effect.

The perspective on power introduced by Lukes (1974) provides a conceptualization that can broaden the scope of political effect. In *Power: A Radical View*, Lukes delineates three approaches to the study of power. His "one-dimensional," "two-dimensional," and "three-dimensional" views of power provide a useful analog for gleaning the potential effects of communication.

The one-dimensional or "pluralist" view is based on the premise that "the locus of power is determined by seeing who prevails in cases of decision making where there is an observable conflict" (Lukes, 1974, p. 11). The one-dimensional view is concerned with explicit behavior, direct decision making, and overt conflict. Lukes points out that this focus confines itself to exercised, not potential, power, as only exerted power can be observed directly. The extent to which A can get B to accept A's beliefs and act in accordance with A's intent demonstrates the exercise of power in the first dimension.

The two-dimensional view of power begins with a critique of one-dimensionality. Its proponents, Bachrach and Baratz (1970), argue that whenever a person or group "creates or reinforces barriers to the public airing of policy conflicts, that person or group has power" (p. 8). Tied to the two-dimensional view is the concept of "mobilisation of bias," which denotes the practice by which some issues are organized into politics while others are organized out (Lukes, 1974, p. 16). The critique is clear: by emphasizing decision making, the one-dimensional view does not account for "the fact that power may be, and often is, exercised by confining the scope of decision-making to relatively 'safe' issues" (Lukes, p. 8). Thus, the two-dimensional view focuses on both decision making and non-decision making, issues and potential issues, and overt or covert conflict. The extent to which A can keep B from deciding on an issue, or can get B to consider some issue that deflects attention from another, measures the exercise of power in the second dimension.

Lukes's (1974) three-dimensional view of power accepts the prior critique of one-dimensionality and develops a critique of the two-dimensional view. His most important point is that power encompasses more than just decision making and non-decision making. For example, A exercises power over B by getting B to do what B does not want to do; however, A also exercises power over B "by influencing, shaping, or determining" B's very wants (p. 23). Further, the three-dimensional view accounts for "latent conflict, which consists in a contradiction between the interests of those exercising power and the real interests of those they exclude" (Lukes, pp. 24–25). Thus, the three-dimensional view moves considerably beyond the two-dimensional by conceiving of control over the political agenda and latent conflict as power issues. To the extent that A prevents B from developing an awareness of B's own policy needs and grievances, A exercises power over B in the third dimension. In addition, whenever A's message operates within a system of communication that prevents B from developing real grievances, there is the occurrence of the third dimension of power.

The third dimension of power is extremely complex and often so subtle that its exercise is difficult to detect. The key to such detection is for one to become critical, that is, aware of all relevant *counterfactual* possibilities (Lukes, 1974, pp. 26–50). A counterfactual situation exists if, were it not for A's power over B, B would develop a different conception of her/his interests. For example, when the vocabulary of A's message throughout time (assuming that A and B have been in a power relationship for some time, as in the case of a government and its public) keeps B from being aware of the underlying and unarticulated assumptions of A's message or of political alternatives, B is prevented from seeing how the very system restricts alternative world views. In exposing this use of power, it must be possible to isolate and justify the relevant counterfactuals, that is, the alternative views and grievances that arguably would be developed if the underlying assumption of A's message was discerned.

A Three-Dimensional Conception of Political Effect: A Rhetorical Analog of Power

For each of Lukes's (1974) three dimensions of power there is a corresponding and analogous conception of communicative effect. Progressing from the first dimension, these conceptions build hierarchically and expand in critical sophistication and abstraction. For example, in each dimension beyond the first, additional mediating variables are introduced that increase the distance between message and outcome. Although at first it may seem intuitively attractive to begin analyses of effect inductively with a consideration of the first dimension, our contention is that, by commencing deductively, starting at the most abstract level, critics may have a greater capacity to guarantee that no possible effect of communication escapes attention. Such a deductive approach may offer a more thorough understanding of why certain first-level effects did or did not occur: third-dimension effects, we posit, may frame second-dimension effects that in turn influence observable results at the first level.

The attraction of inductive criticism is evident in contemporary investigations focusing on the influence of single speeches or media events. Interestingly, the occurrence or absence of effects stemming from isolated artifacts may be predicated upon other, less obviously rhetorical phenomena that take place in advance. On many issues, the process of persuasion (in which a speaker seeks a particular response at one moment in time) is influenced by the existence of antecedent communication that may not explicitly address the issue in question nor overtly solicit audience outcomes. Thus, while analysis of communicative effect at the third level may seem analytically subsequent, our claim is that these effects are sometimes chronologically prior.

To elucidate our three-tiered theory of communicative effect, we draw examples from the ongoing dispute about the Strategic Defense Initiative (hereafter SDI), an issue concerning the proposed expenditure of hundreds of billions of dollars to research, construct, and deploy a laser-guided nuclear missile defense system in space. The SDI controversy is a suitable object for rhetorical analysis for several reasons: SDI would overturn the policy of "mutually assured destruction"[3] that has guided superpower relations; it is a rhetorically rich and complex topic, involving overlapping subissues and a mixture of communication forums; the discourses of both sides reflect unique sets of values, often appearing in clear juxtaposition to one another; and it is a highly charged issue guaranteed to be in the limelight for some time to come. We draw upon this dispute simply to illustrate the kinds of questions to be raised at each of the three

---

3. "Mutually assured destruction" is predicated on the assumption that superpowers, if they maintain the capacity to destroy one another, are deterred from initiating a nuclear attack. The Reagan Administration's SDI rhetoric advocates replacing deterrence, which is offensively based, with a defensive strategy. Art & Jervis (1973) offer a good discussion of traditional deterrence strategy. Current journalistic and academic publications abound with discussion of how SDI would affect traditional policies of deterrence.

levels and to exemplify the potential advantages of a three-dimensional consideration of rhetorical effect.

A one-dimensional analysis of communicative effect focuses on the direct relationship between messages and behavioral outcomes. As made clear in the first section, most discussions of rhetorical effect operate in one dimension, exploring the manner in which empirically verifiable outcomes are causally related to individual messages. In a sense, the relationship between communication and effect is analogous to stimulus and response: rhetors' utterances lead directly to specifiable decisions.

To borrow from our SDI example, a one-dimensional study of communicative effect might analyze a single speech, for example, President Ronald Reagan's (1983) nationally televised speech of March 23, 1983, in which he advocated research and development of a system that would permit the United States to "intercept and destroy ballistic missiles before they reached our own soil or that of our allies" (p. 389). In the first dimension, the communication event subject to scrutiny is Reagan's speech to a clearly specified audience (in this case, immediate and remote). A one-dimensional analysis of his speech might gauge effect by asking: How were audience attitudes and decision making regarding SDI shaped and changed? Specific questions that a one-dimensional critique might pose include: Following Reagan's speech, was the public more favorably disposed toward SDI research and development? Did the president's remarks prompt supportive measures by the Congress? In other words, to what extent did the discourse result in direct (either immediate or remote) actions consistent with Reagan's desire to initiate the SDI project? Criticism is limited to the question of whether or not Reagan's address produced identifiable changes in the audience's thinking about the desirability of a space-based weapons system. Assuming that a shift in audience beliefs, attitudes, or behaviors following the address can be discerned, the problem then becomes one of documenting that it was primarily or even exclusively Reagan's discourse that was responsible for change.

That such a problem arises is not surprising, given the focus of a one-dimensional analysis, for inherent in one-dimensionality is the isolation in time of a particular rhetorical act and a particular set of audience dispositions. Common sense suggests that such a picture of message and audience is static; it freezes one segment of a larger, dynamic interaction. It is not, then, that the critic's question is unimportant or trivial. Rather, the critic's approach is limited: on the one hand, because of the very bracketing of speech and audience, it may be methodologically impossible to show that the communication caused its alleged effect; if, on the other hand, analysis convincingly shows that discourse contributed to changes in audience beliefs and behaviors, it becomes hard to generalize the effect to the ongoing controversy from which the chosen speech is taken. Put differently, if critics can prove that President Reagan's speech resulted in a more favorable public attitude toward the research and development of SDI, then we are still left with the nagging question of how his speech and the effects issuing from it evolve out of and fit into the larger controversy that pre- and post-dates this isolated episode. For example, critics employing a one-dimensional perspective could not inform us as to how the issue of strategic policy—of which SDI is but one aspect— was originally framed, what alternative perspectives on SDI were predetermined by the larger issue of strategic policy that had been articulated in advance of the March 23, 1983, speech, and what institutional and systemic factors exist that may have contextualized disputes of this sort, thus shaping the possibilities for persuasion. This is the problem of generalizability. The methodological difficulty is equally obvious. By restricting analysis to one rhetorical moment in time, how can one ever conclude that Reagan's rhetoric is responsible for particular beliefs and actions?

These problems are not new. At least one scholar has attempted to address the methodological quandary: Arguing that critics should compare language contained within a speech and the language used by those responding to it, Cherwitz (1980) contends that we can discover the contributory effect of discourse. On his analysis, if critics can show not only that there was a shift in audience thinking following Reagan's speech, but that his audience internalized much of his vocabulary and argumentative structure, then it would be reasonable to conclude that the speech contributed to the alleged effect. While Cherwitz's "language-in-use" framework offers a partial redress to the methodological problem of cause and effect, in so doing it accentuates the problem of generalizability. For if the president's audience internalized his language and argument, and that is the standard of effect, then we must wonder what rhetorical antecedents existed for Reagan's particular vocabulary and arguments as well as his audience's. To answer these questions would in turn require a more generalized focus than one-dimensional criticism can give. It requires consideration of how SDI and strategic policy had been framed from the very beginning, and how institutional and systemic forces may have prescribed what potentially could be said and thought on an issue such as this. Only by knowing answers to these questions could we really assess the contributory effect of Reagan's speech on the public's position on the issue.

In summary, one-dimensional analysis of communication may be especially insightful in its microscopic investigation of the rhetorical strategies and techniques contained within speech. Also, it may be quite sensitive in is ability to tap into shifts in audience beliefs, attitudes, and behaviors within limited time frames. However, this approach to assessing effect is incomplete. It is riddled by the inherent methodological problems associated with trying to document direct causal relationships. In addition, because of the difficulty of generalizing from isolated segments of a larger process, one-dimensional criticism cannot explain comprehensively the effects of communication in complex, fluid situations such as the ongoing SDI issue.

The second dimension of effect begins with the previous critique of one-dimensionality. Furthermore, this second conception of communicative effect, like Lukes's (1974) second dimension of power, starts by recognizing the fact that even though communication may not always result in stereotypical persuasion (e.g., attitude change or overt behavior), it may produce other, more subtle types of effect, all issuing from the power communicators exert over audiences.

Rather than being preoccupied with whether or not discourse produces direct behavioral outcomes, two-dimensional criticism considers aspects of the decision-making process that are at least one step removed from public discussion. These would include analysis of how communication establishes barriers to the public airing of policy conflicts, how particular rhetorical acts organize topics into and out of consideration, and how rhetoric produces non-decision making as well as decision making.

Given these foci, a two-dimensional criticism of the SDI issue could take a number of tacks. In terms of the barriers to the public airing of policy conflicts, rhetorical analysis might show how Reagan's initiation of the SDI project shifted attention away from the issue of nuclear disarmament, focusing instead on a technology itself premised upon the continued existence and perhaps growth of offensive nuclear weaponry. In other words, regardless of whether or not Reagan's speech produced support for his SDI proposal (a one-dimensional effect), it could be argued that the very presentation of a supplanting policy alternative had the effect of changing the parameters of public discussion. For example, the public may have devoted less time to the issue of strategic arms reduction and concentrated focus on the specifics of the new space-based technology proposed by Reagan.[4] A potential consequence of this effect is suspension of discussion about, if not de facto support of, the present administration's nuclear weapons policies.

This example reveals an effect moving considerably beyond the scope of one-dimensionality. Rather than looking for direct and obvious public outcomes that are consistent or incongruent with a rhetor's message, two-dimensional criticism seeks to capture more subtle consequences of communication. It recognizes the sometimes unnoticed fact that for every rhetorical act of affirmation, something else is negated, whether unintentionally or by design.[5] Communication is by nature a prioritizing act, one that deemphasizes by emphasizing. Thus, to become preoccupied with whether or not Reagan's speech resulted in support for SDI obscures the more interesting possibility that his rhetoric changed the boundaries of the nuclear arms debate by establishing barriers to the airing of pre-existing viewpoints. Cognizant of this more subtle effect, critics could document how Reagan's discourse may have produced not only public decision making, but non-decision making as well. It may be that the SDI rhetoric so deflected public consideration of negotiated strategic arms reduction that Reagan simply did not have to contend with public pressure in support of an intercontinental ballistic missile treaty when negotiating at Reykjavik and elsewhere. Two-dimensional criticism, therefore, might offer greater understanding of why a strategic arms agreement (that is, one that, unlike the 1988 INF Treaty, substantially reduces or eliminates the kind of long-range weaponry that SDI seems designed to render less threatening) has yet to be reached and why the lack of such an agreement has not produced a visible public outcry. In short, two-dimensional criticism can account for non-decision making. Should a strategic arms treaty be signed in the near future, critics could pose the question: To what extent did Reagan's SDI rhetoric change the parameters of the nuclear arms debate for Soviet policy makers? That is,

---

4. A mere glance at news articles and editorials suggests that SDI has become the centerpiece of discussion concerning intercontinental strategic weaponry.

5. This argument is central to Wander's (1984) argument for an ideological turn in rhetorical criticism. The importance of affirmation/negation (or affirmation/rejection) themes also is discussed by Burke (1937) as well as the Frankfurt School critical theorists (Adorno, 1973).

aside from any in-kind responses to America's SDI project, what effect did Reagan's rhetoric have on the timing and existence of Soviet responses to the pre-existing issue of arms reduction?

It should be noted that two analyses of Reagan's SDI speech have argued for the existence of consequences of communication clearly falling within this second dimension. Goodnight's (1986) textual analysis of the speech underscores the capacity of discourse to produce public agreement over national policy, while simultaneously undermining long-held conceptions of how to deal with the issue of nuclear deterrence. Similarly, Rushing (1986) contends that Reagan's address, entrenched in the "myth of the New Frontier," established new guidelines for future debate. Both of these critiques, although making somewhat different claims, show how the president's rhetoric gives primacy to technical solutions to what traditionally had been seen as a political problem. Thus, while not under the guise of what typically are considered effect studies, Goodnight's and Rushing's research highlights the importance of integrating more sophisticated rhetorical perspectives and methods within a theory of effect. Though not focusing on direct behavioral outcomes of speech, these authors attest to the power communicators exert over audiences. And as we have suggested, it is this notion of power over that rests at the heart of all potential effects of rhetoric.

The value of two-dimensional criticism should be clear: unlike one-dimensional analysis, the indirect, covert, and mobilizing consequences of communication that are revealed by two-dimensional criticism testify to the complexity and fluidity of rhetorical disputes. Sensitive to these aspects of power, critics can get well beyond the stereotypical results of discourse inherent in one-dimensionality. Nevertheless, the most intriguing and often insidious effects of rhetoric remain unelucidated by this second critical dimension.

Two-dimensional criticism, for instance, does not explain how *public grievances are precluded* by communication and how rhetoric may *shape public desires and consent*. Moreover, it does not explicate *latent conflict and/ or enthusiasm*, that is, the yet-to-be-developed public consciousness about rhetorically submerged contradictions between the interests of those in power and the interests of those they govern. Our assumption here is not the crude ideological premise that the public is hopelessly dominated by an "advanced technological capitalism" permeated by exclusive interests, as has been implied by others (Thornburn, 1987). Emphatically to the contrary. The importance of informed rhetoric in a democratic society, and therein of rhetorical criticism (in particular, what we shall now call *third-dimensional* criticism), is to empower the public with knowledge of its real interests and to enable the public to act in accordance with those interests.

Analysis of Reagan's SDI rhetoric provides ample illustration of the inability of two-dimensional criticism to get at the process by which rhetoric precludes grievances or enthusiasms and obscures contradictions between rhetors' interests and those of their publics. While delineating how bias is mobilized and how rhetorical barriers to the airing of policy disputes are established, we may remain unaware of the systemic aspects of communication that subvert public development of grievances and mask conflicting political interests.

In order to expose these systemic consequences, a three-dimensional analysis of rhetoric begins with the claim that to become critical is to become aware of not only the relevant counterfactual possibilities unique to rhetorical disputes, but those germane to specific acts of rhetoric.

Recalling our earlier discussion, the detection by critics of relevant counterfactuals refers to the isolation and justification of alternative views and grievances that arguably would be developed if the unstated and projected implications of the rhetor's message were brought to public consciousness (Lukes, 1974, pp. 48–50). In the case of the SDI issue, there are a number of relevant counterfactuals that, if exposed, would allow the rhetorical analyst to document less obvious, yet highly pronounced effects of Reagan's March 23, 1983, speech. We shall discuss two potential counterfactuals here to secure the importance of three-dimensional criticism.

First, it could be argued that Reagan's placing of SDI on the strategic agenda and the accompanying proliferation of discourse debating the value of space-based weapons systems prevent the development of the primary question, namely, How can humankind solve the political and sociological problems that are the progenitors of nuclear holocaust? Critics might argue that, if the real interest of the public is to find ways to neutralize the potential causes of nuclear war and not just to seek technical deterrents, then one effect of SDI rhetoric is to keep the public from articulating grievances pursuant to that larger question. (Of course, SDI may have the opposite effect, but the point of three-dimensional criticism is to expand consideration of the possible consequences of discourse.)

For example, because Reagan's rhetoric opens the possibility to technological deterrents to nuclear war, the public may no longer find it necessary to think consciously and talk about the political and social causes of war. Instead of debating about what those causes are and how they might best be dealt with, dispute becomes focused on the technological capacity of deterrence. This effect is insidious: the public may unknowingly place all of its eggs in one basket. By diminishing the fervor of the ongoing debate about the ultimate causes of nuclear war, SDI rhetoric may have the effect of lulling the public into believing that a laser-based weapons system, whether SDI or some yet-to-be-advocated mechanism, is the answer to our fears of nuclear nightmare. If we should subsequently discover that these weapons systems are technologically incapable of deterring nuclear war or are circumvented by new offensive weapons, then progress in preventing war will have been impeded because of the restriction of discussion to scientific and mechanistic thinking. What makes this possibility insidious is that our ability to argue about political and social causes may atrophy. To the extent that SDI rhetoric focuses on technological deterrence, therefore, the public may be kept from recognizing its real interest, that is, prevention of nuclear war.

We are not arguing here for the pros or cons of SDI. We are highlighting the fact that the very framing of questions and restricting of alternatives by rhetors can stand in the way of airing other interests. One of the less obvious effects of communication is that it intentionally or unintentionally narrows the parameters of public thought. The only check on this inherent rhetorical narrowing of thinking is criticism. Without the exposure by critics of relevant counterfactuals—in this case, the real interest of the public in remedying the political and social factors that could lead to nuclear war—the hazardous consequences of restricting public discussion become more likely.

Before examining a second relevant counterfactual, we should note that this narrowing of public thought and obfuscation of the public's real interests goes considerably beyond the restricting of parameters of debate that was seen in two-dimensional criticism. In the latter, the alleged effect of Reagan's SDI speech was to alter the agenda of the nuclear arms debate: rather than focusing on the growth of offensive weapons, SDI rhetoric shifts attention to the technological possibility of a space-based defense system. As we have just seen, however, three-dimensional analysts consider not only how the topic of the immediate debate may change, but also how the rhetorical system may keep the public from becoming conscious of its real interest—in this case, a desire to locate and cope with the ultimate causes of nuclear calamity. This, we suggest, may be a more significant consequence of communication than is the shifting of the agenda. For while the latter may be noticeable and strategic, even frequently commented on by the public, the camouflaging of significant alternative interests—which is a three-dimensional effect—is more covert. It involves a subtle yet important change in the way people think, thus keeping a public from expressing some of its interests—interests that might be put forth if the public were alerted to the full range of its options and values.

A second counterfactual concerns the increased concentration of influence over strategic policy in the hands of a defense-industrial establishment. Rhetorical critics might argue, for instance, that one of the real interests of the American public is to avoid placing decision making authority in a small, centralized elite that develops its own interests and becomes isolated from the broader public (Bitzer, 1978). There are those who worry that centralizing the control over strategic policy within a technocratic body increases the possibility of ineffectual, narrow-minded and possibly deleterious decisions (Bitzer; Fisher, 1987). Fear is aroused not only by the possibility of bad outcomes of decision making, but by the process of decision making; the very restriction of authority to an elite, nonrepresentative few threatens the democratic principles of governance upon which the nation is based.

A three-dimensional analysis of Reagan's SDI rhetoric would at least raise the question of whether preoccupation with the specifics of a laser-based weapons system might not make the public lose sight of its real interest of maintaining control over, and checks and balances within, the decision-making process. Beyond the first-dimension effect of securing support for the SDI project and the second-dimension effect of moving the agenda to technological solutions to allegedly political problems, Reagan's rhetoric (and all subsequent rhetoric pursuant to his agenda) may produce several less obvious outcomes.

Such rhetoric makes opposition to America's current and future strategic policy more difficult. SDI, because of its complex scientific and technological nature, engenders a situation in which only those with expert knowledge can engage in argument. A subtle but important effect of the SDI rhetoric, therefore, may be the introduction of a qualitatively different military infrastructure into the strategic system. This infrastructure is a tightly interwoven network of policy, technology, and personnel that perpetuates the already expansive role of the defense-industrial establishment. This is important rhetorically because it is at least possible that those with the necessary expertise to argue against the policies generated by the infrastructure may themselves be a part of the SDI project and thus could be co-opted by the system, becoming incapable of reflecting anything other than the narrow interests their expertise represents.

This effect also is important rhetorically because, under the guise of moving from a policy of mutually assured destruction to one of strategic defense, we may have simply added another abstract layer to the existing military establishment. In so doing, the influence of SDI rhetoric may be longer lasting; it may further insulate those with control over strategic policy from the public. This more systemic effect of the rhetorical dispute over SDI is both latent and covert. The way in which three-dimensional criticism stakes out new ground is by revealing the heretofore camouflaged counterfactual: it can show that often the most pronounced consequence of communication extends beyond the immediate topic and agenda of rhetorical controversies; three-dimensional criticism can explicate the manner in which instances of communication themselves maintain, promote, and expand current institutional values and structures. In other words, a three-dimensional critique of discourse can underscore the institutionally reproductive nature of rhetoric.

In short, by becoming bogged down in the intricacies of the SDI issue, the public unknowingly may keep itself from recognizing its real interest of thwarting efforts to centralize control over strategic policy. And as a result, the public may be precluded in the future from developing grievances against a policy and a system for which they possess insufficient expertise and a subsequent lack of access to the channels of communication. Simply stated, the public will become one step further removed from the institutional elite who control strategic policy. What makes this effect of communication insidious is that it subverts democracy, making what once may have been a political issue in the public domain (namely, how to prevent nuclear war) a technological issue in the hands of a nonrepresentative elite—a possibility that, if understood by the voters of the United States, might alter reactions to SDI and similar proposals.

Implications and Conclusion

Perhaps the most important conclusion to be drawn from our proposed three-dimensional consideration of rhetorical effect is that practically all critiques of discourse are at base concerned with the consequences of communication. At the outset we suggested that the underlying pedagogical and scholarly assumption of our discipline is that communication has the power to elicit effects. Yet as we noted, the problem with most traditional definitions and analyses of effect is that they so narrowly and empirically restrict the concept as to make impossible confirmation of the intuitive assumption that communication has consequences. What the three-dimensional conception of power and its rhetorical analog demonstrate is that a broadened understanding of the power rhetors exert over audiences can yield a more productive and encompassing approach to effect.

There are several important correlates of this implication. To begin with, we observe that there has been a reluctance of late on the part of critics to include judgments of effect pursuant to their rhetorical analyses. Such a reticence is not surprising. Given the restricted, overt, and behavioral character of traditional effect studies, and the methodological problems inherent in them, such judgments are difficult if not impossible to verify. It might be argued, therefore, that the more sophisticated approaches to rhetorical criticism that have evolved over the years have been both a reaction to and a movement beyond traditional effect studies.[6]

---

6. Examples of more sophisticated approaches to rhetorical criticism in the past two decades include the works of Bormann (1985), McGuire (1977), McGee (1980), and Fisher (1987). Our argument here is that, while such innovative approaches to rhetorical criticism as fantasy theme, narrative, and mythic/ideological analysis are not ostensibly effect gauging studies (in the traditional sense of effect), they: either (1) assume as a warrant for producing criticism that communication elicits direct effects, or (2) contain the potential to be able to explain why rhetoric in some instances may be effective and in other instances not be effective. For example, criticism—in seeking to uncover how fantasy themes "chain out," or how mythic structures are implicit within speech texts, or how narrative rationality clarifies the meaning and reception of discourse—presupposes that the value of studying language so microscopically rests on the claim that rhetorical techniques and strategies can make a very real difference for audiences. Thus, although such innovative analyses may not directly address the consequences of communication, it is hard to imagine what other rationale there could be for producing criticism. Moreover, given the expanded notion of effect (which also includes less direct, overt, and empirical gauges) delineated in this essay, the connection between the various contemporary approaches to criticism and the questions of effect should be clear. Our point, then, is that despite the problems associated with traditional effect studies, the speech com-

And yet as this study implies, such newer approaches (e.g., fantasy-theme, narrative, mythic, dramatistic, and ideological analyses) should not be viewed as conceptually divorced from considerations of effect. The three-dimensional conception of power articulated herein allows us to integrate newer and more rhetorically elaborate modes of analysis within one critical perspective—a perspective grounded in the assumption that nearly all analyses of rhetoric are quintessentially appraisals of the effects of communication. In fact, it could be argued that these more sophisticated advances in rhetoric are, though we may not have taken them as such, powerful accounts of the consequences of communication. There is a certain irony, then, in what we believe has been a retreat from the concept of effect. What we hope is at least suggested by this essay is that there is scholarly value in integrating all critiques of discourse within a uniform and expanded theory of effect. This, we believe, is preferable to the current assumption that traditional effect studies constitute one school of thought, while more innovative and advanced analyses form separate and unrelated schools.

An additional correlate of this implication extends beyond the academic merits of effect theory. A major complaint frequently lodged against rhetorical criticism is that it is esoteric and "when it appears, such criticism is available only to limited, usually academic audiences" (Campbell, 1972, p. 12). After reading highly specialized rhetorical accounts of messages, one is often left with the question: Of what value is such criticism to those in society who transmit and receive communication? Or more specifically, To what extent can the insights gleaned by scholarly criticism be used constructively to promote better policies? These questions are more than trivial; for at core, the rhetorical art is a practical one, an art that we intuitively know makes a difference for the vast majority of people not ensconced in academe. It is for this reason that critics cannot sidestep or ignore such questions. The three-dimensional consideration of effect developed in this essay provides a partial answer to these questions. It permits an integration of scholarly

---

munication discipline never may have relinquished the concept and assumption of effect. Part of the value of the power-centered theory of rhetorical effect developed in this paper is that it gives us the potential to make explicit the connection between effect and the many disparate approaches to criticism. And as we argued earlier, there is critical and pedagogical value in discerning how the many perspectives on rhetoric evolve out of a single, uniform, and consistent theory of communication.

methods of criticism with more practical concerns for explaining how discourse affects on people. Unique to all three dimensions of criticism is an emphasis on how communication results in discernible effects: these effects may be overt and empirically instantiated, as one-dimensional criticism emphasizes; they may be covert and related to non-decision making, as two-dimensional criticism shows; and finally, such effects may be latent, impinging on the development of public consciousness, as evidenced by three-dimensional criticism. While the three levels of criticism incorporate different methods and units of analysis, they share an underlying interest in uncovering the impact that messages have on audiences; part of their value is educational—to make us aware of and prevent the untoward consequences of communication. In summary, the theory of effect we offer has important implications for both the public and academic communities.

A second implication of this research relates to our earlier claim that the concept of communicative effect has not been informed by nor kept pace with other purely theoretical advances in rhetoric. One could go so far as to suggest that there has been a virtual separation of the enterprises of rhetorical theory and rhetorical criticism. Nowhere is this more evident than in the growing body of theoretical literature examining the relationship between rhetoric and epistemology. In various and often competing ways, contemporary rhetoricians argue that "rhetoric is epistemic," that communication is essential to the process by which humans come to know (Cherwitz & Hikins, 1986; Scott, 1967). This sort of scholarship is frequently branded as purely theoretical scholarship because its critical implications have not yet been delineated (Hart, 1982). Though space does not permit a fully developed argument, we suggest that one implication of a three-dimensional treatment of rhetorical effect is that it allows, if not demands, an integration of our philosophical and conceptual knowledge of how rhetoric operates with our critical understanding of rhetoric's effects. In their book, *Communication and Knowledge: An Investigation in Rhetorical Epistemology*, Cherwitz and Hikins contend that "rhetoric is the art of describing reality through language" (p. 62). Operating from this definition, they contend that some rhetoric, that which accurately describes reality, functions epistemically. This epistemological perspective on rhetoric is not only germane to but forms the essence of the third dimension of rhetorical effect.

Although one-dimensional and two-dimensional analyses of rhetorical effect focus on what we might call a *psychology of communication* (not to be confused with what we earlier called psychological effect studies), the third dimension underscores the fundamentally epistemological character of communication. The occurrence of overt behaviors and shifting of agendas that are part of the first two dimensions of effect reveal much about how communication shapes what people think and believe about their world. A critic exploring these two dimensions, therefore, is not predominately concerned with reality per se. She or he is merely interested in what people take or perceive reality to be and what consequences perception has on behavior.

A third-dimensional analysis of rhetoric, however, posits that the duty of rhetorical critics is not just to examine the relationship between discourse and the psychological disposition of audiences. Instead, critics must identify and justify what has been termed the relevant counterfactual. It will be recalled that counterfactuals represent interests of the public that become obscured in the course of rhetorical controversies. A three-dimensional criticism, then, must, in addition to discerning the relationship between discourse and perceived reality, uncover those aspects of reality that intentionally or unintentionally have been subverted, ignored, camouflaged, or inaccurately portrayed by rhetors. In essence, the very task of identifying relevant counterfactuals constitutes an epistemological assessment. It is an assessment requiring a full canvassing of the ontological landscape within which the rhetor's message is but one variable. In short, three-dimensional criticism might better be described as epistemic criticism (Hikins, 1983; McKerrow, 1977). By investigating the relationship between rhetoric and reality, epistemic criticism can provide the final piece in the effect puzzle.

It should be noted that this epistemological activity, while unique to the third dimension of effect, relates to and accounts for the effects that make up the other two dimensions. Recall our earlier assertion that while at first glance third-dimensional criticism may seem analytically subsequent, there is a sense in which it may be chronologically prior. In view of the epistemic character of third-dimensional criticism, our claim may be restated: by understanding the broader relationship between discourse and reality (which constitutes effect at the third level) we can better appreciate why messages may or may not have produced the more tangible and visible effects occurring within the first two dimensions. On this analysis, the oft-touted complaint that rhetorical epistemology is devoid of praxis seems perplexing. For what our discussion of effect (where effect is nothing less than a practical concept) implies is that all explorations of the consequences of communication are and can be informed by epistemological analyses.

References

Adorno, T. A. (1973). *Negative dialectics*. London: Routledge & Kegan Paul.

Andrews, J. R. (1969). Confrontation at Columbia: A case study in coercive rhetoric. *Quarterly Journal of Speech, 55*, 9–16.

Art, R. J., & Jervis, R. (Eds.). (1973). *International politics: Anarchy, force, imperialism*. Boston: Little, Brown.

Bachrach, P., & Baratz, M. S. (1970). *Power and poverty*. New York: Oxford University Press.

Bass, J. D., & Cherwitz, R. A. (1978). Imperial mission and manifest destiny: A case study of political myth in rhetorical discourse. *Southern Speech Communication Journal, 43*, 213–232.

Bitzer, L. F. (1978). Rhetoric and public knowledge. In D. M. Burks (Ed.), *Rhetoric, philosophy, and literature* (pp. 67–93). West Lafayette, IN: Purdue University Press.

Bormann, E. G. (1985). *The force of fantasy: Restoring the American dream*. Carbondale: Southern Illinois University Press.

Boss, G. (1976). Essential attributes of the concept of charisma. *Southern Speech Communication Journal, 41*, 300–313.

Brandes, P. D. (1967). The attitude of college audiences to speakers of political extremes. *Southern Speech Communication Journal, 32*, 282–288.

Brock, B. L. (1969). 1968 Democratic campaign: A political upheaval. *Quarterly Journal of Speech, 55*, 26–35.

Brock, B. L., & Scott, R. L. (1980). *Methods of rhetorical criticism: A twentieth-century perspective*. Detroit: Wayne State University Press.

Brooks, W. D. (1967). A field study of the Johnson and Goldwater campaign speeches in Pittsburgh. *Southern Speech Communication Journal, 32*, 273–281.

Burgess, P. G. (1968). The rhetoric of black power: A moral demand? *Quarterly Journal of Speech, 54*, 122-133.

Burke, K. (1937). *Attitudes toward history*. New York: The New Republic.

Campbell, K. K. (1972). *Critiques of contemporary rhetoric*. Belmont, CA: Wadsworth.

Chaffee, S. H., & Hochheimer, J. L. (1982). The beginnings of political communication research in the United States: Origins of the "limited effects" model. In E. Rogers & F. Balle (Eds.), *The Media Revolution in America and Western Europe*. Norwood, NJ: Ablex.

Cherwitz, R. A. (1979). Lyndon Johnson and the "crisis" of Tonkin Gulf: A president's justification of war. *Western Journal of Speech Communication, 42*, 93–105.

Cherwitz, R. A. (1980). The contributory effect of rhetorical discourse: A study of language-in-use. *Quarterly Journal of Speech, 66*, 33–50.

Cherwitz, R. A., & Hikins, J. W. (1986). *Communication and knowledge: An investigation in rhetorical epistemology.* Columbia, SC: University of South Carolina Press.

Cooper, L. (Trans.). (1932). *Rhetoric.* Englewood Cliffs, NJ: Prentice-Hall. (Aristotle's original work published 5th century BC.)

Cragen, J. F., & Shields, D. C. (1977). Foreign policy communication dramas: How mediated rhetoric played in Peoria in campaign '76. *Quarterly Journal of Speech, 60,* 274–289.

Davis, K. M. (1981). A description and analysis of the legislative committee hearing. *Western Journal of Speech Communication, 65,* 88–106.

Davis, M. B., & Quimby, R. W. (1969). Senator Proctor's Cuban speech: Speculations on a cause of the Spanish-American War. *Quarterly Journal of Speech, 55,* 131–141.

Dedmon, D. N. (1966). The functions of discourse in the Hawaiian statehood debates. *Communication Monographs, 33,* 30–39.

Fejes, F. (1984). Critical mass communications research and media effects: The problem of the disappearing audience. *Media, Culture and Society, 6,* 219–232.

Fisher, W. R. (1987). *Human communication as narration: Toward a philosophy of reason, value, and action.* Columbia, SC: University of South Carolina Press.

Goodnight, T. G. (1986). Ronald Reagan's re-formulation of the rhetoric of war: Analysis of the "Zero-Option," "Evil Empire," and "Star Wars" addresses. *Quarterly Journal of Speech, 72,* 390-414.

Gregg, R. B. (1971). The ego-function of the rhetoric of protest. *Philosophy & Rhetoric, 4,* 71–91.

Griffin, L. M. (1952). The rhetoric of historical movements. *Quarterly Journal of Speech, 38,* 184–188.

Griffin, L. M. (1964). The rhetorical structure of the "new left" movement: Part I. *Quarterly Journal of Speech, 50,* 113–135.

Gross, A. G. (1984). Public debates as failed social dramas: The recombinant DNA controversy. *Quarterly Journal of Speech, 70,* 397–409.

Hart, R. P. (1971). The rhetoric of the true believer. *Communication Monographs, 38,* 249–261.

Hart, R. P. (1982, May). *Rhetorical criticism and lay epistemologies: A case study.* Paper presented at the convention of the Eastern Communication Association, Hartford, CT.

Hart, R. P. (1984). The functions of human communication in the maintenance of public values. In C. Arnold & J. Bowers (Eds.), *Handbook of rhetorical and communication theory* (pp.749–791). Boston: Allyn & Bacon.

Hikins, J. W. (1983). The rhetoric of "unconditional surrender" and the decision to drop the atomic bomb. *Quarterly Journal of Speech, 69,* 379–400.

Hill, F. I. (1972). Conventional wisdom—traditional form: The president's message of November 3, 1969. *Quarterly Journal of Speech, 58,* 373–386.

Hillbruner, A. (1974). Archetype and signature: Nixon and the 1973 inaugural. *Central States Speech Journal, 25,* 169–181.

Hogan, J. M. (1986). *The Panama Canal in American politics: Domestic advocacy and the evolution of policy.* Carbondale, IL: Southern Illinois University Press.

Jamieson, K. H. (1976). The rhetorical manifestations of weltanschauung. *Central States Speech Journal, 27,* 4–14.

Lukes, S. (1974). *Power: A radical view.* London: Macmillan.

Lyne, J. R. (1985). Rhetorics of inquiry. *Quarterly Journal of Speech, 71,* 65–73.

McBath, J. H., & Fisher, W. R. (1969). Persuasion in presidential campaign communication. *Quarterly Journal of Speech, 55,* 17–25.

McCloskey, D. (1985). *Rhetoric of economics.* Madison, WI: University of Wisconsin Press.

McGee, M. C. (1980). The "ideograph": A link between rhetoric and ideology. *Quarterly Journal of Speech, 66,* 1–16.

McGuire, M. (1977). Mythic rhetoric in *Mein Kampf*: A structuralist critique. *Quarterly Journal of Speech, 63,* 1–13.

McKerrow, R. E. (1977). Truman and Korea: Rhetoric in the pursuit of victory. *Central States Speech Journal, 28,* 1-12.

Minnick, W. C. (1971). A case study in persuasive effect: Lymon Beecher on duelling. *Speech Monographs, 38,* 262–276.

Nelson, J. S., & Megill, A. (1986). Rhetorics of inquiry: Projects and prospects. *Quarterly Journal of Speech, 72,* 20–37.

Overington, M. A. (1977). The scientific community as audience: Toward a rhetorical analysis of science. *Philosophy and Rhetoric, 10,* 143–163.

Reagan, R. (1983, 15 April). Peace and national security: A new defense. *Vital Speeches of the Day,* 389.

Rushing, J. H. (1986). Ronald Reagan's "Star Wars" address: Mythic containment of technical reasoning. *Quarterly Journal of Speech, 72,* 415–433.

Scott, R. L. (1967) On viewing rhetoric as epistemic. *Central States Speech Journal, 18,* 9–17.

Simons, H. W. (1967). Patterns of persuasion in the civil rights struggle. *Today's Speech, 15,* 25–28.

Simons, H. W. (1969). Confrontation as a pattern in university settings. *Central States Speech Journal, 20,* 163–169.

Simons, H. W. (1970). Requirements, problems, and strategies: A theory of persuasion for social movements. *Quarterly Journal of Speech, 56,* 1–11.

Simons, H. W. (1972). Persuasion in social conflicts: A critique of prevailing conceptions and a framework for future research. *Speech Monographs, 39,* 227–247.

Simons, H. W. (1985). Chronicle and critique of a conference. *Quarterly Journal of Speech, 71,* 52–64.

Simons, H. W., Chesbro, J. W., & Orr, C. J. (1973). A movement perspective on the 1972 presidential campaign. *Quarterly Journal of Speech, 59,* 168–179.

Swanson, D. L. (1977). And that's the way it was? Television covers the 1976 presidential campaign. *Quarterly Journal of Speech, 63,* 239–248.

Thompson, W. N. (1945). A case study of Dewey's Minneapolis speech. *Quarterly Journal of Speech, 31,* 419–423.

Thonssen, L., & Baird, A. C. (1948). *Speech criticism* (1st ed.). New York: Ronald.

Thornburn, D. (1987). Television as aesthetic medium. *Critical Studies in Mass Communication, 4,* 161–173.

Trent, J. S., & Trent, J. D. (1974). The rhetoric of the challenger: George Stanley McGovern. *Central States Speech Journal, 25,* 11–18.

Wander, P. (1984). The third persona: An ideological turn in rhetorical theory. *Central States Speech Journal, 35,* 197-216.

Weimer, W. B. (1977). Science as a rhetorical transaction: Toward a nonjustificational conception of rhetoric. *Philosophy and Rhetoric, 10,* 1–29.

Wichelns, H. W. (1962). The literary criticism of oratory. In Pupils and colleagues (Eds.), *Studies in rhetoric and public speaking in honor of James Albert Winans* (pp. 181–216). New York: Russell & Russell. (Original work published 1925.).

Woodward, G. C. (1979). Prime ministers and presidents: A survey of the differing rhetorical possibilities of high office. *Communication Quarterly, 27,* 41–49.

Zarefsky, D. (1986). *President Johnson's war on poverty: Rhetoric and History.* University, AL: University of Alabama Press.

Zyskind, H. (1968). A case study in philosophic rhetoric: Theodore Roosevelt. *Philosophy & Rhetoric, 1,* 228–254.

• 4 •

Tradition and Resurgence in Public Address Studies

ROBERT S. ILTIS
STEPHEN H. BROWNE

If the history of writing on the subject has told us anything, it is that the history and criticism of public address remains an uncertain enterprise. The best in public address studies remind us, however, that uncertainty is not necessarily a fault; far from despairing over recurrent issues and problems, we have learned to apply them as standards of our scholarship. This willingness to confront the limits of our practice, indeed, represents a collective commitment to public address as a form of humanistic inquiry. In keeping with that commitment, this essay focuses upon certain issues and problems not because they are unprecedented, but because they remain vital in new ways and in fresh contexts. Such an approach, we believe, affirms at once the centrality of tradition to our discipline as well as its capacity for legitimate change.

Our chapter is designed to reflect this contest between the old and the new. We are concerned, accordingly, not with creeds but with rationales for permanence and change. We propose here to evaluate such warrants in terms of the object of study and methods employed. We are thereby led to ask, What is there in our historical and critical practice that deserves steadfast commitment? What new challenges oblige us to reexamine and correct the ways in which we conduct our work? As general as these concerns are, they lend urgency and structure to the observations that follow.

The renascent vitality of public address scholarship can be accounted for, at least in part, by an eagerness to enter into new and unexpected venues of investigation. Such a renewal is important and it is timely, but it presents a fresh challenge to the traditional bases of the discipline. The coherence we seek is now more elusive than ever: the greater the variety of critical objects, the more difficult it is to see relationships between

81

particular discursive phenomena and general patterns of rhetorical activity. This struggle to account for textual specifics, even as we must situate discourse historically, involves an interpretive play common to most forms of humanistic inquiry. But for students of public address the challenge seems especially great: searching for new ways to account for diverse acts, we risk not only fragmenting perspective, but also abandoning the stability that tradition accords.

I

Exploration of what we know about the study of public address requires that we first assert what we mean by "public address." Attempts to cordon off territory for academic studies more often than not amount to academic fighting words. A glance into the tables of contents of recent journals reveals an unsurprising variety of artifacts scholars would no doubt defend as public address if pressed to do so—from Anglican colonial sermons (Enholm, Skaggs & Welsh, 1987) to Israeli youth ceremonials (Katriel, 1987), from Ben Franklin's pictorial representations of the colonies (Olson, 1987), to pop culture parody (Morris, 1987). Thus, our most recent anthologist of American public address excludes visual material only on the grounds of convenience and economy, not because such artifacts are outside the purview of public address (Reid, 1988, p. 7). We are reminded as well that the evolution of public address studies, once concerned primarily with historical individuals and nationalist designations (e.g., British public address) enables us now to cut across such rigid categories. Should we not be comfortable letting the parameters of the subject be broad, so that our understanding of rhetorical processes may be enriched by what we can learn from diverse critical perspectives? Do we not risk snaring ourselves in our own proscription by defining what students of public address ought to study?

Such questions can be answered by first distinguishing rhetorical criticism from the study of public address. The relationship between rhetorical criticism and public address is one between genus and species. Rhetorical critics study symbolic action by means of which humans negotiate social truths and power. Rhetorical criticism encompasses the broad range of rhetorical activities. Folk songs and icons, cartoons and sitcoms, photography and political plays—these and a host of other cultural artifacts can all be fruitfully studied by the methods of rhetorical criticism. The student of public address is a particular type of rhetorical critic. Herbert Wichelns (1925) set the course for studies in public address by arguing that a time bound, effects orientation to the study of oratory separates the field of speech from other disciplines and academically legitimizes it. A review of speech communication journals over the last seventy-five years indicates that scholars of public address have most often concerned themselves with speeches, essays, and public letters. The simplest way of differentiating public address from its fellow studies is to define it by genre. But therein would lie the difficulties of proscription—the inevitable defense of a classification forever vulnerable to this or that exception. It is clear, as we show, that certain genres of rhetorical discourse are "purer" forms of public address than others. But we assume that as regards a definition of public address it is best to cut a broad swath and leave further delineation until we have considered what it means to address a public. Public address may then be understood as discursive symbolic action between rhetors and audiences by means of which humans negotiate social truth and power.

Of course the term *discursive* is stipulative and warrants explanation in light of our intention to cut a broad swath. The objection will be raised that identifying public address with discursive symbolic action alone turns the study away from visual symbols and concentrates on artifacts that have little relevance for the media age and that we are undertaking a reactionary retreat from engaging the communication problems of the modern age to the more genteel study of "old dead orators." What grounds are there for privileging the spoken and written word?

In part, it is the very expansion of mass electronic media that warrants increased attention to discursive symbolic action. A keynote address at a national party convention, that eighty years ago would be available only in newspapers or in pamphlet form, is now instantly broadcast to millions of viewers and can bring heretofore somewhat unknown political figures, such as Mario Cuomo, squarely before the public eye. Televised congressional investigations suddenly make the sermonettes and ideological exhortations of an Oliver North at once the stuff of an American hero and a political pariah, with the result that he now is able to command high fees on the lecture circuit. To the extent that public address studies—including those of dead orators—actually broaden our understanding of the rhetorical function of language in these and any other engagements of the public, they make important contributions to the humanities. Public address responds to, creates, resolves, and sustains tensions between a rhetor and a specific audience. The study of public address is thus charged with discerning and assessing the properties of this distinct and fundamental facet of human behavior.

A public address lives two lives. The first is short. A public address occurs when an individual projects himself or herself into the public space through symbolic action. Such an act is of course ephemeral; it is bred, lives, and dies in a historical moment. After that moment passes, the act, considered in the totality of its situation, is lost forever. This ephemeral nature and its symbolic component are two of the most distinctive characteristics of public address.

The second life of a public address begins when it passes from the control of its creator, the creator's intended audience, and the historical audience by being fixed as a text. The text of a public address, regardless of the original medium of that address or the form it takes as a text, is fixed history; it represents the moment of a rhetor's self-insertion into the public space. Once the public address becomes a text, it is accounted for only by coming into the hands of a secondary auditor, who analyzes and interprets the text through a fresh encounter. The richness of the original moment of communication is lost to the student of public address who deals with only a text. In this loss, the student of public address shares the problem faced by interpreters of any text. Paul Ricoeur (1971) lists elements of the moment of communication that become lost to interpreters. First, the historical moment of communication in its totality is irretrievably lost. Second, the intention of the author is lost, and the interpreter is thereby granted a degree of freedom to attribute meaning. Third, because it stands apart from its moment of expression, the text is freed "from the limits of ostensive reference" and creates a world of its own that the critic is free to discover. Finally, not only is a text freed from ostensive reference, it is freed as well from its real audience and instead addresses audiences created by itself (pp. 531–536).

Ricoeur's third and fourth points are of special importance to public address. The concern with audience effects that grounded early studies in the field centers on these issues of ostensive reference and actual audience. And as the field has developed, questioning of Thonssen and Baird's (1948, pp. 448–461) effects orientation has demonstrated an affinity with Ricoeur's views. Can we measure effect with any accuracy? Do we fool ourselves by thinking we can describe the "real" audience or identify salient features of the situation without implicating ourselves in the description? Should effect or quality constitute the locus of judgment for a discourse? The endurance of such questions as these points precisely to the distinctiveness of public address as a focus in rhetorical studies.

When scholars study the *rhetoric of* or *rhetoric in* some cultural artifact, they concern themselves with how that artifact can be seen as capable of moving an auditor in belief or action at some historical moment. Probably all cultural artifacts can be seen as rhetorical, can be viewed as a text and can thus be discussed as having the same losses of time, author, reference, and audience that Ricoeur indicates for written texts. Here is where public speech, as a form of public address, taken as a text, offers its unique contribution in the happy dilemma it generates for its students.

Unlike films, monuments, records, paintings, cartoons, inscribed music, plays, novels, and other cultural artifacts that come into existence in a form that can be experienced repeatedly over time and can have a wide variety of effects on different audiences, the public speech, once it is fixed as a text, is a purer form of fixed history. The public speech is intended to be an immediate engagement of the public; it is a direct attempt to effect belief or action through symbolic action. Just as important, though it can be the most ephemeral of public symbolic actions, it can be recorded. This aspect of public speeches offers reason for tempering Ricoeur's claims about ostensive reference and real audience. Once the moment of expression passes, the text of a speech remains as the residue of passions, fears, ideals—the *Umwelt* or situation in Ricoeur's terms—of rhetor and interlocutor. Of course, there can be no overlooking the flawed nature of the situation offered in the text of a public speech. As the fixed symbolic action of a situation whose moment is past, the speech text exists in ironic tension between the world created by itself and the situation it represents. Thus, though Ricoeur's observations about the passing of ostensive reference and real audience in a text cannot be denied, it is yet clear that the proximity of speech texts to their original ostensive reference and real audience is closer than that of other rhetorical artifacts. It is the tension between fixity and action, between original audience and the audience of the text, between situation and the world created by the text, that makes public speech so alluring as a form of public address. Hence, it is the mission of public address scholars to both discover and engage in the dialogue—the ironic tension—between meaning and situation. That public speeches provide such a rich vein of such tension is the happy lot of those who seek to understand them. These are by no means the only forms of public address, but students of public address especially commit themselves to understanding speeches, essays, and public letters—traditional modes of public address—that offer clear cases of discursive symbolic action and ironic tension from which to set the plumb line. This charge carries with it questions of method and perspective.

The method that ultimately grounds study of public address is close reading of texts and cross-discourse analysis and interpretation. Roderick Hart (1986) complains of a "conceptual anomie"—the failure to build bridges between investigations—prevalent in the field. Hart's complaint is telling, but it does not go far enough. On the whole, we have ill served the field of rhetorical criticism by failing to develop a body of criticism that rigorously accounts for the rhetorical action of even the acknowledged masterpieces of public address. G. P. Mohrmann (1980), Michael Leff (1980), and, more recently, Stephen Lucas (1988) have persistently drawn attention to this lacuna in the study of canonical public addresses. We compound the problem by failing to develop a body of competing interpretations. Contrast the close readings one can find of Faulkner's novels to those of King's speeches. In the former case, the variety of interpretations has deepened collective understanding of a highly complex set of works. In the latter, one is hard pressed to find competing close readings of even a single speech. As a result we are left short of even Hart's lament regarding conceptual anomie. We suffer from a more basic problem: the lack of critical exchange on the core readings in public address. Our investigations should be taking us into the major texts, showing us how they work, and then bridging among them for theoretical purposes. This kind of interpretation, judgment, and theory development, we believe, will revitalize our study of the art.

II

The values implicit within the discipline provide for the permanence of public address scholarship. These values, in turn, can provide a basis by which disparate forms of inquiry may be ordered. As basic and unsurprising as the following enumeration may be, it nevertheless includes those values that help to constitute a community of interests and a literature of shared scholarship. Because they are so fundamental, these values run the risk of being vague; a few examples, however, should make their meaning more clear. They warrant review, in any case, because they indicate fixity in an otherwise fluid pursuit.

Described in most general terms, our commitment seems to be to directed at the integrity of the public space itself. This belief involves specific commitments to (1) the *public* character of rhetorical practice; (2) the *generic* distinctiveness of public address as a form of symbolic action; and (3) the *ethical* significance of public address and its study. On their face, these commitments may appear to be little more than disciplinary pieties. But for better or worse, we are constantly reminded that commitment to a set of values and successfully engaging them are different— that these are ideals and not givens. And to the extent that they remain problematic, they continue to be relevant aspirations.

That some conception of *public,* however vague, is related in a significant way to the object of our study is patent; it is structured into the very syntax of the phrase *public address*. That relationship is as enduring as culture itself. As a domain of deliberation, celebration, accusation, and defense, the ideal of the public space was central to the meaning of life as it was lived in the polis. The Romans conceived of this space as "the public thing," or *res publica*, and represented it as a place of security and equality. This public space was preeminently a realm where citizens could speak, and in speaking could benefit from those things that public action bestowed. Hence the association of speech with power, which has not gone unrecognized in Western thought. But the key to understanding this relationship is its spatial referent: the *public* describes rhetorical practice not as a will to power, but as a form of action in the presence of others. This description, we believe, is near the heart of contemporary studies in public address. Recently some have sought to embrace this conception by appropriating the theoretical work of Arendt, Habermas, and others; in practice, however, public address scholarship has always assumed, if not explicitly recognized, such a requirement.

But the public, so conceived, is a place of privilege *and* denial. At issue, therefore, is a more salient problem located at the level of historical fact: Since the public space has not been shared, and because it is not always clear just how ingress can be secured, the public remains a location of privilege and jealousy. For this reason, we are obliged by our commitment to call into scrutiny any action that threatens the genuinely public nature of this space. Understandably, perhaps, critics and historians of public address have tended to celebrate those voices that embody the virtues of public action and speech. Thus we deem as exemplars of the art such speakers as Pericles, Demosthenes, Cicero, Burke, Webster, Lincoln, and King. Even with these figures we have far to go before establishing an advanced literature, but until we are able to enrich this canon with voices historically silenced, there is reason to doubt our genuine commitment to public address as a means of empowerment.

For those outside as well as inside, the public represents a realm of possibilities. It guarantees nothing, but it at least grants a hearing, and it gives enduring sanction to a set of values that has come to define the idea of *public* generally. To gain access to the public is first of all to enter a condition of plurality, of speech and action where one may petition for a better life. Understood conceptually and historically, the borders of this public are permeable, and gaining access to it is a rhetorical problem of the first order. But the dynamics of this relationship—ingress to and egress from the public space—are not easily constrained: the conditions within are unstable, and those seeking to enter certain public realms have been dismayed at what they have found.

The public, conceived historically and as an ideal, thus represents a troubled possibility. In giving it a more complete portrayal, students of public address might well address the negative side of the public's legacy. There are at least two lessons in this story: the public may be more attractive as a conceptual field than in actual experience; and whatever coherence it has as a realm of freedom owes as much to its capacity for exclusion as to its capacity for inclusion. As an ideal, the public offers a constellation of incentives and a host of rewards; historically, its offerings have been less sublime. To a significant degree, this difference can be accounted for in motives underlying the arts of public address. The disaffected may employ idioms more appropriate to public orthodoxies as a means of gaining access to the public space—as with Susan Anthony and Elizabeth Stanton's skillful use of legal argot. And yet an essential part of the story of woman suffrage was the consequent disillusionment with the social and moral codes making up that space. Similar experiences can be traced in the discourses of progressivism and black civil rights. For the agents of social change who use language to effect their ends, the question becomes: What price the public?

To recognize the distinctive character of public address is to see that those who wield its power will protect it against intrusion. At the same time, there results a contest of voices representing the ins and the outs. As a dramatic and dramatizing force, public address displays, indeed celebrates, this contest among those in the margins and centers of public life. In the traditions of Western discourse, this seems most apparent when the difference is greatest: hence the systems of proscription from Pericles's Athens through Cicero's Rome, Jefferson's America . . . and beyond. Even in our most sanguine moments, it is difficult to align these traditions of speech and silence. A genuine appreciation of public address will account for that ironic twist whereby the virtues of freedom are proclaimed even as they are withheld from the dispossessed.

If public address is in this way part of a greater tradition of public action, in what manner is it distinctive? As a genre of cultural discourse, its identity rests not on any monolithic properties or singular attributes. It is only one field among many, and there is no gain in claiming for it a privileged or unique status. We are drawn to public address, rather, because it offers a complex rationale for interpretive generalizations. We are, at least by intention, beyond the impulse to reduce this rationale to sheer historicism or analytics of style: a speech is not merely a symptom of history, nor is it a poem—it is an event meaningful as it is situated contextually and investigated with sensitivity to the nuances of language. In this sense, public address is distinctive because its study offers a perspective not available by any other means. That said, a few examples will help establish the point.

Public address scholarship can trace its modern origins to two models. In large part through the efforts of Herbert Wichelns at Cornell and Henry Ewbank at Wisconsin, a historical model informs much of public address scholarship. And, thanks to Kenneth Burke, we can turn with some confidence to a model of analysis and criticism that might be broadly defined as literary. While those models are still very much with us, it is just as clear that we have become more willing to consider psychological and sociological interests. However individuated, whether as oration, essay, manifesto, public letter, etc., public address is traditionally understood and interpreted in at least three ways. One approach sees instances of public address as evidence of cultural representation. In this way, symbolic action is taken as an indication of collective style. Edwin Black's study of anti-Communist rhetoric (1970) is perhaps the best known example of this critical mode. A second convention apprehends public address as symptomatic of character and mind. Such analyses as Kenneth Burke's classic interpretation of *Mein Kampf* and Martha Solomon's study of Emma Goldman (1988) represent efforts to move from the text to the historical actor. A third familiar approach involves public address as a contribution to the climate of value and knowledge surrounding its expression. Stephen Lucas's (1980) explication of the Declaration of Independence thus views that document as it was conditioned by regnant ideas and available idioms. These studies are exemplary, we believe, because they so usefully integrate text and context, and resist a common tendency to efface the text and the critic in historical generalizations. At the same time, each is deeply committed to situating textual specifics within situational constraints; and each looks to practical public discourse as the basis for generalizing about culture, character, and ideas.

The above enumeration suggests that the scope of public address studies extends well beyond issues of type and method. Ultimately, if we are to commit to this conception of public address as a form of symbolic expression and public action, we are obliged to confront its ethical dimension. Whether we enter analysis at the point of intention, act, or effect, we are by the very nature of the phenomena drawn into questions of ethical significance. At the very least, taking public address seriously presumes belief in limited free will *and* recognizing the force of circumstance on individual action. As a constitutive part of democracy itself, public address exists only as its conditions are free. This prerequisite to the art commits us, in turn, to the study of those conditions that foster or threaten it. Such a commitment would entail, for example, a great deal more attention to free speech issues and events, an area that remains, ironically enough, marginalized in our national journals and departmental curricula. The burden that this commitment places upon the critic and historian of public address is inescapable; risking piety, we can only say again that this is no more or less than the burden of citizenship itself.

III

Traditionally and still, many of the most pressing issues surrounding public address scholarship regard method. And while a great deal has been accomplished in clarifying aims and correcting excesses, there remain questions that have yet to lose their salience. It is not enough to admonish against rigid schemes of interpretation, or to promote a given approach as evidence of critical pluralism: underneath these recurrent practices, issues of obligation persist. As a way of ordering these issues, it will help to associate them to the commitments indicated above.

Given our commitment to the public character of the art, we may well ask whether our own practice discourages public access. A pair of tendencies in public address scholarship suggests that we do in fact protect our community of ideas from public scrutiny. The first such practice regards theoretical obscurity. Writing to each other, often using excessively obscure or idiosyncratic methods, we court the danger of narrowing the public for public address scholarship. As methods of investigation deepen in sophistication and broaden to include various intellectual traditions, we lose accessibility and limit severely the appeal of our findings. Second, biases contradict our assumptions about the integrity of public life. Even as we enjoy an association with the discipline that dates to its very inception, public address scholars can be blinded by entrenched assumptions; these assumptions, in turn, can violate our own stated commitments to the integrity of public life. Our failure in the past to incorporate women's public address stands as an obvious example. Finally, does our commitment to the standards of objectivity and scholarly distance displace our obligation to see in public address issues of moral significance? The abiding concern here is not merely for judgments of efficacy or appreciation, but of moral evaluation. Few other disciplines systematically inquire into phenomena of such profound influence; and yet the evident reluctance to issue moral judgment is manifest and enduring. The problem eventually runs to the proper roles of the critic and historian in a democracy. While there can be no satisfactory single answer to such a question, its significance is not thereby diminished. We must, in short, confront our standards of scholarship by accepting the fact that our critical practice itself is a form of public address.

Conclusion

At a primary level, then, we know that students of public address study discursive symbolic action to learn how social truths and power are negotiated within the public space. This public space is a fundamental part of communal life, and it both nurtures and is nurtured by public address. Growth of the field demands simultaneous deepening of analysis and bridging across analyses in order to enrich our critical dialogue. Growth in the field also calls for increased attention to the problems of access and denial to the public space.

This restatement is intended to conserve the discipline, but not to encourage conservatism about the discipline. One sense of the word *conserve* is to keep something in a vibrant and flourishing state. We have expressed an approach to public address that sees the traditional principles and approaches to the field as still useful tools for assessing discursive symbolic action. To conserve and to be conservative are separable modes of thought and action. Conserving the discipline is a form of action that assumes that there is much unknown that warrants future study. To be conservative about the discipline would be to assume an attitude of deference toward the principles as approaches to the art. The only deference implicit in conserving the discipline is the same deference that any student, a professional nihilist notwithstanding, grants to her or his method and objects of study: that they are worthy of pursuit. In short, as it should be with a great redwood, so it should be with the study of public address. We should conserve it, not make a totem of it. Following Emerson's advice to the book lovers, we should turn our energies from mere devotion to the art, toward understanding and enlightening the human constitution that is the source of public address.

References

Black, E. (1970). The second persona. *Quarterly Journal of Speech, 56,* 109–199.

Enholm, D. K., Skaggs, D. C., & Welsh, W. J. (1987). Origins of the Southern mind: The parochial sermons of Thomas Craddock of Maryland, 1744-1770. *Quarterly Journal of Speech, 73,* 200–218.

Hart, R. (1986). Contemporary studies in public address: A research editorial. *Western Journal of Speech Communication, 50,* 286.

Katriel, T. (1987). Rhetoric in flames: Fire inscriptions in Israeli youth movement ceremonials. *Quarterly Journal of Speech, 73,* 444–459.

Leff, M. C. (1980). Interpretation and the art of the rhetorical critic. *Western Journal of Speech Communication, 44,* 33–349.

Lucas, S. E. (1988). The renaissance of American public address: Text and context in rhetorical criticism. *Quarterly Journal of Speech, 74,* 241–260.

Mohrmann, G. P. (1980). Elegy in a critical graveyard. *Western Journal of Speech Communication, 44,* 265–274.

Morris, B. A. (1987). The communal constraints on parody: The symbolic death of Joe Bob Briggs. *Quarterly Journal of Speech, 73,* 460–473.

Olson, L. (1987). Benjamin Franklin's pictorial representations of the British colonies in America: A study in rhetorical iconology. *Quarterly Journal of Speech, 73,* 460–473.

Reid, R. F. (1988). *Three centuries of American rhetorical discourse: An anthology and review.* Prospect Heights, Il: Waveland.

Ricoeur, P. (1971). The model of the text: Meaningful action considered as a text. *Social Research, 38,* 529–562.

Solomon, M. (1988). Ideology as rhetorical constraint: The anarchist agitation of "Red Emma" Goldman. *Quarterly Journal of Speech, 74,* 184–200.

Thonssen, L., & Baird, A. (1948). *Speech criticism.* New York: Ronald.

Wichelns, H. (1925). The literary criticism of oratory. In A. M. Drummond (Ed.), *Studies in rhetoric and public speaking in honor of James A. Winans* (pp. 181–216). New York: Century.

• 5 •

Communication Competence

REBECCA B. RUBIN

The term *communication competence* first appeared in our research journals in 1974, although interest in the idea dates to the ancient Greek philosophers, who spoke of competence in terms of "eloquence" and "the art of speaking." Philosophers and writers such as Plato and Aristotle, Cicero and Quintilian, and Blair, Campbell, and Whately saw communication competence as the ability to perform in a graceful, disciplined manner (Rosenfield & Mader, 1984; Spitzberg & Cupach, 1984). Most of these philosophers thought that knowing how to speak was enough of an achievement for the average person; actual skill in elocution was icing on the cake.

Before delving into specific issues in research on competence, I will provide a quick overview of how competence has been conceived and studied over the years. This overview describes the social movements, the educational features, and the prevailing viewpoints that influenced the trends in how communication competence is treated.

Since its modern beginnings—in 1914, when the National Association of Academic Teachers of Public Speaking was founded—the communication discipline has engaged in a battle for literacy. *Communication literacy* is "the ability to enact all possible behaviors a person needs in order to respond appropriately to communication tasks at hand" (Wiemann, 1978, p. 311). Most early scholars were concerned about how best to teach public speaking and debate, how to distinguish competent public speaking from elocution and other forms of performance, and how to carve out an independent realm of scholarship (Leff & Procario, 1985). Their concerns, therefore, revolved around training communicators to be more effective.

In the mid-1900s, scholars from other disciplines joined the quest for a meaning of communication competence; most of these scholars also drew a distinction between competence and performance. The psychologists Foote and Cottrell (1955) believed communication competence was akin to social adjustment. Argyris (1962), an organizational theorist, examined human relations skills necessary for the management of inter-personal relationships. Chomsky (1965), a linguist, examined innate language structures, and Hymes (1971) expanded the realm of study from linguistics to communication. Hymes argued that communication competence: (a) combines speaking and hearing capabilities, (b) relies on a language and thought system, and (c) includes elements of appropriate-ness and success. Sociologists such as G. H. Mead (1934) and Goffman (1963) explored the development of the self concept and social compe-tence. Also, communication scholars examined competence as an inherent element of source credibility (McCroskey, 1966).

During the 1970s and 1980s, increased writing and research dealt with basic components and definitions of communication competence (e.g., Wiemann & Backlund, 1980). The work of Hart and Burks (1972) and Bochner and Kelly (1974) first focused the attention of the communication discipline on the elements of interpersonal and rhetorical competence. Later, Wiemann's (1977) study of communication compe-tence and McCroskey's (1977b) prolific work in communication appre-hension informed the discipline about the perils associated with dysfunc-tional communication. This research, then, allowed for reasoned dialogue about the meaning and assessment of competence. McCroskey's (1982) essay on communication competence, for instance, was responded to by Jensen (1982), Dance (1982), Duran (1982), Cegala (1982), Backlund (1982), Spitzberg (1983), and Phillips (1984).

Just before this dialogue began, however, the back-to-basics move-ment (with its subsequent emphasis on reading, writing, speaking, and listening) drew our discipline's attention away from eloquence and toward minimal competence. Rather than focus on excellence, as our discipline's tradition suggested, we identified minimal standards for average persons to function effectively in society in communication and other basic skills (Forrest, 1979).

Later research revealed that people can be severely affected by a lack of communication skill. McCroskey (1977a) and others (Powers & Smythe, 1980; Smythe & Powers, 1978), for example, pointed out the debilitating effects of communication apprehension in the classroom. Later research has found that about 25% of the population has substandard communication skills (Vangelisti, Daly, & Mead, in press). A similar study, reporting that over 30% of college students cannot give adequate directions or that almost 50% cannot describe a viewpoint that differs from their own, drives home the point that communication training is sorely needed in our society (R. B. Rubin, 1982).

Our society's current interest in cultural literacy also highlights the need for communication competence. Hirsch (1988) argued that effective communication is predicated on cultural literacy, a broad-based knowledge of subject matter, and skillful use of schemata that allow for interaction with others. This movement back to excellence (i.e., skillful use of schemata) from a minimal competence position is forcing our discipline to develop more rigorous methods of assessment, to realign our attention to methods of teaching students more than just basic skills, and to unite as a discipline in striving toward a common goal.

My purpose in this chapter is to order thinking about communication competence and to promote research on the urgent questions in this area. To do this I have organized the chapter around the following questions: (a) What controversies and areas of disagreement exist in the communication competence literature? (b) What beliefs and understandings have resulted from these controversies? (c) What questions still need research?

Largely because of the variety of contexts and disciplines in which communication competence has been studied, the literature has identified some basic controversies about communication competence. Which viewpoint is most useful for communication competence research? Is communication competence context-bound? What qualities should measures of communication competence have?

Dialogues concerning these disagreements have given rise to common beliefs and an emerging definition of communication competence that seems to be guiding the field. One consensually shared definition is: Communication competence is knowledge about appropriate and effective communication behaviors, development of a repertoire of skills that encompass both appropriate and effective means of communicating, and motivation to behave in ways that are viewed as both appropriate and effective by interactants. This definition implies that communication competence can be taught through enhancing this knowledge, these skills, and this motivation. Future research priorities focus on the questions of which measures of communication competence are most valid and which theories provide the best guidance for future research in communication competence.

My goal is to provide an overview of the major kinds of work that have influenced the field and our current understandings by summarizing scholarship that merits close scrutiny by those seriously interested in communication competence. This review does not discuss particular studies or research programs in detail. I hope to make salient here the broad issues, trends, and problems that are often not discerned by one too enmeshed in the details of research investigations and programs.

What Controversies Exist?

This section will explore three basic controversies. The first focuses on theory: Which of the several theoretical perspectives that have guided communication competence research is most useful? Underlying this controversy is one even more basic: Is communication competence a state or a trait? This leads to the third controversy: What qualities should valid measures of communication competence have? These controversies have guided research in the 1970s and 1980s, and researchers are just now beginning to move past controversy towards agreement.

Which Perspective?

Communication competence has been studied from a variety of perspectives. In the discussion that follows, I classify these perspectives into three main types based on common theoretical bonds—cognitive, social/interpersonal, and communication skills. The controversy that exists revolves around which perspective is most central to scholarship in this area.

Writers employing a *cognitive* perspective view communication competence as a psychological or mental process, either innate or developed, that guides behavior. Linguists (e.g., Chomsky, 1965; Habermas, 1970), for instance, judge utterances on their competence (grammatical structure) or performance (acceptability). They focus on the innate system of grammar and rules by which people master language and generate sentences. Chomsky defined linguistic competence as knowledge of what is acceptable (a system of grammatical rules based on an innate language apparatus) and performance as the use of language in social interaction. According to Chomsky, all potential sentences available to a speaker are within the speaker's domain, given a set of generative rules that allow for novel utterances. Linguists were not interested in language variation owing to culture or other regional features.

Several cognitive theorists have disagreed with this view. Hymes (1971), for instance, agreed with the acceptability notion and argued that community norms determine acceptability of linguistic performance, but believed that this definition lacked an essential element—success. Krauss and Glucksberg (1969) argued that communication competence should be distinguished from linguistic competence because children learn grammatical rules by age 3, show adult-level linguistic performance by age 7 or 8, but do not use cognitive and role-taking skills until much later.

More recent cognitive views focus on congruence of mental images. Powers and Lowry (1984) defined communication competence as basic communication fidelity, a congruence of cognitions that takes place after communication has occurred. This definition of communication competence is not concerned with social appropriateness or accuracy of the communicator, but only on congruence of constructs created in the minds of the participants. Theorists who focus on the coordinated management of meaning would also argue that construct congruence is important for competent communication (Pearce, 1976).

Developmental theorists work mainly from a cognitive perspective. As Cronkhite (1984) noted, they formerly examined how children acquire language (e.g., Bloom, 1978; Ervin-Tripp & Mitchell-Kernan, 1977), but lately have addressed questions of how children develop social skills needed for peer interaction (e.g., Van Hoeven, 1985). Constructivists, for example, point to the importance of cognitive development and construct congruence in children's abilities to understand the perspectives of their peers (e.g., Clark & Delia, 1977, 1979; Delia & Clark, 1977).

Haslett (1984) also examined the development of communication in children and identified four distinct competence areas: understanding the value of communication, using conventional signs, appreciation of dialogue requirements, and development of conversational styles. The study also focused on how mothers facilitate competence in their children by interpreting what they say, serving as models, extending children's communication, providing interaction opportunities, and demonstrating activities. This points to a more social notion of the communication competence development.

Social or *interpersonal* competence stems from a sociological view of an individual's interpersonal interaction and describes the process by which people acquire prosocial behaviors and use them to manage interactions. This line of inquiry appears rooted in dramaturgical theory, which argues that people are actors who play roles during interaction with others. G. H. Mead (1934) viewed role-taking (the ability to take another's perspective) as the constituent element within communication competence, and Goffman (1963, 1967) focused on the development of "face and line" in everyday social, symbolic interaction.

Wiemann (1977) interpreted Goffman's basic views that social rules guide interactions to mean that people must achieve their goals without losing face or breaking the rules governing the situation. Cegala's (1981) work on interaction involvement was also built on these principles; he viewed competence as behavior focused on the other during the interaction. Similarly, Redmond's (1985) work on empathy concluded that other-focused behavior is the essential ingredient in communication competence.

Bochner (1984) referred to social or interpersonal skills as bonding competence. He cited Bochner and Kelly's (1974) treatise on interpersonal communication competence, Hart and Burks's (1972) research on rhetorical sensitivity, Argyle's (1972) work on nonverbal communication, and Wiemann's (1977) study of verbal/nonverbal interpersonal communication as evidence that social skills are important; people must be able to diagnose the situation and plan how to achieve an objective, then achieve the objective through strategic verbal and nonverbal communication.

Relational competence research is an extension of this line of inquiry. It concentrates on adult-adult interactions and the social skills needed for relationship development. Spitzberg and Hecht (1984), for example, developed a model of relational communication based on four components: motivation, knowledge, skill, and relational outcomes.

Reardon (1987) was able to distinguish between cognitive social skills (empathy, social perspective taking, cognitive complexity, sensitivity, situational knowledge, and self-monitoring) and behavioral social skills (interaction involvement, interaction management, behavioral flexibility, listening, social style, and monitoring one's own anxiety). With this model, Reardon suggested that both the cognitive and the social or interpersonal perspectives have sufficient research support. Some communication researchers, however, have adopted a third approach, one that identifies context-specific cognitive and social communication skills.

Communication skills theorists extended their focus beyond broad interpersonal or social contexts and concentrated more on skills specific to a particular context or situation. They identified behaviors that are seen as competent by communication recipients in interpersonal, group, organization, media, and intercultural contexts.

In the interpersonal context, research has examined relational impressions formed by interactants and the interpersonal, prosocial skills that comprise interpersonal competence. Researchers such as Bochner and Kelly (1974) identified empathy, descriptiveness, owning feelings, self-disclosure, and behavioral flexibility as components of interpersonal competence. Other researchers have developed similar schemas and add to this list qualities such as social relaxation, assertiveness, interaction management, altercentrism, expressiveness, supportiveness, behavioral flexibility, immediacy, and control (Argyris, 1962; Duran, 1983; Foote & Cottrell, 1955; Wiemann, 1977).

In group communication, Hirokawa and Pace (1983) looked at the effectiveness of groups in relation to behaviors used by group members and the accuracy of the final decision. Effective groups had members who rigorously evaluated the validity of the group's opinions and alternative courses of action, based decisions on accurate facts and inferences, and had a facilitative leader. Bradley (1980) examined the importance to group members of leaders' task-related knowledge levels (competence). Group members acted toward competent leaders with less dominance, more reasonableness, and less hostility; the highly competent leader was more persuasive.

In organizational settings, researchers have looked at both the communication skills of workers and the rules by which they come to understand their roles in the organization. Research consistently points to three general skill areas necessary in organizations—listening (e.g., understanding directions, distinguishing facts from opinions), speaking (e.g., using appropriate words, pronunciation, and grammar), and human relations (e.g., cooperating, resolving conflict, perspective taking, acting friendly) (DiSalvo, 1980; Monge, Bachman, Dillard, & Eisenberg, 1982; Muchmore & Galvin, 1983; Wheeless & Berryman-Fink, 1985).

Specific organizational communication skills such as advising, persuading, instructing (DiSalvo, Larsen, & Seiler, 1976), business writing, telephone communication, interviewing (Staley & Shockley-Zalabak, 1985), and cognitive differentiation (Sypher, 1984) are also identified in the literature. Rules perspective research distinguished between regulative and constitutive rules used to manage communication in the organizational context (Harris & Cronen, 1979). Wellmon (1988) found the most common rules focused on listening, acting in a friendly manner, good leadership, providing feedback, and using empathic interaction skills.

Other studies have examined communication competence of specific organizational individuals. For instance, research has suggested that:

1. Mediators need to use structuring mediation strategies and reframe the disputant's utterances (Donohue, Allen, & Burrell, 1988).

2. Health-care professionals need interpersonal communication skills to build relationships and listen effectively (DiSalvo, Larsen, & Backus, 1986; Morse & Piland, 1981).

3. Teachers must motivate students, give constructive feedback, be supportive, and establish good rapport with students and coworkers (Swinton & Bassett, 1981), be dramatic, impression-leaving, relaxed, open, and friendly (McLaughlin & Erickson, 1981; R. B. Rubin & Feezel, 1986), and give effective feedback, explain lessons clearly, question effectively, adapt to the audience, and direct others effectively (Cooper, 1986; McCaleb, 1984, 1987; R. B. Rubin & Feezel, 1986).

4. Elementary school children must be able to control others, share feelings, inform, ritualize, and imagine (Allen & Wood, 1978).

5. College students must have both a knowledge of communication principles (Levison, 1976) and ability to listen effectively, use nonverbal codes, evaluate oral messages, express and organize ideas, and take the perspective of others (Bassett, Whittington, & Staton-Spicer, 1978; R. B. Rubin, 1982).

Media or television literacy focuses on critical viewing skills, critical televiewing, and television receivership skills. Anderson (1983) developed a receivership skills project to teach children to interpret and critically understand both their own motives for viewing and the content of the material viewed, and develop strategies to manage viewing amounts and program choices. Lloyd-Kolkin (1981) also identified basic television critical viewing abilities: evaluating and managing one's own television viewing behavior, questioning the reality of programs, recognizing arguments used on television, counterarguing, and recognizing the effect of TV on one's own life.

In cross-cultural settings, interpersonal concepts are stretched across cultures to include elements such as interaction posture, empathy, interaction management, role-oriented behavior, and display of respect (Ruben & Kealey, 1979). Viewing competence as culture-specific, Cooley and Roach (1984) argued that consideration of an individual's cultural background is necessary to assess competence. Context-specific knowledge is instrumental in impressions of communication competence that people form (Pavitt & Haight, 1986). Yet Chen (1988) found support for a culture-general interpretation: Basic communication skills were central to intercultural communication competence for sojourners from a large variety of cultures; interaction involvement, social adjustment, self-consciousness, and self-disclosure were also important.

These three perspectives represent different philosophic positions. The cognitivists (especially the structural sociolinguists) viewed language ability as innate and did not include the social (i.e., appropriateness) nature of communication as an important element. Support for the cognitive view is much more limited than that for the social or communication skills approach. The prevailing developmental view is influenced by the social skills approach; children are seen as perspective takers who develop these social skills as they mature.

The social skills theorists focused mainly on interpersonal relationship skills and the process of taking others' perspectives for increased understanding. This view significantly influenced communication research on interpersonal competence but lacks a practical or training orientation.

The communication skills movement, because of its focus on skill enhancement through instruction, provides instructional guidelines for each of the many skills comprising competence. Some have argued that these skills are much too specific and that the whole impression is more than a sum of the parts. Others have contended that the social skills approach is impractical because instruction cannot change empathy and other personality predispositions.

Thus, there is support for both the social and communication skills approaches; that is, only two of the three perspectives have figured prominently in competence research. Given this, it is appropriate to urge future researchers to use either of the two empirically supported theoretical positions to guide their work and to focus attention in particular on research designed to clarify the relative explanatory power of the two alternatives that have survived initial tests of validity.

The controversy that continues revolves around the issue: Can we dissect communication competence into constituent elements that can be taught individually, or is communication competence basically impressions about others' behavioral predispositions?

State or Trait?

The state or trait debate has received extensive treatment elsewhere (Andersen, 1987; Snyder & Ickes, 1985). The basic issue, stated in communication competence terms, is: Is competence a disposition or cross-situational tendency, or is it an event or state that changes with the situation and can be altered by instruction? Many measures of communication competence assume a cross-situational tendency (e.g., McCroskey's early work on communication apprehension, 1977b), but others argue that a situation-specific measure is mandated (e.g., Phillips, 1984; R. B. Rubin, 1982). This controversial issue is made even more prominent by the measures created to assess communication competence.

State measurement focuses on a particular context, place, or time. For example, Monge et al. (1985) and R. B. Rubin (1982, 1985) created instruments to measure organization communication competence and communication competence in educational settings, respectively. The instruments identify communication skills specific to the situation, and raters assess communicators on these skills. Inherent in these measures is a claim that the specific speaking and listening skills measured can be taught; once taught, employees and students will be perceived as more communicatively competent.

Trait measurement examines personality or predisposition factors that influence communication, and, therefore, perceptions of competence. For example, Hart and Burks (1972) proposed that some people are more rhetorically sensitive than others, and those people exhibit more flexibility and appropriateness in their behavior. Hart, Carlson, and Eadie (1980) developed a scale to test this, one that taps attitudes toward change, not behaviors. Later, Eadie and Paulson (1984) found that there were differences among the rhetorically sensitive, the inflexible "noble selves," and too-flexible "rhetorical reflectors." Noble selves scored higher on impression leaving and dominance, and lower on friendliness, than the other two groups. The rhetorically sensitive and rhetorical reflectors differed in perceived competence and style.

The question remains then, how influential are personality traits and situations in perceptions of communication competence? Is there an element of cross-situational competence, or is the context highly influential in a person's ability to communicate? Cupach and Spitzberg (1983) and Pavitt and Haight (1986) found evidence supporting the situational view. R. B. Rubin (1985) also found evidence that we need to examine communication competence in context. However, traits also exist; both rhetorical sensitivity and communication apprehension exhibit cross-situational consistency.

Spitzberg and Cupach (1984) argued that traits (cognitive complexity, rhetorical sensitivity, etc.) can contribute to situational competence, although the evidence to support this claim is sketchy (R. B. Rubin & Henzl, 1984). Andersen (1987) also suggested that we stop examining traits isolated from other variables and look at these cross-situational and consistent traits (e.g., communication apprehension) in relation to states, situations, feelings, etc. Research continues to point to a need to use both state and trait measures to examine communication competence until we have a firm understanding of which measures assess traits and which estimate state-influenced behaviors. In fact, an interactional research strategy would allow researchers to discern intersecting qualities of states and traits.

Measurement

There are many reviews of instruments for measuring communication competence. For example, Larson, Backlund, Redmond, and Barbour (1978) reviewed ninety measures of functional communication, defined *appropriate* as that which meets the demand of the situation, and detailed types of validity and reliability issues important for measurement. R. B. Rubin, Sisco, Moore, and Quianthy (1983) surveyed forty-five college assessment programs, and D. L. Rubin and Mead (1984) reviewed forty-five instruments suitable for kindergarten through twelfth grade. Though mainly descriptive, these reviews point to a lack of conceptual agreement about communication competence and a dearth of standardized instruments. Many of the instruments reviewed were teacher-constructed tests, and too many used paper-and-pencil techniques

(R. B. Rubin et al., 1983). Disagreements, therefore, exist on what measurement qualities are most desirable.

Three major types of data-gathering techniques are used to measure communication competence. First, self-report measures ask respondents to assess their own abilities or knowledge. These measures are typically of the paper-and-pencil variety, and some scholars question their validity in assessing skills or behavior. Second, trained raters provide objective and reliable observations about how well people communicate. Inter-rater and intra-rater reliability are the main concerns with rater-observed competence measures. Third, others' observations or ratings give interactants' views of their partners' communication abilities. Both validity and inter-rater reliability are concerns with interactant ratings because untrained observers are not always knowledgeable about what constitutes competent communication.

Because of the close relationship between the definition of competence and how it is measured, the measurement technique decidedly helps to define the construct theoretically and operationally. A self-report instrument such as the interaction involvement scale (Cegala, 1981), for example, focuses on an individual's own assessment of how actively perceptive, responsive, and attentive he or she felt in the conversation. Competence, here, is a self-report of one's awareness of being involved; the theoretical base emerges as a cognitive element of competence because of the nature of reported affect or feeling called for by the scale. A knowledge test, however, might tap knowledge of basic speech principles and feelings towards the communication process (Levison, 1976). Additional self-report instruments examine self-reports of appropriateness and effectiveness (Duran, 1983; R. B. Rubin, 1985). Recent evidence suggests that self-reports are invalid when used to assess skill, possibly because people are not sufficiently aware of their own behaviors or the effects of these behaviors on others (Cupach & Spitzberg, 1983; Mc-Croskey & McCroskey, 1986; R. B. Rubin & Graham, 1988; R. B. Rubin, Graham, & Mignerey, 1988).

In contrast are behavioral measures of competence, in which an individual communicates while being rated on standard criteria by either a trained observer (R. B. Rubin, 1982, 1985; Snyder, 1982) or a participant (Spitzberg & Hecht, 1984). These techniques are based on a communication skills approach to competence both theoretically and operationally. For the observer to render a judgment, the skills must first be identified precisely and the observer must then evaluate an individual's competence employing criteria specified for each of the skills. Behavioral measure researchers agree that self-report measures provide unreliable and possibly invalid indicators of communication competence, but they disagree about who should make the judgment. Those who use trained raters would ask: How reliable are the judgments of inexperienced and untrained interactants? Those who use interactants would wonder: How valid are raters not involved in the communication interaction?

Also found in the measurement literature is the controversy over what should be assessed (Spitzberg & Cupach, 1984). Advocates of the *molar* view argue that a holistic impression of competence is both necessary and sufficient for valid measurement. Proponents of *molecular* views favor breaking communication competence into very specific and identifiable behaviors and assessing each of these separately. Although we have demonstrated equivalence of the two techniques (R. B. Rubin, 1985), continuing theoretical disagreements have prevented closure.

The field, however, is beginning to establish guidelines to help resolve these controversial issues. Backlund (1983) described the major types of tests and assessment instruments and organized previously described information (Backlund, Brown, Gurry, & Jandt, 1982) on how competence *should* be assessed. These assessment guidelines, endorsed by the Speech Communication Association Committee on Assessment and Testing, have been further refined and reprinted (Allen, Rubin, & Ridge, 1981; McCaleb, 1987). In essence, the guidelines state that assessment instruments should require people to demonstrate skill as either a speaker or a listener (which argues against self-report instruments for speaking skills), that writing and reading ability should not mediate the assessment, and that assessments should be reliable, valid, and free from bias. They seem to support a molecular view (so that assessment may be both valid and reliable). They do not, however, take a position on who provides the most valid and reliable assessment of communication competence.

The foregoing summary highlights the controversies revolving about communication competence theory and measurement. Because conceptual and operational definitions go hand in hand, competition between different viewpoints on theory and measurement will continue as the discipline sorts through the issues identified above. We have now reached a point in scholarship, however, at which it is appropriate to discriminate between useful and not-so-useful ideas and to highlight significant trajectories for future research.

What Do We Believe?

'l'here appears to be a consensus on four major premises: (a)Communication competence is an impression or judgment formed about behavior; (b) Competence entails both appropriateness and effectiveness; (c) People develop a repertoire of skills, a body of knowledge, and motivation to use both; and (d) Skill can be improved through education. These tenets and research supporting each will be examined in this section.

Impression or Judgment

Communication competence is best conceived as an impression or attribution formed about others (Phillips, 1984; R. B. Rubin, 1985; Spitzberg & Cupach, 1984). Just as with source credibility, communication competence is attributed to a communicator on the basis of those behaviors perceived and judged by others. Several research studies have taken this other-rated approach (rather than using self-report instruments) when examining communication effectiveness (Brandt, 1979; Freimuth, 1976; R. B. Rubin, 1985). Some have compared behaviors with impressions. Street, Brady, and Lee (1984), for example, found that males who spoke faster were evaluated as more socially attractive and competent than those who spoke slower, and females who spoke faster were rated as more competent.

Roloff and Kellermann (1984) also viewed competence as an evaluative judgment of a person's behavior rather than an individual's conception of his or her own skills or traits. They argued that people perceive and evaluate others' communication within the relationship on the basis of both verbal and nonverbal behaviors exhibited in the situation. Interactants have their own standards of performance for use in the evaluation, so different raters may reach different conclusions.

Pavitt and Haight (1985) have detailed the process by which these observations are made. Somewhat like the early philosophers' approach to communication competence as eloquence, Pavitt and Haight argued that past researchers have assumed that people use an "ideal communicator" image to judge another's competence and have relied on the premise that there is only one such image. They argued that there are general prototypes, skill-related prototypes, and logically superordinate prototypes. Which prototype is used depends on what the person is looking for. A follow-up study confirmed that people use an "average person" prototype to form impressions of others (Pavitt & Haight, 1986).

Cooley and Roach (1984), however, argued that "competence itself is neither perceivable nor measurable; it can only be inferred" (p. 15). Phillips (1984) agreed that competence was an inference about a behavior, not the behavior itself. His discussion of labeling theory highlights his position that competence is an inference made about artifacts of speakers; the inference should not be made about the speaker him/herself. Labeling theory research suggests that the label can have a profound effect on the one who is labeled—he/she begins to act in ways consistent with the label and thus makes the prophecy self-fulfilling. So, past controversy that centered on whether competence itself can or should be perceived has resulted in an understanding that communication competence is mainly this perception or judgment and does not exist apart from it.

Appropriateness and Effectiveness

From the early classical views on propriety (Longinus) and taste (Blair) to neo-Aristotelian views on effectiveness as a criterion for discourse (Rosenfield & Mader, 1984), virtually every definition of communication competence includes the mandate that communication be both appropriate and effective. Appropriate behaviors are those that others judge to be consistent with the rules of a particular society, and effective behaviors are those that ensure the accomplishment of a communication goal (Bochner & Kelly, 1974; Phillips, 1984; Wiemann, 1978).

Various communication theories see appropriateness as central to the communication process. For example, in coordinated management of meaning (Pearce, 1976), communicators must invoke the use of social rules to manage meanings created between them. Harris and Cronen (1979) examined these rules in an organization and identified strategic competence as a way of cooperating with others and tactical competence as a way of attaining goals; competence, then, is knowledge of appropriate rules and the skill to accomplish goals while using these rules with others. In constructivism, the concepts of listener-adapted messages and perspective taking focus on the need to use socially appropriate communication.

Modern opinions also concur that communication must be effective to be competent. Bochner and Kelly (1974) viewed communication competence as a combination of appropriateness and effectiveness, and Hale's (1980) study of communication competence emphasized only the effectiveness of communication. McCroskey's (1982) essay, however, argued that effectiveness is an unreliable estimate of competence; he reasoned that it was more important for people to be *able* to communicate in a certain way than actually to do it. He favored a definition more closely tied to the demonstration of knowledge of the appropriate communication behavior without mandating effectiveness. One respondent to McCroskey (Backlund, 1982) agreed with this distinction and described how competence and effectiveness differ in cognitive, psychomotor, and affective domains. Another respondent (Spitzberg, 1983) argued that both appropriateness and effectiveness are necessary for competent communication.

Early distinctions between competence (appropriateness) and effectiveness (goal accomplishment) seem to have faded. Most researchers today agree that both elements must be present. Both appropriateness and effectiveness are context-specific, but effectiveness involves more— the accomplishment of objectives. Spitzberg and Cupach (1984) saw appropriateness as existing if social sanctions are invoked when norms or rules are violated and effectiveness as existing if goals or objectives are achieved. Current interpersonal communication texts adopt these definitions (DeVito, 1989; Reardon, 1987; R. B. Rubin & Nevins, 1988).

Both appropriateness and effectiveness are taken into account when a communicator adapts to the situation; this combination of behaviors is sometimes termed "behavioral flexibility" (Bochner & Kelly, 1974; Duran, 1983). Duran and Zakahi (1984) viewed competence as adaptability, the ability to perceive interpersonal relationships and adjust one's own goals and behaviors to the other's. This strategy assumes a repertoire from which to draw behaviors and the ability to perceive others accurately.

Skill, Knowledge, and Motivation

Humanistic and social science research alike have acknowledged a trilogy of domains: psychomotor, cognitive, and affective. For example, persuasion research has long understood that there is a difference between behavior change, change in knowledge, and attitude change. Also, education consistently distinguishes among teaching a student to do something

well, learning how to do it, and liking it. Translated to the communication competence area, skill, knowledge, and motivation are distinct
elements of communication competence.

Communication competence involves developing both a repertoire
of skills and a body of knowledge (McCroskey, 1982, 1984). The idea
of a repertoire of skills has strong theoretical support. For example,
Goodall (1982) defined communication competence as a repertoire of
skills or strategies used to understand and respond in interactions. Ammon (1981) distinguished skill (knowing how) from knowledge (knowing
about); he saw linguistic competence as a structural representation of
linguistic knowledge rules, and communication competence as both skill
and knowledge. Ammon thought skills were necessary for communication performance, but not sufficient to explain variance in performance
(i.e., knowledge has some effect). As Wiemann (1978) suggested, "It is
not enough 'to know' what is appropriate behavior, but the student
must also 'know how' to perform that behavior. In other words, neither
cognitive nor performance knowledge alone is sufficient for literate behavior" (p. 314). Wiemann and Backlund (1980) identified the rift between
cognitive (e.g., Chomsky, 1965) and behavioral (e.g., Bochner & Kelly,
1974) definitions and argued for a dual approach. People need both
knowledge of rules and skilled, appropriate performance.

There is consensus that competence *requires* performance. Spitzberg
(1983) argued that you cannot tell whether a student has knowledge
unless there is performance (either on a test or in a behavior), so knowledge
and skill are intricately entwined in communication competence through
performance. Likewise, Duran (1982) and Cegala (1981) took the stance
that effectiveness and performance are integral components of communication competence. Cooley and Roach (1984) also accepted the view that
communication competence has both behavioral and cognitive components.

Hirsch (1988, p. 62) adhered to the cognitive view that "expert
performance depends on the quick deployment of schemata" that are
models of operating according to well-known patterns of behavior and
their variations. For example, when people listen, they use short-term
memory for generating meaning for themselves and long-term memory
for later recall. The cognitive schemata used in communicating with
others are highly developed methods of speaking, knowledge of subject
matter, and enough flexibility to share strategies with other and change
strategies when necessary. According to Hirsch, "literate adults have

internalized these shared schemata and have made them second nature" (p. 68).

Reardon's (1987) typology of communication behaviors incorporates this view. Spontaneous behaviors are unplanned, subconscious, and unmonitored; emotional reactions such as sadness and anger are spontaneous. Scripted behaviors are culture-specific; when the behavior is learned, planning and monitoring occur and become automatic with increased practice. Contrived behaviors involve conscious planning and monitoring; they are reasoned behaviors. Instruction is focused on turning effective and appropriate behaviors into scripted or automatic.

Skill, then, is a matter of judgment (choosing correctly from a repertoire), and knowledge is a matter of inference (making connections among bits of information learned about situations and communication). One without the other does not lead to competence; both require some type of behavior to be assessed. R. B. Rubin (1985) found a strong relationship between knowledge and skill in her communication competence research and recommended that both be taught in communication classes.

Some scholars include motivation as a third element in conceptions of competence. Spitzberg and Hecht (1984) developed a model that tested the hypothesis that communication satisfaction is derived from an individual's conversational knowledge, skill, and motivation. They found that skill and motivation were strong predictors of communication satisfaction; conversational knowledge was minimally related. Motivation was also identified by R. B. Rubin (1983) as the third dimension of competence, and evidence suggested that motivation is highly influential in judgments of communication skill (R. B. Rubin et al., 1988).

Research has presented mixed evidence for the existence of motivation (see R. B. Rubin & Feezel, 1985, 1986), but skill and knowledge seem to persist as strong components of communication competence (R. B. Rubin, 1985). However, if motivation is defined as communication apprehension or interaction involvement, then there is considerable evidence that motivation is also a component and may underlie enactment of knowledge and skill (Cegala, 1984; McCroskey, 1977a; R. B. Rubin, 1985).

Communicators must build and consult behavioral repertoires to act in knowledgeable and skillful ways (R. B. Rubin, 1983). Allen and Wood (1978) expanded upon Connolly and Bruner's (1974) definition of competence and developed a model in which competence consisted of:

"(1) developing a repertoire of communication acts, (2) selecting from that repertoire the most appropriate communication acts according to criteria, (3) implementing these choices effectively through verbal and nonverbal means, and (4) evaluating these communication attempts according to elements of appropriateness and effectiveness" (Allen & Wood, p. 289).

Training, Allen and Wood (1978) argued, should focus on these four components. Skill instruction should be coupled with selection strategies for criteria development, practice, and evaluation. "Theoretically, then, the communicatively competent individual is the product of a learning environment which permits the development of appropriate behavioral and cognitive skills, shapes a positive affect for communication, and provides opportunities for use and reinforcement of those abilities. One of our functions as communication professionals is to foster the creation of such environments" (McCroskey, 1984, p. 267).

Training

Training can increase communication competence. Our knowledge of communication has grown to the point where educators today can identify skills that will lead to impressions of competence (e.g., Allen & Wood, 1978) and sharpen skills in those areas (Book, 1978). Communication competence is not comprised solely of inherent personality qualities. There are distinct behaviors that can be changed through education (Trank & Steele, 1983).

Bassett and Boone (1983) have cited a variety of skills that instruction can improve. For example, people have been trained to use nonverbal communication skills (e.g., eye contact, gestures, facial expressions, and paralinguistic features), positive feedback, coping statements, compliments, statements of feeling, refusals, questions and requests, anecdotes, and assertive statements. Many methods are successful in improving these skills: written instructions, quizzes, oral instructions, discussion, modeling, overt rehearsal, and covert modeling/rehearsal.

Following the principles described above, Phillips (1984, p. 29) argued that "instruction could/should be based on a deficit analysis of desired goal and actual accomplishment" and should focus on the learning of skills. "Repertoires of observed behaviors would represent skills. Goal accomplishment would represent effectiveness. Instruction could be evaluated by new goals achieved" (Phillips, 1984, p. 29).

This is consistent with R. B. Rubin's (1983) "learning cube," which proposes that students be evaluated in areas of knowledge, skill, and motivation so that instruction can focus on deficient areas. In this cubic model, knowledge, skill, and motivation (communication apprehension) are assigned as the three dimensions. A student, for example, could be a highly motivated skillful communicator who lacks knowledge of basic principles (i.e., a non-apprehensive natural talent); a knowledge-oriented course would be most helpful for this student. Or a student might be quite knowledgeable but lack motivation and skill; a skills-oriented course would be most beneficial here. Classrooms, however, contain students with various instructional needs and rarely are partitioned into segments to meet students' individual needs.

How can communication competence best be taught? Although some educators advocate either an applied, skills approach or a theoretical orientation, an integrated approach is generally favored. Most would agree that teachers cannot improve skills without also imparting knowledge. Allen and Brown (1976) advocated the teaching of rules, norms, and language conventions. They argued that, although education can modify children's communication behaviors by focusing on education's interactive nature, children themselves must master the rules of communication. Teachers help students master new communication acts by serving as models and expanding the realm of experiences so that repertoires can be developed (Book, 1978; Hopper & Wrather, 1978).

Most education is oriented to increasing students' knowledge, but curricula proposed in several sub-areas within the discipline have focused on the learning of skills. Examples include Goodall's (1982) course in adaptive skills for organizational communication and Hammer's (1984) intercultural communication workshop for increasing intercultural communication competence, based on the seven dimensions of intercultural communication competence described by Ruben (1976) and Ruben and Kealey (1979): display of respect, interaction posture, orientation to knowledge, empathy, self role-oriented behavior, interaction management, and tolerance for ambiguity. Curricula also need to be established to increase motivation (Foss, 1982, 1983).

Spitzberg and Cupach (1984) discussed various social learning theory approaches to improving competent communication. For example, one approach would try to develop self-regulatory systems for encoding strategies. Spitzberg and Cupach argued that teachers should use theory-based knowledge to guide what they teach and that they can assume only a small amount of self-knowledge. Skill development follows the acquisition of knowledge. Pedagogical tools must be developed to facilitate skill development. Teachers must increase students' knowledge about how to achieve goals and help them work on creating repertoires of strategies, social rules, and self-awareness. In skills instruction, teachers can give feedback on skills but must be aware that either too much or too little skill could be seen as inappropriate.

However, Bienvenu (1971) implied that only some aspects of competence can be taught. Those aspects relating to self-concept are central to an individual's personality development and may be beyond instruction in the typical classroom. We need further investigation of the elements of competence that are dispositional and those that can be altered through instruction. Although we cannot easily change predispositions, we can provide the scene for behavior change and positive feedback for the development of a repertoire of skills.

Future Research Directions

Comparison of our disagreements and beliefs results in two main areas in which future research must occur, measurement and theory. A third area—whether communication competence is best conceived as linear or curvilinear—bridges the measurement/theory gap.

Measurement

Perhaps our most urgent question is, How can communication competence best be measured? Because of a lack of strong theoretical underpinnings for the communication competence construct, measurement issues have erupted with the creation of each new scale.

Measurement specialists have attempted to help researchers by identifying basic criteria for assessment. Pottinger (1979), for instance, argued that scale developers must consider a measure's sensitivity (responsiveness to slight as well as gross variations), utility (applicability to a wide range of responses), and uniqueness (lack of redundancy or overlap between measures of different aspects of competence). Also, N. A. Mead

(1980) argued that measures must be feasible, reliable, valid, and free of bias. Test creators must make certain decisions: naturalistic or structured approach, holistic or focused ratings, rater objectivity or subjectivity, and methods of implementing the test. Stiggins, Backlund, and Bridgeford (1985) identified ambiguous items, items based on a narrow cultural perspective, test administration, and scoring procedures as potential sources of bias in assessment instruments and suggested methods for controlling and eliminating them.

Piland (1981) questioned whether the instrument should be criterion-referenced or norm-referenced, and Larson (1978) seemed to advocate a criterion-referenced measure for identifying skills. This point of view reflects adherence to the "ideal" communicator perspective in that standard criteria of excellence are used by raters to judge communication. With norm-referenced instruments, communicators are rank-ordered, so that standards of excellence depend on the person's position in relation to others in the group.

Larson et al. (1978) pointed to additional testing necessities— validity (face, content, construct, concurrent, predictive), and reliability (stability over time, homogeneity of coders). These were also explained by Backlund (1983) and D. L. Rubin and Mead (1984). Spitzberg (1987) proposed that before we can answer the "how to measure" question, we must first address four other questions: What are the components of competent interaction? When should we assess competence? Where is the best place to assess competence? Who should assess competence?

As we have seen earlier in this review, researchers have spent a good deal of effort on defining which skills should be assessed. Spitzberg (1988) broke content into three domains: cognitive, physiological, and motor. Most would argue that physiological (defined as motivation here) and cognitive (knowledge) domains cannot be assessed directly—that only the motor domain (behavior) is observable and, even then, the observation is not without error. He also reviewed instruments that used direct methods, in which the individual actually behaved (e.g., self-observation, naturalistic role play, objective criterion instruments), and indirect methods (e.g., interviews, self-reports and other reports), in which the person recalled past behaviors or behavior was inferred from analysis of past events. We need further research on the construct validity of both direct and indirect methods. What is it they are measuring?

The questions of when and where have not received much attention in our field. Larson (1978) argued that assessment of communication competence is useful only if you can specify the context in which the communication is occurring, the specific aspect of competence to be assessed, the extent to which test items sample that aspect, and which responses are correct and incorrect. Donald Rubin (1981) argued that the ideal assessment procedure would sample performance in a variety of settings. Resolution of this issue depends in large part on further inquiry into the generalizability of competence across situations.

The most salient issue now is who should do the assessment. Research has showed consistently a lack of correlation between self-ratings and perceptions by others. Some researchers suspect that self-concept and self-awareness are moderating variables in the self-assessment process (see R. B. Rubin et al., 1988). That is, those with healthy self-concepts overrate their skills, and those with greater degrees of self-awareness are more accurate in their perceptions. Bochner and Kelly (1974) viewed self-ratings as unreliable. But are peer ratings and observations made by trained raters any more reliable? I believe trained raters make the most reliable observations, yet methodological questions still surround observed ratings of communication competence: How do we account for and control differences in perceptions? What type of demand effects by the examiner or exam itself exist or should exist during measurement? Does anxiety influence the enactment of scripted or contrived behaviors?

Theory development and valid and reliable measurement go hand in hand. The communication skills perspective has helped greatly with content validity of measures, and research is now examining concurrent and predictive validity of state measures of communication competence. Future research must examine the construct validity of instruments; only through this process will theory development be advanced. We need to come to an understanding about the nature of communication competence in everyday life. We also need to know how to adjust our education to produce students who will be perceived as communicatively competent.

Linear or Curvilinear?

One issue that bridges measurement and theory and has practical implications in education is: Is communication competence best conceived as linear, as curvilinear, or some other form? A linear view of communication competence would see competence judged along a straight, flat plane. People would be viewed as either competent, incompetent, or somewhere between. Most writers and measurement specialists have rightly argued that there must be gradations or levels of competence rather than merely a competent-incompetent dichotomy (see the SCA criteria in McCaleb, 1987).

The linear position assumes that criteria for excellence exist so that "ideal" or "eloquent" communication can exist; eloquent communication is superior to both minimal competence (a midpoint, perhaps) and incompetent behavior (R. B. Rubin, 1982, 1985). Pavitt and Haight's (1985, 1986) work on identifying prototypes supports the position that people have concepts of competent communicators in mind when judging others; these concepts fall along a continuum ranging from "ideal" to "incompetent." The "average person" would fall midway along the line connecting the two.

A curvilinear view conceives of incompetent behavior at both ends of a curved plane continuum, while the middle range of behavior is competent. This view follows from psychotherapy principles which advocate training people to act in "normal" ways. Spitzberg and Cupach (1984) argued that there is a curvilinear relationship where too much or too little competence can be perceived negatively. Past research on speaker mistakes increasing a speaker's credibility would support the view that one can be too communicatively competent.

Some research has tested the curvilinear notion. Wiemann (1977), in his research on verbal and nonverbal dimensions of communicative competence, predicted that those with moderate skill level would be perceived as most competent. However, his findings suggested that those high in skill were rated higher on behavioral flexibility, communication competency, empathy, supportiveness, and social relaxation. The results pointed out that norms exist for appropriate behavior and that perhaps the linear view is the better supported position.

Rhetorical sensitivity, a rhetorical view of interpersonal qualities, is inherently curvilinear. A rhetorically sensitive person is one who is flexible and adaptive (unlike the "noble self" who rigidly holds to his/her personal norms), yet not overly changeable (like the "rhetorical reflector" with no self); each situation and person calls for a different image (Hart & Burks, 1972; Hart, Carlson, & Eadie, 1980). This view, then, places competence at a midpoint. McCroskey (1977a), too, warned readers of the dangers of too much or too little communication apprehension. He predicted negative consequences for those who avoid communication and for those who aggressively seek communication situations.

The curvilinear view pervades personality trait research (Steinfatt, 1987) and work on assertiveness (Infante, 1987) and communicator style (Norton, 1983). For example, assertiveness is considered the ideal. A contentious or aggressive style (too much assertiveness) and a non-assertive style (too little) are seen as debilitating, ineffective, and abnormal.

This discussion reveals a possible understanding of how both positions can receive such support. Trait approaches to communication competence naturally follow a curvilinear route. Too much or too little of a predisposition traditionally is seen as abnormal behavior, and people are counselled to the norm. Aggressive and apprehensive students, for example, are given skill training to move them into a normal range of assertiveness.

However, state views of competence, especially those based on objective criteria of excellence, follow a linear approach. We train students to enlarge their repertoires of behavior so that others will see them as ideal communicators, but we know that perfection is rarely achieved. Because instruction is based on principles of excellence and change, the linear view to skill improvement is the most appropriate model. Future research must distinguish between the two positions and examine communication traits in relation to state-measured behaviors. This research will also help in theory development—to understand better how and why communication competence develops.

Theory

Which theory or theories best explain communication competence? Kerlinger (1986) explained that theories must specify relations among variables, explain which variables are related to others, and allow for prediction by means of a set of testable hypotheses. Cooley and Roach (1984) translated these basic principles for communication competence. They stated that a theory of competence must be explicit, empirically relevant, abstract, and logically rigorous, and that it take into account the effect of culture on behavior and specify the relationship between competence and performance.

One model that partially satisfies these criteria is Parks's (1985) model of interpersonal competence. Parks identified a hierarchy of nine control levels and used these to rate degrees of competence. Levels 1 through 4 deal with psychomotor competence, or sensory and motor control. To be competent at this level, people must be able to control speech muscles, sense environmental events and control reactions to them, control combinations of muscles, and to execute these organized combinations of actions.

Most definitions of communication competence assume level 5 competence (sequence control), which focuses on ability to put together actions to achieve goals in the stream of interaction. This includes the more molecular aspects of communication competence: formation of phrases, ability to discriminate between verbal and nonverbal actions and communication, timing, and interaction management strategies. Level 6, relationship control, concerns the behaviors necessary to establish satisfying interactions with others. Included in relationship control are abilities to create and understand interaction rules, constructions, perspectives, and causes of behavior.

Level 7, program control, involves skills such as role-taking and behavioral flexibility. Incompetent communication is that which is damaging to one's self-esteem and physical health, is socially inappropriate, or is violent. Competence requires both cognition, behavior, and evaluation: "To be competent, therefore, we must not only 'know' and 'know how,' we must also 'do' and 'know that we did' " (Parks, 1985, p. 174). Levels 8 and 9 focus specifically on abilities to understand and use basic principles and to consult idealized self-concepts when devising and adjusting goals.

Parks's (1985) model is attractive because it helps us understand the relationship of motor and linguistic skills to more modern conceptions of communication competence. In fact, all the perspectives outlined earlier are understandable in the model. It is also appealing because it identifies the individual as the locus of control, it reposes responsibility for actions in the communicator, and it merges the cognitive and behavioral perspectives. Future research must focus on aspects (such as culture) that impinge on a person's degree of control and explain how self-concepts influence behavior. We would expect persons with a greater degree of control to be better able to adjust images for self-perceived judgments of communication competence, for example.

Another theory, especially useful in understanding how to improve communication competence, is repetition theory (McGuire, 1985). This behavioristic learning theory approach (applied to communication competence) would view competence as a repertoire of behaviors that work as created rewards (stimuli) to produce a response (repeated behavior). Through repetition of behavior in similar situations, a person is gratified, especially if the behavior is rewarded. A student, for example, would receive gratification by positive reactions from friends to behaviors developed in an interpersonal skills class. Once in the repertoire, these interpersonal skills would be used time and time again, as long as they produced gratification.

Through this repetition of behaviors, repertoires or styles are created. The larger the repertoire, the more flexible one can be. Hirsch's (1988) concept of the skillful use of schemata as a basis for cultural literacy is consistent with this position. He would argue that rewards are achieved through intellectual discourse with others. Repetition theory is useful because it helps us understand the logical processes involving communication competence and the relationship between knowledge and skill. It also explains the effect of culture and how socialization affects behavior.

However, propositions and hypotheses need to be developed and tested before we can adopt repetition theory for communication competence. For example, with repetition theory we would expect that: (a) the more different situations an individual experiences, the higher the level of perceived communication competence; (b) the greater the rewards accrued for appropriate or effective behavior (see McCroskey's, 1982, "chicken leg" argument), the greater the communication competence; (c) people will be more motivated to repeat competent behaviors that are rewarded (this will have a profound effect on communication apprehension and reticence training programs); and (d) an increase in knowledge of appropriate and effective behaviors will result in an increase in skill. These expectations lead the way for future research on communication competence. Both control theory and repetition theory provide many promising avenues for research.

In this review, I have attempted to identify some of our current disagreements and issues, understandings, and communication competence research priorities. Exemplary sources are identified with the hope that readers will examine more fully the roots of contemporary viewpoints. The first seventy-five years of study have provided a solid foundation. Future research should provide answers to some of the questions and clarify some of the issues raised here.

References

Allen, R. R., & Brown, K. L. (Eds.). (1976). *Developing communication competence in children*. Skokie, IL: National Textbook.

Allen, R. R., Rubin, R. B., & Ridge, A. A. (1981). Competency based instruction and assessment of communication skills. *Journal of the Wisconsin Communication Association, 11,* 21–24.

Allen, R. R., & Wood, B. S. (1978). Beyond reading and writing to communication competence. *Communication Education, 27,* 286–292.

Ammon, P. (1981). Communication skills and communicative competence: A neo-Piagetian process-structural view. In W. P. Dickson (Ed.), *Children's oral communication skills* (pp. 13–33). New York: Academic Press.

Andersen, P. A. (1987). The trait debate: A critical examination of the individual differences paradigm in interpersonal communication. In B. Dervin & M. J. Voigt (Eds.), *Progress in communication sciences* (Vol. 8, pp. 47–82). Norwood, NJ: Ablex.

Anderson, J. A. (1983). Television literacy and the critical viewer. In J. Bryant & D. R. Anderson (Eds.), *Children's understanding of television: Research on attention and comprehension* (pp. 297–330). New York: Academic Press.

Argyle, M. (1972). *The psychology of interpersonal behavior* (2nd ed.). Baltimore: Penguin.

Argyris, C. (1962). *Interpersonal competence and organizational effectiveness.* Homewood, IL: Irwin-Dorsey.

Backlund, P. (1982). A response to Communication Competence and Performance: A Research and Pedagogical Perspective, by James C. McCroskey, *Communication Education, 31, 1982, 1–8 Communication Education, 31,* 365–366.

Backlund, P. (1983). Methods of assessing speaking and listening skills. In R. B. Rubin (Ed.), *Improving speaking and listening skills* (pp. 59–72). San Francisco: Jossey-Bass.

Backlund, P. M., Brown, K. L., Gurry, J., & Jandt, F. (1982). Recommendations for assessing speaking and listening skills. *Communication Education, 31,* 9–17.

Bassett, R. E., & Boone, M. E. (1983). Improving speech communication skills: An overview of the literature. In R. B. Rubin (Ed.), *Improving speaking and listening skills* (pp. 83–93). San Francisco: Jossey-Bass.

Bassett, R. E., Whittington, N., & Staton-Spicer, A. (1978). The basics in speaking and listening for high school graduates: What should be assessed? *Communication Education, 27,* 293–303.

Bienvenu, M. J., Sr. (1971). An interpersonal communication inventory. *Journal of Communication, 21,* 381–388.

Bloom, L. (Ed.). (1978). *Readings in language development.* New York: Wiley.

Bochner, A. P. (1984). The functions of human communication in interpersonal bonding. In C. C. Arnold & J. W. Bowers (Eds.), *Handbook of rhetorical and communication theory* (pp. 544–621). Boston: Allyn & Bacon.

Bochner, A. P., & Kelly, C. W. (1974). Interpersonal competence: Rationale, philosophy, and implementation of a conceptual framework. *Speech Teacher, 23,* 279–301.

Book, C. L. (1978). Teaching functional communication skills in the secondary classroom. *Communication Education, 27,* 322–327.

Bradley, P. H. (1980). Sex, competence and opinion deviation: An expectation states approach. *Communication Monographs, 47,* 101–110.

Brandt, D. R. (1979). On linking social performance with social competence: Some relations between communicative style and attributions of interpersonal attractiveness and effectiveness. *Human Communication Research, 5,* 223–237.

Cegala, D. J. (1981). Interaction involvement: A cognitive dimension of communicative competence. *Communication Education, 30,* 109–121.

Cegala, D. J. (1982). [Forum response]. *Communication Education, 31,* 247.

Cegala, D. J. (1984). Affective and cognitive manifestations of interaction involvement during unstructured and competitive interactions. *Communication Monographs, 51,* 320–338.

Chen, G. M. (1988). Dimensions of intercultural communication competence (Doctoral dissertation, Kent State University, 1987). *Dissertation Abstracts International, 48,* 2192A.

Chomsky, N. (1965). *Aspects of the theory of syntax.* Cambridge, MA: M.I.T. Press.

Clark, R. A., & Delia, J. G. (1977). Cognitive complexity, social perspective-taking, and functional persuasive skills in second- to ninth- grade children. *Human Communication Research, 3,* 128–134.

Clark, R. A., & Delia, J. G. (1979). *Topoi* and rhetorical competence. *Quarterly Journal of Speech, 65,* 187–206.

Connolly, K. J., & Bruner, J. S. (1974). *The growth of competence.* New York: Academic Press.

Cooley, R. E., & Roach, D. A. (1984). A conceptual framework. In R. N. Bostrom (Ed.), *Competence in communication: A multidisciplinary approach* (pp. 11–32). Beverly Hills, CA: Sage.

Cooper, P. J. (1986). *Communication competencies for teachers: A CAT subcommittee report.* Annandale, VA: Speech Communication Association. (ERIC Document Reproduction Service No. SP 028 649).

Cronkhite, G. (1984). Perception and meaning. In C. C. Arnold & J. W. Bowers (Eds.), *Handbook of rhetorical and communication theory* (pp. 51- 229). Boston: Allyn & Bacon.

Cupach, W. R., & Spitzberg, B. H. (1983). Trait versus state: A comparison of dispositional and situational measures of interpersonal communication competence. *Western Journal of Speech Communication, 47,* 364–379.

Dance, F. E. X. (1982). [Forum response]. *Communication Education, 31,* 246.

Delia, J. G., & Clark, R. A. (1977). Cognitive complexity, social perception, and the development of listener-adapted communication in six-, eight-, ten-, and twelve-year-old boys. *Communication Monographs, 44,* 326–345.

DeVito, J. A. (1989). *The interpersonal communication book* (5th ed.). New York: Harper & Row.

DiSalvo, V. S. (1980). A summary of current research identifying communication skills in various organizational contexts. *Communication Education, 35,* 231–242.

DiSalvo, V. S., Larsen, J. K., & Backus, D. K. (1986). The health care communicator: An identification of skills and problems. *Communication Education, 35,* 231–242.

DiSalvo, V., Larsen, D. C., & Seiler, W. J. (1976). Communication skills needed by persons in business organizations. *Communication Education, 25,* 269–275.

Donohue, W. A., Allen, M., & Burrell, N. (1988). Mediator communicative competence. *Communication Monographs, 55,* 104–119.

Duran, R. L. (1982). [Forum response]. *Communication Education, 31,* 246.

Duran, R. L. (1983). Communicative adaptability: A measure of social communicative competence. *Communication Quarterly, 31,* 320–326.

Duran, R. L., & Zakahi, W. R. (1984). Competence or style: What's in a name. *Communication Research Reports, 1,* 42–47.

Eadie, W. F., & Paulson, J. W. (1984). Communicator attitudes, communicator style, and communication competence. *Western Journal of Speech Communication, 48,* 390–407.

Ervin-Tripp, S., & Mitchell-Kernan, C. (Eds.). (1977). *Child discourse.* New York: Academic Press.

Foote, N. N., & Cottrell, L. S., Jr. (1955). *Identity and interpersonal competence.* Chicago: University of Chicago Press.

Forrest, A. (1979). Competence in the effectively functioning citizen. In P. S. Pottinger & J. Goldsmith (Eds.), *Defining and measuring competence* (pp. 85–93). San Francisco: Jossey-Bass.

Foss, K. A. (1982). Communication apprehension: Resources for the instructor. *Communication Education, 31,* 195–203.

Foss, K. A. (1983). Overcoming communication anxiety. In R. B. Rubin (Ed.), *Improving speaking and listening skills* (pp. 25–35). San Francisco: Jossey-Bass.

Freimuth, V. S. (1976). The effects of communication apprehension on communication effectiveness. *Human Communication Research, 2,* 289–298.

Goffman, E. (1963). *Behavior in public places*. New York: Free Press.

Goffman, E. (1967). *Interaction ritual*. Garden City, NY: Anchor.

Goodall, H. L. (1982). Organizational communication competence: The development of an industrial simulation to teach adaptive skills. *Communication Quarterly, 30,* 282–295.

Habermas, J. (1970). Toward a theory of communicative competence. In H. P. Dreitzel (Ed.), *Recent sociology no. 2: Patterns of communicative behavior* (pp. 114–148). New York: Macmillan.

Hale, C. L. (1980). Cognitive complexity-simplicity as a determinant of communication effectiveness. *Communication Monographs, 47,* 304–311.

Hammer, M. R. (1984). The effects of an intercultural communication workshop on participants' intercultural communication competence: An exploratory study. *Communication Quarterly, 32,* 252–262.

Harris, L., & Cronen, V. E. (1979). A rules-based model for the analysis and evaluation of organizational communication. *Communication Quarterly, 27,* 12–28.

Hart, R. P., & Burks, D. M. (1972). Rhetorical sensitivity and social interaction. *Speech Monographs, 39,* 75–91.

Hart, R. P., Carlson, R. E., & Eadie, W. F. (1980). Attitudes toward communication and the assessment of rhetorical sensitivity. *Communication Monographs, 47,* 1–22.

Haslett, B. (1984). Acquiring conversational competence. *Western Journal of Speech Communication, 48,* 107–124.

Hirokawa, R. Y., & Pace, R. (1983). A descriptive investigation of the possible communication-based reasons for effective and ineffective group decision making. *Communication Monographs, 50,* 363–379.

Hirsch, E. D. (1988). *Cultural literacy: What every American needs to know*. New York: Vintage Press.

Hopper, R., & Wrather, N. (1978). Teaching functional communication skills in the elementary classroom. *Communication Education, 27,* 316–321.

Hymes, D. (1971). Competence and performance in linguistic theory. In R. Huxley & E. Ingram (Eds.), *Language acquisition: Models and methods* (pp. 3–26). New York: Academic Press.

Infante, D. A. (1987). Aggressiveness. In J. C. McCroskey & J. A. Daly (Eds.), *Personality and interpersonal communication* (pp. 157–192). Newbury Park, CA: Sage.

Jensen, M. D. (1982). [Forum response]. *Communication Education, 31,* 245.

Kerlinger, F. N. (1986). *Foundations of behavioral research* (3rd ed.). New York: Holt, Rinehart & Winston.

Krauss, R. M., & Glucksberg, S. (1969). The development of communication: Competence as a function of age. *Child Development, 40,* 255–266.

Larson, C. E. (1978). Problems in assessing functional communication. *Communication Education, 27*, 304–309.

Larson, C., Backlund, P., Redmond, M., & Barbour, A. (1978). *Assessing functional communication*. Urbana, IL: ERIC Clearinghouse on Reading and Communication Skills.

Leff, M. C., & Procario, M. O. (1985). Rhetorical theory in speech communication. In T. W. Benson (Ed.), *Speech communication in the 20th century* (pp. 3–27). Carbondale: Southern Illinois University Press.

Levison, G. K. (1976). The basic speech communication course: Establishing minimal oral competencies and exemption procedures. *Communication Education, 25*, 222–230.

Lloyd-Kolkin, D. (1981). The critical television viewing project for high school students. In M. E. Ploghoft & J. A. Anderson (Eds.), *Education for the television age* (pp. 91–97). Athens, OH: Ohio University Cooperative Center for Social Science Education.

McCaleb, J. (1984). Selecting a measure of oral communication as a predictor of teaching performance. *Journal of Teacher Education, 35*(5), 33–38.

McCaleb, J. L. (1987). A review of communication competencies used in statewide assessments. In J. L. McCaleb (Ed.), *How do teachers communicate? A review and critique of assessment practices* (Teacher Education Monograph No. 7, pp. 7–28). Washington, DC: ERIC Clearinghouse on Teacher Education.

McCroskey, J. C. (1966). Scales for the measurement of ethos. *Speech Monographs, 33*, 65–72.

McCroskey, J. C. (1977a). Classroom consequences of communication apprehension. *Communication Education, 26*, 27–33.

McCroskey, J. C. (1977b). Oral communication apprehension: A summary of recent theory and research. *Human Communication Research, 4*, 78–96.

McCroskey, J. C. (1982). Communication competence and performance: A research and pedagogical perspective. *Communication Education, 31*, 1–7.

McCroskey, J. C. (1984). Communication competence: The elusive construct. In R. N. Bostrom (Ed.), *Competence in communication: A multidisciplinary approach* (pp. 259–268). Beverly Hills, CA: Sage.

McCroskey, J. C., & McCroskey, L. L. (1986, April). *Self-reports as an approach to measuring communication competence*. Paper presented at the meeting of the Central States Speech Association, Cincinnati.

McGuire, W. J. (1985). Attitudes and attitude change. In G. Lindzey & E. Aronson (Eds.), *Handbook of social psychology* (Vol. 2, pp. 233–346). New York: Random House.

McLaughlin, M. L., & Erickson, K. V. (1981). A multidimensional scaling analysis of the "ideal interpersonal communication instructor." *Communication Education, 30*, 393–398.

Mead, G. H. (1934). *Mind, self & society from the standpoint of a social behaviorist.* Chicago: University of Chicago Press.

Mead, N. A. (1980, November). *Assessing speaking skills: Issues of feasibility, reliability, validity and bias.* Paper presented at the meeting of the Speech Communication Association, New York.

Monge, P. R., Bachman, S. G., Dillard, J. P., & Eisenberg, E. M. (1982). Communicator competence in the workplace: Model testing and scale development. *Communication Yearbook, 5,* 505–527.

Morse, B. W., & Piland, R. N. (1981). An assessment of communication competencies needed by intermediate-level health care providers: A study of nurse-patient, nurse-doctor, nurse-nurse communication relationships. *Journal of Applied Communication Research, 9,* 30–41.

Muchmore, J., & Galvin, K. (1983). A report of the task force on career competencies in oral communication skills for community college students seeking immediate entry into the work force. *Communication Education, 32,* 207–220.

Norton, R. (1983). *Communicator style: Theory, applications, and measures.* Beverly Hills, CA: Sage.

Parks, M. R. (1985). Interpersonal communication and the quest for personal competence. In M. L. Knapp & G. R. Miller (Eds.), *Handbook of interpersonal communication* (pp. 171–201). Beverly Hills, CA: Sage.

Pavitt, C., & Haight, L. (1985). The "competent communicator" as a cognitive prototype. *Human Communication Research, 12,* 225–241.

Pavitt, C., & Haight, L. (1986). Implicit theories of communicative competence: Situational and competence level differences in judgments of prototype and target. *Communication Monographs, 53,* 221–235.

Pearce, W. B. (1976). The coordinated management of meaning: A rules-based theory of interpersonal communication. In G. R. Miller (Ed.), *Explorations in interpersonal communication* (pp. 17–35). Beverly Hills, CA: Sage.

Phillips, G. M. (1984). A competent view of "competence." *Communication Education, 33,* 25–36.

Piland, R. N. (1981, October). *Measuring interpersonal communication competence.* Paper presented at the meeting of the Speech Communication Association of Ohio, Columbus.

Pottinger, P. S. (1979). Competence assessment: Comments on current practices. In P. S. Pottinger & J. Goldsmith (Eds.), *Defining and measuring competence* (pp. 25–39). San Francisco: Jossey-Bass.

Powers, W. G., & Lowry, D. N. (1984). Basic communication fidelity: A fundamental approach. In R. N. Bostrom (Ed.), *Competence in communication: A multidisciplinary approach* (pp. 57–71). Beverly Hills, CA: Sage.

Powers, W. G., & Smythe, M. J. (1980). Communication apprehension and achievement in a performance-oriented basic communication course. *Human Communication Research, 6,* 146–152.

Reardon, K. K. (1987). *Interpersonal communication: Where minds meet.* Belmont, CA: Wadsworth.

Redmond, M. V. (1985). The relationship between perceived communication competence and perceived empathy. *Communication Monographs, 52,* 377–382.

Roloff, M. E., & Kellermann, K. (1984). Judgments of interpersonal competency: How you know, what you know, and who you know. In R. N. Bostrom (Ed.), *Competence in communication: A multidisciplinary approach* (pp. 175–218). Beverly Hills, CA: Sage.

Rosenfield, L. W., & Mader, T. F. (1984). The functions of human communication in pleasing. In C. C. Arnold & J. W. Bowers (Eds.), *Handbook of rhetorical and communication theory* (pp. 475–543). Boston: Allyn & Bacon.

Ruben, B. D. (1976). Assessing communication competency for intercultural adaptation. *Group & Organization Studies, 1,* 334–354.

Ruben, B. D., & Kealey, D. J. (1979). Behavioral assessment of communication competency and the prediction of cross-cultural adaptation. *International Journal of Intercultural Relations, 3,* 15–47.

Rubin, D. L. (1981, April). *Using performance rating scales in large scale assessments of oral communication proficiency.* Paper presented at the meeting of the American Educational Research Association, Los Angeles.

Rubin, D. L., & Mead, N. A. (1984). *Large scale assessment of oral communication skills: Kindergarten through grade 12.* Urbana, IL: ERIC Clearinghouse on Reading and Communication Skills

Rubin, R. B. (1982). Assessing speaking and listening competence at the college level: The Communication Competency Assessment Instrument. *Communication Education, 31,* 19–32.

Rubin, R. B. (1983). Conclusions. In R. B. Rubin (Ed.), *Improving speaking and listening skills* (pp. 95–100). San Francisco: Jossey-Bass.

Rubin, R. B. (1985). The validity of the communication competency assessment instrument. *Communication Monographs, 52,* 173–185.

Rubin, R. B., & Feezel, J. D. (1985). Teacher communication competence: Essential skills and assessment procedures. *Central States Speech Journal, 36,* 4–13.

Rubin, R. B., & Feezel, J. D. (1986). Elements of teacher communication competence. *Communication Education, 35,* 254–268.

Rubin, R. B., & Graham, E. E. (1988). Communication correlates of college success: An exploratory investigation. *Communication Education, 37,* 14–27.

Rubin, R. B., Graham, E. E., & Mignerey, J. (1988, November). *A longitudinal study of college students' communication competence.* Paper presented at the meeting of the Speech Communication Association, New Orleans.

Rubin, R. B., & Henzl, S. A. (1984). Cognitive complexity, communication competence and verbal ability. *Communication Quarterly, 32,* 263–270.

Rubin, R. B., & Nevins, R. A. (1988). *The road trip: An interpersonal adventure.* Prospect Heights, IL: Waveland.

Rubin, R. B., Sisco, J., Moore, M. R., & Quianthy, R. (1983). *Oral communication assessment procedures and instrument development in higher education.* Annandale, VA: Speech Communication Association.

Smythe, M. J., & Powers, W. G. (1978). When Galatea is apprehensive: The effect of communication apprehension on teacher expectations. *Communication Yearbook, 2,* 487–491.

Snyder, M., & Ickes, W. (1985). Personality and social behavior. In G. Lindzey & E. Aronson (Eds.), *Handbook of social psychology* (Vol. 2, pp. 883–947). New York: Random House.

Snyder, S. L. (1982). An investigation to develop and validate a rating scale for the assessment of the speaking competence of preservice teachers (Doctoral dissertation, Pennsylvania State University, 1981). *Dissertation Abstracts Interactional, 42,* 3115A–3116A.

Spitzberg, B. H. (1983). Communication competence as knowledge, skill, and impression. *Communication Education, 32,* 323–329.

Spitzberg, B. H. (1987). Issues in the study of communicative competence. In B. Dervin & M. J. Voigt (Eds.), *Progress in communication sciences* (Vol. 8, pp. 1–46). Norwood, NJ: Ablex.

Spitzberg, B. H. (1988). Communication competence: Measures of perceived effectiveness. In C. H. Tardy (Ed.), *A handbook for the study of human communication: Methods and instruments for observing, measuring, and assessing communication processes* (pp. 67–105). Norwood, NJ: Ablex.

Spitzberg, B. H., & Cupach, W. R. (1984). *Interpersonal communication competence.* Beverly Hills, CA: Sage.

Spitzberg, B. H., & Hecht, M. L. (1984). A component model of relational competence. *Human Communication Research, 10,* 575–599.

Staley, C. C., & Shockley-Zalabak, P. (1985). Identifying communication competencies for the undergraduate organizational communication series. *Communication Education, 34,* 156–161.

Steinfatt, T. M. (1987). Personality and communication: Classical approaches. In J. C. McCroskey & J. A. Daly (Eds.), *Personality and interpersonal communication* (pp. 42–126). Newbury Park, CA: Sage.

Stiggins, R. J., Backlund, P. M., & Bridgeford, N. J. (1985). Avoiding bias in the assessment of communication skills. *Communication Education, 34,* 135–141.

Street, R. L., Brady, R. M., & Lee, R. (1984). Evaluative responses to communicators: The effects of speech rate, sex, and interaction context. *Western Journal of Speech Communication, 48,* 14–27.

Swinton, M. M., & Bassett, R. E. (1981). Teachers' perceptions of competencies needed for effective speech communication and drama instruction. *Communication Education, 30,* 146–155.

Sypher, B. D. (1984). The importance of social cognitive abilities in organizations. In R. N. Bostrom (Ed.), *Competence in communication: A multidisciplinary approach* (pp. 103–127). Beverly Hills, CA: Sage.

Trank, D. M., & Steele, J. M. (1983). Measurable effects of a communication skills course: An initial study. *Communication Education, 32,* 227–236.

Vangelisti, A., Daly, J., & Mead, N. (in press). Correlates of speaking skills in the United States: A national assessment. *Communication Education.*

Van Hoeven, S. A. (1985). What we know about the development of communication competence. *Central States Speech Journal, 36,* 33–38.

Wellmon, T. A. (1988). Conceptualizing organizational communication competence: A rules-based perspective. *Management Communication Quarterly, 1,* 515–534.

Wheeless, V. E., & Berryman-Fink, C. (1985). Perceptions of women managers and their communicator competencies. *Communication Quarterly, 33,* 137–148.

Wiemann, J. M. (1977). Explication and test of a model of communicative competence. *Human Communication Research, 3,* 195–213.

Wiemann, J. M. (1978). Needed research and training in speaking and listening literacy. *Communication Education, 27,* 310–315.

Wiemann, J. M., & Backlund, P. (1980). Current theory and research in communicative competence. *Review of Educational Research, 50,* 185–199.

• 6 •

Interpersonal Communication Research:
What Should We Know?

DEAN E. HEWES
MICHAEL E. ROLOFF
SALLY PLANALP
DAVID R. SEIBOLD

The study of interpersonal communication has blossomed during the last two decades. This blooming issues from the enrichment of innovative theory, the immense productivity of researchers, the use of advanced research methodologies, and the cross-fertilization of interpersonal communication research with related efforts in mass communication, social psychology, and sociology. It reflects not only the growth of traditional areas of interpersonal communication research, such as persuasion, but also the germination of new ones, such as relational communication (Fisher, 1978; Rogers, 1981), discourse structure and processing (McLaughlin, 1984; Planalp, 1986; Tracy, 1985), and cognitive approaches to the study of communication (Craig, 1979; Greene, 1984; Planalp & Hewes, 1982). The field of communication should celebrate this flowering and take pride in effort well spent. Still, as any good gardener knows, gardening is a process, not an accomplishment. To garden well requires a vision to guide Nature's growth.

The value of interpersonal communication research, and much of its popularity in the classroom, stems from its applications to everyday life. The study of interpersonal communication must be, first and foremost, practical (Craig, in press)[1]. Yet, to be practical, it must be broadly

---

1. Craig's position on the nature of a "practical discipline" of communication goes beyond the scope of our claims here. We have drawn on his notion of *praxis* as an organizing concern for our field only in the simple sense that we view the important implications of our discipline to derive from its contributions to everyday life.

theoretic, for, without theory, research has little practical value. The problem currently faced by interpersonal communication research is a by-product of its fecundity. Because of its rapid growth, interpersonal communication research seems less like a garden than a wild hedge, beautiful but undisciplined. Even the "theories of the middle range" (Merton, 1968) that dominate interpersonal communication today are insufficient, for they do not provide the breadth of perspective necessary to encompass its disparate branches. Our task is to sketch such a broad theoretical framework that could guide the continuing growth of interpersonal communication research. Some vision of what we need to know, some framework, should tell us what to keep, what to prune, and what to plant. In the discussion to follow we provide an outline of such a vision.

Our discussion centers upon four basic and strongly interrelated questions that define and constrain this vision: What do we know about interpersonal communication? What do we believe? What are the controversies in this field? What are the urgencies for research? We attempt to answer all four questions by embedding our vision of the study of interpersonal communication within a theoretical framework that expresses both what we know and what we believe, thus defining what we do not know and must learn.

What Should We Know?: A Framework for Evaluating Interpersonal Communication Research

In order to guide the growth of interpersonal communication research, we must identify what we should know to feel satisfied with our progress. To know what we should know, we need a theoretical framework to serve interpersonal communication research much as the periodic chart of elements has served chemistry; that is, to organize what we know as well as what we do not, but should expect to find. What we offer here is nothing as brilliant as Mendeleev's and Meyer's accomplishment in chemistry. What we can provide is a framework, anchored in commonly accepted views of interpersonal communication, that serves as a critical device to evaluate and to extend interpersonal communication research.

Anchoring the Framework

To construct our framework, we have focused on interpersonal communication abilities and skills, in particular a set of three that are fundamental and hierarchically ordered.[2] Skills and abilities, as we conceive them, are generalizable complexes of knowledge,[3] perception, and, sometimes, action selection and implementation that provide social actors with a connection, or a perceived connection, between their goals and their attempts to achieve those goals—goals that may or may not be consciously accessible. Following Hewes and Graham (1988), we also distinguish between skills and abilities, where the former are learned, as is the skill to persuade or the skill to interpret messages, and the latter are biologically innate, as are the abilities to integrate information, to attend to it, and to recall it. Thus, skills are learned in order to aid in the pursuit of personal, often socially situated, goals. Both skills and abilities are essential to all human endeavors; obviously, abilities make the most general contributions to human conduct, while skills, being essential to the performance of specific goals, are more contextualized.

We adopted this theoretical framework for three reasons. First, we focused on *skills* and the abilities that support them because they constitute the most pragmatic way to view interpersonal communication. It is skills that we teach; therefore it is a framework for studying interpersonal communication skills that we need. Second, we chose to look at *fundamen-*

---

2. While we do claim that the skills we discuss are hierarchically ordered, we do not claim that they form a *complete* hierarchy. That is, it is entirely possible that there may exist more levels in a more complete hierarchy of interpersonal skills than we present here, either between, above and/or below our levels. For instance, *information-seeking skills* might be inserted between impact skills and influence skills. (Also see Footnote 7 for a discussion of ways of elaborating the current levels.)

3. Skills are also anchored in knowledge—knowledge of initiating conditions, goal/path linkages, etc. Knowledge may come from many sources, sources that affect how we view the skill being displayed. At least three such sources seem relevant to interpersonal communication skills; biological, conventional, and idiosyncratic. For instance, we can affect others through their innate aversion to pain or their innate limitations in processing information. We also may be able to influence them or negotiate with them more effectively on the basis of conventional understanding of the rules of bargaining or the ethics of public speaking. Finally, we may find that our knowledge of them as individuals allows us to understand highly indexical exchanges with them or to reach a common understanding on the resolution to some problem more effectively. While we will not explore the implications of these three sources of knowledge here for structuring skills, in the future some consideration of them would be desirable.

tal skills to preserve theoretical parsimony. Skills can be conceived at many levels of abstraction and degrees of specificity. We have identified a set of fundamental skills that we believe logically undergird all communication processes, not merely those relevant to interpersonal communication (Hewes & Planalp, 1987; Planalp & Hewes, 1982; Poole, Folger, & Hewes, 1987). Finally, we sought a *hierarchically ordered* set of skills because this seemed to be the most natural and useful way to view them. Certainly this is so for most developmental theorists (Erikson, 1963; Piaget & Inhelder, 1969) and for many interpersonal communication researchers as well (Delia, O'Keefe, & O'Keefe, 1982; Pearce & Cronen, 1980). More importantly, by selecting hierarchically ordered skills for our framework, we put ourselves in a better position to critique interpersonal communication research. Hierarchically organized skills carry more explanatory value than do those ordered collaterally. Failures of more highly ordered skills may be explained by failures at lower levels; theories aimed at higher ordered skills thus assume responsibility for explanations of lower ordered skills; explanations of social processes based on higher ordered skills are potentially subject to reduction to explanations of lower ordered skills. Of course, the reverse might be true also. Skills or abilities incorrectly identified as fundamental might show connections to higher ordered skills. In order to identify key areas of both agreement and controversy in the study of interpersonal communication, we advance such a hierarchy of skills. At the lowest level are *impact skills*, which include those skills of interpretation and production that are basic to all forms of communication, however nonconscious and undirected. At the next level in the hierarchy are *influence skills*, which are employed in attempts by one communicator to bend another to his or her will. Finally, at the highest level are *coordination skills*. These are skills that make it possible for dyads or larger aggregates to reach consensus concerning joint goals and intersubjective understandings about the social world. The successful operation of skills at each level of the hierarchy presumes the successful operation of skills at lower levels. Conversely, skills at higher levels guide the knowledge and constraints placed on the applications of skills at the lower levels.[4]

---

4. In this chapter, we do not provide sufficient attention to the influence of higher levels of the hierarchy on lower levels. In very general terms, we see this influence as taking at least three forms. Higher levels may influence the *relevance* of certain lower level skills; they may influence the *resources available* for

A Hierarchy of Skills

Level 1: Impact Skills. Interpersonal communication skills can be arranged hierarchically in many ways. The developmental theorist Jerome Bruner (1975), for example, examined the roots of language skills in the nonverbal and paralinguistic skills that evolve in parent-infant interaction. Interpersonal theorists such as Delia and O'Keefe (1979) have developed a hierarchy of persuasive messages based on their adaptiveness to the targets of those messages. Similar moves have been made by Burleson (1982) in the study of empathic skills and by O'Keefe (1988) in the study of discourse styles. In each of these cases, however, an even more basic set of skills, not directly included in their hierarchies, is presumed implicitly. Central to these skills is the ability to identify stimuli, assign meaning to them, and, perhaps, to react to them. Such skills form the basis of "responsiveness," the minimum component necessary for social interaction (D. Davis, 1982). In fact, responsiveness is often cited as a minimum requirement for a definition of communication, where communication is said to have taken place if the probability of B's behavior is dependent on A's behavior at some prior time (Hewes, Planalp, & Streibel, 1980). Only if B has the skills to attend to A's behavior, to identify it, and to produce behavior in return, has communication occurred. Note, however, that we are not assuming in this definition of impact skills that A intends to affect B, or B to affect A, nor are we assuming that A and B share a common goal or interpretive frame. Thus impact skills require only a minimal amount of mutual attention to the exchange, or "mutual engagement" as we choose to call it.[5] Indeed,

---

the operation of lower level skills; they may influence the *content* of lower level skills as in cases in which coordination skills are employed to negotiate rules for interaction.

5. Our hierarchy is anchored in two interrelated notions. The first of these is the specificity of the goals. By degrees each succeeding level of the hierarchy involves much greater constraints on the nature of the goals being pursued by an interactant. For instance, *impact skills* are guided only by system goals (cognitive, physiological), not goals of a social actor, conscious or nonconscious. *Influence skills* involve efforts on the part of at least one party to gain compliance on the part of another party. The subject of that compliance is left unspecified. *Coordination skills,* on the other hand, involve the more specific goal of joint agreement on motivations, the state of the world, and/or behaviors. Our hierarchy is also grounded in another notion, that of *engagement*. Engagement is a relational term, perhaps better rendered as *mutual engagement* (Hewes & Graham,

impact skills are guided only by cognitive and physiological "system" goals, such as the efficiency goal in the former case (Hewes & Graham, 1988; Planalp & Hewes, 1982) and the need for arousal within anticipated ranges in the latter (Cappella & Greene, 1982). Explanations based on either of these two types of goals require no reference to the intent, conscious or habitual, of *A* or *B*.

Drawing on work in cognitive psychology and artificial intelligence, Planalp and Hewes (1982) linked this set of skills, impact skills, to Bruner's (1978) work in their discussion of the cognitive bases of communication. Interpersonal researchers such as Roloff and Berger (1982), Berger & Roloff (1982), Greene (1984), and Pavitt (1982), to name but a few, have all argued for the primacy of such impact skills as attention, information integration, inference, storage, retrieval, selection, and implementation as fundamental to any complete explanation of communication. This set of skills, coupled with the driving forces behind their successful application (goals/motivations, affect, task complexity, and cognitive capacity), provides a necessary but not sufficient foundation for interpersonal communication.

Level 2: Influence Skills. Next in our hierarchy, and necessarily dependent on impact skills, are *influence skills*. Influence skills go beyond mere

---

1988). Like similar concepts such as *involvement* and *intensity* (Bell, 1987), it concerns the amount of effort devoted by each member of a social exchange to the other members of that exchange. Note, however that it is not assumed, as it often is with these other concepts, that engagement is necessarily reflected behaviorally, although it may be. We are much more concerned here with the cognitive resources being used by all parties to the interaction devoted to each other. Thus, we see impact skills as requiring the least engagement because no specific, actor-controlled goals are required, whereas coordination skills involve the highest level of engagement because both parties are trying to achieve joint ends with the help of both impact and influence skills, *ceteris paribus*. Note, however, that while the concept of engagement serves us well intuitively, it is a bit fuzzy. For example, it exists by degrees whereas our sets of skills are considered qualitatively distinct. What is it that leads to those specific qualitative breaks? Obviously, it is the specific goal that defines each skill set. But if that is it, then the hierarchy depends very strongly on the distinction between system goals and actor goals, between single-actor goals and mutual goals. The former distinction may prove problematic upon further analysis, while the latter is weakest in mixed-motive situations. Still, we believe that our hierarchy serves a useful function as a critical device even if it may need to undergo revision as a theoretical framework.

responsiveness. They are employed in the service of a specific, though not necessarily shared, goal—to gain or maintain control of beliefs, affective states, and/or behaviors through the use of messages that affect information, motivation, and/or direction. Thus, influence skills include those skills normally treated in discussions of social influence (Siebold, Cantrill, & Meyers, 1985).

Influence skills involve more engagement with the other than do impact skills because they serve to satisfy specific goals of a social actor, not just the general needs of cognitive and physiological systems. As a consequence, in describing influence skills, we add to the minimal definition of communication introduced in our discussion of impact skills the intuitively appealing requirement that A's behavior is intended, consciously or nonconsciously, to affect B even if it does not have the intended consequences on B. It then follows naturally that A must have the requisite impact skills as a precondition for possessing influence skills.[6]

For instance, A must use his or her impact skills concerned with interpretation (attention, integration, etc.), coupled with knowledge specific to the process of influence, to determine which aspects of self (credibility, social identity, role, resources, etc.), of B (social identity, role, goals, resources, etc.), and of the context (as perceived by either A or B) affect the exigencies of the situation. These exigencies then determine which general impact skills (selection, production), coupled with specific performance-oriented influence skills, are deployed to effect A's messages. Failures in the deployment of influence skills are thus attributable to deficiencies either in those skills or in the impact skills that undergird them. Note however, that the application of influence skills does not require that A and B share an understanding of A's intent or B's goals, nor does it imply that B utilizes any impact skills to affect A.

Level 3: Coordination Skills.   Finally, the highest on our hierarchy are *coordination skills*. Coordination skills are necessary for individuals to reach

---

6. Without appending this intuitively appealing assumption concerning A's intent, we would merely be asserting that B must have the requisite interpretive skills in order for successful impact to have occurred. For example, a falling stone C might change B's behavior. B must still recognize the implication of C's behavior but no intent of C's is necessary for B to do so. It also follows that, if B does infer a person A's intent to control rightly or wrongly and attempts to counter that intent, the skills with which he or she does so fall under the definition of influence skill offered here.

a common understanding, or believe that they have reached a common understanding, concerning some issue of joint importance.[7] Thus, coordination skills involve the highest level of engagement in our hierarchy. Whereas impact skills are general and operate in the service of all specific goals a social actor might have, and whereas influence skills need involve only the specific goal of one social actor, coordination skills involve the interdependence or two or more social actors. Coordination skills might be applied to establishing common terms of reference, common definitions of a relationship, or a jointly acceptable settlement of a problem. Research related to coordination skills typically appears under such headings as relational communication (Fisher, 1978; Rogers, 1981), symbolic interactionism (Stryker, 1980), sociological approaches to emotion (Denzin, 1984; Gordon, 1981), and bargaining and equity (Roloff, 1981).

Coordination skills are dependent on both impact and influence skills. In a relational conflict, for instance, each member of a couple must first be able to understand what he or she counts as costs and rewards, as well as what the other counts as costs and rewards in the relationship (impact skills). Each must also be able to influence the other, informationally and otherwise, as a logical prerequisite to coordination (impact and influence skills). Only with these skills in place can the couple begin to achieve some joint resolution of the inequity (coordination skills). And just as in the case of influence skills, failure in the application of coordination skills may be attributable to failures in skills at lower levels in the hierarchy.

In the remainder of our discussion we return to these three sets of skills and their associated abilities. With them, we assess what we should know in the study of interpersonal communication. In particular, we ask two questions of current research: (1) In what ways does it enhance our understanding of each of these three skill sets—impact, influence, and coordination—and the subskills of which each is composed? (2) To

---

7. Actually, coordination skills might be differentiated into two hierarchically ordered levels. In the lower, skills are used to attempt to attain common understandings on issues of joint interest. In the higher, one or more of the individuals involved in the exchange attempts to create the impression in others that a common understanding exists, when in fact that impression is incorrect. For example, in a bargaining situation, *A* may try to manipulate *B's* impression of his or her bargaining power in order to gain advantage. This requires that *A* understand and execute those skills necessary to accomplish a real sense of common understanding, while at the same time employing skills necessary to deceive *B* concerning *A's* actual beliefs, motives, resources, etc.

what extent and in what ways does current research furnish a clear understanding of the interrelationship among interpersonal communication skills? That is, does this research in addressing higher ordered skills reflect the importance of lower ordered skills that anchor them? By answering these two questions we come one step closer to knowing what we should know to guide the growth of the study of interpersonal communication.

What We Know: A Precis and Critical Assessment

Impact Skills

In its most basic form, communication occurs when A produces a message that affects B's behaviors, thoughts, or emotions. Regardless of what individual and collective goals are pursued through communication, no goals can be realized without impact. We persuade others by influencing their behaviors, their beliefs, and their feelings. We coordinate on tasks by aligning behaviors, following joint plans, and generating shared enthusiasm. If communicators do not have the skills to effect *some* impact, they cannot have the skills to effect a *specific* impact or to effect a *joint* impact on each other.

To say that impact is basic, however, is not to say that it is simple. The principal components are simple enough—an A, a B, and a message (some would add feedback, but one person's feedback is another person's message). The complexity within each of those components that makes impact possible, however, has been traced in detail by Greene (1984), Hewes and Planalp (1982), and Planalp and Hewes (1982), to name a few. A simplified version of their analyses is as follows. At the very least, *speakers* must have some thought or feeling to be expressed or enacted, design a message to express or enact it, and assess its impact on the listener (by becoming listeners themselves). *Listeners,* in turn, must focus attention on the message, assign meaning to it, assimilate that meaning with current awareness and prior knowledge, and select and implement a response to it (thus becoming speakers themselves).

Moreover, skillful speakers and listeners do not always communicate spontaneously, hoping for impact; they also anticipate the degree of impact their messages are likely to have and try to regulate it. In order to design messages with optimal impact, *speakers* anticipate what listeners will focus their attention on, what meanings are likely to be assigned, how the meaning will impact on current awareness and prior knowledge, and how listeners are likely to respond. At the same time, in order to fully appreciate the impact of the message, *listeners* must infer from the message what the thought or feeling of the speaker was, why it was expressed as it was, and what feedback the speaker seeks.

Consider the statement, "It's raining outside." The *speaker*, noticing rain outside, chooses to express that thought to the listener. To design the appropriate message, the speaker must know that the listener will be able to direct his attention to the appropriate window, will assign the correct meaning to the words (he knows English, knows what rain is), and will draw the correct inferences based on his own state (change in current view of weather) and prior knowledge (that the car's windows are open). She must then monitor the listener's response to determine what the impact of the message actually was.

At the same time the *listener* must focus his attention on the message. He must assign the appropriate meaning to it by determining why the message took the form it did (an item of information) and what thought or feeling was being expressed (statement of information or request for action). He then must assimilate the meaning of the message into his own current awareness (the current weather) and prior knowledge (that car windows are down). Finally, he must decide how to respond, taking into account how the speaker expects him to respond (by performing the requested act, ignoring the request, refusing it, responding vacuously, etc.).

This analysis is useful for several reasons. First, it makes clear the true complexity of the most simple messages. Analyzing impact alone is an ambitious task, even without including the more sophisticated analyses of influence and coordination. The elaboration of that complexity also provides a framework for assessing the strengths and weaknesses of the research literature in several different domains in accounting for impact. Second, it serves as groundwork for making links among impact, influence, and coordination. Third, it may be used to identify ways in which impact has been glossed over in research on influence and coordination.

The analysis of impact is most relevant to communication that is not guided by any specific goal of the actor's (or is general enough to serve as the basis for pursuing a broad range of goals), though it may be guided by the "system" (cognitive, physiological) goals discussed previously. For example, it would include expression and interpretation of thoughts and emotions (Bowers, Metts, & Duncanson, 1985), responsiveness (D. Davis, 1982), deception (Knapp, Cody, & Reardon, 1987; Zuckerman, DePaulo, & Rosenthal, 1981), basic regulatory patterns such as turn-taking (Cappella, 1985; Wiemann, 1985), basic conversation patterns such as information exchange (Kellermann, 1987), and self-disclosure (Chelune, 1979), etc.

Different domains of research also benefit in different ways from the analysis of impact. For example, work on deception might be extended to include concerns for how a deceiver monitors the target's response to determine whether the deception has been successful. Similarly, links between impact and influence might be explored by analyzing how spontaneous self-disclosure is modified in the service of particular goals such as self-clarification, relationship development, or manipulation. Phenomena studied at the level of coordination, such as consensus building, might be analyzed in terms of their component impact skills, such as expressing one's own thoughts and feelings, monitoring those of the other, or drawing appropriate inferences about the other's position. In the sections that follow, each of these types of analysis is illustrated in a different domain of research in interpersonal communication.

Impact and the Communication of Emotion.   Of the many areas of interpersonal communication that deserve further exploration, the study of emotion is among the most fruitful and ripe for research. In the words of Berscheid (1987, p. 77), "what is now not known about the role emotion plays in interpersonal communication will some day fill books." It is not that emotion has been neglected entirely (e. g., Bowers, Metts, & Duncanson, 1985), but that new approaches, theories, and research have re-energized the area dramatically during the past decade. Our analysis of impact provides a framework for organizing and assessing these developments.

First, person *A* must have an emotion to communicate to *B*. Some researchers have studied how emotions arise from interaction. Drawing on work by Mandler (1984), Berscheid (1983) has developed the hypothesis that strong emotions occur when well-established patterns of interaction are interrupted. Conflict, for instance, interrupts routine interaction patterns (except for conflict-habituated dyads) and results in emotions, as found by Levenson and Gottman (1983). Moreover, the better established the pattern is, the stronger the emotional response is likely to be when it is broken (Berscheid, 1983; Simpson, 1987). Much work is still needed, however, to identify specific events *within* interactions that elicit emotions (e. g., interruptions, disagreements, compliments).

Sometimes specific stimuli do elicit specific emotions. "Threats of pain, hunger, or cold cause fear; insults and frustrations cause anger; personal loss causes grief; satisfactions cause joy" (Frijda, 1986, p. 263). More often, however, the type and intensity of emotions that people feel depend on their interpretations of the stimulus (Roseman, 1984), changing circumstances (Folkman & Lazarus, 1985), their personal concerns and dispositions (Frijda, 1986, pp. 333–378; Larsen, Diener & Emmons, 1986), and the relevance of events to their self-concepts (Higgins, 1987; Strauman & Higgins, 1987). Socialization processes also influence what emotions are appropriate to feel in certain circumstances and in different cultures (Coulter, 1986; Gordon, 1981; Hochschild, 1983). Thus, individual and cultural differences in how people respond to communicative events must be studied as well.

Second, A must express the emotion. A vast amount of research over decades has provided very sophisticated knowledge about how emotions are encoded through facial expressions (Ekman, 1982; Frijda, 1986; Izard, 1977). Some work has also been devoted to other nonverbal cues, especially paralinguistic cues (Bowers, Metts, & Duncanson, 1985; Burgoon, 1985; Frick, 1985). Most investigation of verbal expressions of emotion have focused on single words that label different types of emotion (Clore, Ortony, & Foss, 1987; Davitz, 1969; Storm & Storm, 1987), although there is some work on other verbal expressions (such as metaphor) and expression through action (such as crying) (Bowers, Metts, & Duncanson, 1985; Shaver, Schwartz, Kirson, & O'Connor, 1987, Study 2). Very little is known, however, about how complex emotions are described in extended discourse such as conversation.

Third, A assesses whether the expressed emotion has had an affect on B. One way to do this is to assess whether the emotion has been expressed successfully and, if so, to assume that it has impacted B. Feedback from facial muscles can be used for this purpose. Another way to assess the impact of emotional expression is for A to monitor B's messages and behavior for evidence that the emotion has registered. Research does not tell us what that evidence might be, but B's emotional expressions or direct verbal acknowledgments or rejections would be good starting points.

Next, we turn to the role of the receiver, B, in communicating emotion. First, he must attend to cues that emotions are being felt by

A. Picking cues out of the ongoing stream of behavior is no mean feat, and we have only begun to understand how it is done. To study naturally occurring emotions, Rutherford and Leto (n.d.) asked people to record displays of emotion from their roommates. In preliminary analyses, they found evidence for a number of different cues, including actions (throwing a plate), indicators of physiological arousal (blushing), situational cues (trouble with classes), and cues related to partners' habitual behaviors that helped identify emotions, in addition to a number of verbal and nonverbal cues identified in previous research (facial expression, vocal cues). Moreover, spontaneous, situated emotional expression has also been found to be more ambiguous and difficult to interpret than posed expressions (Motley & Camden, 1988; Wagner, MacDonald, & Manstead, 1986). These findings taken together indicate that identifying emotion as it occurs naturally may be much more complex and subtle than has been suggested by laboratory studies.

B must also use cues to identify the appropriate emotion. There is a very close parallel between work on interpreting emotion and work on expressing emotion. Most of this research has dealt with the interpretation of facial cues to emotion, some with other nonverbal cues, and still less with verbal cues (Bowers, Metts & Duncanson, 1985; Ekman, 1982). Especially interesting are studies that compare sending and receiving abilities. For example, Halberstadt (1984, 1986) found that people from low-expressive families were better at judging emotions than at expressing them, whereas people from high-expressive families were better at expressing emotions than at judging them.

Once emotions are identified, *B* must then relate that information to his current awareness and prior states and make appropriate inferences. Dyer (1983) had investigated how people make inferences about the motives, goals, and likely reactions of characters in stories based on the characters' emotional states. Halberstadt (1984) also has linked degrees of emotional expressiveness to trait inferences; strongly expressive people were more likely than weakly expressive people to be judged as warm, friendly, loud, assertive, outgoing and excitable. A virtually unexplored area is how people make even more complex judgments of the fit between role and emotion (such as whether Michael Dukakis was sufficiently passionate to be a viable presidential candidate), or of the legitimacy of emotional reactions (such as whether Oliver North was justified in feeling defiant at the Senate hearings on the Iran-Contra scandal).

Finally, *B* responds to *A's* emotion in whatever ways he sees fit. For example, *B* may show empathy by literally feeling *A's* embarrassment (R. S. Miller, 1987). Even if *B* does not feel what *A* is feeling, he may mimic *A's* emotional display to show that he knows or cares how *A* feels (Bavelas, Black, Chovil, Lemery, & Mullett, 1988; Bavelas, Black, Lemery, & Mullet, 1986). Another way is to reciprocate positive feelings with positive feelings or negative feelings with negative feelings. Accurate reciprocity depends, of course, on accurate perceptions of *A's* feelings—and this may not always be the case (Gaelick, Bodenhausen, & Wyer, 1985; Pike & Sillars, 1985). Levenson and Gottman (1983) also found evidence for strong relationships between married couples' physiological states, indicating each spouse's visceral responses to the other's messages. A final type of response is to try to change *A's* affect in desirable ways, such as converting anger to productive action, or fear into hope. (More on this later).

Meta-levels of production and interpretation do not seem to have great import for the spontaneous expression and interpretation of emotion. If spontaneous communication is biologically shared and nonvoluntary, as defined by Buck (1984, p. 7), neither *A* nor *B* need take the other's perspective to produce impact, since impact is guaranteed. Nonspontaneous communication of emotion, however, is another matter. When people are judged on the basis of the social appropriateness of their emotional expressions (as in the Dukakis and North examples), it is extremely important to anticipate how others will interpret those expressions and to control them accordingly (Hochschild, 1983). Moreover, emotion may be the only example of biologically grounded impact. All verbal communication is arbitrarily coded, not biologically given, so that any communication with a significant verbal component requires more of the skills that we have discussed in order to produce impact.

Links to Influence and Coordination. If *A* wants more than just impact, but also wants to control or influence the kind of impact she has on *B*, meta-perspectives become increasingly important. For instance, if *A* wants to change *B's* emotions, she must understand *B's* emotions and what she can do to change them. This requires sophisticated meta-level analyses, which have been described by Thoits (1984). She argues that emotions have four elements: situational cues, physiological sensations, expressive gestures, and a label or interpretation. A skillful *A* could manipulate any or all of these components to change *B's* emotions. If *B* were angry with *A*, for instance, *A* could: leave, thus removing herself as a source of anger, calm *B* down by giving him a drink (preferably not coffee), try to get B to laugh, and/or explain how B should reinterpret the situation to blame circumstances or himself instead of her. Analyzing impact skills, then, may contribute to understanding various types of influence skills, including comforting communication (Burleson & Samter, 1985; Samter & Burleson, 1984), social support (Albrecht & Adelman, 1987), influencing responses to mass media (Wilson, 1987), and controlling employees' emotions (Hochschild, 1983).

Similarly, one might analyze how responsiveness skills (D. Davis, 1982) underlie consensus building. To be responsive to A, B must pay attention to what A is saying, juxtapose that information with his own position, and draw inferences about how the two might be reconciled. B then takes on the speaker's role to develop and present his own position, then assesses A's reaction. To the extent that both parties are able to understand and take the other's position into account *and* to communicate their responsiveness to the other's position in their own messages, consensus building is likely to be facilitated. Conversely, to the extent that A and B have poor responsiveness skills at any point in the cycle, consensus making would be impeded.

A final way in which our analysis of impact might inform research is by providing an understanding of what issues have been glossed over by moving to higher levels of skills without building a foundation at lower levels. The most striking example is work on relational control, as previously analyzed by Planalp and Hewes (1982). They argued that a model of negotiated control in close relationships must be consistent with research at the level of basic production and interpretation (impact) processes.

Since the publication of Planalp and Hewes' work, researchers have begun to investigate the ways in which relational communication is grounded in basic message production and comprehension processes. As a starting point, Planalp (1985) argued that what is being communicated is a working but tentative definition of the relationship. That definition may come from social roles (K. E. Davis & Todd, 1985; La Gaipa, 1987) or previous interactions with the partner. A must design a message to communicate that definition. Precisely how this is done is unclear, but Planalp (1985) found that appropriate messages for professors and students were consistent with a definition of the relationship based on a system of mutual rights and obligations. On the other side of the transaction, B attends, in turn, to aspects of the interaction that are relevant to a relational definition and assimilates them into his own definition if they fit or accommodates his own definition to them if they do not (Planalp, 1987). Finally *B* responds with a bid for his own definition of the relationship and the cycle continues. How *A* and *B* come to a mutually negotiated, compatible definition of the relationship, if at all, is still unclear. Nevertheless, it is unlikely that the process of communicating bids and counterbids can be glossed over in arriving at an explanatory account of coordination.

Influence Skills

Our discussion thus far has emphasized that even impact skills, requiring comparatively less engagement (see Footnote 5) than higher order influence and coordination skills, entail complex processes of message production and interpretation. At the impact level of our framework, interactants' interpretation and production activities need not be directed toward specific goals. They may undergird influence and coordination activities (that are goal-directed and require more relational engagement) or they may serve no goal at all. Thus, communicative influence and coordination practices (directed toward individual and joint impacts, respectively) presume and follow from communicators' skills at effecting *some* impact.

At the same time, experience, theory, and research make it clear that persons use communication to pursue a variety of instrumental and regulative objectives. Beyond simply impacting others' message receptiveness, actors seek to *influence* others—to affect their beliefs, affective states, and/or behaviors through communication that informs, motivates, directs, persuades, and so on. Viewed at this level of the three-tiered hierarchy, interpersonal communication involves message selection and other subskills intentionally and strategically enacted in the service of the goals of at least one party in the interaction. Furthermore, influence message skills (1) are directed toward goals that may not be attained and of which even the influencer may not be consciously or fully aware; (2) may result in other, unintended or less central consequences; (3) presuppose enactment of the impact skills discussed thus far; and (4) are foundational to higher order, coordinative communication.

To say that influence skills are not as complicated as coordinative communication skills should not imply that communicative influence is simple—any more than impact is. However, additional considerations make communication at the influence level even more complex than the interpretation and production processes necessary for achieving impact and engaging responsiveness. Various descriptions of the intricacies and skills of interpersonal influence have been offered by theorists and reviewers (e. g., Bochner, 1984; R. A. Clark, 1984; R. A. Clark & Delia, 1979; Delia, O'Keefe, & O'Keefe, 1982; Goffman, 1969; Grimshaw, 1981; Kelman, 1974; G. R. Miller, Burgoon, & Burgoon, 1984; Schlenker, 1980; Seibold et al., 1985; Tedeschi & Lindskild, 1976), but there is a basic silhouette that emerges from their analyses. At a minimum, communicative influence entails cognitive and emotional processes that lead *influencers* to identify personal objectives that can be satisfied only by reinforcing or altering the cognitions, emotions, and/or behaviors of another. Thus they formulate a plan, a strategy or, at least, an intended line of action that precludes some communication options, but involves choice and implementation of other communication tactics that are perceived to be situationally responsive, socioculturally appropriate, and linguistically competent. It is desirable that this plan be capable of simultaneously achieving impact, interaction efficiency, and attendant identity and interpersonal goals (e. g., face protection and preservation).

But communicative influence may not occur without influence targets, so influence processes and skills must also be considered from a meta-perspective. Just as speakers' strategies are structured by their communication goals, message choices are affected by the speakers' perceptions of the intentions and objectives of those whom they seek to influence. The influence skills identified above may be used in the pursuit of personal goals, but effectiveness is contingent upon recognizing and accommodating to others' goals—especially if they are discrepant from the ends sought by influencers. Furthermore, influence reflects actors' successive adaptations to others' responses to prior message tactics. These adaptations are, of course, based on previous messages in the current episode. Relational history may also affect strategy selection. Communicative influence must therefore be analyzed, at both direct and meta-levels, as a process in which influencers enmesh personal plans and potential lines of action within knowledge born of relational histories with targets or their awareness of targets' behaviors in episodes like the current one, and their interpretations of targets' purposes and anticipated reactions in the present situation.

And what of these *listeners/targets?* While not as central as in communication at the coordination level, in which listener engagement needed to achieve accommodation is most apparent, more aspects of listeners are salient in communicative influence processes and skills than in communication at the impact level. Above and beyond the attention, interpretation, assimilation, and responsiveness that listeners inherently provide when impacted by speakers' communication, in influence processes listeners must directly relate the impacted message to their own behavioral routines and to their own general purposes. At a meta-level, targets of influence attempts must try to determine the goal(s) underlying speakers' messages and relate that assessment to their own specific goals. From speakers' perspectives, for influence to occur, listeners must concur, feel, or comply in ways that are consistent (if not commensurate in magnitude) with those sought by speakers, irrespective of listeners' objectives and level of awareness of speakers' true aims. But this is a limited and limiting view of communicative influence. Influence effects may not be isomorphic with influence attempts. Because listeners may be affected in ways other than those intended, a complete analysis of influence processes must focus on the full range of intended and other cognitive, emotional, and behavioral effects on listeners, not merely on speakers' aims and skills.

As is our analysis of impact, this assessment is useful for several reasons. It underscores the complexity of communicative influence processes, even before considering the intricacies of interpersonal communication as coordination. Too, it aids in making links among impact, influence, and coordination. Third, it offers a schema for examining the strengths and limitations of previous research in a variety of areas in which communicative influence occurs. Finally, it can help to determine whether influence has been adequately recognized in research on impact or coordination.

An analysis of influence skills is most germane to communication that serves as a goal in and of itself. For example, the subskills identified would be particularly applicable for assaying studies of messages aimed at eliciting a particular emotion (namely, comforting) (Burleson, 1984), or in studies of compliance gaining (Boster & Stiff, 1984), altercasting (Weinstein & Deutschenbergen, 1963), embarrassment (Modigliani, 1968, 1971), ingratiation (Jones & Wortman, 1973), and sequential perspective requests (Cantrill & Seibold, 1987). But the framework provided can also aid in assessments of studies not focused solely on influence messages but in which influence is apparent; politeness (Brown & Levinson, 1978), self-disclosure (Derlega, Winstead, Wong, & Greenspan, 1987), information exchange (Kellerman, 1987), self-presentation

(Baumeister, 1982; Blumstein, 1973), impression management (Tedeschi & Reiss, 1981), and conflict reduction (Sillars & Weisberg, 1987), to name but a few. We next review research in an area centrally concerned with communication at the influence level—compliance-gaining message strategies.

Influence and Compliance-Gaining Communication. During the last two decades communication researchers have increasingly turned away from investigations of persuasion in public contexts and toward the study of instrumental communication in interpersonal settings (G. R. Miller, Boster, Roloff, & Seibold, 1987). In the last decade alone more than fifty published studies and conference papers have examined compliance-gaining communication—anticipated and actual persuasive and regulative discourse performed in the service of personal agendas within interpersonal contexts and interactions (Seibold et al., 1985). By applying the analytic framework sketched above, it is possible to determine what we know about the antecedents, causes, processes, performance, correlates, and effects of compliance gaining messages, and what we still need to know.

First, cognitive and emotional responses to proximal stimuli lead speakers toward personal influence objectives and strategies. In some cases, speakers' perceptions of the immediate situation may stimulate and shape particular purposes. But, more generally, speakers' needs, values, general goals, and relational histories with listeners are likely to be enmeshed in the formulation of influence aims. At times, these factors may derive and determine undifferentiated and crosssituational objectives; more often, these factors interact with perceptions of situational exigencies to affect speakers' communicative purposes and strategic lines.

Many reviewers have noted the theoretical character of research on compliance gaining (R. A. Clark, 1979; Cody & Mclaughlin, 1985; Tracy, Craig, Smith, & Spisak, 1984) and the fact that little attention has been paid to understanding the cognitive and motivational determinants of influence objectives. Still, there are notable exceptions, including well-grounded theoretical explanations of cognitive and emotional antecedents of communicative influence. O'Keefe (1988) has located the genesis of communicative objectives and strategies in different "message design logics," reflecting systematic individual differences in reliance on alternative sets of premises that generate messages through ends-to-means reasoning. Berger (1985) proposed a cognitive model consisting of two schemata. One schema (SAS) is theorized to generate influence strategies by employing configurations of strategy attributes (e. g., "approach-avoidance," "positive-negative," "direct-indirect"). The other schema (SSS), more closely related to speakers' objectives, drives the first and contains a number of variables ("intimacy," "relative power," "personality predispositions," etc.) that control the likelihood that certain paths will be chosen in SAS. Wheeless, Barraclough, and Stewart (1983) positioned compliance-gaining attempts within a framework of "interpersonal power." They suggested that the exercise of power emanates from influencers' "needs" and draws upon the bases of control that influencers are perceived by targets to have. Others have invoked different theoretical perspectives to explain the cognitive and emotional antecedents of compliance-gaining objectives and strategies; constructivism (Delia, Kline, & Burleson, 1979), Brown and Levinson's (1978) theory of politeness (Baxter, 1984), subjective expected utility theory (Sillars, 1980), contingency rules theory (Smith, 1984), and extensions of social exchange theory (Roloff, Janiszewski, McGrath, Burns, & Manrai, 1988). Finally, studies have found that predispositions associated with certain personality variables correlate with stronger influence attempts; Machiavellianism (Kaminski, McDermott, & Boster, 1977; Roloff & Barnicott, 1978; but see Williams & Boster, 1981 for contrary evidence), dogmatism (Roloff & Barnicott, 1979), and negativism (William & Boster, 1981).

Second, personal influence objectives must be transformed into plans, strategies, or at least lines of action. A great deal of our knowledge of influencers' plans and strategic lines comes from studies in which subjects are asked either to contrast written, oral, or role-play responses to hypothetical influence situations, or to select from among preformulated lists of strategies adapted to hypothetical influence situations (see Seibold, 1988, p. 154 for a survey of alternate methods). In constructionists, studies, free responses are analyzed within coding systems hierarchically organized to reflect increasing amounts of person-centeredness (Delia, O'Keefe, & O'Keefe, 1982) and listener-adaptedness (Delia, Kline & Burleson, 1979). Results have revealed that individuals capable of forming complex interpersonal impressions formulate more diverse and well-developed lines of action. Results from selectionists' studies, following higher order secondary analyses of specific choices, indicate that influencers are more likely to develop lines of action that are affectively positive before relying on strategies that are negative (Hunter & Boster, 1987).

Critics have argued that these results may be an artifact of the construction and selection procedures used to elicit subjects' strategies, and that they may bear little resemblance to influence strategies in natural contexts (Burleson, Wilson, Waltman, Goering, Ely, & Whaley, 1988; but see Boster, 1988; Hunter, 1988). In view of the fact that *both* procedures virtually ensure that respondents will consciously focus their attention on certain cues when making the message choice (G. R. Miller et al., 1987, p. 103), it is important to consider whether influencers' behaviors (in whatever form) are always as premeditated as research in the area would imply. At a general level, Berger and Douglas (1982) have cautioned against viewing most communicative exchanges as deliberate activities. Because most behavior is enacted "mindlessly" (Langer, 1978) and directed unconsciously (Hinde, 1979), it will be important to understand the mechanisms at work when influence attempts are not consciously planned. We also need a better understanding of the processes moderating purpose-plan-intention-message choice relationships when influence *is* thoughtful. For example, O'Keefe and Delia (1982) portray a multistage process in which message designs are functionally resolved in the generation and reconciliation of multiple message objectives and obstacles, especially: (1) speakers' possession of multiple aims and recognition of obstacles to their primary objective and (2) their reconciliation of principal aims with perceived obstacles and with subsidiary aims. Alternatively, Berger's (1985) cognitive model of social influence includes a "buffer" between strategy formulation and an instantiation of the strategy. The inclusion of this buffer acknowledges that, even in planned communicative influence, considerable cognitive effort and self-awareness may be needed to direct attention to the intention-choice/performance relationship.

Third, influence involves the choice and competent implementation of situationally responsive and appropriate communication tactics. Studies of compliance-gaining situations have focused on (1) uncovering the dimensional structure of persons' perceptual evaluations of influence situations and (2) discerning situational effects of message choices. Reviews of research in both areas may be found in Cody and McLaughlin (1985), Jackson and Backus (1982), Seibold et al. (1985), and Wheeless et al. (1983). The central findings emerging from research in the second area are that persons employ message strategies that they perceive will be most effective in influencing targets, and that strategy choices are guided by speakers' desires to maximize expected gains and minimize potential costs (Cody & McLaughlin, 1985). Furthermore, research reveals that situations in which it is clear that listener compliance will benefit the listener have the most consistent effects on message choices (and somewhat less consistent effects for situations in which listener compliance will benefit the influencer), while the relative intimacy of the influencer-listener relationship and the implication of listener compliance for the duration of that relationship appear to have little effect on message choices (Boster & Stiff, 1984). But we need to know much more. Since many studies in this area assess message construction and selection strategies in hypothetical scenarios, routinized message choices are elicited. Beyond the threats to ecological validity associated with use of these stimuli and restrictive modes of responding, we need much more knowledge about how initial plans and orientations to influence situations (functions of long-term knowledge and present perceptions) are modified as the interaction unfolds and the situation changes (because of speakers' recognition of emerging constraints). Further, since few of these studies have investigated the impact of two or more factors, we know little about the complexities of situations that affect communicators' choice and performance of influence strategies.

Fourth, speakers who seek to influence must simultaneously manage attendant identity and interpersonal goals. Researchers have recognized that many messages are enacted as means for balancing the goal of clear communication (impact goal) with the influence goal of maintaining another's identity (i. e., the analysis of politeness forms by Brown & Levinson, 1978). But instrumental influence attempts increase the complexity of multiple goal management. While pursuing instrumental goals, influencers usually must also maintain interactional efficiency, deal with others' identity needs, and manage self presentation as well. For example, Tracy et al. (1984) examined request discourse and found considerable complexity in speakers' efforts to anticipate and resolve potential conflicts among multiple interactional goals, especially, satisfying the "face wants" of others, while still securing their compliance.

As noted earlier, O'Keefe and Delia's (1982) analysis of influence processes (and reinterpretation of previous constructivist research) was rooted in one factor: the degree to which messages address multiple aims and objectives, and therefore how communication is organized to accomplish multiple intentions. In several experiments in which subjects' goal sets were manipulated, Kline (1985) found that differences in the strategies used were attributable to differences in the number and variety of speakers' goals. O'Keefe and Shepard (1987) also found that differential reliance on strategies for managing multiple objectives in argumentative interactions (communication clarity, issue on the position in dispute, explicitness with which conflict was acknowledged, and attention to fact protection) was, in turn, related to differing degrees of interpersonal success.

Finally, communicative influence also reflects actors' successive adaptations to others' responses to initial (usually unsuccessful) bids by the speaker. Although this may be apparent from a practical standpoint, research on compliance gaining has produced very little knowledge about these successive adaptations. In part, that is because compliance-gaining strategy studies have provided insight only into the *initial*, or entry, strategies that subjects construct or select. Without (1) *a priori* theory about how speakers' message choice decision processes are affected by responses they receive to their influence attempts (see Berger, 1985, for a notable exception), (2) more data on targets' typical modes of influence resistance (for another exception see McLaughlin, Cody, & Robey, 1980), and (3) further research on influence interactions *in situ,* studies like those reviewed above shed little light on the dynamics of influence message production. Isolated studies (Chemielewski, 1982) suggest that individuals will strategically retreat from using initial tactics when presented with subsequent opportunities to influence others. Too, there is a substantial body of literature on alternative forms of "sequential request" persuasive communication such as foot-in-the-door, low-ball, door-in-the-face (Seibold et al., 1985), but very little of this research has been extended to interactional contexts. Since such strategies clearly operate within dynamic episodes, scholarship must explain their nature and effects there.

Links to Impact and Coordination Skills.   Our analysis of impact skills revealed that they are rooted in *both* speakers' and listeners' attention, assimilation, and signification processes. While compliance-gaining researchers acknowledge these underpinnings of influence skills (Cody & McLaughlin, 1985), we know very little about *how* impact-related processes interface with influence dynamics. How do influencers scan the environment with respect to their purposes, and how do they construct different situations? What is the link between this attention to, and processing of, relevant information about targets and situations and speakers' objectives, strategic lines, and message tactics? Only recently have investigators begun to examine how listeners' impact skills are related to influence. For example, researchers have examined how listeners' predispositions toward nonverbal communication cues, especially their abilities to decode speakers' vocalic patterns, affect compliance (Buller & Burgoon, 1986).

At the same time, many influence episodes may actually be mixed-motive situations or evolve into episodes requiring coordinative communication skills. Despite speakers' initial orientations, objectives, and plans, the stream of interaction may make it obvious that they must adjust their own expectations and accommodate to those of listeners. We have very little empirical information about how speakers attempting regulative and instrumental influence proceed past these aims to define a common goal, recognize the extent to which others' objectives are discrepant from that common goal (and persuade them to change), adjust their own goals, and enact these adjustments in light of the common goal. We turn next to a fuller exposition of these skills.

Coordination Skills

Thus far, we have reviewed evidence that interpersonal communication is affected by impact skills, such as information processing and retrieval, and by influence skills, through which communicators seek to achieve specific goals. While these skill domains apply to both participants within a conversation, coordination skills appear to be more truly dyadic. They are evident in the linkages that exist between the actions of two communicators. We believe these connected behaviors represent the attempts of interactants to coordinate their actions so as to achieve a common view. As noted earlier, this implies that coordination skills reflect the greatest degree of engagement, since each interactant must consider the antecedent actions of the other and respond in a fashion that achieves consensus within a given domain.[8]

In this section, we examine theory and research that delineates an underlying goal toward which this mutual contingency is aimed and the skills that are necessary to accomplish it. Specifically, we will examine three conditional premises of this argument. First, a fundamental objec-

---

8. By placing coordination at the highest tier of our hierarchy, we do not mean to ignore highly involving but nontransactive communication episodes in which listeners try to discern the meaning of messages without the benefits of interaction with the speaker. These nontransactional situations are an important part of interpersonal communication and might be placed in an information-

tive of interpersonal communicators is to build a consensus for understanding their prior, current, and future actions. Second, in order to
achieve and maintain consensus, communicators must be able to coordinate their interaction behaviors. Finally, establishing and maintaining
consensus also depends upon impact and influence skills; the coordination
of behaviors is not sufficient to develop and reinforce consensus. Support
for each of these arguments is analyzed in turn.

Achieving and Maintaining Consensus. Cushman and Craig (1976)
have noted that societal interest in communication has emerged as we
have come to realize that the diversity among people is matched only by
their interdependence. Communication has come to be seen as the most
humane means of building and regulating consensus among people holding disparate views.

Interdependency has been hypothesized to be a primary characteristic of an interpersonal relationship (Kelley, 1979; Kelley & Thibaut,
1978). Particularly in intimate relationships, there is an expectation of
coordinated action, mutual concern, and shared interests (Argyle &
Henderson, 1984; La Gaipa, 1977). However, achieving these goals is
rendered problematic by the often diverse individual characteristics,
values, and needs of relational partners. Indeed, there is evidence that
individuals find close relationships to be important sources of both satisfaction and conflict (Argyle & Furnham, 1983).

Interpersonal communication serves as an important mechanism for
facilitating relational consensus. Relational partners can and often do
negotiate agreements that allow them to explain and predict their behaviors in domains in which they are interdependent. This view is evident in
models of marriage that highlight the importance of explicit negotiations
(Scanzoni & Polonko, 1980) and relational contracts (Jacobson, 1977;
Weiss, Birchler, & Vincent, 1974).

Interestingly, not only is interpersonal communication a means of
building consensus but it is a process that *depends upon* consensus. Scholars

---

seeking skills level of a hierarchy (see Footnote 2). Several lines of research have
focused on this facet of communication (e. g., Berger & Douglas, 1981; Hewes
& Graham, 1988). In addition, we do not mean to imply that all coordination
situations require equal amounts of engagement. For instance, initial interactions
may prompt sufficient uncertainty so that communicators must expend more
energy than in subsequent encounters (Berger & Calabrese, 1975). Our only
argument is that coordination skills generally require greater engagement than
do impact or influence skills.

have argued that to communicate successfully, individuals must *initially* reach agreement about a variety of factors. Pearce (1976b) claims that in the initial stages of an interaction, communicators are attempting to negotiate a common episodic definition that will then guide subsequent conversation. Similarly, McCall and Simmons (1978) posit that interactants must first develop at least a tentative working agreement as to their respective social identities or roles *before* they can enact communicative behaviors aimed at achieving consensus on more pragmatic issues. Finally, rules theorists suggest that initial interactions are attempts to generate consensus about the rules that will guide later conversations (Cushman, Valentinsen, & Dietrich, 1982).

Once some preliminary accord is reached, interactive behavior presumably reflects each individual's understanding of the agreement. Hence, scholars have argued that relatively objective linguistic and nonverbal features of interaction might be coded into interpretive categories reflecting relational definitions (e. g., Millar & Rogers, 1976, 1987; Sillars, Weisberg, Burggraf, & Wilson, 1987) or self-presentational images (e.g., McCall, 1987; Schneider, 1981). Moreover, if these conversational cues appear to deviate from the tentative accords, interactants may have to suspend discussion of pragmatic concerns in order to restore or renegotiate consensus (McCall & Simmons, 1978).

Thus, on a theoretical level, consensus building seems fundamental to the processes and goals of interpersonal communication, but this proposition is not without ambiguities. First, the basic nature of consensus is not entirely clear. More often than not, consensus is treated as a primitive term requiring no explication. On the basis of coorientation models (Laing, Phillipson, & Lee, 1966; McLeod & Chaffee, 1973), one could argue that consensus should be operationalized as actual agreement between two people, perceived agreement by one or both partners, and/ or mutual understanding. Since these various measures are not always positively correlated (Sillars & Scott, 1983), one might speculate as to whether any one of them is fundamental to communication or if their importance and interrelationship might vary with the situation. Because the acceptance of any one of them as an indicator of consensus could have profound implications for skill recommendations, one clearly urgent matter for theoretical advancement is clarifying the concept of consensus.

A second ambiguity concerns the *focus* of consensus. As noted earlier, theorists have argued that interactants are attempting to build or maintain consensus about role-identities, rules, episodic definitions, relational dimensions, and presumably, any number of task-related domains. Unclear is the interrelationship among these various constructs. Are they to be arranged hierarchically (Cronen, Pearce, & Harris, 1982)? Could several be the same construct but with different labels, or are they unrelated domains? If these factors are different, under what conditions do communicators address them? Can we identify topics on which consensus must be reached (e. g., use of the same language) before any communication can take place? Unfortunately, theoretical perspectives do not always provide clear answers to these questions, and when they do, empirical research has not evaluated the veracity of their answers. So, further work is much needed in order for us to identify and to understand the critical phenomena about which communicators must reach consensus.

Finally, there is the neglected issue of whether consensus facilitates the achievement of *other* positively valenced outcomes. Does consensus (however it may be defined) maximize the satisfaction and well being of relational partners? Our arguments assumed that it should. Unfortunately, the evidence is mixed. For example, *actual* agreement on relational definitions, roles, and issues is not always significantly related to measures of marital satisfaction, while *perceived* agreement and/or the infrequency of *overt* disagreements are often significant predictors of marital satisfaction (e. g., Arias & O'Leary, 1985; Chadwick, Albrecht, & Kunz, 1976; Sillars, Pike, Jones, & Murphy, 1984). Does this imply that the "illusion of consensus" is the critical variable (Bochner & Krueger, 1979)? Moreover, research has not found a consistent association between understanding and relational satisfaction (e. g., Sillars et al., 1984; Sillars & Scott, 1983; Tiggle, Peters, Kelley, & Vincent, 1982). Why does it appear that in some cases ignorance is bliss but in others accurate perceptions seem to facilitate satisfaction?

Until we clarify the essential nature of consensus, our research and recommendations will also be fraught with ambiguity. The inability to specify the precise nature of consensus may make it difficult to falsify perspectives based upon it. For example, if we observed communicators acting in a manner so as to decrease rather than increase actual agreement, does that mean that consensus building is unimportant, that actual agreement is not the critical form of consensus (perhaps understanding is), or that the particular issue about which we measured consensus is not the central one (e. g., we focused on topic agreement when the central issue was consensus on a rule of honesty)? The aforementioned ambiguities do not undercut the importance of consensus building for understanding interpersonal communication. Instead, they highlight areas of needed conceptual and empirical work.

Coordination and Consensus Building. At the outset, we posited that the mutual contingency observed in interaction is aimed at developing and maintaining consensus. However, we have not described the nature of mutual contingency itself. This description is of great importance since it highlights the skills that are necessary for consensus building.

Scholars have noted that to accomplish their goals, interactants must engage in conversational management (e. g., Pearce, 1976b; Tracy, 1985; Wiemann, 1977). The essential feature of this process is the mutual coordination, or meshing, of interaction behaviors. Communicators adjust their own actions in such a fashion so as to be responsive to those of their partner. Behavioral responsiveness is related to consensus building in three ways. First, it is a sign that both parties acknowledge that an interaction is taking place. Without some mutual adaptation, it is hard to discern whether symbolic behavior is part of a conversation or merely a soliloquy. Second, responsive behavior provides a minimum mutual acknowledgment of mutual engagement. If individuals seek to confirm their self-concepts by initiating interaction, then discriminable responses to their communication should provide at least minimum confirmation. Finally, coordinated behaviors add a measure of coherency to the conversation. Without adaptation, the point of the conversation may remain obscure and consensus unrealized.

One can identify three behavioral subskills of responsiveness. First, responsive communicators must minimally engage in actions that acknowledge the occurrence of a partner's prior behaviors (D. Davis & Perkowitz, 1979). This subskill is essential to maintaining a shared view that there is mutual engagement in the conversation. For example, backchannel responses (Duncan, 1975) may signal that one is paying attention to what the other is saying. At worst, the absence of such cues might be viewed by the speaker as a disconfirmation of his or her very existence (Watzlawick, Beavin, & Jackson, 1967). It is not surprising that the enactment of recognition cues such as "Mmhmm" or "Really?" is positively related to social approval from one's partner (Rosenfeld, 1966). Moreover, communicating signals of acknowledgement, approval, or acceptance (e. g., "I realize that," "I agree") is positively related to satisfaction with conversational outcomes and, more importantly, to the ability to settle conflicts (Koren, Carlton, & Shaw, 1980). While undoubtedly such cues are often communicated to give the mere appearance of responsiveness (Hewes, 1986), the ability to supply them is an important social skill.

Second, responsive communicators must adapt their messages so as to take into account the *content* of a partner's communications (D. Davis & Perkowitz, 1979). While such behaviors imply acknowledgment of the speaker, they also indicate a willingness to let the other person define the topic of the conversation and may be an essential condition for creating a coherent conversation (Tracy, 1985). Consistent with the latter observation, Kraut, Lewis, and Swezey (1982) found that communicators who were encouraged to be responsive and to be inquisitive about the content of their partners' statements developed a superior understanding of the topic of conversation in comparison to those communicators who were less responsive. This advantage stemmed from the ability of the speakers who received feedback to tailor their message to the needs of the listener. Research also indicates that, in general, responses that extend the immediate topic of conversation are viewed as more appropriate than those related to events external to the interaction (Planalp & Tracy, 1980). Thus, communicators who are able to relate the content of their messages to that of their partners' are more likely to develop superior comprehension.

Finally, responsive communicators should adapt their messages so as to take into account the *intent* behind a partner's conversational behaviors. Not all communicators directly state what they mean. Concern for self-presentation (Folkes, 1982), politeness (H. H. Clark & Schunk, 1980), conflict avoidance (Wagner & Pease, 1976), or manipulation (Christie & Geis, 1970; Hunter, Gerbing, & Boster, 1982) may cause an individual to produce a message that expresses an intent that is to some degree discrepant from what is actually meant. To create consensus, communicators must construct a response that reflects not just the stated content of a prior message but the intent behind it. For example, research on indirect requests demonstrated that receivers are able to construct responses that take into consideration both the literal meaning and the implied intent of a message (H. H. Clark & Schunk, 1980; Gibbs, 1983). While the ability to recognize outright deception is more problematic (Zuckerman et al., 1981), communicators appear to be able to discern and respond to benign indirectness.

The responsiveness subskills attract scholarly attention because they encompass behaviors that might be incorporated into teaching and training. Following the lead of marital negotiation skill training (e. g.,

Peterson, Frederiksen, & Rosenbaum, 1981), scholars might be tempted to provide students with models of responsive behavior, the opportunity to rehearse those behaviors, and feedback about their skill level; yet, such a move may be premature.

While we have highlighted potential skill domains and exemplars within each, researchers have generally ignored whether specific behaviors within a given domain will necessarily lead to consensus. For example, one could reasonably argue that allowing an interactant to complete a speaking turn without interruption implies a recognition of the person's desire and right to communicate as well as an intent to avoid the confusion produced by simultaneous speech. In some contexts, however, interruptions may be perceived positively by the speaker (Wiemann, 1985) and could even be evidence of involvement in the interaction. Furthermore, subgroups of communicators seem to differ as to what they consider to be signs of social skills (Romano & Bellack, 1980). If so, researchers need to identify what responsive behaviors might be either universal or context specific before broad prescriptions can be made.

The latter observation implies that an exclusive focus on behavioral manifestations of coordination may obscure equally important impact and influence skills. It is ill-advised to study responsiveness without addressing cognitive processes and other communication processes. In fact, our failure to take into consideration how interaction processes are perceived has led to ambiguous results (Folger & Poole, 1982) and incomplete knowledge (Planalp & Hewes, 1982). In the next section, we explore the role of impact and influence skills in greater detail.

Impact and Influence Skills as Predictors of Consensus

Our earlier discussion implies that to be a responsive communicator, one must be able to recognize that a cue has been encoded, categorize it by topic, and infer the intent behind it. Hence, if a person's impact skills are deficient or inadequately employed, then the attainment of coordination and consensus will be problematic. Also, the simple ability of communicators to coordinate their behavior so that the conversation is coherent does not imply that they will find the content of each others' communication sufficiently attractive so that consensus will be reached. Communicators must know how to negotiate consensus (Cushman & Craig, 1976; Pearce, 1976a). Hence, we believe that scholars need to study both impact and influence skills as additional determinants of consensus.

Impact Skills and Consensus Building.   While we believe that impact skills provide the foundation for the three behavioral subskills of responsiveness, it is not entirely clear what approach should be taken to identify the appropriate cognitive processes. One answer might stem from identifying individual difference characteristics or traits that predispose individuals to be responsive. Individuals vary in their predispositions to be attentive (Norton, 1983), involved (Cegala, 1981; Cegala, Savage, Brunner, & Conrad, 1982), or interpersonally oriented (Street & Murphy, 1987; Swap & Rubin, 1983) during a conversation. However, as noted by Hewes and Planalp (1987), trait approaches frequently do not provide the underlying reason for the relationship between traits and interaction behavior. Often the self-descriptive statements used to assess traits do not provide insight into the cognitive processes that facilitate the achievement of the goals those traits reflect.

An alternative approach focuses on specific cognitive activities as explanations and predictors of responsiveness. This perspective examines the influence of cognitive processes (integration and inference) and knowledge structures (schemata) on the attainment of coordinated behavior (Hewes & Planalp, 1987). For example, Tracy (1985) has advanced a cognitively based perspective about the management of conversation, and psycholinguists have described the cognitive processes that affect the interpretation of indirect requests (e. g., H. H. Clark, 1979; H. H. Clark & Lucy, 1975). This approach may provide insight into deficiencies that lead to less effective responsiveness. For example, social cognition research indicates that human inference making is not infallible (Fiske & Taylor, 1984; Nisbett & Ross, 1980). While these skill deficits are often forgivable (Hewes & Planalp, 1982) and individuals are sometimes aware that these deficits exist (Hewes, Graham, Doelger, & Pavitt, 1985), such deficits may still impede our ability to interpret stimuli. This misunderstanding could result in either false conflict (Deutsch, 1977) or the illusion of agreement (e. g., Levinger & Breedlove, 1966).

Weiss (1980, 1984) has developed a "sentiment-override" hypothesis that focuses on the effect of cognitive skills on how marital partners interpret their communication. He argues that some couples are relatively insensitive to the actual affective quality and message content of their spouses' communication. Hence, spouses' perceptions of their own communication behavior often deviate from the judgments made by observers of the interaction (e. g., Birchler, Clopton, & Adams, 1984; Margolin, Hattem, John, & Yost, 1985), and spouses do not always closely agree about their own interaction behaviors (Margolin et al., 1985). Instead, these couples interpret incoming messages on the basis of their feelings toward each other at the time. If they have positive feelings toward their spouse or relationship, then their attributions of intent will be shaded in that direction; if the feelings are negative, negative interpretations should follow (e. g., Camper, Jacobson, Holtzworth-Munroe, & Schmaling, 1988; Fincham & O'Leary, 1983). Since communication responses are thought to be determined by the interpretations, spouses may have difficulty coordinating their behavior, since their attributions do not reflect either the actual content or intentions of their partner's communication. Although not completely tested, there is partial support for this position (e. g., Floyd, 1988).

This perspective suggests that beyond training individuals to coordinate behavior, instructors need to improve impact skills. This implies that the identification of techniques that can heighten awareness and control of interpretive bias is a critical research area (e. g., Dailey, 1986; Lord, Lepper, & Preston, 1984).

Influence Skills and Consensus Building.   Scholars have noted that influence and, in particular, negotiation skills are an important part of consensus building. For example, Pearce (1976a) argues that communicators must have the ability to negotiate in order to achieve consensus about the episode in which they are engaged and to respond appropriately to their partners' negotiation strategies. He further suggests that this skill is manifested in the use of negotiation strategies such as presentation of self, altercasting, nonverbal cues, and metacommunication. Similarly, McCall and Simmons (1978) assert that a basic social skill is proficiency in negotiating or manipulating interaction so as to achieve one's own ends. They hypothesize that this social skill stems from the use of principles or rules of interaction to overcome resistance from another. In essence, the skillful negotiator uses his or her social knowledge to construct messages that overcome obstacles to persuasion (Francik & Clark, 1985; Gibbs, 1986).

Research has identified certain negotiation behaviors that seem to be effective means of overcoming disagreement. For example, Koren et al. (1980) found that married couples were better able to resolve their conflicts when they proposed many alternative solutions and avoided criticism of each other. Importantly, these two sets of cues accounted for more variance in conflict resolution than did a measure of responsiveness. Moreover, Sillars (1980) discovered that conflict resolution between college roommates was positively related to their use of integrative strategies such as self-disclosure and problem solving, and negatively related to conflict avoidance.

While these studies are useful, they provide limited insight into the cognitive variables (both beliefs and processes) that guide the construction of effective interpersonal negotiation strategies. Although not often employed in interpersonal communication research, bargaining models may be helpful in this regard. For example, Pruitt (1983) has argued that the ability to achieve an integrative agreement (one in which both parties achieve their goals) is a function of dual concern. In essence, effective bargainers are concerned about their own outcomes and those of their partners. This position seems congruent with the relational obligation to help and care for one's intimate partners (Roloff, 1987). Successful bargainers are also hypothesized to employ search models from which they create a variety of plans in order to achieve their own goals. These various plans are presented until it becomes apparent that none is mutually acceptable. If so, then goals are lowered and new alternatives are created. This process results in the proposal of a variety of solutions and appears to be reflected in the findings of Koren et al. (1980).

While these beliefs concerning obligations and cognitive search processes are both good starting points for studying negotiation skills, they do have some drawbacks. First, they imply that relational partners are sufficiently self-aware of their goals to create alternative packages. Sillars and Weisberg (1987) suggest that interpersonal disagreements are often muddled affairs in which issues and goals may at best be only partly understood by the disputants. If this is accurate, then integrative bargaining would be difficult since the relational partners have little understanding of what they want, let alone how to attain it.

Second, these beliefs and search processes imply that negotiation is directed cognitively rather than affectively. Indeed, a rational search process might be seriously impeded by the emotional nature of interpersonal relationships (Berscheid, 1987) and conflicts (Resick, Barr, Sweet, Kieffer, Ruby, & Spiegel, 1981). For example, Sillars and Parry (1982) discovered that nonverbal indicators of stress are negatively related to the degree to which a disputant's communications expressed the recognition and foundation of multiple viewpoints. This implies that under high levels of stress, individuals are less concerned with their partner's position than under lower levels of stress. On the other hand, Fry, Firestone, and Williams (1983) observed that positive emotions such as romantic love also interfered with integrative bargaining. In essence, romantic love prompts self-sacrifice rather than the search for solutions that benefit both partners. While both outrage and love may at times be advantageous (Frank, 1988), they also may reduce the likelihood of a systematic search for a mutually beneficial solution to the problem at hand.

Finally, the model assumes that relational partners have the where-withal to plan and carry out optimal solutions to their problems. Time pressure, or limited resources, could easily discourage the use of such bargaining processes in interpersonal settings. Moreover, one might question whether individuals have the cognitive capacity to consider the full range of issues that might need to be addressed by a given solution (Norman & Bobrow, 1975).

Regardless of the merits of this or any other cognitive model, it should be apparent that the impact skills implicit in such models inform our understanding of coordination successes and failures. More generally, researchers need to focus on coordination, impact, and influence skills *as a set* when examining consensus building. To ignore any one provides an incomplete and perhaps distorted picture of interpersonal communication.

Conclusions

The field of interpersonal communication has, indeed, undergone explosive growth during the last two decades, growth in both the quantity and the quality of research, in the traditional areas of concern and in new ones. For example, the discipline's long-standing commitment to persuasion research is reflected in our comments on influence skills, while an emerging focus on conflict management appears in our discussion of coordination skills. Despite its foundations in ancient rhetoric, the study of the communicative bases and effects of emotion contained in our exposition of impact skills deserves much more attention by communication researchers than it has yet received.

If viewed against the backdrop of our hierarchical skills framework, this juxtaposition of traditional and new research areas in interpersonal communication is informative both for its coherence and its lack thereof. Consider, first, the latter. Growth, in either a discipline or a garden, does not imply *systematic* growth. The growth of interpersonal communication research is better characterized as interspecies competition than as managed completion.

The quantitative study of interpersonal communication began with a social psychological emphasis on influence skills. Subsequently this emphasis was challenged by a sociological focus on the processes of meaning construction as exemplified in relational communication research, conversational analysis, and theories such as coordinated management of meaning (Pearce & Cronen, 1980). Current interest in the basic information-processing strategies (covered in our discussion of impact skills) represents a reaction to the deficiencies of sociological treatments of interpersonal communication, while at the same time it introduces a whole new set of complexities, chief among which is the issue of meta-perspectives (see Hewes & Planalp, 1987, for details; also see Hewes & Graham, 1988, on "second-guessing" as an example of a meta-perspective). Thus the growth of interpersonal communication is marked more by reaction than by integration of perspectives; yet integration is needed desperately.

If there is one point that our framework is designed to make, it is this: *Interpersonal communication must be approached from theoretical positions that integrate both the individual processes and the social forces that shape social interaction.* Our discussions of influence and coordination skills make constant reference to their anchor in impact skills. By the same token, though less often emphasized, impact skills, though more basic, are frequently anchored in socially constructed agreements that both shape the content of cognitive representations and guide the ways that information-processing skills are brought to bear on understanding and producing messages (see Footnote 4). One valid criticism of our framework is that it does not go nearly far enough in articulating this interplay among levels of skills. Another is that we are unable at present to offer a precise depiction of skills at the highest level of our hierarchy, in part because to describe coordination skills thoroughly we must understand more fully how to integrate processes, both psychological and social, within the same theoretical perspective. Of course, neither of these criticisms is limited to our framework. Instead, they reflect the very difficulty that all of the social sciences have in proffering explanations that cross the boundary between individual and social forces. But whatever the failures of the other social sciences, this boundary is on our turf. We have the responsibility to find a way across it. The lack of coherence in the development of interpersonal communication theory and research cannot be allowed to obscure the importance—for our discipline's raison d'etre—of crossing this boundary.

If there are gaps in the coherence of interpersonal communication research, there are areas of congruity as well, areas on either side of the boundary between social and psychological processes. For instance, most interpersonal communication researchers now recognize the complexity of the communication process as portrayed throughout this chapter. Our discussions of consensus and influence illustrate that the study of messages or patterns of messages per se is insufficient to yield an explanation of how communication functions in these domains of interpersonal exchange. As a result, there is an emerging appreciation of the importance of cognitive processes such as attention, memory, planning, and decision making for the study of social interaction. While these cognitive processes may be relatively transparent in some areas of study, it is doubtful that they can ever be wholly ignored in any interpersonal theory. Certainly, they have proven central to our explications of emotion, relational communication, persuasion, conflict, and bargaining.

At the other end of the theoretical spectrum, we perceive a growing recognition that interpersonal communication researchers must exert more effort in clarifying our notions of consensus and intersubjectivity (Hewes & Planalp, 1987; Poole, Folger, & Hewes, 1987). These notions operate at the dyadic (or higher) level. Thus they embody the social aspects of communication, just as cognitive processes embody the individual aspects. Unfortunately, only one communication theorist in recent years has given serious attention to the conceptual problem of intersubjectivity (Grossberg, 1982). Others of us need to follow his lead, turning to hermeneutics, literary criticism, critical theory, and Continental philosophy for insights to augment our investigations into this fundamental problem. Further, this conceptual work needs to go hand in hand with research that addresses the following questions: What kinds of and how much mutual understanding are necessary to the successful application of impact, influence, and coordination skills? How is this intersubjective understanding signalled, maintained, and/or achieved? What are the circumstances that promote and sustain mutual misunderstanding? Under what circumstances is this misunderstanding pernicious, and how is it recognized and overcome? Each of these questions directs us to fundamental issues in the social aspects of interpersonal communication. The answer to each requires a serious reexamination of the nature and function of interpersonal communication. The process of answering these questions, as well as exploring the interrelationships of impact, influence, and coordination skills, should lead to two decades of interpersonal communication research as bountiful as the past two have been.

References

Albrecht, T. L., & Adelman, M. B. (1987). *Communicating social support.* Newbury Park, CA: Sage.

Argyle, M., & Furnham, A. (1983). Sources of satisfaction and conflict in long-term relationships. *Journal of Marriage and the Family, 45,* 481–493.

Argyle, M., & Henderson, M. (1984). The rules of friendship. *Journal of Social and Personal Relationships, 1,* 211–237.

Arias, I., & O'Leary, D. (1985). Semantic and perceptual discrepancies in discordant and nondiscordant marriages. *Cognitive Therapy and Research, 9,* 51–60.

Baumeister, R. F. (1982). A self-presentational view of social phenomena. *Psychological Bulletin, 91,* 3–26.

Bavelas, J. B., Black, A., Chovil, N., Lemery, C. R., & Mullett, J. (1988). Form and function in motor mimicry: Topographic evidence that the primary function is communicative. *Human Communication Research, 14,* 275–299.

Bavelas, J. B., Black, A., Lemery, C. R., & Mullett, J. (1986). "I *show* how you feel": Motor mimicry as a communicative act. *Journal of Personality and Social Psychology, 50,* 322–329.

Baxter, L. A. (1984). An investigation of compliance-gaining as politeness. *Human Communication Research, 10,* 427–456.

Bell, R. A. (1987). Social involvement. In J. C. McCroskey & J. A. Daly (Eds.), *Personality and interpersonal communication* (pp. 195–242). Newbury Park, CA: Sage.

Berger, C. R. (1985). Social power and interpersonal communication. In M. L. Knapp & G. R. Miller (Eds.), *Handbook of interpersonal communication* (pp. 439–499). Newbury Park, CA: Sage.

Berger, C. R., & Calabrese, R. J. (1975). Some explorations in initial interaction: Toward a developmental theory of interpersonal communication. *Human Communication Research, 1,* 99–112.

Berger, C. R., & Douglas, W. (1982). Thought and talk: "Excuse me, but have I been talking to myself?" In F. E. X. Dance (Ed.), *Human communication theory* (pp. 42–60). New York: Harper & Row.

Berger, C. R., & Roloff, M. E. (1982). Thinking about friends and lovers: Social cognition and relational trajectories. In M. E. Roloff & C. R. Berger (Eds.), *Social cognition and communication* (pp. 151–192). Beverly Hills, CA: Sage.

Berscheid, E. (1983). Emotion. In H. H. Kelley, E. Berscheid, A. Christensen, J. H. Harvey, T. L. Huston, G. Levinger, E. McClintock, L. A. Peplau, & D. R. Peterson (Eds.), *Close relationships* (pp. 110–168). New York: W. H. Freeman.

Berscheid, E. (1987). Emotion in interpersonal communication. In M. E. Roloff

& G. R. Miller (Eds.), *Interpersonal processes: New directions in communication research* (pp. 77–88). Newbury Park, CA: Sage.

Birchler, G. R., Clopton, P. L., & Adams, N. L. (1984). Marital conflict resolution: Factors influencing concordance between partners and trained coders. *American Journal of Family Therapy, 12,* 15–28.

Blumstein, P. W. (1973). Audience, Machiavellianism, and tactics of identity bargaining. *Sociometry, 36,* 346–365.

Bochner, A. P. (1984). The functions of human communication in interpersonal bonding. In C. C. Arnold & J. W. Bowers (Eds.), *Handbook of rhetorical and communication theory* (pp. 544–621). Boston: Allyn & Bacon.

Bochner, A., & Krueger, D. I. (1979). Interpersonal communication theory and research: An overview of inscrutable epistemologies and muddled concepts. *Communication Yearbook, 3,* 197–210.

Boster, F. J. (1988). Comments on the utility of compliance-gaining message selection tasks. *Human Communication Research, 15,* 169–177.

Boster, F. J., & Stiff, J. B. (1984). Compliance-gaining message selection behavior. *Human Communication Research, 10,* 539–556.

Bowers, J. W., Metts, S. M., & Duncanson, W. T. (1985). Emotion and interpersonal communication. In M. L. Knapp & G. R. Miller (Eds.), *Handbook of interpersonal communication* (pp. 500–550). Beverly Hills, CA: Sage.

Brown, P., & Levinson S. (1978). Universals in language usage: Politeness phenomena. In E. N. Goody (Ed.), *Questions and politeness: Strategies in social interaction* (pp. 56–289). New York: Cambridge University Press.

Bruner, J. S. (1975). From communication to language—psychological perspective. *Cognition, 3,* 255–287.

Buck, R. (1984). *The communication of emotion.* New York: Guilford Press.

Buller, D. B., & Burgoon, J. K. (1986). The effects of vocalics and nonverbal sensitivity on compliance: A replication and extension. *Human Communication Research, 13,* 126–144.

Burgoon, J. K. (1985). Nonverbal signals. In M. L. Knapp & G. R. Miller (Eds.), *Handbook of interpersonal communication* (pp. 344–390). Beverly Hills, CA: Sage.

Burleson, B. R. (1982). The affective perspective-taking process: A test of Turiel's role-taking model. *Communication Yearbook, 6,* 473–488.

Burleson, B. R. (1984). Comforting communication. In H. E. Sypher & J. L. Applegate (Eds.), *Communication by children and adults: Social cognitive and strategic processes* (pp. 63–104). Beverly Hills, CA: Sage.

Burleson, B. R., & Samter, W. (1985). Consistencies in theoretical and naive evaluations of comforting messages. *Communication Monographs, 52,* 103–123.

Burleson, B. R., Wilson, S. R., Waltman, M. S., Goering, E. M., Ely, T.

K., & Whaley, B. B. (1988). Item desirability effects in compliance-gaining research: Seven studies documenting artifacts in the strategy selection procedure. *Human Communication Research, 14,* 429–486.

Camper, P. M., Jacobson, N. S., Holtzworth-Munroe, A., & Schmaling, K. B. (1988). Causal attributions for interactional behaviors in married couples. *Cognitive Therapy and Research, 12,* 195–209.

Cantrill, J. G., & Seibold, D. R. (1987). The perceptual contrast explanation of sequential request strategy effectiveness. *Human Communication Research, 13,* 253–267.

Cappella, J. N. (1985). The management of conversations. In M. L. Knapp & G. R. Miller (Eds.), *Handbook of interpersonal communication.* Beverly Hills, CA: Sage.

Cappella, J. N., & Greene, J. (1982). A discrepancy-arousal explanation of mutual influence in expressive behavior for adult and infant-infant interaction. *Communication Monographs, 49,* 89–114.

Cegala, D. (1981). Interaction involvement: A cognitive dimension of communicative competence. *Communication Education, 30,* 109–121.

Cegala, D., Savage, G., Brunner, C., & Conrad, A. (1982) An elaboration of the meaning of interaction involvement: Toward the development of a theoretical concept. *Communication Monographs, 49,* 229–248.

Chadwick, B. A., Albrecht, S. L., & Kunz, P. R. (1976). Marital and family role satisfaction. *Journal of Marriage and the Family, 38,* 431–440.

Chelune, G. J., and Assoc. (1979). *Self-disclosure.* San Francisco: Jossey-Bass.

Chemielewski, T. J. (1982). A test of a model for predicting strategy choice. *Central States Speech Journal, 33,* 505–518.

Christie, R., & Geis, F. C. (1970). *Studies in Machiavellianism.* New York: Academic Press.

Clark, H. H. (1979). Responding to indirect speech acts. *Cognitive Psychology, 11,* 430–477.

Clark, H. H., & Lucy, P. (1975). Understanding what is meant from what is said: A study in conversationally conveyed requests. *Journal of Verbal Learning and Verbal Behavior, 14,* 56–72.

Clark, H. H., & Schunk, D. H. (1980). Polite responses to polite requests. *Cognition, 8,* 111–143.

Clark, R. A. (1979). The impact of self-interest and desired liking on selection of persuasive strategies. *Communication Monographs, 46.* 257–273.

Clark, R. A. (1984). *Persuasive messages.* New York: Harper & Row.

Clark, R. A., & Delia, J. G. (1979). Topoi and rhetorical competence. *Quarterly Journal of Speech, 65,* 187–206.

Clore, G. L., Ortony, A., & Foss, M. A. (1987). The psychological foundations of the affective lexicon. *Journal of Personality and Social Psychology, 53,* 751–766.

Cody, M. J., & McLaughlin, M. L. (1985). The situation as a construct in communication research. In M. L. Knapp & G. R. Miller (Eds.), *Handbook of interpersonal communication* (pp. 263–312.) Newbury Park, CA: Sage.

Coulter, J. (1986). Affect and social context: Emotion definition as a social task. In R. Harre (Ed.), *The social construction of emotion* (pp. 120–134). Oxford, Eng.: Basil Blackwell.

Craig, R. T. (1979). Information systems theory and research: An overview of individual information processing. *Communication Yearbook, 3,* 99–123.

Craig, R. T. (in press). Communication as a practical discipline. In B. Dervin, L. Grossberg, B. O'Keefe, & E. Wartella (Eds.), *Rethinking communication,* Vol. 1. Newbury Park, CA: Sage.

Cronen, V. E., Pearce, W. B., & Harris, L. M. (1982). The coordinated management of meaning: A theory of communication. In F. E. X. Dance (Ed.), *Human communication theory: Comparative essays* (pp. 61–89). New York: Harper & Row.

Cushman, D. P., & Craig, R. T. (1976). Communication systems: Interpersonal implications. In G. R. Miller (Ed.), *Explorations in interpersonal communication* (pp. 37–58). Beverly Hills, CA: Sage.

Cushman, D. P., Valentinsen, B., & Dietrich, D. (1982). A rules theory of interpersonal relationships. In F. E. X. Dance (Ed.), *Human communication theory: Comparative essays* (pp. 90–107). New York: Harper & Row.

Dailey, W. O. (1986, November). *The effects of discussion on debiasing judgment: Two pilot studies.* Paper presented at the annual convention of the Speech Communication Association, Denver.

Davis, D. (1982). Determinants of responsiveness in dyadic interaction. In W. Ickes & E. S. Knowles (Eds.), *Personality, roles & social behavior* (pp. 85–140). New York: Springer-Verlag.

Davis, D., & Perkowitz, W. T. (1979). Consequences of responsiveness in dyadic interaction: Effects of probability of response and proportion of content-related responses on interpersonal attraction. *Journal of Personality and Social Psychology, 37,* 534–550.

Davis, K. E., & Todd, M. J. (1985). Assessing friendship: Prototypes, paradigm cases and relationship description. In S. Duck & D. Perlman (Eds.), *Understanding personal relationships: An interdisciplinary approach* (pp. 17–38). Beverly Hills, CA: Sage.

Davitz, J. R. (1969). *The language of emotion.* New York: Academic Press.

Delia, J. G., Kline, S. L., & Burleson, B. R. (1979). The development of persuasive communication strategies in kindergartners through twelfth-graders. *Communication Monographs, 46,* 241–256.

Delia, J. G., & O'Keefe, B. J. (1979). Constructivism: the development of communication. In E. Wartella (Ed.), *Children communicating* (pp. 157–185). Beverly Hills, CA: Sage.

Delia, J. G., O'Keefe, B. J., & O'Keefe, D. J. (1982). The constructivist approach to communication. In F. E. X. Dance (Ed.), *Human communication theory: Comparative essays* (pp. 147–191). New York: Harper & Row.

Denzin, N. K. (1984). *On understanding emotion*. San Francisco: Jossey-Bass.

Derlega, V. J., Winstead, B. A., Wong, P. T. P., & Greenspan, M. (1987). Self-disclosure and relationship development: An attributional analysis. In M. E. Roloff & G. R. Miller (Eds.), *Interpersonal processes: New directions in communication research* (pp. 172–187). Newbury Park, CA: Sage.

Deutsch, M. (1977). *The resolution of conflict: Constructive and destructive processes*. New Haven, CT: Yale University Press.

Duncan, S. (1975). On the structure of speaker-auditor interaction during speaking turns. *Language in Society, 2*, 161–180.

Dyer, M. G. (1983). The role of affect in narratives. *Cognitive Science, 7*, 211–242.

Ekman, P. (Ed.). (1982). *Emotion in the human face*. Cambridge, Eng.: Cambridge University Press.

Erikson, E. H. (1963). *Childhood and society* (2nd ed.). New York: W. W. Norton.

Fincham, F., & O'Leary, K. D. (1983). Causal inferences for spouse behavior in maritally distressed and nondistressed couples. *Journal of Social and Clinical Psychology, 1*, 42–57.

Fisher, B. A. (1978). *Perspectives on human communication*. New York: Macmillan.

Fiske, S. T., & Taylor, S. E. (1984). *Social cognition*. Reading, MA: Addison-Wesley.

Floyd, F. J. (1988). Couples' cognitive/affective reactions to communication behaviors. *Journal of Marriage and the Family, 50*, 523–532.

Folger, J. P., & Poole, M. S. (1982). Relational coding schemes: The question of validity. *Communication Yearbook, 5*, 235–248.

Folkes, V. S. (1982). Communicating the reasons for social rejection. *Journal of Experimental Social Psychology, 18*, 235–252.

Folkman, S., & Lazarus, R. S. (1985). If it changes it must be a process: Study of emotion and coping during three stages of a college examination. *Journal of Personality and Social Psychology, 48*, 150–170.

Francik, E. P. & Clark, H. H. (1985). How to make requests that overcome obstacles to compliance. *Journal of Memory and Language, 24*, 560–568.

Frank, R. H. (1988). *Passions within reason*. New York: W. W. Norton.

Frick, R. W. (1985). Communicating emotion: The role of prosodic features. *Psychological Bulletin, 97*, 412–429.

Fridja, N. H. (1986). *The emotions*. Cambridge, Eng.: Cambridge University Press.

Fry, W. R., Firestone, I. J., & Williams, D. L. (1983). Negotiation process and outcome of stranger dyads and dating couples: Do lovers lose? *Basic and Applied Social Psychology, 4*, 1–16.

Gaelick, L., Bodenhausen, G. V., & Wyer, R. S., Jr. (1985). Emotional communication in close relationships. *Journal of Personality and Social Psychology, 49*, 1246–1265.

Gibbs, R. W., Jr. (1983). Do people always process the literal meaning of indirect requests? *Journal of Experimental Psychology: Learning, Memory, and Cognition, 9*, 524–533.

Gibbs, R. W., Jr. (1986). What makes some indirect speech acts conventional? *Journal of Memory and Language, 25*, 181–196.

Goffman, E. (1969). *Strategic interaction.* Philadelphia: University of Pennsylvania Press.

Gordon, S. L. (1981). The sociology of sentiments and emotions. In M. Rosenberg & R. Turner (Eds.), *Social psychology: sociological perspectives,* (pp. 562–592). New York: Basic Books.

Greene, J. O. (1984). A cognitive approach to human communication: An action assembly theory. *Communication Monographs, 51*, 289–306.

Grimshaw, A. D. (1981). Talk and social control. In M. Rosenberg & R. H. Turner (Eds.), *Social psychology: sociological perspectives* (pp. 200–232). New York: Basic Books.

Grossberg, L. (1982). Does communication theory need intersubjectivity? Toward an immanent philosophy of interpersonal relationships. *Communication Yearbook, 6*, 171–205.

Halberstadt, A. G. (1984). Family expression of emotion. In C. Z. Malatesta & C. E. Izard (Eds.), *Emotion in adult development.* Beverly Hills, CA: Sage.

Halberstadt, A. G. (1986). Family socialization of emotional expression and nonverbal communication styles and skills. *Journal of Personality and Social Psychology, 51*, 827–836.

Hewes, D. E. (1986). A socio-egocentric model of group decision-making. In R. Y. Hirokawa and M. S. Poole (Eds.), *Communication and group decision-making* (pp. 265–291). Beverly Hills, CA: Sage.

Hewes, D. E., & Graham, M. L. (1988). Second-guessing theory: Review and extension. *Communication Yearbook, 12*, (pp.).

Hewes, D. E., Graham, M. L., Doelger, J., & Pavitt, C. (1985). "Second-guessing": message interpretation in social networks. *Human Communication Research, 11*, 299–334.

Hewes, D. E., & Planalp, S. (1982). There is nothing as useful as a good theory . . . : The influence of social knowledge on interpersonal communication. In M. E. Roloff & C. R. Berger (Eds.), *Social cognition and communication* (pp. 107–150). Beverly Hills, CA: Sage.

Hewes, D. E., & Planalp, S. (1987). The individual's place in communication science. In C. R. Berger & S. H. Chaffee (Eds.), *The handbook of communication science* (pp. 146–183). Newbury Park, CA: Sage.

Hewes, D. E., Planalp, S., & Streibel, M. J. (1980). Analyzing social interaction: Some excruciating models and exhilarating results. *Communication Yearbook, 4,* 123–142.

Higgins, E. T. (1987). Self-discrepancy: A theory relating self and affect. *Psychological Review, 94,* 319–340.

Hinde, R. A. (1979). *Toward understanding relationships.* Orlando, FL: Academic Press.

Hochschild, A. R. (1983). *The managed heart: Commercialization of human feeling.* Berkeley, CA: University of California Press.

Hunter, J. E. (1988). Failure of the social desirability response set hypothesis. *Human Communication Research, 15,* 162–168.

Hunter, J. E., & Boster, F. J. (1987). A model of compliance-gaining message selection. *Communication Monographs, 54,* 63–84.

Hunter, J. E., Gerbing, D. W., & Boster, F. J. (1982). Machiavellian beliefs and personality: Construct invalidity of the Machiavellianism dimension. *Journal of Personality and Social Psychology, 43,* 1293–1305.

Izard, C. E. (1977). *Human emotions.* New York: Plenum.

Jackson. S., & Backus, D. (1982). Are compliance-gaining strategies dependent on situational variables? *Central States Speech Journal, 33,* 469–479.

Jacobson, N. S. (1977). Problem solving and contingency contracting in the treatment of marital discord. *Journal of Consulting and Clinical Psychology, 45,* 92–100.

Jones, E. E., & Wortman, C. (1973). *Ingratiation: An attributional approach.* Morristown, NJ: General Learning Press.

Kaminski, E., McDermott, S., & Boster, F. (1977). *The use of compliance-gaining strategies as a function of Machiavellianism and situation.* Paper presented at the annual meeting of the Central States Speech Association, Southfield, MI.

Kellerman, K. (1987). Information exchange in social interaction. In M. E. Roloff & G. R. Miller (Eds.), Interpersonal processes: New directions in communication research, (pp. 188–219). Newbury Park, CA: Sage.

Kelley, H. H. (1979). *Personal relationships: Their structures and processes.* Hillsdale, NJ: Lawrence Erlbaum and Associates.

Kelley, H. H., & Thibaut, J. W. (1978). *Interpersonal relations: A theory of interdependence.* New York: Wiley.

Kelman, H. C. (1974). Further thoughts on the processes of compliance, identification and internalization. In J. T. Tedeschi (Ed.), *Perspectives on social power* (pp. 125–171). Chicago: Aldine.

Kline, S. L. (1985). Social cognitive determinants of face support in persuasive messages (Doctoral dissertation, University of Illinois at Urbana-Champaign, 1984). *Dissertation Abstracts International, 45,* 3238–3239.

Knapp, M. L., Cody, M. J., & Reardon, K. K. (1987). Nonverbal signals. In C. R. Berger & S. H. Chaffee (Eds.), *Handbook of communication science.* Newbury Park, CA: Sage.

Koren, P., Carlton, K., & Shaw, D. (1980). Marital conflict: Relations among behaviors, outcomes, and distress. *Journal of Consulting and Clinical Psychology, 48,* 460–468.

Kraut, R. E., Lewis, S. H., & Swezey, L. W. (1982). Listener responsiveness and the coordination of conversation. *Journal of Personality and Social Psychology, 43,* 718–731.

La Gaipa, J. J. (1977). Testing a multidimensional approach to friendship. In S. Duck (Ed.), *Theory and practice in interpersonal attraction* (pp. 249–270). New York: Academic Press.

La Gaipa, J. J. (1987). Friendship expectations. In R. Burnett, P. McGhee, & D. Clarke (Eds.), *Accounting for relationships: Explanation, representation, and knowledge* (pp. 134–157). London: Methuen.

Laing, R. D., Phillipson, H., & Lee, A. R. (1966). *Interpersonal perception: A theory and a method of research.* New York: Springer-Verlag.

Langer, E. J. (1978). Rethinking the role of thought in social interaction. In H. Harvey, W. Ickes, & R. Kidd (Eds.), *New directions in attribution research* (Vol. 2, pp. 35–58). Hillsdale, NJ: Lawrence Erlbaum and Associates.

Larsen, R. J., Diener, E., & Emmons, R. A. (1986). Affect intensity and reactions to daily life events. *Journal of Personality and Social Psychology, 51,* 803–814.

Levenson, R. W., & Gottman, J. M. (1983). Marital interaction: Physiological linkage and affective exchange. *Journal of Personality and Social Psychology, 45,* 587–597.

Levinger, G., & Breedlove, J. (1966). Interpersonal attraction and agreement. *Journal of Personality and Social Psychology, 3,* 367–372.

Lewis, D. K. (1969). *Convention: A philosophical study.* Cambridge, MA: Harvard University Press.

Lord, C. G., Lepper, M. R., & Preston, E. (1984). Considering the opposite: A corrective strategy for social judgment. *Journal of Personality and Social Psychology, 47,* 1231–1243.

Mandler, G. (1984). *Mind and body.* New York: W. W. Norton.

Margolin, G., Hattem, D., John, R. S., & Yost, K. (1985). Perceptual agreement between spouses and outside observers when coding themselves and a stranger dyad. *Behavioral Assessment, 7,* 235–247.

McCall, G. J. (1987). The self-concept and interpersonal communication. In M. E. Roloff & G. R. Miller (Eds.), *Interpersonal processes: New directions in communication research* (pp. 63–76). Newbury Park, CA: Sage.

McCall, G. J., & Simmons, J. L. (1978). *Identities and interactions: An examination of human association in everyday life* (2nd ed.). New York: Free Press.

McLaughlin, M. L. (1984). *Conversation: How talk is organized.* Beverly Hills, CA: Sage.

McLaughlin, M. L., Cody, M. J. & Robey, C. S. (1980). Situational influences on the selection of strategies to resist compliance-gaining attempts. *Human Communication Research, 7,* 14–36.

McLeod, J., & Chaffee, S. H. (1973). Interpersonal approaches to communication research. *American Behavioral Scientist, 16,* 469–499.

Merton, R. K. (1968). *Social theory and structure.* New York: Free Press.

Millar, F. E., & Rogers, L. E. (1976). A relational approach to interpersonal communication. In G. R. Miller (Ed.), *Explorations in interpersonal communication* (pp. 87–104). Beverly Hills, CA: Sage.

Millar, F. E., & Rogers, L. E. (1987). Relational dimensions of interpersonal dynamics. In M. E. Roloff & G. R. Miller (Eds.), *Interpersonal processes: New directions in communication research* (pp. 117–139). Newbury Park, CA: Sage.

Miller, G. R., Boster, F. J., Roloff, M. E., & Seibold, D. R. (1987). MBRS rekindled: Some thoughts on compliance gaining in interpersonal settings. In M. E. Roloff & G. R. Miller (Eds.), *Interpersonal processes: New directions in communication research,* pp. 89–116). Newbury Park, CA: Sage.

Miller, G. R., Burgoon, M., & Burgoon, J. K. (1984). The functions of human communication in changing attitudes and gaining compliance. In C. C. Arnold & J. W. Bowers (Eds.), *Handbook of rhetorical and communication theory* (pp. 400–474). Boston: Allyn & Bacon.

Miller, R. S. (1987). Empathic embarrassment: Situational and personal determinants of reactions to the embarrassment of another. *Journal of Personality and Social Psychology, 53,* 1061–1069.

Modigliani, A. (1968). Embarrassment and embarrassability. *Sociometry, 31,* 316–326.

Modigliani, A. (1971). Embarrassment, facework, and eye contact: Testing a theory of embarrassment. *Journal of Personality and Social Psychology, 17,* 15–24.

Motley, M. T., & Camden, C. T. (1988). Facial expression of emotion: a comparison of posed expressions versus spontaneous expressions in an interpersonal communication setting. *Western Journal of Speech Communication, 52,* 1–22.

Nisbett, R., & Ross, L. (1980). *Human inference: Strategies and shortcomings of social judgment.* Englewood Cliffs, NJ: Prentice-Hall.

Norman, D. A., & Bobrow, D. G. (1975). On data-limited and resource-limited processes. *Cognitive Psychology, 7,* 44–64.

Norton, R. (1983). *Communication style: Theory, applications, and measures.* Beverly Hills, CA: Sage.

O'Keefe, B. J. (1988). The logic of message design: Individual differences in reasoning about communication. *Communication Monographs, 55*, 80–103.

O'Keefe, B. J., & Delia, J. G. (1982). Impression formation and message production. In M. E. Roloff & C. R. Berger (Eds.), *Social cognition and communication* (pp. 33–72). Beverly Hills, CA: Sage.

O'Keefe, B. J., & Shepard, G. J. (1987). The pursuit of multiple objectives in face-to-face persuasive interactions: Effect of construct differentiation on message organization. *Communication Monographs, 54*, 396–419.

Pavitt, C. (1982). Preliminaries to a theory of communication: A system for the cognitive representation of person and object based information. *Communication Yearbook, 5*, 211–232.

Pearce, W. B. (1976a). *An overview of communication and interpersonal relationships.* Chicago: Science Research Associates.

Pearce, W. B. (1976b). The coordinated management of meaning: A rules-based theory of interpersonal communication. In G. R. Miller (Ed.), *Explorations in interpersonal communication* (pp. 17–36). Beverly Hills, CA: Sage.

Pearce, W. B., & Cronen, V. (1980). *Communication, action, and meaning.* New York: Praeger.

Peterson, G. L., Frederiksen, L. W., & Rosenbaum, M. S. (1981). Developing behavioral competencies in distressed marital couples. *American Journal of Family Therapy, 9*, 13–23.

Piaget, J., & Inhelder, B. (1969). *The psychology of the child.* New York: Basic Books.

Pike, G. R., & Sillars, A. L. (1985). Reciprocity of marital communication. *Journal of Social and Personal Relationships, 2*, 303–324.

Planalp, S. (1985). Relational schemata: A test of alternative forms of relational knowledge as guides to communication. *Human Communication Research, 12*, 3–29.

Planalp, S. (1986). Scripts, story grammars, and causal schemas. In D. G. Ellis & W. A. Donohue (Eds.), *Contemporary issues in language and discourse processes* (pp. 111–125). Hillsdale, NJ: Lawrence Erlbaum and Associates.

Planalp, S. (1987). Interplay between relational knowledge and events. In R. Burnett, P. McGhee, and D. Clarke (Eds.), *Accounting for relationships: Explanation, representation, and knowledge* (pp. 175–191). London: Methuen.

Planalp, S., & Hewes, D. E. (1982). A cognitive approach to communication theory: *Cogito Ergo Dico? Communication Yearbook, 5*, 49–78.

Planalp, S., & Tracy, K. (1980). Not to change the topic but . . . : A cognitive approach to the management of conversation. *Communication Yearbook, 4*, 237–258.

Poole, M. S., Folger, J. P., & Hewes, D. E. (1986). The analysis of interpersonal interaction. In M. E. Roloff & G. R. Miller (Eds.), *Interpersonal processes:*

New directions in communication research (pp. 220–256). Beverly Hills, CA: Sage.

Pruitt, D. G. (1983). Strategic choice in negotiation. *American Behavioral Scientist, 27,* 167–194.

Resnick, P. A., Barr, P. K., Sweet, J. J., Kieffer, K. M., Ruby, N. L., & Spiegel, D. K. (1981). Perceived and actual discriminators of conflict from accord in marital communication. *American Journal of Family Therapy, 9,* 58–68.

Rogers, L. E. (1981). Symmetry and complementarity: Evolution and evaluation of an idea. In C. Wilder & J. H. Weakland (Eds.), *Rigor and imagination: Essays from the legacy of Gregory Bateson* (pp. 231–252). New York: Praeger.

Roloff, M. E. (1981). *Interpersonal communication.* Beverly Hills: Sage.

Roloff, M. E. (1987). Communication and reciprocity within intimate relationships. In M. E. Roloff & G. R. Miller (Eds.), *Interpersonal processes: New directions in communication research* (pp. 11–38). Newbury Park, CA: Sage.

Roloff, M. E., & Barnicott, E. (1978). The situational use of pro- and anti-social compliance-gaining strategies by high and low Machiavellians. *Communication Yearbook, 2,* 193–208.

Roloff, M. E., & Barnicott, E. (1979). The influence of dogmatism on the situational use of pro- and anti-social compliance-gaining strategies. *Southern Speech Communication Journal, 45,* 37–54.

Roloff, M. E., & Berger, C. R. (Eds.) (1982). *Social cognition and communication.* Beverly Hills, CA: Sage.

Roloff, M. E., Janiszewski, C. A., McGrath, M. A., Burns, C. S., & Manrai, L. A. (1988). Acquiring resources from intimates: When obligation substitutes for persuasion. *Human Communication Research, 14,* 364–396.

Romano, J. M., & Bellack, A. S. (1980). Social validation of a component model of assertive behavior. *Journal of Consulting and Clinical Psychology, 48,* 478–490.

Roseman, I. J. (1984). Cognitive determinants of emotion: A structural theory. In P. Shaver (Ed.), *Review of personality and social psychology* (Vol. 5, pp. 11–36). Beverly Hills, CA: Sage.

Rosenfeld, H. M. (1966). Approval-seeking and approval-inducing functions of verbal and nonverbal responses in the dyad. *Journal of Personality and Social Psychology, 4,* 597–605.

Rutherford, D., & Leto, V. (n. d.). *The communication of emotion: A qualitative study with college roommates.* Unpublished manuscript, University of Illinois.

Samter, W., & Burleson, B. R. (1984). Cognitive and motivational influences on spontaneous comforting behavior. *Human Communication Research, 11,* 231–260.

Scanzoni, J., & Polonko, K. (1980). A conceptual approach to explicit marital negotiation. *Journal of Marriage and the Family, 42,* 31–44.

Schlenker, B. R. (1980). *Impression management.* Belmont, CA: Wadsworth.

Schneider, D. J. (1981). Tactical self-presentation: Toward a broader conception. In J. T. Tedeschi (Ed.), *Impression management theory and social psychological research* (pp. 23–40). New York: Academic Press.

Seibold, D. R. (1988). A response to "Item desirability in compliance-gaining research." *Human Communication Research, 15,* 152–161.

Seibold, D. R., Cantrill, J. G., & Meyers, R. A. (1985). Communication and interpersonal influence. In M. L. Knapp and G. R. Miller (Eds.), *Handbook of interpersonal communication* (pp. 551–611). Newbury Park, CA: Sage.

Shaver, P., Schwartz, J., Kirson, D., & O'Connor, C. (1987). Emotion knowledge: Further explorations of a prototype approach. *Journal of Personality and Social Psychology, 52,* 1061–1086.

Sillars, A. L. (1980). Attributions and communication in roommate conflicts. *Communication Monographs, 47,* 180–200.

Sillars, A. L., & Parry, D. (1982). Stress, cognition, and communication in interpersonal conflicts. *Communication Research, 9,* 201–226.

Sillars, A. L., Pike, G. R., Jones, T. S., & Murphy, M. A. (1984). Communication and understanding in marriage. *Human Communication Research, 10,* 317–350.

Sillars, A. L., & Scott, M. D. (1983). Interpersonal perception between intimates: An integrative review. *Human Communication Research, 10,* 153–176.

Sillars, A. L., & Weisberg, J. (1987). Conflict as social skill. In M. E. Roloff & G. R. Miller (Eds.), *Interpersonal processes: New directions in communication research* (pp. 140–171). Newbury Park, CA: Sage.

Sillars, A. L., Weisberg, J., Burggraf, C. S., & Wilson, E. A. (1987). Content themes in marital conversations. *Human Communication Research, 13,* 495–528.

Simpson, J. A. (1987). The dissolution of romantic relationships: Factors involved in relationship stability and emotional distress. *Journal of Personality and Social Psychology, 53,* 683–692.

Smith, M. J. (1984). Contingency rules theory, context, and compliance behaviors. *Human Communication Research, 10,* 489–512.

Storm, C., & Storm, T. (1987). A taxonomic study of the vocabulary of emotions. *Journal of Personality and Social Psychology, 53,* 805–816.

Strauman, T. J., & Higgins, E. T. (1987). Automatic activation of self-discrepancies and emotional syndromes: When cognitive structures influence affect. *Journal of Personality and Social Psychology, 53,* 1004–1014.

Street, R. L., Jr., & Murphy, T. L. (1987). Interpersonal orientation and speech behavior. *Communication Monographs, 54,* 42–62.

Stryker, S. (1980). *Symbolic interactionism.* Menlo Park, CA: Benjamin/Cummings.

Swap, W. C., & Rubin, J. Z. (1983). Measurement of interpersonal orientation. *Journal of Personality and Social Psychology, 44,* 208– 219.

Tedeschi, J. T., & Lindskold, S. (1976). *Social psychology: Interdependence, interaction, and influence.* New York: Wiley.

Tedeschi, J. T., & Reiss, M. (1981). Verbal strategies in impression management. In C. Antaki (Ed.), *The psychology of ordinary explanations of social behavior* (pp. 271–309). New York: Academic Press.

Thoits, P. A. (1984). Coping, social support, and psychological outcomes. In P. Shaver (Ed.), *Review of personality and social psychology* (Vol. 5., pp. 219–238). Beverly Hills, CA: Sage.

Tiggle, R. B., Peters, M. D., Kelley, H. H., & Vincent, J. (1982). Correlational and discrepancy indices of understanding and their relation to marital satisfaction. *Journal of Marriage and the Family, 44,* 209–215.

Tracy, K. (1985). Regulating conversational coherence: A cognitively grounded rules approach. In R. L. Street, Jr., & J. N. Cappella (Eds.), *Sequence and pattern in communicative behaviour* (pp. 30–49). Baltimore: Edward Arnold.

Tracy, K., Craig, R. T., Smith, M., & Spisak, F. (1984). The discourse of requests: Assessment of a compliance-gaining approach. *Human Communication Research, 10,* 513–538.

Wagner, H., MacDonald, C., & Manstead, A. (1986). Communication of individual emotions by spontaneous facial expressions. *Journal of Personality and Social Psychology, 50,* 737–743.

Wagner, H., & Pease, K. (1976). The verbal communication of inconsistency between attitudes held and attitudes expressed. *Journal of Personality, 44,* 1–15.

Watzlawick, P., Beavin, J., & Jackson, D. D. (1976). *Pragmatics of human communication: A study of interactional patterns, pathologies, and paradoxes.* New York: W. W. Norton.

Weiss, R. L. (1980). Strategic behavioral marital therapy: Toward a model for assessment and intervention. In J. P. Vincent (Ed.), *Advances in family intervention, assessment, and theory* (Vol. 1, pp. 337–355). Greenwich, CT: JAI Press.

Weiss, R. L. (1984). Cognitive and strategic interventions in behavioral marital therapy. In K. Hahlweg & N. S. Jacobson (Eds.), *Marital interaction: Analysis and modification* (pp. 229–271). New York: Guilford Press.

Weiss, R. L., Birchler, G. R., & Vincent, J. P. (1974). Contractual models for negotiation training in marital dyads. *Journal of Marriage and the Family, 36,* 321–330.

Wheeless, L. R., Barraclough, R., & Stewart, R. (1983). Compliance-gaining and power in persuasion. *Communication Yearbook, 7,* 105–145.

Wiemann, J. M. (1977). Explication and test of a model of communicative competence. *Human Communication Research, 3,* 195–213.

Wiemann, J. M. (1985). Interpersonal control and regulation in conversation. In R. L. Street, Jr., & J. N. Cappella (Eds.), *Sequence and pattern in communicative behaviour* (pp. 85–102). London: Edward Arnold.

Williams, D., & Boster, F. (1981). *The effects of beneficial situational characteristics, negativism, and dogmatism on compliance-gaining message selection.* Paper presented at the annual meeting of the International Communication Association, Minneapolis.

Wilson, B. J. (1987). Reducing children's emotional reactions to mass media through rehearsed explanation and exposure to a replica of a fear object. *Human Communication Research, 14,* 3–26.

Zuckerman, M., DePaulo, B., & Rosenthal, R. (1981). Verbal and nonverbal communication of deception. In L. Berkowitz (Ed.), *Advances in experimental social psychology* (Vol. 14, pp. 2–59). New York: Academic Press.

• 7 •

Research in Interpretation and
Performance Studies:
Trends, Issues, Priorities

MARY S. STRINE
BEVERLY WHITAKER LONG
MARY FRANCES HOPKINS

[A] field, no less than a discipline, defines itself—as, say, a subject area alone does not—chiefly in relation to the questions it asks, the problems it poses, the arguments it encourages; while none of these matters can be contemplated in isolation from actual research, the research that is actually produced within any field ultimately matters, in the sense of being susceptible to definition and assessment, only in relation to such things—only by virtue of the way it refines the questions, clarifies the problems, and deepens the arguments.

G. Gunn, *The Culture of
Criticism and the
Criticism of Culture*

Trends

Research in interpretation and performance studies focuses on the constitutive elements of texts, performers, and audiences, individually or in some combination, in order to advance understanding of the aesthetic, psychological, historical, sociocultural, and political dimensions of performance. As with most fields whose subject matter is historically emergent and variable, research emphases—the questions asked, the problems posed, and the arguments encouraged—over the last seventy-five years have been responsive to the supporting cultural climates, both academic and professional, that generate and foster performance activities (e.g., Thompson, 1983). From the 1950s through the early 1970s, for example,

181

oral interpretation within the academy flourished as a method of literary study, one considered unique and invaluable. The principal model of scholarship was text-centered, with research efforts focused on the study of the writings of particular authors and literary genres. Research programs focusing on major literary figures or literary genres include the work of Wallace Bacon (1973a, 1973b, 1987) on Shakespeare, Thomas Sloan (1962, 1963, 1965) on John Donne, Katherine Loesch (1968, 1979) on Dylan Thomas, Francine Merritt (1969a, 1969b) on concrete poetry, Lilla Heston (1972, 1973, 1975, 1981) on narrative fiction, and Robert Post (1967, 1969, 1973, 1977) on drama, to mention but a few noteworthy examples.

Providing the conceptual framework for text-centered studies that draw on performance-related insights to supplement the textual analysis of conventional literary scholarship were the following: Wallace Bacon's definitive exposition of the humanizing values inherent in the oral interpretation of literature in his co-authored (with Robert Breen) *Literature as Experience* (Bacon & Breen, 1959) and *The Art of Interpretation* (Bacon, 1966), Don Geiger's (1963, 1967) theoretical integration of American New Criticism and principles of dramatism in *The Sound, Sense, and Performance of Literature* and *The Dramatic Impulse in Modern Poetics*, and Thomas Sloan's (1966) agenda-setting argument for the interrelationships among oral performance, rhetoric, and literary criticism in *The Oral Study of Literature*. The common presuppositions here were that literary texts are repositories of enduring insight and value, and that latent meanings and values embedded within literary texts become manifest and most fully accessible when experienced holistically through the act of performance. These assumptions continued in the research of the 1970s; they remain largely unchallenged in the pedagogical practices of the present (e.g., HopKins, 1982; Lee & Gura, 1987; Long and HopKins, 1982; Maclay, 1983).

Issues

During the 1970s and early 1980s much research in interpretation and performance studies built upon the theoretical foundation laid by Geiger, Bacon, and Sloan. However, the full potential for scholarship implicit in their theorizing has yet to be realized. The purpose of this essay is to clarify and extend the boundaries of performance studies in order to address that potential. We begin by reformulating the concept and action of performance so as to problematize its nature and functions. Three interrelated perspectives organize this discussion: *performance viewed as an essentially contested concept, performance viewed as text*, and *performance viewed as metaphor and as metonymy*. An explanation of what is implied by each of these perspectives follows.

Performance Viewed as an Essentially Contested Concept

Performance, like art and democracy, is what W. B. Gallie (1964) calls an *essentially contested concept*, meaning that its very existence is bound up in disagreement about what it is, and that the disagreement over its essence is itself part of that essence. As Gallie explains, "Recognition of a given concept as essentially contested implies recognition of rival uses of it (such as oneself repudiates) as not only logically possible and humanly 'likely,' but as of permanent potential critical value to one's own use or interpretation of the concept in question" (pp. 187-188). Scholars in interpretation and performance studies value performance as process, activity, achievement, and as an object of study. Although they place performance in a valorized category, they recognize and expect disagreement not only about the qualities that make a performance "good" or "bad" in certain contexts, but also about what activities and behaviors appropriately constitute performance and not something else.

Recognizing performance as an essentially contested concept has positive value because that recognition energizes scholarly discussion. Thus, we understand not just that others disagree, but that this disagreement is inevitable and healthy. In such an atmosphere of sophisticated disagreement, arguments are likely to occur on a higher plane. Factions in the controversy do not expect to defeat or silence opposing positions, but rather through continuing dialogue to attain a sharper articulation of all positions and therefore a fuller understanding of the conceptual richness of performance.[1]

---

1. For an indication of the diverse conceptualizations of performance currently in circulation see Benamou and Caramello (1977); Fine and Speer (1977); Bauman (1977); Taylor (1982); Battock and Nickas (1984); Gentile (1985); Gray (1985); Schechner (1985); Issacharoff and Jones (1988); Maclean (1988); and Bowman and Pollock (1989).

Performance Viewed as "Text"

Recent poststructuralist emphasis on the nature of *texts* and their complex interrelationships challenges all of the human sciences, including interpretation and performance studies. Roland Barthes (1979, 1981) provides an especially useful explanation of what the theoretical shift "from work to text" entails. Rather than approaching the object of analysis as a *work*, a concrete, relatively stable entity with inherent meanings and values, an interpreter approaches a *text* in its etymological sense as a tissue or weave of always potential meanings and values. A work is self-contained and determinate; scholars discover meanings in works. Whereas a text, according to Barthes, is conceptualized as an open methodological field, a grid of signifying practice or sense-making. Scholars construct the meanings of texts in relation to other texts within the interwoven social fabric.

Two important implications for performance scholarship follow from this conceptual shift. First, when understood as text, performance phenomena assume variable proportions. That is, the dimensions and meanings of performances are always post hoc constructions drawn from affiliations that performances have with other cultural and social phenomena. Second, the concept of text allows for useful distinctions between scholarship that clearly foregrounds performance within the research process and scholarship for which performance is of associational, not central, importance. For most research in interpretation and performance studies to date performance functions as an enabling "pre-text" and/or enabled "post-text" in relation to the construction of the primary research text. As a consequence, research texts in the field have tended to presuppose or anticipate, rather than feature, actual performance events and practices in their discussion.

Performance Viewed as Metaphor and as Metonymy

Both the fact and the act of performance (Strine, 1986), or both performance as concept and as processual event have often been viewed as a transformation, as metaphor. So formulated, the performance exchanges or displaces a "literary work" with a "performed text." The critic-researcher looks to the work as the guide or blueprint that sustains authority for whatever meaning is produced in performance. The performed text is both constructed and judged in terms of its adequacy, its fidelity, its similarity to aspects or elements of the (typically) written literature (Geiger, 1963; HopKins, 1981; Hudson, 1973; Long, 1977; Roloff, 1973; Schneider, 1976).

For example, Robert Breen (1980), adapter and director of Somerset Maugham's *Of Human Bondage*, reflects on the production as satisfying, in large part, because it encouraged audiences to watch it as a novel. The aspect metaphorically, or comparatively, realized here is generic. In other instances it might be structural, semantic, scenic, and so on. Whatever the comparison, the performance paradoxically declares both subordination to and power over the written work: even while approximating, representing, substituting for, the performance nonetheless clarifies and illuminates to the point of resolving, for a time, the work's ambiguities.

Metonymy, less well established in the discourse of performance than its companion trope, metaphor, is also of practical and theoretical use to the researcher. When the performance is considered metonymically, its meaning emerges as relational rather than representational. The performance is contiguous to; it is partial, thus opening the study to a wide range of associations or affiliations—part of a biography, part of another text, part of an institution, part of a social reality, and so on (Said, 1983). The performed text achieves meaning in terms of its relations, some near, some remote, and all somehow different from the literary work (Evans, 1986; Johnson, 1986).

Linda Park-Fuller (1986) alone and in collaboration with Tillie Olsen (Park-Fuller & Olsen, 1983) comments, for example, on her production of Olsen's *Yonnondio* as an event that, of course, owed to the printed novella, but it attached just as much and even more in a constitutive sense to Olsen's early work and to the unrelenting social forces of the American Depression. Her alternative to "closing" Olsen's work to a realization of selected elements in the fiction was "opening" it to a variety of pressures that impinge on the literature, the writer, and even the contemporary audience. Experienced meaning was associational, not fixed in the work that inspired the relational event.

Sites of Performance

To make the spectrum of performances more clearly a focus for a variety of research questions, we offer a description of eight representative sites of performance. This taxonomy strives to differentiate without reducing or separating the acts and events that performance embraces. Researchers may construe sites in various ways, depending on the nature and function of the performance as well as questions the researcher chooses to address.

For many critic-researchers as well as performers and audiences, performances will remain in large part *sites of aesthetic enjoyment*, opportunities like musical concerts that offer terminal values (Beardsley, 1980; Taft-Kaufman, 1983). Critic-researchers of the future are likely to find aesthetic enjoyment part of a larger configuration of questions, such as why notions of aesthetic response change over time, how aesthetic values are produced or reproduced in performance, and how non-aesthetic factors operating in performances influence and are influenced by aesthetic factors.

Performance may also be construed as a *site of intellectual inquiry*. Researchers ask what ideas are mobilized in the performance—ideas about the performed text itself or ideas raised independently by the written text and the performance. A performance, particularly one that takes a variety of perspectives toward its material, may question that written work by underscoring its implicit ideologies, ambiguities, and contradictions. Scripting itself can function as a mode of inquiry. The several contemporary performances of Jane Austen's work provide clear examples. In each case, the performer assumes the role of Austen—as author and as character—speaking her words from both nonfictional and fictional sources, juxtaposing inquiries into the author's life and work (P. C. Miller, 1988; Schneider, 1985).

Some performances, like some works of art, are approached as *sites of affective play*. Greenblatt (1980, p. 24) says, in describing Holbein's painting "The Ambassadors" and More's *Utopia*: "This [affective] play is not conceived by humanists as an escape from the serious, but as a mode of civility, an enhancement of specifically human powers." The notion of art as play enjoys a history supported by considerable theoretical and applied criticism, studies that describe the possibilities for play in various media, the contextual requirements for play, its basic psychological motives, and its effects (e.g., Skinner, 1986; Turner, 1982). Poems as riddles, poems that contain in their very physical shape on the page the suggestion of a joke or pun, and devices in metafiction that break the frame are all texts that invite performers and audiences to play, to engage in gaming.

Some performances, both of fiction and nonfiction, might best be construed by the critic-researcher as *sites of cultural memory*. The Denver Center Theatre Company's regional tour of *Quilters* is a ready example. One reviewer of this production notes, "Oral history narrative, quilts, songs, a six-member cast, and presentational staging comprise *Quilters*. . . . The script originated from a collection of oral historical narratives that tell about quilting and about the lives of pioneer women of the Southwest" (Carlin, 1985). Audiences of such performances find themselves experiencing a past that they may have lived or known only through stories, participating in occasions that go beyond pleasures of the text as language to become significant factors in the creation of a common sense of past. This sense, what Cox (1987, p. 4) refers to as cultural memory, is vital to the maintenance of public space, "a locus of uninstitutionalized power" where "people can engage freely in informed and vital talk about the possibilities for action that lie before them." When researchers recognize that history must be constructed rather than discovered, they tend to privilege performances that feature cultural memory, since it contextualizes the past in the present.

Especially for ethnographic researchers, performances may be approached as *sites of participatory ritual*. Dwight Conquergood's field work with performance traditions of the Hmong refugees (1986a, 1986b, 1988) provides an especially compelling example of extended research focused on performance as communicative ritual.[2] Other examples of ethnographic research programs concentrated on performance as ritual process include the work of Elizabeth Fine (1984), Barbara Myerhoff (1984), and Jean Speer (1985).

The nine-hour stage adaptation of the Indian epic, *The Mahabharata*, devised by Jean-Claude Carriere and Peter Brook (Carriere in French and Brook in English translation), successfully performed in Europe and the United States, offers a powerful example of stage performance as a representation of celebratory participatory ritual. Brook (1985, p. xvi) wrote in the introduction to the published version of *The Mahabharata*: "the many nationalities who have gathered together [for this production] are trying to reflect *The Mahabharata* by bringing to it something of their own. In this way, we are trying to celebrate echoes for all mankind."

---

2. Jean Haskell Speer (1988) reviews the award-winning video-documentary, "Between Two Worlds: The Hmong Shaman in America" that Conquergood made in collaboration with the film-maker Taggart Siegel. Conquergood

Many performances function as *sites of social commentary*. At two recent conventions, SSCA in Memphis and SCA in New Orleans, productions dealt with the AIDS crisis (Downs, 1988; Martin, 1988). Such events have as a primary aim the shaping and sharpening of attitudes to the point of at least incipient action. The script for the Memphis production derived from interviews with AIDS patients. The New Orleans production used a wide range of published materials on the subject.

Some performances, even more directly instrumental, go a step further to become *sites of political action* (e.g., Capo, 1983a, 1983b; Deetz, 1983; Langellier, 1983). For example, public poetry readings during the Vietnam War often served to strengthen political protest against American involvement in Southeast Asia, mobilizing anti-war energies. More recently, creation of "trigger scripts" (Rassullo & Hecht, 1988; Valentine, 1979; Valentine and Valentine, 1983) has functioned to dramatize real-life situations so as to move audiences to action. Performers' scripts are based on taped interviews and personal narratives of troubled or oppressed groups. Legislative bodies who witnessed such performances have enacted laws to deal with the dramatized problems (Hartman & Alho, 1979).

Some performances function on an individual rather than public level as *sites of psychological probe*. Poetry therapy, a practice in harmony with the strong contemporary interest in the relationship between literature and health, is an obvious example. This relationship has evolved into a field of study in the 1980s, with its own journal, *Literature and Medicine*, and with several collections of essays. *Healing Arts in Dialogue: Medicine and Literature* is a report of discussions that resulted when "The Institute of Human Values in Medicine" brought ten people together over a period of two years to explore the therapeutic functions of poetry (Trautmann, 1981). Articles published in these and other sources are concerned with images of illness and healers in fiction and poetry as well as with the power of literature to restore psychological health (Kleinau, 1987; Leedy, 1969, 1985; Roloff, 1983).

Leland Zahner-Roloff, a performance studies scholar and practicing Jungian analyst, has worked extensively with poetry therapy, which he calls "the curing of psyche by the making and sounding of image." According to psychiatrists and psychologists, participants in poetry ther-

---

(1985) explores the ethical implications of performance-related ethnographic field work.

apy find help both from composing poems and from reading the poems of others. Zahner-Roloff (1986, p. 19) explains this process as follows: "Poetry therapy is a model interpenetration, particularly in the imagery of myth. . . . [T]he premise of archetypal psychology is that myths are the carriers of *psychological* realities, images of psychological processes and states, once perhaps worshipped, now psychologized. It is therapeutic to sing, it is therapeutic to listen, it is therapeutic to perform." David Williams (1986) supports this view in his personal account of working with poetry therapy in classrooms and various other settings.

These eight sites offer a variety of ways to construe cultural performances studied by researchers. Factors that operate to characterize these sites include the material being performed, the audience, and primarily the presuppositions of the researcher. Notably, the same performance event may qualify as more than one site, and sites may be mixed or alternating within a single performance event (e.g., Pollock, 1987–1988).

Modes of Representing Performance-Related Research

Much of the foregoing discussion suggests that researchers in interpretation and performance studies may need to extend the modalities of representing their research to include alternatives to the traditional research essay.[3] For performance-centered research, a grid of possibilities emerges, taking the form of three continua:

1. REPORTING
   Summary ....Evocation
2. DRAMATIZING
   Declarative..Interrogative
3. CRITIQUING
   Theoretical..Applied

First, the research might be communicated in a *report*, one that could range from a *summary* of findings to an *evocation* of the performance process or product. One example among many of research that falls

---

3. There is evidence that others, including scholars in speech communication, see a need to loosen constraints that limit the appropriate vehicles for communicating scholarly insights. See Strine and Pacanowsky (1985); Clifford and Marcus (1986); Clifford (1988); and Pacanowsky (1988).

mainly in the summary zone is Jean Speer's (1985) detailed account of women's folk performances in the Scottish isles; another instance is Lea Queener's (1972) indexical study of contiguity in the poetry of W. H. Auden.

Also in part summary but leaning more toward evocation is Elias Canetti's (1978) recreation of the Moroccan storyteller or Queener's (1986) depiction of a recent production of *Vienna: Lusthaus*. In both Canetti's and Queener's versions of the performances, the imagistic world of the performance and the uneffaced presence of the researcher are not only allowed, they are featured. Other examples of evocative reporting sometimes appear in reviews in the *Theatre Journal*, often in Walter Kerr's columns for the *New York Times*, and consistently in Andrew Porter's comments on music in *The New Yorker*. Such a mode of representing research, less rare in speech communication than it was a decade ago, humanizes the scholarly effort (e.g., Bowden, 1982).

Second, the researcher who *dramatizes* findings also enjoys a range of options (Espinola, 1977). Investigation of, say, Ibsen's *Hedda Gabler* may lead to a production in which the text of the play is allowed to control meaning, resulting in a *declarative* performance, consistent with what Belsey (1980) calls expressive or classic realism. Instead of such an enactment of Ibsen's play, the researcher may choose to dramatize her/his argument with the drama or questioning of it, the research thus moving on the continuum from declarative to *interrogative* (Long, 1987, 1988). One recent instance of the latter was Paul Gray's (1983) feminist deconstruction of *Hedda Gabler*, in which a male actor was cast in the role of Hedda and a female as Judge Brock.

The third continuum, *critiquing*, with its *theoretical* and *applied* end points, is fairly standardized and requires less explanation. Still, examples may emphasize its distinctiveness. A critique in performance-centered research that lies primarily on the theoretical end of the range is John Allison's (1985) "Rehearsal in the Performance Process," in which theories of reader-response criticism and symbolic interactionism are combined to produce a dialogic rehearsal stance. Other examples are Fabian Gudas' (1983a, 1983b) essays on dramatism. Lying much closer to the other end of the continuum is Donna Nudd's (1987, 1988) recent work, which presupposes a feminist critical theory while focusing on an applied critique of differences in male and female student performers' responses to fiction.

Although these modes of representing research on performance are not mutually exclusive, they do remind us that in the 1990s we may expect considerable variation in the form of represented research, thus granting greater latitude and increased empowerment to the researcher.

Priorities

Three research priorities follow from the issues elaborated above. In setting these priorities, we are not excluding the many ongoing research programs that do not fall explicitly within our agenda. Rather, our aim is to describe three directions that foster better understanding and integration of diverse research programs.

Historical Studies of the Role of Performance in Culture

Traditional historical scholarship in interpretation and performance studies focused on reconstructing the careers of prominent performers in order to systematize the distinctive performance strategies and practices that made these figures exemplary for their particular times. While some attention was given to the historical context, these studies typically conceived of context as a stable setting or background, socially ordered and unproblematically given, within which individual performers' careers were made. The effect of such studies was to dehistoricize their subject, that is, to extract formal performance characteristics as if their cultural meanings and values could be understood and appreciated apart from the network of social activity in and through which performances occur (DeNeef, 1987).

Historical scholarship informed by the "new historicism," on the other hand, would focus on performances and performance genres as situated intertextual phenomena, the meanings of which are informed by the ideas, values, and interpretive practices in circulation within a given society during a particular time period. According to Greenblatt (1988), the overarching goal of new historicist research is "study of the collective making of distinct cultural practices and inquiry into the relations among these practices—a poetics of culture" (p. 5). Greenblatt sets forth questions that might direct the development of a poetics of performance as follows:

[W]e can ask how collective beliefs and experiences were shaped, moved from one medium to another, concentrated in manageable aesthetic form, offered for consumption. We can examine how the boundaries were marked between cultural practices understood to be art forms and other, contiguous, forms of expression. We can attempt to determine how these specifically demarcated zones were invested with power to confer pleasure or excite interest or generate anxiety. The idea is not to strip away and discard the enchanted impression of aesthetic autonomy but to inquire into the objective conditions of this enchantment, to discover how the traces of social circulation were effaced. (p. 5)

Such studies within interpretation and performance studies would require detailed historical reconstructions of performances as strategic sites of cultural formation and contest embedded within, though not wholly determined by, a network of social, economic, and political contingencies. In response to the questions: When and where was performance valued? With what effects?, new historicist scholarship would elaborate the multilayered and interactive dynamics. It would chart how performances were collaboratively sustained and imbued with particular cultural meanings and values, and how they achieved social resonance and power (e.g., Levine, 1988; Mullaney, 1988; Stallybrass & White, 1986).

Empirical Studies of Performers and Audiences

Some research projects simply must wait until the proper time, until situation and methodology are appropriate to the questions. Such has been the case with what may be the most pressing research need for performance studies: to know how performance affects the performer. Beginning in the 1950s and reaching a high level of confidence in the 1960s and 1970s was the conviction that studying literature through performance yielded knowledge about the text and something else— sensitivity, appreciation, values, perspectives, and so forth—as well. Research on the often ineffable "something else" has been so infrequent as to be negligible. Now, a host of studies from such diverse disciplines as art, sociology, and American studies have, in effect, cleared the space for us to ask those questions that have long been central but, we thought, unmeasurable with the tools we possessed. The empirically grounded theorizing of Pierre Bourdieu, among others, may be especially instructive for us.

For more than a decade, Bourdieu and his colleagues at the Centre de Sociologie Européene in Paris have studied French culture in various guises and reported their findings, largely in the journal *Actes de las Recherche en Science Sociale*. More recently, a summary of that work has become available in an English translation of Bourdieu's (1984) book, *La Distinction* [*Distinction: A Social Critique of the Judgement of Taste*]. His empirical studies of the responses of more than 1,200 French people to events and artifacts such as cinema, painting, music, literature, theatre, and photography led to a sustained body of theorizing regarding the ways in which social origin and education create "cultural capital" for exchanges that reproduce values. Seen as a problem on both material and symbolic levels, the reproduction of values entails a certain but largely invisible coordination of social and cultural practices that elevates or rewards some practices while denying or devaluing others (Smith, 1988). For Bourdieu, those works of art that by definition have little or no value in relieving the urgencies of everyday living, nevertheless achieve enormous value— and power—through various forms of reproduction: transformations, analyses, circulations, celebrations, preservations, and recordings. Bourdieu (1986, p. 163) writes: "The ideology of the inexhaustible work of art, or of 'reading' as recreation masks . . . the fact that the work is indeed made not twice, but a hundred times, by all those who are interested in it, who find a material or symbolic profit in reading it, classifying it, deciphering it, commenting on it, combating it, knowing it, possessing it."

Researchers in interpretation and performance studies seem ready to examine the multiple ways we encourage and inhibit the reproduction of values (whatever they are) in our performance classes and other performance situations. Our students' choices of texts to perform and their responses to their own and others' performances offer a natural repository of largely unexamined data, information that could be assembled through focused, self-reflective probes recorded in journals and supplemented with questionnaires and interviews (e.g., Athanases, 1988). Thus, we might study in some detail the cultural practices that characterize individual students as well as groups. Students' choices of texts—and of performance styles, as well—may be telling us far more than we recognize about affirmations as well as denials of values we consciously or unconsciously ask them to reproduce in performance. Part of such a project would explore how these evaluators' interests, their dynamics of valuing, alter over time. Such an aim is resonantly in tune with a much larger project, described earlier, of studying performance history in terms of the value attached to its instances by its performers and its publics (Long, 1988).

Intertextual Studies of the Relationship between Performance and Other Cultural Texts

Intertextuality focuses on the dialogue of one text with another. It refers to the interpretation of texts in relation to other texts. Insofar as cultural "texts" implicitly respond to one another, their meanings are linked to that implied interaction (Bakhtin, 1981; Hutcheon, 1985; Todorov, 1984). Yet, intertextual relations, their emergent meanings and values, are dependent on the discursive practices and interpretive frameworks of a given culture. As Jonathan Culler (1981, p. 103) explains: "Intertextuality thus becomes less a name for a work's relation to particular prior texts than a designation of its participation in the discursive space of culture: the relationship between a text and the various languages or signifying practices of a culture and its relation to those texts which articulate for it the possibilities of that culture." When diverse texts, such as paintings, poems, letters, stories, diaries, films, and so on, are combined for study or for solo or group performance, a unique forum is created for exploring the broad range of intertextual possibilities and emergent meanings and values that go into the making of the composite cultural "(con)text" (e.g., HopKins, 1989; Strine, 1989).

Performance-focused research questions that intertextual studies might address are: How does one text (cultural, social, or personal) reappear in other texts? If intertextuality is conscious and intentional, what are the formal and rhetorical effects of the new/re-contextualizing of the earlier text? How does the individual performer's memory of other texts function in an intertextual dialogue? In what respects is a performance by definition an intertext?

Such questions complement the historical and empirical studies discussed above. By focusing on performance at its inception rather than as a fait accompli—as a vehicle for creative and variable formations rather than as a completed form of expression—intertextual studies direct critical attention to the inherent potential of performance in its many forms for effecting cultural change and transformation. Most importantly, intertextual studies provide an avenue for research tied directly to innovation at various stages of the performance process.

Conclusion

Throughout this essay, we attempt to describe trends, clarify issues, and set priorities for performance-related research, for the purpose of broadening and deepening the boundaries that have traditionally framed scholarship in oral interpretation. That reframing requires a greatly expanded understanding of the core issues of disciplinary concern; it also necessitates certain changes in how we conceive of the research process.[4] In addition to studies in *reinforcement* that serve to validate and underscore our common beliefs and assumptions about the nature and function of performance, the field needs studies in *exploration* that strive to grasp the shifting—at times ephemeral—meanings and values associated with performances within the continually changing symbolic landscape.

Reinforcement and exploration entail significantly different research styles or postures. Typically, studies in reinforcement are directed toward discovery, the researcher assuming a detached and passive role in the process of *sense-finding*. Studies in exploration, on the other hand, are directed toward original construal, implicating the researcher in immediate and active *sense-making* in relation to the performance event.

By foregrounding the researcher's stance as a constitutive feature of performance centered scholarship, we draw attention to what Frank Lentricchia (1983) refers to as "the cultural work of words" and to what Strine (1987) calls "the vitality of interpretive communities." Interpretation and performance studies, no less than any other subunit within speech communication, requires a vigorous dialogue that turns on the differing perspectives and insights researchers bring to the process of disciplinary knowledge construction. This essay is dedicated to advancing that common but richly diversified enterprise.

---

4. In this sense our essay complements but differs from Taft-Kaufman's (1985), Langellier's (1986), and Pelias and VanOosting's (1987) recent articles on research directions in the field.

References

Allison, J. M., Jr. (1985). *Rehearsal in the performance process: A description of selected works in transactional theory, symbolic interactionism, and performance studies.* Unpublished master's thesis, University of North Carolina, Chapel Hill, NC.

Athanases, S. (1988, November). *The articulation of value contingencies in the performance of literature class.* Paper presented at the meeting of the Speech Communication Association, New Orleans.

Bacon, W. A. (1966). *The art of interpretation.* New York: Holt, Rinehart & Winston.

Bacon, W. A. (1973a). The Margery Bailey memorial lectures. *Speech Monographs, 40*, 75–100.

Bacon, W. A. (1973b). Problems in the interpretation of Shakespeare. *Speech Teacher, 22*, 273–281.

Bacon, W. A. (1980) An aesthetics of performance. *Literature in Performance, 1(1)*, 1–9.

Bacon, W. A. (1987). The lion, the fox, and the pelican: Shakespeare and power politics. *Literature in Performance, 7(2)*, 1–22.

Bacon, W. A., & Breen, R. S. (1959). *Literature as experience.* New York: McGraw-Hill.

Bakhtin, M. M. (1981). *The dialogic imagination: Four essays by M. M. Bakhtin.* (M. Holquist, Ed.; C. Emerson & M. Holquist, Trans.). Austin, TX: University of Texas Press.

Bakhtin, M. M. (1986). *Speech genres and other late essays* (C. Emerson & M. Holquist, Eds.; V. W. McGee, Trans.). Austin, TX: University of Texas Press.

Barthes, R. (1979). From work to text. In J. V. Harari (Ed.), *Textual strategies: Perspectives in post-structuralist criticism.* Ithaca, NY: Cornell University Press.

Barthes, R. (1981). Theory of the text. In R. Young (Ed. and Trans.), *Untying the text: A post-structuralist reader* (pp. 31–47). Boston: Routledge & Kegan Paul.

Battock, G., & Nickas, R. (Eds.). (1984). *The art of performance: A critical anthology.* New York: E. P. Dutton.

Bauman, R. (1977). *Verbal art as performance.* Prospect Heights, IL: Waveland.

Bauman, R. (1986). *Story, performance, and event: Contextual studies of oral narrative.* Cambridge, Eng.: Cambridge University Press.

Beardsley, M. C. (1980). Right readings and good readings. *Literature in Performance, 1(1)*, 10–22.

Belsey, C. (1980). *Critical practice.* London: Methuen.

Benamou, M. & Caramello, C. (Eds.). (1977). *Performance in postmodern culture.* Madison, WI: University of Wisconsin-Milwaukee.

Bourdieu, P. (1984). *Distinction: A social critique of the judgement of taste* (R. Nice, Trans.). Cambridge, MA: Harvard University Press.

Bourdieu, P. (1986). The production of belief: Contribution to an economy of symbolic goods (R. Nice, Trans.). In R. Collins, J. Curran, N. Garnham, P. Scannell, P. Schlesinger, & C. Sparks (Eds.), *Media, culture and society: A critical reader* (pp. 131–163). Beverly Hills: CA: Sage.

Bowden, B. (1982). Performed literature: A case study of Bob Dylan's "Hard rain." *Literature in Performance*, 3(1). 35–48.

Bowman, M., & Pollock, D. (1989). "This spectacular visible body": Politics and postmodernism in Pina Bausch's Tanztheater. *Text and Performance Quarterly* 9(2), 113–118.

Breen, R. S. (1978). *Chamber theatre*. Englewood Cliffs, NJ: Prentice-Hall.

Breen, R. S. (1980). A chamber theatre production of W. Somerset Maugham's *Of Human Bondage*. *Literature in Performance*, 1(1). 62–67.

Brook, P. (Trans.). (1985) *The Mahabharata: A play*. New York: Harper & Row.

Canetti, Elias. (1978). *The Voices of Marrakesh; A Record of a Visit* (J. A. Underwood, Trans.). New York: Seabury Press.

Capo, K. E. (1983a). Performance of literature as social dialectic. In M. S. Strine (Ed.), Symposium: Post-Structuralism and Performance. *Literature in Performance*, 4(1), 31–36.

Capo, K. E. (1983b). From academic to social-political uses of performance. In D. W. Thompson (Ed.), *Performance of literature in historical perspectives* (pp. 437–457). Lanham, MD: University Press of America.

Carlin, P. S. (1985). [Review of *Quilters*]. *Literature in Performance*, 6(1), 82–84.

Carlin, P. S. (1986). Performance of verbal art: Expanding conceptual and curricular territory. In T. Colson (Ed.), *Renewal and revision: The future of interpretation* (pp. 116–131). Denton, TX: NB Omega.

Clifford, J. (1988). *The predicament of culture: Twentieth-century ethnography, literature, and art*. Cambridge, MA: Harvard University Press.

Clifford, J., & Marcus, G. (Eds.). (1986). *Writing culture: The poetics and politics of ethnography*. Berkeley, CA: University of California Press.

Conquergood, D. (1983). Communication as performance: Dramaturgical dimensions of everyday life. In J. Sisco (Ed.), *The Jensen lectures: Contemporary communication studies* (pp. 24–43). Tampa, FL: University of South Florida.

Conquergood, D. (1985). Performing as a moral act: Ethical dimensions of the ethnography of performance. *Literature in Performance*, 5(2), 1–13.

Conquergood, D. (1986a). Performing cultures: Ethnography, epistemology, and ethics. In E. Iembek (Ed.), *Miteinander sprechen und handeln: Festschrift für Hellmut Geissner* (pp. 55–66). Frankfurt: Scriptor.

Conquergood, D. (1986b). Performance and dialogical understanding: In quest of the other. In J. L. Palmer (Ed.)., *Communication as performance* (pp. 30–37). Tempe, AZ: Arizona State University.

Conquergood, D. (1988). Health theatre in a Hmong refugee camp: Performance, communication, and culture. *TDR: The Drama Review, 32*, 174–208.

Cox, R. J. (1987). *Cultural memory and public moral argument* (Van Zelst lecture in communication). Evanston, IL: Northwestern University School of Speech.

Culler, J. (1981). *The pursuit of signs: Semiotics, literature, deconstruction*. Ithaca, NY: Cornell University Press.

Dailey, S. (Ed.). (1983). Forum: The authentic voice. *Literature in Performance, 3(2)*, 110–118.

Deetz, S. (1983). Response: The politics of the oral interpretation of literature. In M. S. Strine (Ed.), Symposium: Post-structuralism and Performance. *Literature in Performance, 4(1)*, 60–64.

DeNeef, A. L. (1987). Of dialogues and historicisms. *South Atlantic Quarterly, 86*, 497–517.

Downs, B. (Adaptor and Director). (1988, April). *The splendid ones: narratives of the AIDS experience* [Performance]. Presented at the annual meeting of the Southern Speech Communication Association, Memphis, TN.

Edwards, P. C. (1985). Transforming Cheever: Three failures in reimagination. *Literature in Performance, 5(2)*, 14–26.

Espinola, J. (1977). Oral interpretation performance: An act of publication. *Western Journal of Speech Communication, 41*, 90–97.

E[vans], R. O. (1986). (W. Martin, Rev.). Metonymy. In A. Preminger (Ed.), *The Princeton handbook of poetic terms* (p. 144). Princeton, NJ: Princeton University Press.

Fine, E. C. (1984). *The folklore text: From performance to print*. Bloomington, IN: Indiana University Press.

Fine, E. C., & Speer, J. H. (1977). A new look at performance. *Communication Monographs, 44*, 374–389.

Fiske, J. (1987). *Television culture*. New York: Methuen.

Flynn, E. A., & Schweickart, P. P. (Eds.). (1986). *Gender and reading: Essays on readers, texts, and contexts*. Baltimore: Johns Hopkins University Press.

Gallie, W. B. (1964). *Philosophy and the historical understanding*. New York: Schocken Books.

Geertz, C. (1980). Blurred genres: The reconfiguration of social thought. *American Scholar, 49*, 165–179.

Geiger, D. (1958). *Oral interpretation and literary study*. San Francisco: P. Van Vloten.

Geiger, D. (1963). *The sound, sense, and performance of literature*. Chicago: Scott, Foresman.

Geiger, D. (1967). *The dramatic impulse in modern poetics.* Baton Rouge, LA: Louisiana State University Press.

Geiger, D. (1972). Poetry as awareness of what? In E. M. Doyle & V. H. Floyd (Eds.), *Studies in interpretation* (pp. 287–305). Amsterdam: Rodopi.

Gentile, J. S. (1985). Early examples of the biographical one-person show genre: "Emlyn Williams as Charles Dickens" and Hal Holbrook's "Mark Twain Tonight!" *Literature in Performance,* 6(1), 42–53.

Gray, P. H. (Director). (October, 1983). *Hedda Tesman based on a play by Henrik Ibsen* [Performance]. Presented at the University of Texas, Austin, TX.

Gray, P. H. (1984). Poet as entertainer: Will Carleton, James Whitcomb Riley, and the rise of the poet-performer movement. *Literature in Performance,* 5(1), 1–12.

Gray, P. H. (1985). Preparing for popularity: origins of the poet-performer movement. *Literature in Performance,* 6(1), 34–41.

Greenblatt, S. (1980). *Renaissance self-fashioning: From More to Shakespeare.* Chicago: University of Chicago Press.

Greenblatt, S. (1988). *Shakespearean negotiations: The circulation of social energy in renaissance England.* Berkeley, CA: University of California Press.

Gudas, F. (1983a). The vitality of dramatism. *Literature in Performance,* 3(2), 1–12.

Gudas, F. (1983b). Dramatism and modern theories of interpretation. In D. W. Thompson (Ed.), *Performance of literature in historical perspectives* (pp. 589–628). Lanham, MD: University Press of America.

Gunn, G. (1987). *The culture of criticism and the criticism of culture.* New York: Oxford University Press.

Hamera, J. (1986). Postmodern performance, postmodern criticism. *Literature in Performance,* 7(1), 13–20.

Hartman, B., & Alho, B. (1979). The power of common experience: The living text. *Readers Theatre News,* 7(1), 5–6, 18, 48.

Heston, L. (1972). The interpreter and the structure of the novel. In E. M. Doyle & V. H. Floyd (Eds.), *Studies in Interpretation* (pp. 137–154). Amsterdam: Rodopi.

Heston, L. (1973). An exploration of the narrator in Robbe-Grillet's *Jealousy. Central States Speech Journal,* 24, 178–182.

Heston, L. (1975). The solo performance of prose fiction. *Speech Teacher,* 24, 269–277.

Heston, L. (1981). The very oral Henry James. *Literature in Performance,* 1(2), 1–12.

Hill, R. T. (1988, November). L'écriture feminine: Alternative texts, alternative performance possibilities. Paper presented at the meeting of the Speech Communication Association, New Orleans.

HopKins, M. F. (1981). From page to stage: The burden of proof. *Southern Speech Communication Journal, 47,* 1–9.

HopKins, M. F. (1982). [Interview with Wayne C. Booth]. *Literature in Performance, 2(2),* 46–63.

HopKins, M. F. (in press). The rhetoric of heteroglossia in flannery o'Connor's *Wise Blood. Quarterly Journal of Speech 75,* 198–211.

Hudson, L. (1973). Oral interpretation as metaphorical expression. *Speech Teacher. 22,* 27–31.

Hunter, J. (1987). *Image and word: The interaction of twentieth-century photographs and texts.* Cambridge, MA: Harvard University Press.

Hutcheon, L. (1985). *A theory of parody: The teachings of twentieth-century art forms.* New York: Methuen.

Issacharoff, M., & Jones, R. F. (Eds.). (1988). *Performing texts.* Philadelphia: University of Pennsylvania Press.

Johnson, B. (1986). Metaphor, metonymy, and voice in Zora Neale Hurston's *Their Eyes were Watching God.* In M. A. Caws (Ed.), *Textual analysis: Some readers reading* (pp. 233–244). New York: Modern Language Association of America.

Kleinau, M. (1987). Notes on the "encounter": Toward a model of performance process. In W. A. Bacon (Ed.), *Festschrift for Isabel Crouch: Essays on the theory, practice, and criticism of performance* (pp. 1–20). Las Cruces, NM: New Mexico State University.

Langellier, K. M. (1983). Doing deconstruction: Sexuality and interpretation. In M. S. Strine (Ed.), Symposium: Post-structuralism and performance. *Literature in Performance, 4(1),* 45–50.

Langellier, K. M. (1986). From text to social context. *Literature in Performance, 6(2),* 60–70.

Lee, C. I., & Gura, T. (1987). *Oral interpretation* (7th ed.). Boston: Houghton Mifflin.

Leedy, J. J. (Ed.). (1969). *Poetry therapy: The use of poetry in the treatment of emotional disorders.* Philadelphia: J. B. Lippincott.

Leedy, J. J. (Ed.). (1985). *Poetry as healer: Mending the troubled mind.* New York: Vanguard Press.

Lentricchia, F. (1983). *Criticism and social change.* Chicago: University of Chicago Press.

Levine, L. W. (1988). *Highbrow/lowbrow: The emergence of cultural hierarchy in America.* Cambridge, MA: Harvard University Press.

Loesch, K. T. (1968). The shape of sound: Configurational rime in the poetry of Dylan Thomas. *Speech Monographs, 35,* 407–424.

Loesch, K. T. (1979). Welsh poetic syntax and the poetry of Dylan Thomas. Reprinted from *The transactions of the honourable society of Cymmrodorion.* Denbigh, U.K.: Gee & Son.

Long, B. W. (1977). Evaluating performed literature. In E. M. Doyle and V. H. Floyd (Eds.), *Studies in interpretation, Vol. II* (pp. 267–282). Amsterdam: Rodopi.

Long, B. W. (1987). Performance as doing: A reconsideration of evaluating performed literature. In W. A. Bacon (Ed.), *Festschrift for Isabel Crouch: Essays on the theory, practice, and criticism of performance* (pp. 21–32). Las Cruces, NM: New Mexico State University.

Long, B. W. (1988, November). *Performance criticism as valuing/evaluating performance criticism*. Paper presented at the meeting of the Speech Communication Association, New Orleans.

Long, B. W., & HopKins, M. F. (1982). *Performing literature: An introduction to oral interpretation*. Englewood Cliffs: Prentice-Hall.

Maclay, J. H. (1983). Group performances in academic settings. In D. W. Thompson (Ed.), *Performance of literature in historical perspectives* (pp. 393–417). Lanham, MD: University Press of America.

Maclean, M. (1988). *Narrative as performance: The Baudelairean experiment*. New York: Routledge.

Martin, A. (Adaptor & Director). (1988, November). *"Things fall apart": Literature that speaks to AIDS* [Performance]. Presented at the annual meeting of the Speech Communication Association, New Orleans.

Merritt, F. (1969a). Eyear: Shape/sound of concrete poetry. *Southern Speech Journal, 34*, 213–224.

Merritt, F. (1969b). Concrete poetry—*verbivococivual*. *Speech Teacher, 18*, 109–114.

Miller, L. C. (1987). The evolution of a production concept: *Three Americans in Paris*. *Communication Education, 36*, 172–177.

Miller, O. (1985). Intertextual identity. In M. J. Valdes & O. Miller (Eds.), *Identity of the literary text* (pp. 19–40). Toronto: University of Toronto Press.

Miller, P. C. (1988). "Will you dance, Miss Austen?": A one woman show. *Literature in Performance, 8(1)*, 65–75.

Minister, K. (1983). Doing deconstruction: The extra-institutional performance of literature. In M. S. Strine (Ed.), Symposium: Post-structuralism and Performance. *Literature in Performance, 4(1)*, 51–54.

Mitchell, W. J. T. (1986). *Iconology: Image, text, ideology*. Chicago: University of Chicago Press.

Mullaney, S. (1988). *The place of the stage: License, play and power in renaissance England*. Chicago: University of Chicago Press.

Myerhoff, B. G. (1984). A death in due time: Construction of self and culture in ritual drama. In J. J. MacAloon (Ed.), *Rite, drama, festival, spectacle: Rehearsals toward a theory of cultural performance*. Philadelphia: Institute for the Study of Human Issues.

Nudd, D. M. (1987, November). *Is there sex in the text? An analysis of undergraduates' interpretation of Katherine Anne Porter's "Rope" and James Thurber's "A Couple of Hamburgers."* Paper presented at the meeting of the Speech Communication Association, Boston.

Nudd, D. M. (1988). [Response in Forum: *Cross-gender performance*]. *Literature in Performance, 8(1)*, 123–125.

Pacanowsky, M. E. (1988). Slouching towards Chicago. *Quarterly Journal of Speech, 74*, 453–467.

Park-Fuller, L. M. (1986a). Between the reflection and the act: A response to Mary S. Strine's essay, "Between meaning and representation: Dialogic aspects of interpretation scholarship. In T. Colson (Ed.), *Renewal and revision: The future of interpretation* (pp. 92–99). Denton, TX: NB Omega.

Park-Fuller, L. M. (1986b). Voices: Bakhtin's heteroglossia and polyphony, and the performance of narrative literature. *Literature in Performance, 7(1)*, 1–12.

Park-Fuller, L. M., & Olsen, T. (1983). Understanding what we know: *Yonnondio: From the thirties. Literature in Performance, 4(1)*, 65–77.

Pelias, R. J., & VanOosting, J. (1987). A paradigm for performance studies. *Quarterly Journal of Speech, 73*, 219–231.

Peterson, E. E. (Intro.). (1983). Symposium: The audience in interpretation theory. *Literature in Performance, 3(2)*, 33.

Pollock, D. (1987–1988). Playing for keeps: The trickster in oral traditions. *Carolinas Speech Communication Annual, 3–4*, 1–19.

Post, R. M. (1967). Albee's *Alice. Western Speech, 31*, 260–265.

Post, R. M. (1969). Cognitive dissonance in the plays of Edward Albee. *Quarterly Journal of Speech, 55*, 54–60.

Post, R. M. (1973). The outsider in the plays of John Osborne. *Southern Speech Communication Journal, 39*, 63–74.

Post, R. M. (1977). Impotency in Pinter's *No Man's Land. Central States Speech Journal, 28*, 214–219.

Queener, L. G. (1972). Contiguity figures: An index to the language-world relationship in Auden's poetry. In E. M. Doyle & V. H. Floyd (Eds.), *Studies in interpretation* (pp. 67–98). Amsterdam: Rodopi.

Queener, L. G. (1986). [Review of *Vienna: Lusthaus*]. *Literature in Performance, 7(1)*, 66–68.

Rassulo, M. M., & Hecht, M. L. (1988). Performance as persuasion: Trigger scripting as a tool for education and persuasion. *Literature in Performance, 8(2)*, 40–55.

Ray, W. (1984). *Literary meaning: From phenomenology to deconstruction.* Oxford, Eng.: Basil Blackwell.

Roloff, L. H. (1973). *The perception and evocation of literature.* Glenview, IL: Scott, Foresman.

Roloff, L. H. (1983). Performer, performing, performance: Toward a psychologicalization of theory. *Literature in Performance, 3(2),* 13–24.

Said, E. W. (1983). *The world, the text, and the critic.* Cambridge, MA: Harvard University Press.

Schechner, R. (1985). *Between theater and anthropology.* Philadelphia: University of Pennsylvania Press.

Schechner, R. (1988). *Performance theory* (rev. ed.). New York: Routledge.

Schneider, R. J. (1976). The visible metaphor. *Communication Education, 25,* 121–126.

Schneider, R. J. (1985). A conversation with Geraldine McEwan. *Literature in Performance, 5(2),* 56–67.

Scholes, R. (1985). *Textual power: Literary theory and the teaching of English.* New Haven, CT: Yale University Press.

Shattuck, R. (1980, April 17). How to rescue literature. *The New York Review of Books,* pp. 29–35.

Skinner, J. F. (1986). Semantic play in the poetry of Howard Nemerov. *Literature in Performance. 6(2),* 44–59.

Sloan, T. O. (1962). A rhetorical analysis of John Donne's "The Prohibition." *Quarterly Journal of Speech, 48,* 38–44.

Sloan, T. O. (1963, Winter). The rhetoric in the poetry of John Donne. *Studies in English Literature, 3,* 31–44.

Sloan, T. O. (1965). Persona as rhetor: An interpretation of Donne's "Satyre III." *Quarterly Journal of Speech, 51,* 14–27.

Sloan, T. O. (Ed.). (1966). *The Oral Study of Literature.* New York: Random House.

Sloan, T. O. (1967). Restoration of rhetoric to literary study. *Speech Teacher, 16,* 91–97.

Smith, B. H. (1988). *Contingencies of value: Alternative perspectives for critical theory.* Cambridge, MA: Harvard University Press.

Speer, J. H. (1985). Waulking o' the web: Women's folk performances in the Scottish isles. *Literature in Performance, 6(1),* 24–33.

Speer, J. H. (1988). [Review of *Between two worlds: The Hmong shaman in America}. Literature in Performance, 8(2),* 105–107.

Stallybrass, P., & White, A. (1986). *The politics and poetics of transgression.* Ithaca, NY: Cornell University Press.

Steiner, W. (1982). *The colors of rhetoric: Problems in the relation between modern literature and painting.* Chicago: University of Chicago Press.

Strine, M. S. (1986). Between meaning and representation: Dialogic aspects of interpretation scholarship. In Ted Colson (Ed.), *Renewal and revision: The future of interpretation* (pp. 69–91). Denton, TX: NB Omega.

Strine, M. S. (1987). Art, argument, and the vitality of interpretative communities. In W. A. Bacon (Ed.), *Festschrift for Isabel Crouch: Essays on the theory, practice, and criticism of performance* (pp. 58–70). Las Cruces, NM: New Mexico State University.

Strine, M. S. (1989). The politics of asking women's questions: Voice and value in the poetry of Adrienne Rich. *Text and Performance Quarterly, 9(1)*, 24–41.

Strine, M. S., & Pacanowsky, M. E. (1985). How to read interpretive accounts of organizational life: Narrative bases of textual authority. *Southern Speech Communication Journal, 50*, 283–297.

Taft-Kaufman, J. (1983). Deconstructing the text: Performance implications. In M. S. Strine (Ed.), Symposium: Post-structuralism and performance. *Literature in Performance, 4(1)*, 55–59.

Taft-Kaufman, J. (1985). Oral interpretation: Twentieth-century theory and practice. In T. W. Benson (Ed.), *Speech communication in the 20th century* (pp. 157–183). Carbondale, IL: Southern Illinois University Press.

Taylor, J. (1982). Narrative Strategies in fiction and film: Flannery O'Connor's "The Displaced Person." *Literature in Performance, 2(2)*, 1–11.

Thompson, D. W. (Ed.). (1983). *Performance of literature in historical perspectives.* Lanham, MD: University Press of America.

Todorov, T. (1984). *Mikhail Bakhtin: The dialogic principle* (W. Godzich,Trans.). Minneapolis, MN: University of Minnesota Press.

Tompkins, J. P. (Ed.). (1980). *Reader-response criticism: From formalism to post-structuralism.* Baltimore: Johns Hopkins University Press.

Trautmann, J. (Ed.). (1981). *Healing arts in dialogue: Medicine and literature.* Carbondale, IL: Southern Illinois University Press.

Turner, V. (1982). *From ritual to theatre: The human seriousness of play.* New York: Performing Arts Journal Publications.

Turner, V. W., & Bruner, E. M. (1986). *The anthropology of experience.* Urbana, IL: University of Illinois Press.

Valentine, K. B. (1979). Interpretation trigger scripting: An effective communication strategy. *Readers Theatre News, 6*, 7–8, 46–47.

Valentine, K. B., & Valentine, E. E. (1983). Facilitation of intercultural communication through performed literature. *Communication Education, 32*, 303–306.

Wicks, S. A. (1981). Music, meaning, and the adaptation of literature. *Literature in Performance, 2(1)*, 89–97.

Williams, D. A. (1986). Poetry for patients and physicians. *Literature in Performance, 7(1)*, 36–44.

Wolff, J. (1984). *The social production of art.* New York: New York University Press.

Zahner-Roloff, L. H. (1986). *The therapies of performance: The Dionysian, Hermetic, and Apollonian archetypes of poetry therapy.* Unpublished manuscript.

· 8 ·

Communication Technology and Society

STUART J. KAPLAN

In less than half a century, modern communication technologies have significantly altered the environments for work, play, learning, government, and personal relations. The rate of technological change in communication media appears to be following an "acceleration curve" (F. Williams, pp. 24–35) as intense competitive pressures drive innovation in computing technology, new communication industries attract an increasing share of investment capital, consumers adapt to new modes of message transmission and reception, and the United States shifts to an information-based economy (Dizard, 1985, pp. 1–18).

The personal and societal implications of accelerating change and innovation in communication technology have been the subject of a rapidly growing research literature. Attention has been given to questions of economic impact (Dizard, 1985), public policy for new media (Ferguson, 1986), constitutional implications (Pool, 1983), applications of technology in organizational settings (Rice, 1984), and behavioral effects (Rogers, 1986; F. Williams, 1987). An important trend in the literature is the increasing emphasis on studying the role played by human capabilities and social values in the relationship between technology and communication behavior (Rafaeli, 1988; F. Williams, 1985).

This essay seeks to make a distinctive contribution by focusing on rhetorical phenomena, including public policy discourse. Its primary goals are to identify broad features and qualities of new technologies that may significantly affect rhetorical behaviors and processes, examine the major themes and arguments in research on this topic, and advance some analytical concepts for future research. The review of research literature will be selective, with an emphasis on those materials and themes that

Suggestions by Thomas Benson and Thomas Lindlof were extremely helpful in the preparation of this chapter.

seem, in this writer's opinion, to be most helpful for advancing our knowledge about the rhetorical implications of new communication technology.

Throughout this chapter, the term *communication technology* will be used in a broad sense to encompass application and social context as well as hardware. This definition is consistent with Rogers's (1986) recommendation that communication technology include the "hardware equipment, organizational structures, and social values by which individuals collect, process, and exchange information with other individuals" (p. 2).

The chapter is organized into four parts. The first briefly describes the new communication technologies and classifies them with reference to some relevant analytical dimensions. The second part addresses the question of how technological change in communication media may affect communication behavior and forms of personal expression. The third part examines some implications of technology for persuasion and public policy discourse. A concluding part presents several questions for future research.

The New Technologies

The following brief description of new media includes those technologies that currently seem to have the greatest potential for substantially enlarging the consumer's choices of entertainment and information programming. The list excludes applications that have been introduced into the marketplace but show little promise of achieving commercial viability. For example, multipoint distribution service (which uses microwave signals to transmit television programs directly to residences) and subscription television (using broadcast signals) are excluded from this section because they appear to be interim applications of technology that have been superseded by cable television in those markets where they directly compete with cable. Also excluded are technologies that appear to be limited to highly specialized use by small segments of the population. More complete (nontechnical) descriptions of these communication technologies can be found in recent books by Aumente (1987) and Whitehouse (1986).

Cable Television

At the end of 1987, half of the households in the United States were cable television subscribers (*CableVision*, 1988a). Although the technology for distributing television signals to the home via coaxial cable has been in commercial use since the late 1940s, advanced applications, including two-way transmission of messages, have been available only within the last ten years and generally only to subscribers of the large urban cable systems. The most advanced cable systems in current operation offer up to 100 channels of mass-appeal and specialized programming. A number of those systems provide extensive community program services, including public-access channels that carry programs produced by local residents and organizations. Interactive (two-way) applications of cable technology allow subscribers to order entertainment and informational programs, respond to public opinion polls, and participate in telecourses. The current market reach and growth rate of cable television, coupled with the increasing political clout of the cable industry, assure that it will be the dominant new medium for at least the next fifteen years. Various combinations of cable with other technologies (e.g., satellite, fiber optic transmission) have enabled cable to increase its capability and efficiency.

Integrated Services Digital Network

The term *integrated services digital network* (ISDN) denotes a marriage of computing, fiber optics, and video technologies that will enable a comprehensive wired network to transport telephone, television, radio, mail, and data services into homes, businesses, and institutions (Harrold & Strock, 1987; Rothamel, 1986). In simple terms, ISDN can be visualized as a combination of cable television and the telephone system, using digital transmission via glass fiber cables. As presently conceived, ISDN would incorporate several nested networks: a network that is similar to current cable television systems would carry radio and television programs and switched (point-to-point) networks would be used for telephone conversations, electronic mail, data, and other forms of interactive communication. The initial, narrowband form of ISDN would be limited to telephone, facsimile, and data services. The broadband version, which would be introduced five to ten years later, could provide a variety of video services, including teleconferencing, videophone, and television entertainment programming.

Because of the enormous expense of research, development, and construction, the telephone industry is probably best positioned to build a national ISDN system. Indeed, the telephone industry has already established fiber optic networks for internal communications, including video teleconferencing, and is slowly converting its current distribution system to fiber optic and digital technology. According to current estimates, fiber optic transmission to the home will be equivalent in cost to conventional telephone technology by the mid-1990s (Daley, 1988). The question of when ISDN systems will become widely available hinges on regulatory policy and economic incentives. If the telephone industry is allowed to compete with cable television systems in the delivery of video entertainment to the home, a substantial portion of the nation could be served by ISDN in twenty or thirty years.

The proposal to put virtually all electronic communication services on one integrated network raises a number of difficult and extremely important political issues and public policy questions. Some implications of this controversy for public policy discourse will be discussed later in the chapter.

Compact Disc

Compact disc-read only memory (CD-ROM) technology represents a stunning advance in the ability to store and retrieve information. Discs in current use hold the equivalent of 250,000 pages of data. Various combinations of text and video images, including moving pictures, can also be stored on CD-ROM. Although the best known current application of CD-ROM is high quality audio recording for the consumer market, its use for data is expanding rapidly. Test versions for home use (e.g., encyclopedias on CD-ROM) are becoming available.

At the present time, CD-ROM is not an interactive medium. However, a blending of CD-ROM, computers, and centralized databases—accessed through the telephone system—makes it possible to rapidly update information stored on the disc (Aumente, 1987, pp. 85–88; Bruno, 1987). As telephone line charges rise and the cost of computers drops, it may be more efficient to mail large amounts of information to consumers on discs and use telecommunication for updating.

Satellites

Satellite technology is an integral component of nearly every major electronic communications network currently in operation. The ability of satellites to transport audio, video, and data over great distances at low cost, combined with the capability of telephone and cable to selectively serve specific users, has made it possible to develop extremely efficient and flexible new communication networks. The applications range from international satellite carriage of the Olympic Games to hundreds of millions of viewers to a public-access cable-satellite network called "Deep Dish TV," which links local cable public-access facilities throughout the United States. Business and institutional uses of satellite for teleconferencing, data transmission, and the distribution of videotaped programs are growing rapidly.

The development of satellite program networks for basic and premium cable television in the mid-1970s is probably the most significant factor driving the expansion of cable television during the 1980s. By early 1988, more than seventy satellite-cable national program distribution networks were in operation, most of them on a full-time basis (*CableVision*, 1988b).

Direct broadcast satellite (DBS), which is a system for transmitting television programs directly to home satellite antennas, has been a subject of much interest and controversy. Although DBS is inherently more efficient than cable for distributing national programming to individual households, cable can provide local programs and interactive services. With the completion of cable system construction in nearly every major population center in the United States, it now seems unlikely that a full-scale national DBS service could be commercially feasible. Instead, with the advent of signal scrambling in 1986, a new business has developed to sell satellite programming to the nearly 2 million households with backyard antennas (Gerber, 1987).

Videocassettes in the Home

More than half of the American households now have at least one VCR (Lachenbruch, 1987); that is, VCRs have achieved a market penetration equivalent to that for cable television. By mid-1987, approximately one-third of the households had both VCRs and cable (Behrens,

1987). Although the major portion of the software market for home VCRs simply consists of taped versions of feature films, a growing segment involves special-interest cassettes such as instructional tapes for hobbyists and video versions of children's literature. The latter form has been termed "video publishing" because it has some of the characteristics of traditional print publishing, most notably the relative ease of entry into the business because production and distribution costs tend to be low in comparison to broadcasting and cable.

Video Information Services via Home Computers

Video information services sold to the home consumer market fall into two categories: videotex, which involves two-way communication between the user and an information source, and the less interactive teletext. Videotex systems use the telephone system or cable television to connect the user's home computer to information sources. Teletext systems rely on unused portions of commercial broadcast television channels to "download" several hundred pages of text to a home terminal.

Videotex, the more successful of the two methods, has a consumer base of 1 million American households (Arlen, 1987). A French videotex system, Minitel, has achieved a much greater degree of consumer acceptance, probably because of its government subsidy and the extraordinary variety of information services offered (Aumente, 1987).

Classification of the New Technologies

Figure 8–1 categorizes the major technologies of electronic mass communication and several of their applications with reference to two analytic dimensions: degree of interactivity and centralization of production and editorial control. No attempt has been made to order these technologies within each of the four cells in Figure 8–1. That is, the variance in Figure 8–1 occurs only between cells. It should be further noted that some of the category placements in Figure 8–1 are tentative and based on assumptions that will be explained below. Future technological and economic developments in the telecommunication marketplace and changes in regulatory policy may result in a different picture in five or ten years. Nevertheless, the relationships depicted in Figure 8–1 are useful for analytic purposes and for the argument presented in this chapter.

Centralized Production
& Editorial Control

Broadcast network TV	Two-way cable TV
Teletext	Some forms of marketing
One-way cable TV	research (see text)
Satellite networks	

Low   High

Interactivity   Interactivity

Videotex	Teleconferencing
Public-access cable	Bulletin boards
Video publishing	CB radio
ISDN	ISDN (interactive services)
CD-ROM	

Decentralized Production
& Editorial Control

Figure 8-1. Communication technologies classified by degree of centralization and editorial control, and extent of interactivity.

Interactivity is a widely discussed characteristic of new communication technologies. However, its meaning varies among writers. Nearly any form of electronic mass communication technology involves at least a minimal amount of interactivity to the extent that audience members are able to select different channels. The highest level of interactivity is provided by systems that enable audiences to also become sources. In the scheme shown in Figure 8–1, the technologies and applications assigned to the right side of the diagram allow users to *create or modify a message that can be accessed by other users.*

Centralization of production and editorial control is a key issue in regulatory policy for new forms of mass communication. As a general principle, advances in technology have facilitated decentralization. However, the high cost of developing and building new communication systems and the economic benefits of large scale ownership create pressures toward greater centralization. Several important implications of that tendency will be considered in the section on public policy discourse.

In the following discussion of the relationships depicted in Figure 8–1, it should be noted that interactivity and extent of centralization are not inherent characteristics of particular media. Rather, these characteristics result from a combination of factors that includes regulatory trends, economic incentives, and social and political history (e.g., public-access cable television), as well as the technical capabilities of a medium.

Centralized Production and Editorial Control/Low Interactivity.   Broadcast television, particularly the network programming service, is the clearest example of a centralized non-interactive medium. Teletext (using broadcast signals or cable), one-way cable television, and satellite program networks are more interactive in the sense that audiences have greater choice of content, and they tend to offer programming from a broad range of sources. However, the extent of decentralization and degree of interactivity for these media is insufficient to warrant their placement in any of the other categories in Figure 8–1.

Centralized Production and Editorial Control/High Interactivity.   Generally, decentralization of production and editorial control is associated with highly interactive communication technology. However, communication systems that use interactive hardware to obtain information from (or about) users—that is then incorporated into programs or other types of messages under the control of the system—are properly placed in this category. One type of example is interactive systems that collect information from their consumers and either use it for marketing purposes or supply it to third parties.

Certain applications of two-way cable television also belong in this category because they allow audience members to create information that is then made available to other viewers, though editorial control over format, timing, and emphasis is retained by the cable system. An example is the public opinion polling channel provided by some two-way cable facilities. Another illustration of this application of technology is the live interactive drama, in which viewers are periodically polled concerning their preferences among a variety of plot options and story outcomes, and the live program is modified accordingly.

Decentralized Production and Editorial Control/Low Interactivity.   The technologies and applications associated with this combination of characteristics can be subdivided into three subcategories. Video cassettes and CD-ROM are characterized by considerable decentralization of production and editorial control, particularly in the case of video cassettes created for small speciality markets (video publishing), and the use of nonelectronic means for the final link of the distribution chain connecting content sources and end users. In the second subcategory, ISDN and videotex services can be thought of as electronic "gateways" that give consumers virtually direct access to the products of a great many information and entertainment providers.

Public-access cable television, the third subcategory, is a unique application of technology in several respects. It came about as a result of unusual historical and political circumstances (Stoney, 1986), and its continued existence owes more to regulatory fiat than to consumer demand. Public access combines the technically sophisticated distribution media of cable and (in some instances) satellite with inexpensive and unsophisticated production technology. A very high degree of editorial decentralization is inherent in the public-access concept. Some rhetorical implications of that concept will be discussed later in the chapter.

Decentralized Production and Editorial Control/High Interactivity. The technologies in this category combine elements of interpersonal and mass communication. They are interpersonal in the sense that individual users are able to have a conversational relationship. Yet, in some applications the message created by that conversational activity can be accessed by other persons, either as the conversation occurs or, in the case of computer bulletin boards or teleconferences that are recorded, at a later time.

Knowledge, Consciousness, and Expression

This section deals with informational, perceptual, and expressive implications of recent trends in communication technology. It is intended to supply premises for the subsequent discussion of rhetorical implications of technological change in communication media. The section is organized around a series of assertions concerning personal and social effects. In some cases, there is modest research support for these assertions. For the most part, however, they should be considered speculative and based mainly on the author's interpretation of trends. They are offered as a stimulus for discussion and research.

Adoption of New Communication Technologies Will Lead to a Further
Synthesis of Oral and Literate Modes of Thought and Discourse

Walter Ong's (1982) discussion of *secondary orality* provides the conceptual basis for the assertion made in the title of this subsection. According to Ong's argument, the electronic media are fostering new modes of thought and discourse that partake of some of the qualities of primary oral culture, yet, at the same time, are highly dependent on literate modes of communication. Secondary orality resembles the older oral mode chiefly in its participatory aspects, its fostering of a communal sense, and its emphasis on the present moment; but the process of designing, producing, and distributing the content of the electronic media is dominated by the technology of writing and the analytic thought processes of literate culture (pp. 135–138).

The television display itself plays a significant role in the historic process of altering the modes of thought and consciousness that had evolved with the technology of writing. Unlike the linear presentation of ideas and arguments in written form, the single frame of video can simultaneously present associations and multiple levels of information (Chesebro, 1984). Haynes (1988) observes that the television experience more closely approximates the existential quality of experiencing actual events because the video representation is readily changed and revised. That characteristic of mutability gives the video producer great freedom to alter viewers' perceptions of reality (Haynes, p. 96).

Although a number of scholars have given considerable attention to these differences between writing and the electronic media, particularly television, relatively little has been written about the possible role of the newer communication technologies in the evolution of secondary orality. It is argued here that recent technological trends will accelerate the synthesis of oral and literate modes of thought and discourse.

The computer appears to be a significant element in the evolution of a distinctive communication mode, taking its place between the oral and the literate. At first it might seem that computing, with its reliance upon sequential and hierarchical ordering of information, is simply an extension of the linear mode of thought that is characteristic of print literacy. However, the ability of computers to store vast amounts of information and quickly rearrange the organization and presentation of that information makes it possible to simulate the continual reshaping and revising of ideas that are characteristic of oral discourse. Noblitt (1988) observes that a dialogical form of reasoning may be facilitated by the use of computers for writing: "Wordprocessing seems to provide a medium that makes it easy to record the loose associative material which occurs rather spontaneously in oral mode; it then provides assistance in shaping this material into the more disciplined prose we are accustomed to seeing in print" (p. 35).

The use of computing technology to overcome the linearity of print and foster a more oral mode of thought is taken a step further with a technology called *hypertext* (Perry, 1987). Hypertext systems use extensive cross-referencing capability to link documents that are on the screen with related documents, which could be in the form of text, visual images, or audio. The user of a hypertext system is able to freely explore possibly relevant associations and search for novel connections between ideas.

Several attributes of the new communication technologies put the user in a participatory role that is more closely akin to oral discourse than to print. Computer bulletin boards and videotex systems designed to facilitate a high degree of interactivity between individual users are two examples. Rafaeli's (1988) classification of types of interactivity provides a good foundation for understanding interpersonal processes in electronically mediated communication.

Word-processing systems that are linked in a network facilitate collaborative development and refinement of a document. When those linked word processors are also connected to data bases containing research materials, the result is a powerful tool for collaborative exploration and reasoning (Noblitt, 1988).

The recent introduction of computerized architectual modeling systems into architectural education provides another example of participatory use of advanced communication technology. The speed with which a computer model of a building design can be revised encourages students to develop and test a large number of design alternatives in interaction with other students and the teacher:

> Rather than being asked to work on another approach and present it tomorrow, students can develop alternatives immediately and interactively with the studio critic. Also, students can more directly interact with each other in the design process. They do not hesitate to change their fellow students' computer work, whereas they will rarely touch another student's drawing in a conventional studio. The number of idea/design/evaluation cycles increases manyfold. (Zdepski and Goldman, 1988, p. 125)

The development of inexpensive and simple video cameras, recorders, and editing equipment makes an important contribution to secondary orality's synthesis of oral and literate modes of discourse. A video cooperative in India teaches self-employed women the rudiments of video production so that they can document their poor working conditions and their problems with the local police (Stuart, 1988). These women, many of whom are illiterate, are thus able to transcend barriers of linguistic competence and social class by communicating their needs to government councils with their own video documentaries.

Another illustration of the participatory attributes of new communication technology is provided by public-access cable in the United States. The public-access movement was stimulated by two important technological developments: broadband cable television and low cost video production equipment. Public access has turned out to be particularly attractive to small ethnic populations in large urban areas, who use the production facilities and access channels to help maintain their group identity and compensate for lack of coverage by existing media. In one case that I (Kaplan, 1988) observed in a large public-access organization, the Korean community was especially active in access programming, and its members freely exchanged the roles of program creator and viewer. To ensure continued participation in those roles, a Korean-language newsletter—containing access program listings and other news about programming activities—was established by members of that community.

Decentralization of Production and Editorial Control Leads to Greater Content Diversity and More Highly Differentiated Audiences

As a result of cable television, home VCRs, and videotex networks linked to home computers, there has been a considerable increase in the amount and variety of information and entertainment available to consumers. Although many of the new service providers are subsidiaries of established major communications organizations, there has also been a substantial growth in independent production (Koch, 1987). The decentralization that new distribution technologies make possible has started to occur to a significant degree.

When no more than five or six television channels were available to the home audience, the networks and stations competed for large segments of that audience by offering programs that differed only marginally from one another. Now that the average cable television household is able to receive at least thirty channels and VCR owners can select among many thousands of tapes, competition among program producers and suppliers results in more meaningful variations of content and form (Webster, 1986).

Greater content diversity both divides and unites audiences. Audiences divide along program preference lines and develop loyalties to particular cable channels or presentation formats, types of taped material, or specialized videotex forums and information services. A study of cable television viewing habits (Webster, 1986) found that fragmentation of the audience was accompanied, as well, by a type of polarization. On the whole, cable viewers divided, or fragmented, their viewing time among a larger set of choices than is available in households without cable television. However, distinct subgroups of viewers committed substantial portions of their viewing time to certain specialized cable channels. Webster reports that "the users of music video, sports, and news channels devoted from 12 to 15 times more attention to those services than did the larger cable audience" (p. 88).

The audience polarization attributable to content that is suggested by Webster's data is also a unifying force. Audience groups defined by their loyalty to distinctive content and communication forms share common mass-mediated experiences and perceptions of the world. Lindlof (1988) uses the term *interpretive communities* to refer to group affiliations that arise from the "sharing of media technologies, content or software, codes, and occasions" (p. 92), rather than the more conventional group categories based on demographic and occupational factors. Audience groups that devote significant portions of their available viewing time to specialized cable television channels exemplify one interpretive community. Computer bulletin board users provide another example.

The fact that audiences for the electronic media are now more likely to be differentiated by message content and form does not mean that socioeconomic factors and occupation will cease to be consequential. Rather, income, education, and occupation are likely to be threshold variables that determine who gets to benefit from the new technologies and who is denied access. For example, videotex delivered via home computers may exist as an elite medium because of its cost and the skills needed to fully participate in the technology (Carey, 1982). Reese (1988) reports data showing a significant occupational factor in the adoption of home computers.

Differential access to the benefits of communication technology is an important social policy issue. Some dimensions of that issue will be considered in the section of this chapter on public policy discourse.

Another significant policy issue to be taken up later in this chapter is the use of government regulation to assure decentralization of editorial control in new forms of mass media. My prediction, in this section, concerning content diversity is based on the assumption that new communication technologies will continue to foster decentralization of editorial control. That assumption is based on current trends, however. Raymond Williams (1975, pp. 135–152) suggests that it may be a risky assumption in the light of historical experience with earlier forms of electronic media.

The Process of Forming Codes of Communication Will Be More Fluid and Dynamic in an Age of Decentralized and Interactive Mass Media

Codes constitute a socially based system of rules for giving meaning to communicative behavior (Fiske, 1982, pp. 68–87; Hall, 1980). They create the symbolic links between message sources, message texts, and audiences. For example, the codes of television incorporate the social codes that arise from human behavior in real life (such as appearance and gesture), representational and technical codes that are medium-specific (e.g., camera angle, editing), and the ideological codes (e.g., capitalism, individualism) that establish the meaning of a television message within a context of cultural beliefs (Fiske, 1987, pp. 4–13). In addition to their role in message production and interpretation, codes serve an evaluative function in providing the terms for determining which messages are useful, important, and aesthetically pleasing (Hartley, 1982, pp. 32, 180–181). Codes are inherent in all social practices and forms of conduct, including communication behavior.

Mass-media messages are encoded according to the frameworks of knowledge, ideologies, production techniques and routines, and organizational priorities of the producing organizations (Hall, 1980, p. 129). Messages, once received and interpreted (decoded) by audience members, eventually influence the larger system of social practices from which producing organizations draw their ideas and values. From this analytic perspective, then, mass communication can be thought of as a discursive process in which meaning is circulated between producers and receivers. Because of the discursive nature of mass communication, codes of meaning are not static. Instead, codes may undergo change as audiences respond to variations in topics, themes, visual treatments, and other aspects of content and form. In this model, audiences are both sources and receivers.

It follows from this theoretical argument that the increased diversity in mass communication content and form due to technological change will result in a more variable and fluid process of code formation and change. In addition, interactivity between audiences and content sources should speed up the discursive process by which codes of meaning are created and revised.

Another example from my (Kaplan, 1988) research with public-access cable organizations will help clarify this point. I found that three distinct aesthetic codes were influencing program producers' choices of materials and production techniques. Those codes developed in an ideological context formed by the political values and aesthetic standards of the broader culture in combination with the political value-system of the public access movement. For example, access producers whose work is defined by a "documentation" code consciously avoided manipulating form. Instead, they presented events with a naturalistic technique that made almost no use of graphics, editing, closeups, or narration. Although the resulting programs looked amateurish, the approach of the producers could not be explained away as mere sloppiness or ineptitude. Rather, producers who adhered to the documentation code made deliberate choices out of a sincere belief that their programs achieved a higher degree of fidelity to the televised event than is the case with conventional television. The political values of the public access movement provide a supportive context for this expression of "alternative TV." Thus, conscious avoidance of the conventional aesthetic code of professional television, in this circumstance, can be considered to be ideologically based. Because public-access producers and viewers frequently swap roles (a form of interactivity), production practices within the access organization might influence external definitions of television aesthetics by enlarging the range of acceptable forms.

Some types of codes are more stable than others, however, and this variation qualifies my assertion that trends toward decentralization and interactivity in mass communication will lead to greater fluidity in code formation and change. Fiske (1987) notes that ideological codes are highly resistant to change, in part because different audiences are able to interpret any given text in ways that support their existing ideologies. It seems likely, therefore, that the representational codes of mass communication will be the most susceptible to change as a result of the phenomena described in this section.

Recent Advances in Communication Technology Will Broaden the Base of Artistic Literacy and Enhance Opportunities for Personal Expression

The ability of new communication technologies to foster more widespread participation in the artistic and expressive activity of a culture is generally overlooked in the literature on new media. Most of the attention has focused on information gain and on access to a more diverse menu of programming. Yet, the technologies of inexpensive video production and storage of images, computer graphics, broadband video distribution systems (e.g., cable television and ISDN), and interactive media of various types can facilitate the spread of artistic literacy in a population. At the most obvious level of effect, new communication media offer new ways of seeing and hearing (Turim, 1983; Winston, 1987).

Aesthetic empowerment is a less obvious benefit of recent technology. As noted earlier, aesthetic empowerment is a primary theme in the ideology and practices of the public-access cable movement. Several hundred public-access centers currently provide free or low-cost training in the use of video production equipment (Epler-Wood & D'Ari, 1987). Architecture students who use three-dimensional architectural modeling systems, based on microcomputer technology, tend to generate a greater variety of design concepts and to experiment more with form and site organization (Zdepski & Goldman, 1988). Inexpensive electronic music systems for personal computers encourage more widespread learning of compositional skills. Work is currently under way on visual interfaces for electronic music systems that will make it easier for persons who have not learned musical notation to compose intuitively (Acker & Dias, 1988).

These examples illustrate the use of communication technology to develop artistic competence (Gross, 1973) and encourage participation in creative activity. The more optimistic predictions concerning the use of technology in creative activity envision a burgeoning of artistic endeavor: "art will flourish as a popular means by which a literate, if not necessarily a print-literate, population can express with images and sounds its innermost thoughts and feelings" (Conant, 1981, p. 94).

Other applications of interactive media (e.g., videodiscs) give art consumers greater access to creative works and a more participatory role in the viewing or listening experience.

Several caveats concerning the possible effects of communication technology on artistic literacy should be introduced at this point. Although the advent of inexpensive video equipment (and earlier introductions of 16-mm and 8-mm film equipment), has made access to the tools of mass-media production more democratic, the means of distribution are still largely under centralized control by major economic interests (Monaco, 1981, pp. 411–416). If institutional and economic barriers to distribution and exhibition remain high, new artists will be discouraged. The new electronic tools of artistic expression are most effective in the hands of capable artists (Turim, 1983; Winston, 1987). Whether the untrained person can or will fully utilize the aesthetic potential of new communication technologies remains to be seen. A final caveat concerns the effect that increasing the number of channels and media may have on the economic base for content production. When a finite audience is distributed across a broader range of content options, the financial resources that are available to individual producers and channels may diminish. As a consequence, production values and program standards slip. This phenomenon seems to have already affected commercial broadcast television, which has been losing its audience to cable television and home VCR use. In response to the erosion in their revenue base, broadcast television networks have cut production budgets and turned to more sensational programming aimed at the lowest levels of taste in the audience. Thus, the amount of content at both extremes of the quality spectrum has increased: more fine arts material can now be obtained on cable channels, videodiscs, and tape, while the medium that is available to the largest segment of the population has increased its share of "trash TV."

Rhetorical Implications

The four propositions concerning broad social effects of recent developments in communication technology that were discussed in the preceding section—increasing integration of oral and literate modes, greater differentiation of content and audiences, more variable processes of social code formation, and aesthetic empowerment—provide a starting point for speculation about rhetorical implications. Two aspects of this question are considered: (1) effects of new technologies on persuasion and (2) effects of technological change on a particular type of public discourse, namely, communication policy debate.

Persuasion

Specialized and Adaptive Persuasive Media and Messages.   The proliferation of specialized cable television channels directed at particular viewing interests that also coincide with specialized consumer interests (e.g., health information channels), provides a unique opportunity for advertisers (Kaplan, 1981). Political candidates are finding that cable is a relatively inexpensive medium for appeals directed at particular voter groups. Because of its efficiency and ability to target voters, cable was used for a substantial portion of the advertising during the presidential primary campaigns of 1988.

Computers are also starting to play a significant role in political persuasion. A videotex network is used by the Democratic Party national office to transmit campaign information each day to news organizations (Sabato & Beiler, 1988). Political campaigns also make extensive use of computers in fund raising and in the recruitment and management of campaign volunteers (Meadow, 1985). An application of data base technology to the task of identifying and communicating with voters is described by Tobe (1985): "Using political databases and today's other new campaign technologies, computers have made it possible to select voters and voter households precisely and economically, and to produce phenomenally successful response-provoking voter contacts which add further names and data into the base" (p. 55). The interactive characteristics of some new communication technologies lend an adaptive and participatory quality to persuasion via the electronic media that simulates face-to-face dialogue between sales representatives and their customers. For example, videotex marketing systems can adjust a sales presentation in accord with the viewer's response to a series of consumer-preference questions. These applications of technology further illustrate how persuasive practices may change as a consequence of the merging of oral and literate modes of discourse (Haynes, 1988). Beniger (1987) warns that increasingly effective means for personalizing mass-media messages and creating a type of pseudo-intimacy may lead to undesirable forms of societal control.

Persuasive theory and practice will also change to accommodate the increasing diversity of audiences. A wider spectrum of interpretive communities (Lindlof, 1988) and more use of specialized media will result in more heterogeneous codes of meaning and social perspectives (Chesebro, 1984; Gumpert & Cathcart, 1985). The greater variation in aesthetic form that is facilitated by new technologies may lead to more diverse preferences for presentation format and style. Advertising and political persuasion will have to become more finely tuned to these differences between audiences.

Diffuse Sources of Authority and Credibility. The fragmentation and polarization of audiences, together with a vast increase in the quantity of available information, makes the definition of authority and source credibility problematic. Meyrowitz (1985, pp. 160–163, 322) believes that the electronic media flatten authority (and status) structures by giving average people access to information that formerly was not available to them. But Klapp (1982) argues that advances in information-processing technology have led to an increasing meaning gap because our ability to discern the significance of facts and understand how units of information are related lags the sheer gain in its quantity.

Thus, the stage is set for the emergence of new types of credible sources who are adept at seeing patterns and interrelationships and skilled in contextualizing information (Meyrowitz, 1985, pp. 327–328). Perhaps future advances in information technology will also help society cope with meaning lag. For example, very powerful interactive databases, such as hypertext, make it easier for users to explore possible connections among seemingly unrelated facts and ideas.

Broad Participation in Public Discourse. The new technologies lower the threshold for participation in public discourse. Inexpensive video production equipment and the availability of public-access channels on cable gives many more citizens the opportunity to use television to persuade voters and local officials. Video materials produced by local political groups are also played at public meetings and in public forums such as shopping malls. In one example that I observed, a series of videotapes produced by a neighborhood group with virtually no prior experience in television production significantly influenced the outcome of a controversial zoning decision.

At a more sophisticated technical level, many national, politically oriented organizations (e.g., labor unions) use their own satellite networks to distribute text materials and video programs designed for lobbying purposes. Political advocacy groups use computers and videotex for research, fund raising, and recruitment. Ball-Rokeach and Reardon (1988) coined the term "debate telelog" to refer to uses of interactive videotex and electronic bulletin boards by individual participants in persuasive exchanges.

An important potential limitation on this prediction concerning technology and participation in public discourse is posed by income and education barriers. Public-access cable is, by design, able to surmount those obstacles. But adoption or use of many information technologies is constrained by their cost or requisite levels of literacy. Without effective policies to assure ready access to communication technology, its use to participate in public discourse may be limited to elite segments of the population.

Narrow Consensus.   One corollary of more widespread participation in public discourse is the increasing difficulty of achieving broad consensus on political issues. All of the major special interest groups have access to sophisticated communication technologies. As a result of the diversity of special interests with access to powerful means of political communication, the likelihood of successfully seeking the common interest may be diminished (Hauser, 1981). This historic political trend may be accelerated by the advanced communication technologies.

The use of sophisticated methods of political persuasion may be contributing to a related trend: less representative elections. Because of generally declining voter turnout and large differences in political participation by various sectors of the population, political candidates are making more use of appeals precisely aimed at those citizens who are most likely to vote. Some political campaign analysts have suggested that the emphasis on demographic research and more efficient campaign communication may also be a causal factor in the decline in turnout. According to their argument, those voters who are predisposed to vote for a candidate receive substantial encouragement through precisely directed messages, while the less interested citizens get contacted less and are also discouraged by negative advertising (Frantzich, 1988; Sabato, 1988). As a consequence, election outcomes are being decided by relatively small groups of voters who may not be representative of the general population.

Communication Policy Discourse

The discourse of communications policy making is being driven and shaped by the rapid and revolutionary changes in technology that have occurred within the last decade. The significance of this phenomenon for rhetorical study should not be overlooked. Streeter's (1987) investigation of the formulation of cable television policy is a good example of the value of analyzing the process of making policy in the context of the discursive practices that help shape that process.

Several of the key issues in current telecommunication policy discourse are identified below. They are presented in dialectical form in order to highlight the main competing interests and values.

Applying the First Amendment: Bulwark against Government Intervention versus Stimulus for Diversity. Recent advances in communications technology have severely challenged the ability of the courts to apply First Amendment theory and principles. For more than 200 years, the American legal system has done a good job of maintaining the First Amendment's prohibition against governmental abridgement of expression. However, unprecedented monopoly characteristics of some electronic mass media have forced Congress, the Federal Communications Commission, and the courts to balance the First Amendment rights of media owners against society's interest in receiving a wide range of ideas. The current debate over cable television regulation nicely illustrates this clash of values (Kaplan, 1986). Under current national policy for cable, local governments have the option of requiring cable operators to set aside some of their channels for community programming, including public access. The justification is to prevent local cable monopolies from controlling all of the content on their systems. But the courts have given inconsistent answers to the question of whether community channel regulations are an impermissible abridgement of the cable operators' "speech" (Van Eaton, 1987, pp. 43–47). Integrated services digital networks may also challenge our ability to adapt the First Amendment to changing technology. If ISDN should become the single conduit into the home for television, voice, and data, its ownership structure will become a matter of substantial concern for Congress and the FCC.

The inherent monopoly characteristics of cable television (at the local system level) and ISDN have led some observers to recommend that ownership and control of programming services should be separated from system ownership, as a matter of national policy (Pool, 1983). Under this application of the common carrier regulatory model, large comprehensive networks like ISDN would be required to lease transmission channels to program producers and networks (U.S. Department of Commerce, National Telecommunications and Information Administration, 1988, pp. 32–60).

Access to Information: Private versus Public "Goods."   Increasingly, information is being sold as a commodity and priced according to its market value. In that sense, publicly distributed information that used to be treated as a public good is now being privatized. As a consequence of this trend, there is a justifiable concern that some portions of the population will miss out on the benefits of the information age. The rosier predictions concerning the democratizing and liberating effects of new communication technology are based on the assumption that income and social position will not be barriers to access (Cleveland, 1985). But current trends in videotex and some aspects of cable television indicate that information technology may discriminate among social sectors, thus creating barriers to economic and political participation. This has led some observers to propose that government-subsidized public videotex terminals be made widely available (Carey, 1982). The current controversy over "universal service" requirements in telephone regulation is another theme in the debate over access to technology (Aufderheide, 1987). The recent trend toward deregulation of the electronic media jeopardizes requirements like low cost basic phone service and universal availability of basic cable service within franchise areas, which, traditionally, were based on the concept of information as a public good. This has become a significant topic for public discourse about communications policy.

Liability for Injurious Information: Access versus Responsibility.   It used to be easier to identify "the press," and thereby assign responsibility for the effects of harmful messages (e.g., libel). Broadcast station owners and publishers were relatively few and generally visible within their communities. Responsibility for injurious communication becomes vastly more difficult to establish, however, when information becomes decentralized and editorial control gets widely dispersed. Under those conditions, regulatory or legal efforts to maintain editorial accountability may threaten the benefits of decentralization in communications media. Videotex illustrates the dilemma. Videotex systems that operate as gateways to thousands of information providers can offer an unprecedented degree of content diversity. But if the videotex system, or intermediate networks that combine and package the services of several information providers, are required to do the kinds of verifying and supervising expected of more traditional publishers, the concept of open access may be jeopardized and the growth of the technology inhibited (U.S. Congress, Office of Technology Assessment, 1988).

Privacy Protection: Efficiency versus Personal Autonomy. A great deal of concern has been voiced about the intrusiveness of new technologies and their ability to gather huge amounts of information about people without express authorization. As a result of widespread concern over the potential abuse of two-way cable television technology, Congress included privacy protection provisions in its 1984 cable law. However, advances in information-gathering technology are outstripping the ability of government to address the privacy problem (Peck, 1984). Adding to this problem is the lack of well-developed legal theory concerning the distinction between public and private information. Highly restrictive regulations concerning the gathering and dissemination of personal information may inhibit the growth of some communication technologies, add costs of compliance that will be passed on to consumers, and threaten society's legitimate interests in certain kinds of information (e.g., for crime investigation).

Optimizing the Benefits of Technology: Distributed versus Hierarchical Communication Technologies. Traditionally, the large electronic communication networks have been centralized and hierarchical organizations. In the case of the telephone system, for example, central control was deemed necessary to assure standardized universal service at a reasonable rate (Noam, 1987). The enormous investment needed to construct a national communication network similarly favors some form of monopoly ownership. Potential abuses of monopoly power are curbed through governmental regulation of rates and services. This model of centrally controlled, but government-regulated, communication technology is currently undergoing change as a result of numerous factors, including the decreasing cost of technology and the increase in demand for a wide variety of specialized telecommunication services (Noam, 1987). A great variety of new telecommunication services for business and residential consumers are now available in the marketplace as a result of decentralization. ISDN promises even greater technical capacity and flexibility. However, the pending transition to digital technology (ISDN) creates new pressures for centralization, chiefly because of the huge start-up costs. The debate concerns the structure of a nationwide digital network. A hierarchical system is built on technical standards and requirements that protect the owner's investment by discouraging competition. "Open network architecture" is an alternative structure that is technically open to a broad range of communication technologies and service providers (Noam, p. 30). Our ability to realize the full benefits of new technologies and decentralization in the communications marketplace may depend greatly on the outcome of this debate (Pool, 1983).

Conclusion

The trends toward greater interactivity and decentralization of electronic mass media are basic changes with far-reaching implications for theory and practice. Some existing theories of mass communication effects will need to be reconceptualized to account for new types of content and usage patterns. Traditional conceptual distinctions between interpersonal and mass communication require reexamination (Ball-Rokeach and Reardon, 1988; Beniger, 1987). Several rhetorical implications of technological change in communication media were discussed in the preceding section. Attention was also given to the various ways that the new technologies are testing our ability to adequately define the public interest in mass communication and to craft appropriate public policy. Harlan Cleveland (1985) has noted the recent increase in debate concerning the social impacts of science and technology (e.g., national environmental policy). The telecommunications policy debate is a rich source of discourse deserving of close study by communication scholars.

The trends and issues discussed in this chapter suggest several questions for future research. First, we need more basic research on the question of how people obtain and interpret information from the new media. Do people varying in economic status and educational attainment differ in the way they conceptualize and value "information"? What are the analytic dimensions that people use to differentiate among types of information? How is information-seeking behavior affected by the range and nature of the information choices available in mass communication? What mechanisms are used to cope with an overabundance of information? Have the dimensions and characteristics of source credibility changed as a result of the greater diversity of sources and distribution channels?

Second, the effects of technological change on cultural and artistic expression warrant research. Will greater artistic diversity result from decentralization in mass communication, or is standardization of content an inevitable consequence of the economic characteristics of mass media? To what extent are aesthetic values medium-specific (e.g., will unique video aesthetics develop in the more specialized television media and applications?)?

A third general area for exploration is interpersonal communication on interactive media. For example, will language-behavior rules change in response to interactivity? We need to learn more about the communication of socioemotional content in electronically mediated information systems. Rice and Love's (1987) study of message content in a computer-based bulletin board forum illustrates this type of research.

Finally, the continuing dilemma of privacy protection provokes a variety of questions for behavioral research. Has the psychological construct of personal privacy (or personal autonomy) changed or been redefined with the introduction of interactive media and more powerful methods for obtaining information? The answer to that question has considerable legal significance because the courts now use the average person's reasonable expectation for privacy as the standard in assessing privacy abuse.

Scholars in all areas of the speech communication field can be engaged in research on the implications of technological change for communication behavior. The research effort to date may have suffered from an excessive future orientation. As Frederick Williams (1985) and others have pointed out, recent technological developments should be considered extensions of older technologies, created to serve long-established human communication needs, rather than a revolutionary break with the past. Therefore, historical and critical research on the development and maintenance of communication values, norms, and practices are both highly relevant to the issues raised in this chapter. As a specific example on this point, Smith (1982) argues that the current emphasis on channel diversity and specialized content should be seen as an evolutionary outgrowth of social trends toward individualism and differentiated consumer interests that began in the previous century. Rather than attribute observable changes like the recent growth in media and channels solely to the push of technology, it may be more fruitful to examine the role of demand based on established social trends and communication needs.

Another consequence of the preoccupation with hardware and future applications is the tendency to focus research on the communication behavior of small and elite segments of the population comprised of innovators or people with a strong personal or occupational need for new information services. Rafaeli (1988, pp. 112–113) urges researchers to focus more attention on the use of new media by casual, average users rather than expert consumers and innovators. Again, more widespread participation in this research effort by specialists in many different aspects of speech communication would be a healthy development.

The need to inform public policy making for new media with the findings of our research is especially pressing now (R. Williams, 1975, pp. 147–152). Significant policy and regulatory decisions are currently being made, within a relatively short time period. Speech communication scholars should be contributing to the policy debate.

References

Acker, S. R., & Dias, J. A. (1988, June). *Spatializing temporal events: The visual language of electronic music composition.* Paper presented at the Visual Communication Conference, Calistoga, CA.

Arlen, G. (1987, December). People still don't know just what they're missing. *Channels*, p. 123.

Aufderheide, P. (1987). Universal service: Telephone policy in the public interest. *Journal of Communication, 37*(1), 81–96.

Aumente, J. (1987). *New electronic pathways.* Newbury Park, CA: SAGE Publications, Inc.

Ball-Rokeach, S. J., & Reardon, K. (1988). Monologue, dialogue, and telelog: Comparing an emergent form of communication with traditional forms. In R. P. Hawkins, J. M. Wiemann, & S. Pingree (Eds.), *Advancing Communication Science: Merging Mass and Interpersonal Processes* (pp. 135–161). Newbury Park, CA: SAGE Publications.

Behrens, S. (1987, December). A finer grind from the ratings mill. *Channels*, pp. 10–12, 16.

Beniger, J. R. (1987). Personalization of mass media and the growth of pseudo-community. *Communication Research, 14*(3), 352–371.

Bruno, R. (1987, November). Making compact disks interactive. *IEEE Spectrum*, pp. 40–45.

CableVision. (1988a, January 18). Cable stats, p. 64.

CableVision. (1988b, March 28). Cable stats, p. 64.

Carey, J. (1982). Videotex: The past as prologue. *Journal of Communication, 32*(2), 80–85.

Chesebro, J. W. (1984). The media reality: Epistemological functions of media in cultural systems. *Critical Studies in Mass Communication, 1*(2), 111–130.

Cleveland, H. (1985, January/February). The twilight of hierarchy: Speculations on the global information society. *Public Administration Review*, pp. 185–195.

Conant, T. R. (1981). Art, the artist, and the new technologies. *Journal of Broadcasting, 25*(1), 92–95.

Daley, A. (1988, July). *Will the single wire home be a reality in 20 years?* Paper presented at the annual meeting of the National Federation of Local Cable Programmers, Tampa, FL.

Dizard, W. P., Jr. (1985). *The coming information age* (2nd ed.). New York: Longman.

Epler-Wood, G., & D'Ari, P. (1987). *Cable programming resource directory.* Washington, DC: Communication Press, Broadcasting Publications, Inc.

Ferguson, M. (Ed.). (1986). *New communication technologies and the public interest.* London: SAGE Publications.

Fiske, J. (1982). *Introduction to communication studies.* London: Methuen.

Fiske, J. (1987). *Television Culture*. London: Methuen.

Frantzich, S. E. (1988). The rise of the service-vendor party. In J. L. Swerdlow (Ed.), *Media Technology and the Vote: A Source Book* (pp. 173–177). Washington, DC: Annenberg Washington Program in Communications Policy Studies.

Gerber, C. (1987, December). The dish crowd fights for a pipeline in the sky. *Channels*, p. 99.

Gross, L. (1973). Art as the communication of competence. *Social Science Information, 12*(5), 115–141.

Gumpert, G., & Cathcart, R. (1985). Media grammars, generations, and media gaps. *Critical Studies in Mass Communication, 2*(1), 23–35.

Hall, S. (1980). Encoding/decoding. In S. Hall, D. Hobson, A. Lowe, & P. Willis (Eds.), *Culture, Media, Language*. London: Hutchinson.

Harrold, D. J., & Strock, R. D. (1987). The broadband universal telecommunications network. *IEEE Communications Magazine, 25*(1), 69–79.

Hartley, J. (1982). *Understanding News*. London: Methuen.

Hauser, G. A. (1981). Trends in public discourse: Political rhetoric and social action. *The Pennsylvania Speech Communication Annual, 37*, 7–12.

Haynes, W. L. (1988). Of that which we cannot write: Some notes on the phenomenology of media. *Quarterly Journal of Speech, 74*, 71–101.

Kaplan, S. J. (1981). Trends in persuasion on the media: The electronic salesman and its relationship to the viewer. *The Pennsylvania Speech Communication Annual, 37*, 25–31.

Kaplan, S. J. (1986, November). *Freedom of speech on cable television: First Amendment implications of recent legislation and court rulings*. Paper presented at the meeting of the Speech Communication Association, Chicago.

Kaplan, S. J. (1988, June). *Development of an aesthetic code in public access cable television*. Paper presented at the Visual Communication Conference, Calistoga, CA.

Klapp, O. E. (1982). Meaning lag in the information society. *Journal of Communication, 32*(2), 56–66.

Koch, N. (1987, December). Splashing new realities onto an old Hollywood. *Channels*, p. 32.

Lachenbruch, D. (1987, December). Sharp and super: A new VCR's got the picture. *Channels*, pp. 124–125.

Lindlof, T. R. (1988). Media audiences as interpretive communities. *Communication Yearbook, 11*, 81–107.

Meadow, R. G. (1985). Political campaigns, new technologies and political competition. In R. G. Meadow (Ed.), *New Communication Technologies in Politics* (pp. 5–16). Washington, DC: The Washington Program of the Annenberg School of Communications.

Meyrowitz, J. (1985). *No Sense of Place*. New York: Oxford University Press.

Monaco, J. (1981). *How To Read a Film*. New York: Oxford University Press.

Noam, E. M. (1987). The public telecommunications network: A concept in transition. *Journal of Communication, 37*(1), 30–47.

Noblitt, J. S. (1988, February). Writing, technology and secondary orality. *Academic Computing*, 34–35, 56–57.

Ong, W. J. (1982). *Orality and Literacy*. London: Methuen.

Peck, R. S. (1984). Extending the constitutional right to privacy in the new technological age. *Hofstra Law Review*, 12(4), 893–912.

Perry, T. S. (1987, November). Hypermedia: Finally here. *IEEE Spectrum*, pp. 38–39.

Pool, I. de Sola (1983). *Technologies of Freedom*. Cambridge, MA: Harvard University Press, Belknap Press.

Rafaeli, S. (1988). Interactivity: From new media to communication. In R. P. Hawkins, J. M. Wiemann, & S. Pingree (Eds.), *Advancing Communication Science: Merging Mass and Interpersonal Processes* (pp. 110–134). Newbury Park, CA: SAGE Publications.

Reese, S. D. (1988). New communication technologies and the information worker: The influence of occupation. *Journal of Communication, 38*(2), 59–70.

Rice, R. E. (1984). *The New Media*. Beverly Hills, CA: SAGE Publications.

Rice, R. E., & Love, G. (1987). Electronic emotion. *Communication Research, 14*(1), 85–108.

Rogers, E. M. (1986). *Communication Technology*. New York: Free Press.

Rothamel, H. J. (1986, November 17). A blueprint for broadband ISDN services. *Telephony*, pp. 50–58.

Sabato, L. (1988). Consultant service: The new campaign technology. In J. L. Swerdlow (Ed.), *Media Technology and the Vote: A Source Book* (pp. 182–184). Washington, DC: The Annenberg Washington Program in Communications Policy Studies.

Sabato, L., & Beiler, D. (1988). *Magic . . . Or Blue Smoke and Mirrors?* Washington, DC: The Annenberg Washington Program in Communications Policy Studies.

Smith, A. (1982). Information technology and the myth of abundance. *Daedalus, 111*(4), 1–16.

Stoney, G. (1986). Public access: A word about pioneers. *Community Television Review*, 9(2), 7–11.

Streeter, T. (1987). The cable fable revisited: Discourse, policy, and the making of cable television. *Critical Studies in Mass Communication*, 4(2), 174–200.

Stuart, S. (1988, July 14). Keynote address to annual meeting of the National Federation of Local Cable Programmers, Tampa, FL.

Tobe, F. L. (1985). New techniques in computerized voter contact. In R. G. Meadow (Ed.), *New Communication Technologies in Politics* (pp. 53–68).

Washington, DC: The Washington Program of the Annenberg School of Communications.

Turim, M. (1983). Video art: Theory for a future. In E. A. Kaplan (Ed.), *Regarding Television* (pp. 130–137). Frederick, MD: University Publications of America.

U.S. Congress, Office of Technology Assessment. (1988, January). *Science, Technology, and the First Amendment* (OTA-CIT–369). Washington, DC: U.S. Government Printing Office.

U.S. Department of Commerce, National Telecommunications and Information Administration. (1988, June). *Video Program Distribution and Cable Television: Current Policy Issues and Recommendations* (NTIA Report 88–233). Washington, DC: U.S. Government Printing Office.

Van Eaton, J. (1987). Old franchises never die? Denying renewal under the First Amendment and the Cable Act. *Cardozo Arts & Entertainment Law Journal, 6*(1), 37–73.

Webster, J. G. (1986). Audience behavior in the new media environment. *Journal of Communication, 36*(3), 77–91.

Whitehouse, G. E. (1986). *Understanding the New Technologies of the Mass Media.* Englewood Cliffs, NJ: Prentice-Hall.

Williams, F. (1983). *The Communications Revolution.* New York: Mentor.

Williams, F. (1985). Technology and communication. In T. W. Benson (Ed.), *Speech communication in the 20th century* (pp. 184–195). Carbondale, IL: Southern Illinois University Press.

Williams, F. (1987). *Technology and Communication Behavior.* Belmont, CA: Wadsworth.

Williams, R. (1975). *Television: Technology and Cultural Form.* New York: Schocken Books.

Winston, B. (1987). A mirror for Brunelleschi. *Daedalus, 116*(3), 187–201.

Zdepski, S. M., & Goldman, G. (1988, January) Computers: Beyond working drawings. *Architectural Record,* pp. 125–127, 129.

• 9 •

Legal Constraints on Communication

PETER E. KANE

All study of communication is in one way or another the study of constraints on communication. The student of interpersonal communication examines psychological elements within the individual that create barriers to effective communication. The semanticist looks at the barriers created through the inappropriate or ambiguous use of words. Studies in organizational communication seek to identify and correct those factors that inhibit the flow of communication. Rhetorical studies focus on what the rhetor may or may not be able to do in a given situation. Still another communication barrier is that of custom and law that prevents or punishes some types of communication in particular circumstances. The study of freedom of speech is the study of these legal and cultural barriers to communication.

There are two fundamental kinds of communication constraints. First are those that prevent the communication from taking place. Because of personal inhibitions something is not said. The rhetor examines the situation and consciously concludes that an effective appeal should avoid certain arguments. The government issues an order that certain information may not be publicly disclosed. The second kind of constraint involves punishment for what has been communicated. A spouse reacts with disgust to what has been said. The voters reject the candidate whose appeals are not effective. Through court action the communicator whose communication has been found improper must pay money damages and/or a fine and/or may suffer imprisonment.

This essay will examine legal constraints on communication. Each nation of the world has developed its own set of rules and customs

The author wishes to acknowledge the assistance received from members of The Speech Communication Association's Commission on Freedom of Speech and in particular the many helpful suggestions offered by Raymond S. Rogers.

regarding the suppression and punishment of communication; this study
will be limited to the United States of America. In the United States these
communication constraints are far more extensive than seems necessary on
the basis of present understanding of the communication process. This
fact will be demonstrated through an examination of the apparent understanding of communication processes by the justices of the Supreme
Court of the United States and illustrations of the application of that
understanding in a variety of situations. These views will then be con-
trasted with those of communication scholars. This comparison leads to
the identification of a number of problems for future study.

The Law's Understanding of Communication

The study of freedom of expression begins with the task of describing
as accurately as possible the legal and social constraints that limit complete freedom of communication. The paradox with which students of
this subject in the United States are forced to deal is the apparent conflict
between principles and reality. The first article of the Bill of Rights
attached to our Constitution in 1791 seems to make freedom of expression
absolute. The simple language says that "Congress shall make no law
. . . abridging freedom of speech or of the press." Other rights granted
in this document are stated in qualified terms such as "unreasonable," "due
process," "speedy," and "excessive." However, the history of litigation
regarding this seeming absolute right has demonstrated that the words,
as judicially interpreted, do not mean what they seem to say. In our legal
system it is the Supreme Court of the United States that has become the
final arbiter of the meaning of the words. Thus an understanding of that
pragmatic meaning must be based upon an examination of the Court's
opinions in the freedom of expression cases that have come before it.
The major cases can be grouped in five areas: 1) efforts to prevent
communication; actions to punish unacceptable communication in the
areas of 2) sedition, 3) libel, and 4) obscenity; and 5) the articulation of
special rules for particular forms of communication.

The process of arriving at conclusions about the extent of freedom
of communication in these several areas demonstrates basic principles
of judicial thinking about commmunication. These principles can be
illustrated through a close examination of the way the techniques of
definition and balancing are used in freedom of expression cases.

The process of definition is one in which the courts decide arbitrarily that some form of communication or come communicators are not protected by the guarantees of the First Amendment. For example, in *Chaplinsky v. New Hampshire* (1942, at 571–572) the Supreme Court observed, "There are certain well-defined and narrowly limited classes of speech, the prevention and punishment of which have never been thought to raise any Constitutional problem. These include the lewd and obscene, the profane, the libelous, and the insulting or 'fighting' words. . . ."

While there are many formulations of this defining process, all clearly rest on a value system that differentiates among communications and communicators. The idea is that some communication is worthwhile and other is not. The list offered in *Chaplinsky* enumerates those communications the content of which the Court in 1942 considered to have no individual or social value. The assertion here is that there has always been agreement that such communication is worthless and thus legitimately punished or suppressed. This assumption, like many of our most basic assumptions, has gone largely unexamined. When conflicts producing examination have arisen, they have focused on the problem of drawing the line between worthless and worthwhile communication. The question of whether there really is such a thing as worthless communication remains unasked.

The assumption that some classes of communicators can be excluded from First Amendment protection has also gone unexamined. The assumption is simply an extension of a principle that has extended throughout our Constitutional history regarding civil liberties. For two centuries courts have ruled that some people may be excluded from the full rights of U.S. citizenship because of age, color, national origin, race, religion, sex, or sexual preference. In the field of freedom of communication age is the principal criterion used by the courts today to place some communication sources outside of the protection of the First Amendment. To paraphrase John Stuart Mill (1859/1947), such communicators lack the maturity of their faculties and therefore their communication can be labeled worthless. A startling recent example of such thinking is the case of *Bethel School District v. Fraser* (1986), in which Chief Justice Warren Burger labeled a gifted senior honor student a "confused boy" in order to justify punishment for a brilliant political speech (at 683).

In the process of balancing, the courts weigh the value of free communication against other social values. For example, in the area of sedition, the courts balance society's right to protect itself against the individual's right to communicate. Various formulas such as the "clear and present danger" test have been used over the years to help determine where the proper balance should be struck.

The underlying assumption in cases where balancing techniques are used is that communication is inherently dangerous and damaging. Such assumptions rest on a push-button model of communication. Simply stated, the idea is that we can draw firm conclusions about the effect or result of communication by looking at its content. It is assumed that communication whose content advocates the overthrow of the government by violent force will lead to that act, or at least the attempt. Since the courts assume that the act is very undesirable, the punishment of such communication is clearly the lesser evil. The assumptions about communication efficacy that underlie the technique of balancing remain unexamined.

With this outline of judicial thinking about communication and freedom of expression it is now possible to turn to the five specific communication areas listed previously and see how these understandings translate themselves into case law.

Prior Restraint

One widely held assumption is that the language of the First Amendment surely means that the government may not legally prevent communication from taking place. However, this assumption, like most assumptions about legal freedom of expression, is only partially true. The record created by the courts is mixed. Major cases seem to lend support to the assumption, while a large number of subsidiary cases point in an opposite direction.

The landmark case in this area, usually referred to as the area of prior restraints, is that of *Near v. Minnesota* (1931). This case arose from the state of Minnesota's response to a scurrilous newspaper called *The Saturday Press,* published in Minneapolis by R. M. Near. This paper was viciously anti-Semitic, its stories and editorials week after week attacking the "Jew gangsters" running Minneapolis and responsible for all the crime in the city. Finally, charges were brought against the paper and its publisher under a Minnesota public nuisance law. The government successfully moved in court to forbid further publication of *The Saturday Press* and any other publication by Near. The state appeals courts upheld this ruling, and Near asked the Supreme Court of the United States to review the case on the grounds that Minnesota was violating his First Amendment rights. In a 5 to 4 decision the Court agreed with Near that the Minnesota law as applied in his case was a prior restraint on communication in violation of the First Amendment. Thus the Court rejected the balance that had been struck by the Minnesota courts between freedom of communication and the elimination of a "public nuisance."

The decision in the Near case is of special interest for several reasons. First, the majority opinion, written by Chief Justice Charles Evans Hughes, states clearly that the First Amendment "guaranty of liberty of the press gives immunity from previous restraints. . . ." Second, the opinion reaffirms the concept of incorporation that had been originally stated in another freedom of expression case six years earlier (*Gitlow v. New York,* 1925). According to this concept, the Fourteenth Amendment to the United States Constitution has the effect of applying the right of freedom of expression to actions of state governments as well those of the federal government. Third, had it not been for two changes in the makeup of the court a year earlier, the decision might well have gone against Near by a vote of 6 to 3. Fred W. Friendly (1981) has provided a full discussion of this possibility as well as a detailed background of the case in his book *Minnesota Rag.* Had the Court ruled against Near, the history of freedom of expression in the United States would have been markedly different: government at all levels would have been able to forbid communication of which it did not approve.

The second landmark case in the area of prior restraint is that known as the "Pentagon Papers" case. In fact, the Supreme Court of the United States considered two cases to arrive at one decision. The first was an appeal by *The New York Times* of a decision by the Second Circuit Court of Appeals in favor of the federal government's attempt at prior restraint; the second was an appeal by the government of a decision in favor of *The Washington Post* by the Fourth Circuit Court of Appeals. Once again the Supreme Court ruled in favor of freedom of expression, this time by a vote of 6 to 3. However, the opinions in this case offer little comfort to those seeking protection from government attempts at prior restraint. Only Justice Hugo Black stated unequivocally that all prior restraints are unconstitutional. Justice William Douglas's opinion left open the possibility of a wartime exception, and Justice William Brennan made this exception explicit. Justice Potter Stewart would expand the exception to include national defense and international diplomacy, while Justice

Byron White would include any material not in "the national interest" (which was undefined) as well. Justice Thurgood Marshall would conclude only that prior restraint was improper in this specific case because Congress had not authorized it. Clearly the six justices of the majority were anything but forceful supporters of freedom of expression. All but Justice Black were willing to balance some societal interest against a claim of freedom to communicate (*New York Times v. United States, United States v. The Washington Post,* 1971). Thus, while the two landmark cases in this area appear to protect expression from prior restraint by government, a close examination of the opinions written in these cases demonstrates how tenuous that protection really is.

In addition there are a number of minor cases dealing with prior restraint. These can generally be characterized as special-situation cases. A recent example is *Hazelwood School District v. Kuhlmeier* (1988), in which a high school principal forbade publication in a student newspaper of articles that he found objectionable. By a vote of 5 to 3, the Supreme Court of the United States reversed the Court of Appeals and upheld the constitutionality of this prior restraint. The fundamental basis for this decision was that an official high school newspaper is a special situation to which the First Amendment does not apply. The reasoning that the Court applied is typical of these cases. The process of definition is used to distinguish between protected and unprotected expression. Thus, by a definition formulated by the Court, the First Amendment does not apply to high school journalists.

Further illustrations of this category are the cases in which the federal government attempts to forbid communication by its employees, particularly those who work for the Central Intelligence Agency. As a condition of employment C.I.A. agents sign a contract granting to the agency the right to review and censor prior to publication anything ever written by the agent. In two cases dealing with former agents James Agee and Frank Snepp, the courts have upheld the validity of these contracts. Here again, by definition, the issue is viewed not as a First Amendment one but rather a simple question of enforcing a contract (*Snepp v. United States,* 1980).

From this group of cases it is possible to conclude that the Supreme Court of the United States has generally decided that government cannot forbid communication from taking place. However, the many exceptions suggested by various justices and those that have been supported by decisions of the Court seem to indicate that this conclusion is less than firmly established. Although the precedent has been established, the language of decisions indicates a willingness to balance the freedom to communicate against a number of other desirable social ends. Given the general deference that the Supreme Court of the United States has shown toward government action in general and the exercise of presidential power in particular, it is not difficult to envision the Court's responding favorably to a forceful claim that damage to the country will result unless communication is suppressed. Furthermore, the Snepp case demonstrates that through defining the issue as something else the Court is willing to authorize government suppression of communication.

Sedition

The second major communication case area is that labeled sedition. Sedition—defined as speaking, acting, or writing against the established government—is a term that is not widely used today. No law naming sedition as a crime has been passed in the United States since the Sedition Act of 1798, which automatically expired in 1800. Nevertheless, prosecutions for what is in effect sedition are numerous enough to be worth noting and have produced some landmark decisions by the Supreme Court of the United States. In these decisions the Court has engaged in the process of balancing individual rights of freedom of expression against the rights of the government to protect itself. In almost every case the rights of the government have been viewed as the more important. The best-known of these cases is *Schenck v. United States* (1919). This case arose out of the prosecution of Charles Schenck for violating the Espionage Act of 1917 by advocating draft resistance during World War I. While Schenck's communication crime clearly fits the definition of sedition, the Court accepted the Congressional claim that the activity constituted wartime espionage. This case is the one in which Justice Oliver Wendell Holmes first stated the idea that communication could be a crime if there was a "clear and present danger that will bring about the substantive evil that Congress has a right to prevent" (*Schenck v. United States,* at 52). This doctrine was used to send Schenck to prison, even though the facts of the case suggested that Schenck's pamphleting was substantially less than a "clear and present danger" to the country's military effort. This decision, sustaining the conviction of Schenck, a leader of the Socialist Party in the United States, was followed in short order by other decisions

upholding Espionage Act convictions of those on the political left, including Jacob Abrams and Socialist Party presidential candidate Eugene V.
Debs.

Among the laws used to justify sedition prosecutions of those on
the left was the New York State criminal anarchy statute that made it a
crime to teach "that organized government should be overthrown by force
or violence . . . . The advocacy of such doctrine either by word of
mouth or writing is a felony." The language of this statute criminalized
communication alone, without reference to any physical acts. Benjamin
Gitlow, who was convicted under this law for publishing 16,000 socialist
pamphlets, appealed his conviction which was sustained by the Supreme
Court of the United States (*Gitlow v. New York,* 1925). While the
continued suppression of left wing thought is not noteworthy, this case
did produce an important advance for freedom of expression in that the
Court used this case to establish the doctrine of incorporation. The First
Amendment, "*Congress* shall make no law. . . ," is silent regarding what
state governments may do in this area. However, in the Gitlow case the
Supreme Court recognized that the Fourteenth Amendment's due process
clause made the First Amendment guarantee applicable to state as well
as federal action. This principle was the one used to reverse the conviction
of R. M. Near in *Near v. Minnesota.*

The next major group of sedition prosecutions, following World
War II, were those based on a law usually identified as the Smith Act of
1940. This statute clearly stated that communication advocating the
overthrow of the government of the United States by force was criminal.
The law had been drafted to criminalize the teachings of members of the
Communist Party in the United States. The first major prosecution came
during the height of the Cold War, in 1948, when Eugene Dennis
and ten other leaders of the Communist Party were convicted for this
communication crime. The constitutionality of the Smith Act and these
convictions were upheld by the Supreme Court in *Dennis v. United States*
(1951). However, the vigorous dissenting opinions of Justices Hugo
Black and William O. Douglas eventually prevailed, and by 1957 almost
all of the Smith Act had been declared unconstitutional (*Yates v. United
States,* 1957).

The most recent consideration of sedition by the Supreme Court is
one of the few cases dealing with far-right- rather than left-wing politics.
This 1969 case arose from the conviction of Clarence Brandenburg, a Ku
Klux Klan leader, for violating the Ohio criminal syndicalism law that

made it a crime to advocate political change by "unlawful methods." His speech to a group of followers had been recorded and broadcast by a television news team. In an unanimous, unsigned opinion the Court reversed this conviction and stated a new test for criminally seditious communication. Rather than "clear and present danger," the prosecution would need to prove that the "advocacy is directed to inciting or producing imminent lawless action and is likely to incite or produce such action" (*Brandenburg v. Ohio,* 1969).

Over the fifty years considered here sedition prosecution has largely been used to silence left-wing political advocacy. As this area of law has evolved, the Court has come to enunciate two very important protections for political communication. First, the Court clearly established and has repeatedly reaffirmed that the constitutional guarantee of freedom of expression is a protection against state as well as federal acts of suppression. Second, the level of proof needed for successful prosecution of seditious communication has been substantially tightened to the standard that exists today—clear proof that the communication will result in an imminent lawless act likely to occur.

Defamation

The third group of court cases dealing with communication to be considered consists of those dealing with defamation. Defamation is the general legal term for what is popularly identified as libel and covers both the written word (libel) and the spoken word (slander). Although libel was included in the *Chaplinsky* list of communications excluded by definition from Constitutional protection, actual Court decisions in this area have depended on the technique of balancing. Communication that can lead to a successful suit for damages must have the following characteristics: 1) it must be communicated to some third party, 2) it must identify a person or persons or business, and 3) it must contain false information that injures the person or group identified.

The central issue in libel suits in recent decades has been that of fault, the kind of mistake that a communicator has made that led to the communication of false information. Strict liability rules can lead to a judgment against the communicator for any mistake, regardless of how accidental or unintended. Negligence as a standard for liability is commonly defined as failure to take the care that would be expected of the

average prudent person. The fault standard of gross irresponsibility allows
for even greater carelessness. Finally, there is the standard that the courts
call malice, which does not mean hatred, but rather the communication
of known falsehoods or with reckless disregard for whether the communication is true or false.

Since it is obvious that each of these four standards of fault places
a different burden of proof on the person claiming to be libeled and
each provides a different degree of protection to the communicator, the
question of which standard should apply becomes a critical question in
libel suits. Defamation case law has attempted to answer this question
by determining the qualities of those to whom these different standards
apply. On the theory that accidental errors in communication are inevitable, the fault standard of strict liability has been virtually abandoned.
The area of controversy today is in large part confined to the differences
between negligence and malice, and it is this controversy that has been
addressed by a series of major cases decided by the Supreme Court of the
United States.

The landmark libel case is that of *The New York Times v. Sullivan,*
decided in 1964. This case arose from a suit filed against *The New York
Times* by Montgomery, Alabama, Commissioner L. B. Sullivan, who
claimed that he had been libeled by an ad placed in *The Times* by a group
of supporters of Martin Luther King, Jr. The ad was critical of Southern
white political leadership for racist government policies. The ad, which
did not mention Commissioner Sullivan, contained four minor errors of
fact. The Alabama trial court judge instructed the jury that *The Times*
could be held responsible for any error and that it could assume that the
ad was about Commissioner Sullivan since it mentioned a governmental
agency for which he was responsible. The jury was told that if it found
the statements to be false it could also assume injury even though no
evidence of injury had been presented. On the basis of these instructions
the jury gave Commissioner Sullivan the largest libel damage award in
Alabama court history.

The appeals by *The New York Times* in this case eventually reached
the Supreme Court of the United States, which set aside the verdict and
award against *The Times.* The opinion in this case, written by Justice
Brennan, enunciated a new standard for determining fault in a specific
class of cases. Brennan identified Sullivan as a public official whose official
conduct was being criticized and concluded that such a person must prove
that a defamatory falsehood has been communicated with knowledge that

it is false or with reckless disregard for its truth or falsity—the malice standard of fault. Since there was no proof of knowing falsehood or reckless disregard in this case, The Times was exonerated.

The central question left open by the decision of the Supreme Court in *The New York Times v. Sullivan* was, To whom does the malice standard of fault apply? Since 1964, in a series of cases, the Court has attempted to answer this question. From its initial application to public officials, the application of the malice standard was expanded to include celebrities and other public persons (*Curtis Publishing Company v. Butts, Associated Press v. Walker,* 1967) and eventually included virtually anyone whose name might appear in the news—any newsworthy person (*Rosenbloom v. Metromedia,* 1971). Finally, after ten years of struggle with the issue, the Court arrived at a formula for determining which people must prove reckless disregard or knowing falsehood in order to be awarded damages. In *Gertz v. Welch* (1974) the Court defined a public person as one who thrusts her/himself into the vortex of public affairs and/or attempts to influence the outcome of public policy controversy. Using this formula, the Court also said that someone could be a public person for some matters and still be a private person for other matters. Finally, the Court added that even a private person must prove reckless disregard or knowing falsehood—that is, malice—in order to receive punitive damages beyond compensation for that actual damage that the false statements caused.

Because the standards of proof required for public and private persons are substantially different, a central issue in many defamation cases is whether the plaintiff should be considered a public or private person. Clearly, the communicator of the alleged defamation would like everyone who sues to be a public person, while those who sue often claim to be private persons. Application of the Gertz rules has not been a simple matter, and the Supreme Court has dealt with a series of cases in an effort to clarify this application of the rules (*Hutchinson v. Proxmire,* 1979; *Time, Inc. v. Firestone,* 1976; *Wolston v. Reader's Digest Association,* 1979). The general conclusion that can be drawn from the Court's opinions in these cases is that the rules are to be strictly applied. Public persons are really those who thrust themselves into current public controversies as opposed to being drawn into them.

While the Sullivan and Gertz decisions by the Supreme Court of the United States established who was a public person and the level of proof of fault that such a person must provide, state courts and legislatures remain free to establish levels of proof of fault for private persons. The negligence standard is common, but a number of states have adopted more rigid proof-of-fault requirements. For example, the New Jersey Supreme Court has adopted the reckless disregard or knowing falsehood (malice) standard for private as well as public plaintiffs. The New York State Court of Appeals has enunciated a gross irresponsibility standard that, while undefined, appears to be very much like the malice standard, even though the Court of Appeals said that the two are different.

The fact that these standards are confusing and subject to individual judgment is nowhere better illustrated than in the case of *Tavoulareas v. The Washington Post* (1983). In this case William Tavoulareas and his son Peter sued *The Washington Post* for stories that discussed business favors done for Peter by William as president of Mobil Oil. The trial court judge ruled that William was a public person but that Peter was a private person. The jury gave a defamation award to William but not Peter, a verdict that the trial court judge set aside as contrary to the evidence. A survey of the jurors after the trial showed that they had not understood the judge's instructions about levels of fault that must be proven by these two different types of plaintiffs (Brill, 1982). The jury had somehow reached the conclusion that a higher level of proof was needed by the private person than was needed by the public person—the exact opposite of the legal principle that the judge had explained. While, as Brill reveals, the jury was led astray by its foreman, who incorrectly interpreted the judge's instructions, this case demonstrates the complexity of detail that is a part of much freedom of communication study. Basic principles can be stated with clarity, but their application in specific situations may be far more complex. Nowhere is that complexity more pronounced than in the area of libel. It is for this reason that commentators such as Haiman (1981) and Smolla (1986) have called for major restructuring of the law in this area.

Two highly publicized cases illuminate a final problem in the area of defamation—the political use of libel suits. These two cases are *Westmoreland v. CBS* (1984) and *Sharon v. Time* (1983). In both cases the plaintiffs were clearly public persons, and in both the evidence was clearly insufficient to prove knowing falsehoods or reckless disregard for whether the information was true or not. The two trials established that, in spite of carefully checking, *Time* had made a relatively minor factual error in a cover story about Ariel Sharon; and that the CBS broadcast about William Westmoreland was basically true. Since neither plaintiff had a realistic chance of winning his suit, the motive for suing lay elsewhere.

For Sharon, the goal was to salvage some political reputation after the government of Israel released an investigative report that found Sharon bore responsibility for the killing of civilians in refugee camps in Beirut, Lebanon. The Westmoreland suit had been solicited by a right-wing legal group that sought to punish CBS by forcing it to spend millions to defend itself against the meritless suit.

Thus, in the area of defamation the courts of the United States have sought to strike a balance between a communicator's right to spread information and the individual's right to protect reputation and to receive financial compensation when false statements have damaged that reputation. Simple errors are generally tolerated. A private person must show that the communicator has not exercised due care in checking the facts. People who thrust themselves into public controversy and/or seek to influence public policy thereby become public persons and must prove that the communicator knowingly published falsehoods or showed a reckless disregard for whether the information was true or false. In spite of what would seem to be an appropriate balance, defamation suits are still used as an improper means of punishing communication.

Obscenity

The fourth area to be considered in this review of what we know about legal constraints on communication is that of obscenity. Here, as the *Chaplinsky* list suggests, the basic decision-making technique of the Supreme Court of the United States is that of definition. In all the cases considered in this area, the Court seeks to establish and apply definitions to decide what is and is not obscene. Although the language of the First Amendment appears to allow no exception, Justice Brennan, writing for the majority of the Court in *Roth v. United States* (1957, at 481), observed "that this Court has always assumed that obscenity is not protected by the freedoms of speech and press." Given this majority position, the problem is to determine the difference between protected nonobscene communication and unprotected obscene communication. This problem is one that the Court has considered in a substantial body of cases and has not yet resolved.

In the Roth case the majority opinion by Justice Brennan made the first modern attempt to define the difference between what is and is not obscene. This definition was embodied in what has come to be known as the *Roth test*. According to this test, the material was obscene if "to the average person, applying contemporary community standards, the dominant theme of the material taken as a whole appeals to prurient interest" (*Roth v. United States,* at 489). Although this test clearly broadened protection for communication with sexual content, its inherent vagueness and subjectivity are easy to recognize. Confusing the matter still further, Brennan had early in this opinion placed the whole question of obscenity in the context that "all ideas having even the slightest redeeming social importance" are protected by the First Amendment (*Roth v. United States,* at 484).

Ever since Roth the Supreme Court has been trying without great success to clarify the distinction between obscene and nonobscene communication. These efforts to improve and refine the verbal formulas provoked one justice, Potter Stewart, to comment, "I shall not today attempt further to define [obscenity]. . .; and perhaps I could never succeed in intelligibly doing so. But I know it when I see it, and the motion picture involved in this case is not that" (*Jacobellis v. Ohio,* 1964, at 197). Justice Stewart's exasperated comment directs attention to one of the major problems with the Court's attempts at definition: It is impossible to say for certain what is or is not obscene until after the justices of the Supreme Court have seen it and arrived at their individual subjective conclusions.

One attempt to deal with this problem of vagueness and subjectivity can be found in *Ginzburg v. United States* (1966). Following a suggestion that had been repeatedly made by Chief Justice Earl Warren in obscenity cases, the Court majority decided to look at the apparent intent of the communicator rather than the content of the communication. The Court looked at Ginzburg's promotional activities for his publications, including attempts to secure mailing permits from the villages of Intercourse and Blue Ball in Pennsylvania, and concluded that he intended his audience to believe that the materials he was selling were obscene. This approach eliminated the subjective evaluation of one body of communication but required the vague and subjective evaluation of a second.

Finally, in 1973, a different group of justices of the Supreme Court attempted still another refinement of the Roth test in *Miller v. California.* Writing for the Court majority, Chief Justice Warren Burger stated the new *Miller test* as follows: The basic guidelines for the trier of fact must be: (a) whether "the average person, applying contemporary community standards" would find the work, taken as a whole, appeals to prurient interest . . . , (b) whether the work depicts or describes, in a patently offensive way, sexual conduct specifically defined by the applicable state law, and (c) whether the work, taken as a whole, lacks serious literary, artistic, political, or scientific value (*Miller v. California,* 1973, at 24). Justice Burger also added the explanation that community standards were to be interpreted as local community standards.

While some of the language of this formulation was different from that of the Roth test, it is still clear than this formulation does not resolve the problems of vagueness and subjectivity. This fact was underlined by the forceful dissenting opinion written by Justice Brennan in a companion case to *Miller (Paris Adult Theatre I v. Slaton,* 1973). He asserted that his efforts in Roth and all subsequent cases (including Miller) failed to resolve this problem. He rejected both greater suppression of communication with sexual content and the elimination of all laws in this area. In this situation he advocated the adoption of the recommendations that appeared in a 1970 report by a presidential commission that had spent three years studying the problem of communication with sexual content (*Paris Adult Theatre I v. Slaton,* at 60). The effect of these recommendations would be the elimination of all laws restricting communication with sexual content among consenting adults.

The lack of clarity in determining what is or is not obscene has been further complicated by Court opinions that have made obscenity a function of circumstances and made possible the punishment and suppression of material that the Court agrees is not legally obscene. Obscenity convictions can be sustained on the basis of the nature of the communication audience (*Ginsberg v. New York,* 1968) or the medium of communication (*Federal Communications Commission v. Pacifica Foundation,* 1978). In addition some indecent communication can be criminalized even though it cannot be clearly defined and is not legally obscene (*New York v. Ferber,* 1982; *Bethel School District v. Fraser,* 1986).

In the United States many groups and individuals feel threatened and/or distressed that others may have access to sexually explicit communication of which they do not approve. The result has been ongoing legal action against such communication, so that the Supreme Court of the United States has been forced to try to define which communication can be criminalized and which cannot. As this brief review has shown, from 1957 to the present this effort has been largely unsuccessful. In fact, the situation has become more rather than less confused. On the basis of all this litigation it is impossible to say today exactly what sexually explicit communication can be criminalized.

Commercial Speech and Broadcasts

Finally, there are those areas where special rules have been developed for particular forms of communication. The two special rule areas to be considered here are those of commercial speech and broadcasting. In both of these areas the rule development process begins with defining these forms of communication as special ones not subject to the normal application of First Amendment principles. Commercial communication has been one of those forms that the Supreme Court of the United States has generally recognized as not subject to constitutional protection. The broad range of government regulation of commercial communication, through a variety of regulatory agencies such as the Federal Trade Commission and the Securities and Exchange Commission, has withstood constitutional challenges. As early as 1915 (*Mutual Film Corp. v. Industrial Commission of Ohio*), the Supreme Court clearly stated that commercial communication was not protected by the First Amendment. However, in a series of cases beginning with *Bigelow v. Virginia* (1975), the Court began to extend constitutional protection to commercial communication. They decided that pharmacies and lawyers could not be forbidden to advertise prices and services (*Virginia State Board of Pharmacy v. Virginia Citizens Consumer Council,* 1976; *Bates v. State Bar of Arizona,* 1977) and that corporate advertising on public issues could not be restricted (*First National Bank of Boston v. Bellotti,* 1978).

This established pattern of expanding protection for commercial speech was called into question by the Supreme Court's decision in *Posadas de Puerto Rico v. Tourism Company* (1986). At issue in this case was a Puerto Rico law that prohibited gambling casinos from advertising in any communication medium aimed as residents of Puerto Rico. Chief Justice William Rehnquist, writing for a five-justice majority in this case, argued that since Puerto Rico could legally ban casino gambling it certainly could constitutionally limit advertising, even though the activity being advertised was legal. The implication of Rehnquist's position is that communication concerning any product or service that government might legally regulate may also be regulated, restricted, or banned.

Broadcast communication is another area in which special rules have evolved. The basic premise underlying the regulation of broadcasting is that the broadcast communicator is using leased public property, the airwaves, as the channel of communication. On this grounds Congress has passed laws establishing performance standards for broadcasters, and the Supreme Court has upheld these laws (*Red Lion Broadcasting Co. v. Federal Communications Commission,* 1969). The two most significant areas of broadcast communication regulation are political communication and the discussion of controversial issues. The regulations on political communication are relatively straightforward: All candidates for office must be treated the same by the broadcaster, who may not interfere with the candidates' communication. If the broadcaster provides air time without charge, it must be equal for all candidates, with the major exception of broadcasts identified as bona fide news events. The same terms and conditions for purchasing air time must be available to all candidates.

The present status of the so-called fairness doctrine regulating broadcasting on controversial issues is unclear. In *Red Lion* the Supreme Court upheld the constitutionality of the regulations. Many in Congress assumed that the regulations were part of the broadcast communication law. However, the Federal Communications Commission, abandoning its statutory role of trustee for the public at large, rescinded these regulations. To recodify the fairness doctrine Congress passed new legislation that was vetoed by President Ronald Reagan. Suits have been filed, and the issue is now in the courts.

The regulations being contested place on broadcasters an affirmative obligation to include in their programming, communication dealing with matters of significant public controversy. They are required to do so in a balanced manner, hence the term fairness. On the question of balance the FCC and the courts have always taken an expansive view, looking at overall programming patterns rather than a single broadcast or stopwatch measurement of broadcasting time. Only in the area of the personal-attack rule are the regulations quite specific. Here the broadcaster must notify promptly a person attacked and make available equivalent time to reply.

Recapitulation: Interpretations of the First Amendment

The foregoing review of what we know about present legal constraints on communication has considered prior restraint and the punishment of unacceptable communication. Even though the language of the first article of the Bill of Rights seems to protect all communication, the Supreme Court of the United States has said this view is not correct. Although most of us are free to communicate, the Court has determined that there are large classes of communicators whose communication can be prohibited, that there are a number of situations in which such prohibitions are appropriate, and that regulations may be placed on time, place, and manner of communication. As First Amendment absolutist Justice Hugo Black put it, "It is a myth to say that any person has a constitutional right to say what he pleases, where he pleases, and when he pleases. Our Court has decided precisely the opposite" (*Tinker v. Des Moines School District,* 1968, at 522). In general the courts have recognized the right of government to place reasonable restrictions on time, place, and manner of communication, providing that such regulations are administered in an equitable and content-neutral manner for all who seek to communicate.

In addition broad classes of communication can be punished. Today there is substantial but not complete protection for threatening statements made against the government. The real problem in this area continues to be the relationship between communication and action. For example, in the trial of a group of white supremacists who were accused of a large number of criminal acts, the defense claimed that the prosecution was based on communication rather than physical acts. One of the admitted "political heretics" said in his defense, "I was under the impression that I could say what I wanted to say" (Bishop, 1988). The government was apparently unable to persuade the trial jury that the defendants had committed criminal acts, and they were all acquitted.

The punishment of communication in the areas of defamation and obscenity presents many problems. For defamatory communication the problems lie in the area of the subject of the communication. Different levels of care apply to communication about people with different public status. In addition, the "malicious" use of libel statutes is an ongoing concern. Distinguishing with any precision obscene communication from nonobscene communication has been a problem that to date the Supreme Court of the United States has been unable to solve.

Special rules have been developed to deal with special forms of communication. In the two areas considered here, commercial communication and broadcasting, established and settled principles have recently been called into question. The expanding constitutional protection for commercial communication has been placed in some doubt by the Supreme Court's reversal of position in *Posadas de Puerto Rico v. Tourism Company* (1986). This decision seems to indicate that the Court will once again accept tightened control on commercial communication.

In contrast, the FCC has moved to ease some of the restrictions on communications by broadcasters. While equal time rules for political candidates remain in force, the status of the fairness doctrine is unclear. If the present position of the FCC is sustained, broadcasters will no longer be required to communicate on controversial issues or to do so in a balanced manner.

In addition to providing a catalog of Court-determined rules for permissible communication, the foregoing review provides an insight to judicial understanding of communication. First, the Supreme Court of the United States has imposed a value system on communication. Some communication is defined as worthwhile and granted First Amendment protection, while other, worthless communication is denied that protection. Personally offensive words, commercial communication, and some sexually explicit messages, particularly visual ones, can be punished or restricted because they are worthless. Regardless of the content of the message, some communication can be punished because of its source. In particular the age of the communicator can be taken into consideration to determine whether the communication has value and should be protected.

Second, the Court also uses a value system balancing the individual's right to communicate against other social values. Underlying this balancing process is a push-button view of communication that assumes direct effect based on the content of the communication. The claim is made that some undesirable action will result from the communication. The Court then decides whether national security requires the suppression of communication or the degree to which seemingly defamatory statements should be protected as a necessary component of political discourse.

What We Believe

The beliefs of communication scholars regarding legal and social constraints have been clearly stated in the "Credo for Free and Responsible Communication in a Democratic Society" adopted as a formal policy statement by the Speech Communication Association in 1972. The full text of that statement is as follows:

> Recognizing the essential place of free and responsible communication in a democratic society, and recognizing the distinction between the freedoms our legal system should respect and the responsibilities our educational

system should cultivate, we members of the Speech Communication Association endorse the following statement of principles:

We believe that freedom of speech and assembly must hold a central position
among American constitutional principles, and we express our determined support for the right of peaceful expression by any means
available.

We support the proposition that a free society can absorb with equanimity
speech which exceeds the boundaries of generally accepted beliefs
and mores; that much good and little harm can ensue if we err on
the side of freedom, whereas much harm and little good may follow
if we err on the side of suppression.

We criticize as misguided those who believe that the justice of their cause
confers license to interfere physically and coercively with the speech
of others, and we condemn intimidation, whether by powerful major-
ities or strident minorities, which attempts to restrict free expression.

We accept the responsibility of cultivating by precept and example, in our
classrooms and in our communities, enlightened uses of communication; of developing in our students a respect for precision and accuracy
in communication, and for reasoning based upon evidence and a
judicious discrimination among values.

We encourage our students to accept the role of well-informed and articulate
citizens, to defend the communication rights of those with whom
they may disagree, and to expose abuses of the communication
process.

We dedicate ourselves fully to these principles, confident in the belief that
reason will ultmately prevail in a free marketplace of ideas (*spectra*,
1973).

The final sentence in this statement of principles makes explicit the
philosophy that underlies the statement—the concept of a free marketplace of ideas. This concept views the basic purpose of freedom of
communication as the provision of as broad a diversity of views as possible,
so that every individual can make fully informed decisions in all areas of
human thought and activity. As is the case with the "perfect" economic
market, it is recognized that such an ideal does not really exist. However,
as with the perfect economic market, the free marketplace of ideas is an
ideal that can be used to measure the desirability of communication
policies. The S.C.A. Credo is meant to provide a precise measuring
instrument. As Franklyn Haiman (1981) observes, "Reliance is placed
on a free marketplace of ideas trusting that, even if the wisest decisions
do not always emerge victorious, the likelihood is greater of approximat-

ing truth and avoiding the most serious errors when communication is free than when it is restricted" (p. 7).

Support for the concept of a marketplace of ideas rests on a rejection of a push-button model of communication. Response to communication is the result of a large number of factors in addition to the content of that communication, and one of the more important factors is other communication. We select among competing messages those that we find most compatible with our existing attitudes, knowledge, and values. Only when a single message is allowed in the marketplace to the exclusion of all others can the push-button model have any validity.

The S. C. A. Credo also expresses a careful awareness of the difference between the symbolic activity of communication and physical acts. There is a difference between advocacy of an act and performing the act. When communication is followed by criminal activity, responsibility for the activity rests with those who undertake it.

The question of the locus of personal responsibility is one dealt with in the Credo and our understanding of the communication process. Haiman (1981) notes, "Words and pictures per se do not do injury. It is the meaning and values with which they are endowed by those who see or hear them that may cause pleasure or pain and that is a *symbolic* [Haiman's emphasis] transaction mediated through consciousness" (pp. 20–21). The semanticists frequently observe that meanings are in people rather than words. In sum, this statement of belief by communication scholars shows a sophisticated awareness of the complexity of the communication process, an awareness evidently not shared by the justices of the Supreme Court of the United States.

What Are the Problems?

The gap between the current status of freedom of expression in the United States, as shown in the review of Supreme Court decisions, and the statement of what the Speech Communication Association believes about freedom of expression illuminates the current problems in this area. In many areas real communication activities depart significantly from the ideal model. The causes of these departures can be identified as financial, ideological, and legal.

Financial limitations on the effective working of a free marketplace of ideas are easy to see. One of the conclusions of Jerome Barron's *Freedom of the Press for Whom?* (1973) is that freedom of the press belongs only to those who own the press. It is obvious that the average person does not have the access to the public that the publishers of *The New York Times* or *The Washington Post* do. All voices do not have equal opportunity to be heard because economic power can control access to the marketplace of ideas just as it controls access to the marketplace for other goods. Robin Wood (1986) forcefully makes this point when he observes, "A culture committed to freedom of speech but built on money and private enterprise has a very simple means of repressing the former by using the latter, with no inconvenient or disturbing sense of hypocrisy" (p. 212).

Some owners of major information sources have recognized that their positions of special privilege can create special responsibilities for maintaining the marketplace of ideas. This philosophy can be seen in the policy of some newspapers of unrestricted acceptance of editorial advertising so that many voices can be heard. While commendable, such action is only a partial redress of the balance. First, the press has no legal obligation to accept editorial advertising (*Chicago Joint Board, Amalgamated Clothing Workers of America v. Chicago Tribune,* 1970). Second, an editorial ad can never realistically carry the same weight as a news story or regular editorial. Third, even where unrestricted access exists, ads cost money that not all communicators have. Thus, it is clear that financial considerations do create barriers that inhibit the operation of the marketplace of ideas.

The ideological constraints on the free marketplace of ideas are perhaps more numerous and in some ways more difficult to identify than the financial constraints. For example, as just noted, publishers can and do reject editorial advertising whose content they find ideologically objectionable. Over the years various legislative bodies have criminalized communication that the legislators found iedologically objectionable. Many religious groups require strict ideological conformity of their members, prohibit communication that does not conform, and enforce that prohibition through the expulsion of those whose communication is considered ideologically improper. For example, Sonia Johnson, a leader in the Mormons for ERA (the Equal Rights Amendment) movement, was excommunicated from her church because the church hierarchy opposed the idea of equal rights for women (Jensen, 1983).

Other ideological constraints are far more subtle. The society in which we live can play a significant role in conditioning its members to reject any communication that does not conform with the prevailing ideology of that society. In fact, for many people certain ideas are literally unthinkable. Many institutions, but in particular the schools, play a role in the ideological indoctrination that is often described as socialization. The ongoing battles across the country regarding the ideological content of school curricula are clear recognition of the crucial role of the schools in this process. School board responses to these pressures have not been encouraging. In an effort to avoid problems critical and controversial ideas are removed from texts and curricula; the result has been increased ideological conformity and decreased freedom in the marketplace of ideas. For example, in an effort to avoid the anger of religious fundamentalists, school boards and textbook publishers purged the word *evolution* from junior high and high school biology texts, even though evolution is the fundamental organizing principle of the science. Even after years of counterpressure from the scientific community, the treatment of evolution in most texts is only marginally adequate.

The social constriction of ideological vision is the central issue addressed by Herbert Marcuse (1964, 1969) in the book *One-Dimensional Man* and the essay "Repressive Tolerance." Many who might agree with Marcuse's analysis of the way in which society represses communication so as to prevent free and autonomous thinking are nevertheless unwilling to accept Marcuse's proposed solution—the systematic suppression of all communication that interferes with the promotion of a truly free marketplace for all ideas. Seeing no further than Marcuse's proposal to suppress communication, may students of freedom of expression reject his ideas out of hand. What goes unnoticed is Marcuse's belief in the marketplace of ideas. However, his analysis leads him to the conclusion that this marketplace has been so completely corrupted that only radical restructuring can save it. Even though his solution may be unpalatable, Marcuse deserves recognition for his detailed analysis of our society's ideologically based interference with the marketplace of ideas.

Many of the legal restraints on the free operation of the marketplace of ideas have been detailed previously. The difficulty with many of these restraints is that they are based on concepts of communication that are not consistent with communication scholars' understanding of the process. This fundamental point has been explored in depth by William E. Bailey (1981) in an award winning study that first appeared in the *Free Speech Yearbook 1980*. Bailey points out that the opinions of the Supreme Court of the United States in communication cases view the communication process as a mechanistic injection of communication into an audience that responds predictably to the stimulus. This model obviously ignores the many variables other than the communication that have significant effect upon audience response to that communication.

On the basis of years of study the communication scholar knows that the Court's concept of communication is dead wrong. However, the cases discussed previously provide repeated examples of the application of this false concept. So-called obscene communication is viewed as dangerous and therefore criminal because it causes antisocial behavior. Advocates of draft resistance can be punished because the targets of their communication are seen as incapable of resisting this communication.

In addition, there are very real philosophical and theoretical problems regarding personal responsibility for actions. The philosophical issue is that if we act in a lawless manner after being urged to do so, should we not be responsible for that action rather than the communicator who urged the action? To blame the communicator for the illegal action is to abrogate the principle of personal responsibility, and that is precisely what the Court does when it upholds the conviction of those who advocate the overthrow of the government. The principle of personal responsibility should direct legal action against those who act to overthrow the government rather than those who advocate such action. Theoretically, most rulings are at odds with our carefully developed and documented knowledge of communication as a complex reciprocal exchange of information among more or less willing communicators.

The principle of a free marketplace of ideas offers additional direction for dealing with the legal constraints on communication. This principle has been eloquently stated by Haiman (1981), who argues that the best solution to bad communication is more and better communication. With this principle Haiman has confronted the legal morass of defamation with the simple idea that legal action for defamation should be prohibited if a right to reply has been granted. If the person defamed is given the opportunity to present her/his case in the publication in which the alleged defamation appeared, no legal action would be allowed. In a similar manner communication advocating violent and illegal action is best answered by more communication that shows the error in such action. In the area of obscenity Haiman is joined by Surgeon General C. Everett Koop, who has concluded that the best answer to obscenity is education in media literacy (Office of the Surgeon General, 1986). The Surgeon General's report on obscenity recommends that schools teach the nature and function of mass communication and appropriate ways to interpret and use such communication.

Summary

This essay has looked at the present state of the law of freedom of expression to determine what we know about this subject. What we believe about freedom of expression has been clearly stated in the Credo of the Speech Communication Association. The problems lie in the marked gap between what we know and what we believe. Communication scholars are making a contribution to the closing of this gap by calling attention to the judiciary's faulty understanding of the communication process and the need for education in this area. Franklyn Haiman's *Speech and Law in a Free Society* (1981) is being read by the legal community and has received a Silver Gavel award from the American Bar Association. S. C. A. is a participating organization in the National Coalition Against Censorship and in this capacity has participated in preparing briefs submitted to the Supreme Court of the United States in major freedom of communication cases. Surgeon General Koop's recommendations on obscenity reflect the influence of communication scholars. While much more can and should be done, recommendations for dealing with "bad" communication have been offered that, if adopted, will contribute to reconciling the freedom of communication facts and our beliefs.

References

Bailey, W. (1981). The Supreme Court and communication theory: Contrasting models of speech efficacy. *Free Speech Yearbook 1980, 20.* 1–15.

Barron, J. A. (1973) *Freedom of the press for whom?* Bloomington, IN: Indiana University Press.

Barron, J. A., & Dienes, T. C. (1979). *Handbook of free speech and free press.* Boston: Little, Brown.

Bates v. State Bar of Arizona, 433 U.S. 350 (1977).

Bethel School District v. Fraser, 478 U.S. 675 (1986).

Bigelow v. Virginia, 421 U.S. 809 (1975).

Bishop, K. (1988, February 19). White supremacists at trial, charge persecution of beliefs. *The New York Times,* p. A13.

Bosmajian, H. A. (Ed.). (1976) *Obscenity and freedom of expression.* New York: Burt Franklin.

Brandenburg v. Ohio, 395 U.S. 444 (1969).

Brill, S. (1982, November). Inside the jury room at the *Washington Post* libel trial. *The American Lawyer, 1.* 88–94.

Chafee, Z., Jr. (1941). *Free speech in the United States,* Cambridge, MA: Harvard University Press.

Chaplinsky v. New Hamshire, 315 U.S. 568 (1942).

Chicago Joint Board, Amalgamated Clothing Workers of America v. Chicago Tribune, 307 F.2d 470 (1970).

Commission on Obscenity and Pornography (1970). *Report of the commission on obscenity and pornography.* Washington, D.C: U.S. Government Printing Office.

Cox, A. (1981) *Freedom of expression.* Cambridge, MA: Harvard University Press.

Credo for free and responsible communication in a democratic society. 1973, April). *spectra.* p. 5.

Curtis Publishing Company v. Butts, Associated Press v. Walker, 388 U.S. 130 (1967).

DeGrazia, E., & Newman, R. (1982) *Banned films,* New York: Bowker.

Dennis v. United States, 341 U.S. 494 (1951).

Emerson, T.I. (1966). *Toward a general theory of the first amendment.* New York: Random House.

Emerson, T.I. (1970). *The system of freedom of expression.* New York: Random House.

Federal Communications Commission v. Pacifica Foundation, 438 U.S. 726 (1978).

First National Bank of Boston v. Bellotti, 435 U.S. 765 (1978).

Fowler, D.G. (1977). *Unmailable: Congress and the Post Office.* Athens, GA: University of Georgia Press.

Friendly, F. W. (1975). *The good guys, the bad guys, and the First Amendment,* New York: Random House.

Friendly, F. W. (1981) *Minnesota rag: The dramatic story of the landmark Supreme Court case that gave new meaning to freedom of the press.* New York:Random House.

Gertz v. Robert Welch, Inc., 418 U.S. 323 (1974).

Ginsberg v. New York, 390 U.S. 629 (1968).

Ginzburg v. United States, 383 U.S. 463 (1966).

Gitlow v. New York, 268 U.S. 652 (1925).

Haiman, F.S. (1981). *Speech and law in a free society,* Chicago: University of Chicago Press.

Hazelwood School District v. Kuhlmeier, 56 LW 4079 (1988).

Hentoff, N. (1980). *The first freedom.* New York: Delacorte Press.

Hutchinson v. Proxmire, 443 U.S. 111 (1979).

Jacobellis v. Ohio, 378 U.S. 184 (1964).

Jenkinson, E. B. (1979) *Censors in the classroom.* Carbondale, IL: Southern Illinois University Press.

Jensen R. J. (1983). Freedom of expression: The Mormons for ERA. *Free Speech Yearbook. 1982, 23,* 1–14.

Kane P. E. (1986). M*urder, courts, and the press.* Carbondale, IL: Southern Illinois University Press.

Kurland P. B. (Ed.). (1976). *Free speech and association: The Supreme Court and the first amendment.* Chicago: University of Chicago Press.

Levy, L. W. (Ed.). (1966). *Freedom of the press from Zenger to Jefferson.* Indianapolis: Bobbs-Merrill.

Levy, L. W. (1985). *Emergence of a free press.* New York: Oxford University Press.

Lofton, J. (1980). *The press as guardian of the first amendment.* Columbia, SC: University of South Carolina Press.

Marcuse, H. (1964). *One-dimensional man.* Boston: Beacon Press.

Marcuse, H. (1969). Repressive tolerance. In *A critique of pure tolerance* (pp. 81–123). Boston: Beacon Press.

McCoy, R. E. (1968). *Freedom of the press: An annotated bibliography.* Carbondale, IL: Southern Illinois University Press.

McCoy, R. E. (1979). *Freedom of the press: Ten-year supplement (1967–1977).* Carbondale, IL: Southern Illinois University Press.

Mill, J.S. (1947). *On liberty.* New York: Appleton-Century-Crofts. (Original work published 1859.)

Miller v. California, 413 U.S 15 (1973).

Mutual Film Corporation v. Industrial Commission of Ohio, 236 U.S. 230 (1915).

Near v. Minnesota, 291 U.S. 503 (1931).

Nelson, H.L. (Ed.). (1967). *Freedom of the press from Hamilton to the Warren court.* Indianapolis: Bobbs-Merrill.

New York v. Ferber, 458 U.S. 747 (1982).

New York Times v. Sullivan, 376 U.S. 254 (1964).

New York Times v. United States, United States v. Washington Post, 303 U.S. 713 (1971).

Office of the Surgeon General (1986). *Report of the Surgeon General's workshop on pornography and public health.* Washington, DC: U.S. Department of Health and Human Services.

O'Neil, R. M. (1981). *Classrooms in the crossfire.* Bloomington, IN: Indiana University Press.

Paris Adult Theatre I v. Slaton, 413 U.S. 49 (1973).

Porter, W. E. (1975). *Assault on the media: The Nixon years,* Ann Arbor, MI: University of Michigan Press.

Posadas de Peurto Rico v. Tourism Company, 478 U.S 328 (1986).

Red Lion Broadcasting Co. v. Federal Communications Commission, 395 U.S. 367 (1969).

Rosenbloom v. Metromedia, 403 U.S. 29 (1971).

Roth v. United States, 354 U.S. 476 (1957).

Sanford, B. W. (1985). *Libel and privacy.* New York: Harcourt Brace Jovanovich.

Schenck v. United States, 249 U.S. 47 (1919).

Schmidt, B. C., Jr. (1976). *Freedom of the press v. public access.* New York: Praeger.

Sharon v. Time, Inc., 575 F. Supp 1162 (1983).

Simmons, S. J. (1978). *The fairness doctrine and the media.* Berkeley, CA: University of California Press.

Smolla, R. A. (1986). *Suing the press.* New York: Oxford University Press.

Snepp v. United States, 444 U.S. (507) (1980).

Speech Communication Association (1961–1986). *Free speech yearbook* (Vols. 1–25). Annandale, VA. Speech Communication Association.

Speech Communication Association (1987–   ). *Free speech yearbook* (Vols. 26–   ). Carbondale, IL: Southern Illinois University Press.

Tavoulareas v. Washington Post, 567 F. Supp. 651 (D. D.C. 1983).

Tedford, T. L. (1985). *Freedom of speech in the United States.* Carbondale, IL: Southern Illinois University Press.

Tedford, T.L., Makay, J. J., & Jamison, D. L. (Eds.). (1987). *Perspective on freedom of speech.* Carbondale, IL: Southern Illinois University Press.

Time, Inc. v. Firestone, 424 U.S. 448 (1976).

Tinker v. Des Moines School District, 393 U.S. 503 (1968).

Virginia State Board of Pharmacy v. Virginia Citizens Consumer Council, 425 U.S. 748 (1976).

Westmoreland v. CBS, 10 Med.L.Rep. (BNA) 2417 (S.D.N.Y., 1984).

Wolston v. Reader's Digest Assocaition, 443 U.S. 157 (1979).

Wood, R. (1986). *Hollywood from Vietman to Regan.* New York: Columbia University Press.

Yates v. United States, 354 U.S. 298 (1957).

• 10 •

A Cultural Inquiry Concerning
the Ontological and Epistemic Dimensions
of Self, Other, and Context in Communication
Scholarship

H. L. GOODALL, JR.

In the concluding section of an essay entitled " 'What We Need Is Communication': 'Communication' as a Cultural Category in Some American Speech," Tamar Katriel and Gerry Philipsen (1981) offer the following observation:

> Our study of American "communication" has led us to think of ethnography less as a journey into a foreign land or culture, and more as a journey into a no-man's land, which is neither the territory of the self nor of the other. As every Israeli child who was taken on that mandatory field trip to the border knows, one cannot risk more than a few steps into unsettled territory. In doing so, however, one becomes aware not only of the existence of the other's territory, but of one's own, and the concept of territory in general. The ethnographer, like the careful tourist, pays his or her tribute to the border at designated spots, but the border stretches and winds between these spots as well, and it is in this unmarked territory that the "person" searches for a sense of personal meaning. (p. 316)

My essay begins with this observation for three reasons. First, I want to use the metaphor of the border and its place in relational definitions of self and other to further an argument about the centrality of context to both processes and products of human understanding. Second, I will examine our professional literature as a cultural artifact that reveals both ontological and epistemic dimensions of the problems of self, other, and context that are inherently connected to accepted forms of scholarly research and writing. Third, I invoke a Brockriedeian interpretation of *human understanding* as a dialectical bridge between readings of the cultural category of American communication and the personal experiences and reporting habits of communication researchers as a source of critique.

My purpose in this chapter is to build on rich, existing intellectual traditions to suggest that a new frontier of communication research and writing is available for scholarly exploration. At this frontier, new questions arise about the relationships between and among researcher, subject, and context within the broader scope of historical, cultural, and social processes that create and constitute *meaning* as the core human experience of "communication."[1] Toward this general objective I will derive major assumptions, questions, and methods from the enterprises of cultural ethnography, anthropology, family systems psychology, and the philosophy of communication that are at this historical juncture converging on meaning-centered, postmodern conceptions of the connection between knowledge and its representation. By attending to the promise of this new frontier I will show that all accounts of "communication," "understanding," and "research" are interpretive episodes capable of providing readers with narrative details about how we know about what we see when we situate the study of communication in contexts marked by the presence of self and other.

No-Man's-Land: The Absence of Context and the Negation of Self and Other in Communication Research Practices

Victor Turner observes that "meaning arises when we try to put what culture and language have crystallized from the past together with what we feel, wish, and think about our present point in life" (1986, p. 33). Viewed this way, meaning can be both a constrained response to a situation (as when a certain language "fits" a ritual) and an inventional opportunity to overcome or replace those constraints (as when a revolu-

---

1. This essay must acknowledge a heavy intellectual debt to George Herbert Mead and Herbert Blumer. While most readers will recognize that most of these arguments are embedded within the scholarly traditions that have worn the label of "symbolic interactionism," my formal acknowledgement here is intended to extend these ontologic and epistemic traditions to include the considerations of literary, relational, and representational concerns that are featured in this essay.

tion, innovation, or discovery is articulated as such). Meaning, then, suggests an array of possibilities in any situation, that array being limited by cultural standards, personal history and preferences, and whatever occurs within the situation that prompts a meaningful response.

To be meaningful, experience must include three sources of potential information: knowledge of and about self, knowledge of and about others, and knowledge of and about the context in which meaning can be attributed to the experience. This is not to suggest that each one of these sources of information is real, complete, or accurate. No matter how completely we believe we know ourselves or others or understand a situation, such knowledge is at some level always necessarily ego-centered and is therefore, by definition, partial.

Self

Viewed monistically a self is contained within an individual, and the nature of self, while never open to purely empirical scrutiny, is nevertheless a category under which falls, depending upon your linguistic assets (theory), a variety of sentences, phrases, and descriptors. For some knowledge of self is "organic" and may be located in a particular region of the brain. For others knowledge of self is a linguistic category shaped by cultural and environmental influences, definable only by its outward manifestations of behavior. For still others, knowledge of self is a product of organic and environmental influences, an analytical category that nevertheless maintains that the individual actor is the hero-villain capable of exercising choice to overcome negative predispositions, a poor economy, illness, or family neglect.

Each of these conceptions of self is grounded in a preference for individuality. In them an individual self is the inheritor of certain traits and capacities, and has the native ability to develop, change, or maintain them. Knowledge *about* the self, then, is knowledge *about* an individual actor, a person, a choice maker, a user of words, observable behaviors.

Viewed dialectically, however, knowledge of self is never achieved alone. The self is not presented to the world in isolation but in consort with other selves. For family systems theorists (Haley, 1976; Kerr & Bowen, 1988; Phillips & Wood, 1983), "the individual" is a convenient linguistic construction that often obscures the fact that a structure of interlocking relationships—rather than autonomous psychological entities—is the base for whatever empirical, behavioral, or internal states are used to describe a self.

This view of a self as an actor within webs of relationships reveals that knowledge *about* the self is always interdependent with knowledge *about* others (Blumer, 1969; Mead, 1934). It also reveals the centrality of communication as a bridge between or among selves, and places at the forefront of communication theory the issue of linguistic representation of human experience. Knowledge of and about how a person, a self, interacts within a particular web should proceed dialectically within an evolving context, and therefore confronts two issues simultaneously. First, how can we make sense out of the action? And second, how can we make the action sentence-able?

The primary issue of sense making, then, is relational, not individual. What are the structures of family, friends, enemies, etc., that contribute to the observed performances? If meaning is a broad cognitive construct, and if situated meaning among persons is at least partly aimed at reducing the uncertainty of the setting and partly aimed at reducing the anxiety of the self, then dialectical conceptions of self—Who am I in relation to the other? What are the likely reponses the other will make to me? etc.— seem far more appropriate than individual ones.

The second issue is as important as the first, at least as far as scholarship is concerned. The issue is not merely how to make sense out of a performance, but how to make such a performance sentence-able.

First, it seems clear that to capture multiple selves within contexts requires fuller participation of the selves being captured whose experience can and should be articulated *by* them rather than *for* them. Several options are currently available, including multiple authorship of the essay or book; a written account of the experience from those used to generate the researcher's conclusions included within, or as an appendix to the text; and experimentation with alternative genres for writing scholarship, including drama, dialogue, fiction, interview, and debate.

Second, knowledge of the researcher/writer's self must be included in scholarly accounts of other's experiences. If we insert ourselves into the context we will learn to see our observational and critical processes as part of the reading we give to whatever happens, and the written (or other form of) account will provide richer testimony to the complexity and connectedness of how meanings are constructed through communication.

Third, alternative media may be cultivated for presentation of scholarly work. Ours is a generation of scholars that has available to us forms of expression previous generations did not, including all forms of electronic media. Consider, for example, a video of a corporate culture as a way of revealing what the discussed persons and things look like and do, complete with oral endnotes, if you like. The result would be a new use of an available means of persuasion that could further our understanding of what an individual self took as data for interpretive conclusions, as well as a permanent account of both the data and conclusions which could easily be made available to others for critical scrunity.

So, in summary, a knowledge of and about self is understood within a web of relationships. To get at those relationships, to bring to their internal dynamic a source of external critique, should be a natural aspect of communication research. To do such research requires expanding the way in which research projects are carried out and reported by actively engaging the participation of those studied, the articulated acknowledgement of the researcher's knowledge of self into the experience, and broadening the scope of what constitutes a scholarly contribution.

Other

Knowledge of and about the other in communication research is one of the most troublesome concepts in our literature. Historically, speech scholars defined the other as the audience, a collective group of generally passive listeners about whom the speaker had attitudes, strategies, and motives and toward whom the message of the speech was directed. With the advent of group and interpersonal research, the concept of audience shifted—mostly along the lines of the individual psychology discussed above—and the interpersonal other became, in the communication process, a partner whose personal needs, desires, goals, and motives were to be assessed.

There are both ontological and epistemic concerns that guide research about knowledge of and about the other. Rawlins (1985), for example, discusses three phases of interpersonal communication research that occurred from the 1940s to the 1970s using the labels of social integration, individual integration, and situational integration eras to chart changes in the what and how of our discipline's research.

In his review, he develops an extensive critique of the terms most often used to describe the ontological dimensions of our knowledge—effectiveness, social conventions and idiosyncratic rules, communication skills and attitudes toward communication, persuasion versus individual freedom, and interactional control—yet curiously absent from his list is any coherent concept of *other*. It is as if despite our claims to a fundamental concern for communication as the substance of human *relationships*, we carry over into the realm of relational research the intellectual baggage of an individualized, nonintegrative view of the self and other that form relationships.

The question of the ontological dimensions of the other—What is this person to the relationship, and what can be known about him or her?—is reduced to a categorical mirroring of our similarly narrow view of the self-as-behavior: What we are is that portion of what we say and do that can be measured. A more comprehensive, holistic, and dialectical perspective would modify that statement to read: What we are includes what we say and do as well as the *meanings* we (self and other) have for the experience of those actions within contexts and relationships that we maintain. Viewed this way, the other is a full partner to the relationship and an equal contributor to the ways in which contexts are understood.

The epistemic issue has been handled primarily as a question of methods for conducting the research, rather than as a question that connects those methods with their results—the written research report. If our knowledge exists in sentences, and if our sentences are constrained by traditional scholarly formats and formulas for reporting research, then the issue of how we come to knowledge is isomorphic with how we represent that which we have come to know. Unfortunately, most graduate training—both texts and course structures—creates an unnecessary and inaccurate bifurcation between "doing research" and "writing up the report," which fails to recognize the connection between knowledge and its representation. The result is, in part, that we have developed sophisticated methods that fit into the traditions of scholarly writing without examining how that writing has likewise contributed to (and obscured) our knowledge. Consider, for example, the representative depth of a good dramatic enactment of a relationship, particularly what it suggests about the self and other in a context, against any published essay in our literature. Which one better depicts relational reality?[2]

---

2. Some graduate programs within our discipline allow performance theses that attempt to accomplish precisely these objectives. Specifically, I am here thinking about the area of performance of literature, in which the actor's ability

The issue is not whether the questions we ask as scholars can be accomodated by alternative genres and media, for surely an answer— regardless of which one you give—is too superficial. Some very sophisticated questions about human relationships have been evident in plays, novels, biographies, and films for quite some time, but not everyone who has mastered the methods of sophisticated inquiry can write that well. The issue, however, is deeper than that: Whoever is able to define the other is ultimately in charge of what is known.

As researcher/writers we have a relationship with those whom we study. In that relationship we also have the power of the pen, and the authority of our role in society as seekers of truth and beauty, knowledge and understanding, to control what is made known. If our knowledge is constrained by the genre of our endeavors, and if our understanding of others is narrowed by our treatment of them as objects to be seen, counted, accounted for, or manipulated, then we are back to a concept of knowledge of and about the other as audience for our sophisticated rhetorical charms. We still don't know who the others are, or what meanings they bring to our—and their own—relationships.

Context

If our research literature reveals anything about the concept of context, it is that we have reduced it to one of mere *role*, occasionally coupled with the researcher's descriptions of a physical environment. Studies are done in which X number of roles (roommates, friends, superiors/subordinates, students, and volunteers) define the context in which the study is to have meaning. Similarly, other studies focus on the artifacts within an environment as clues to what a context is, despite the fact, as Sackmann (1987) points out, that the presence of the same or even similar artifacts in two distinct cultures (for example, the pyramids in Egypt and in Mexico) may give a false sense of shared meaning (the former are to honor the dead, the latter, for worshiping the sun).

Similarly, to define context as the role enacted within a physical environment is to ignore the functions of communication in creating and constituting, as Marshall Sahlins puts it, "the meaningful orders of

---

to research and to produce relational understanding within a definable context is paramount.

persons and things" (1976). If the researcher is the key definer of the role, as well as the physical aspects of the environment, the meanings ascribed to the relationships manifested in the context by the participants are essentially lost. Think about the well-intentioned but nevertheless neocolonial attitude of early cultural anthropology as analogue to our research experience. We are learned and trained observers; they are our naive subjects. We give to them a context of our devising, and seldom ask if they have thoughts concerning it beyond the narrow purposes of our particular research project. We are interested in findings and conclusions, in rounding out the research experience in a way that will further our scholarly goals.

The conceptualization of knowledge of and about a context is often rendered in the static language of photography—we are taking pictures of a scene, this is what you see in it. But the scene was not the same before the photographer entered and it changes after the picture is taken. A context is not the picture any more than "the word is the thing" (Korzybski, 1933). What is even more confounding is that a context is given meaning in sentences uttered by the participants, who, in turn, are influenced by those utterances to "see" the context in their own interpretive ways. What one person "sees" as the context is not necessarily what another person "sees" (or responds to) in it, even though their roles may be clear to the researcher and to them and despite the fact that they share precisely the same physical environment.

Here again we confront the ontological and epistemic problems of ordinary, everyday experience. There are no easy answers unless we reduce the complexity of the experience, in which case, to what questions are we actually providing answers? Furthermore, if our overall agenda is to take apart naturally occurring experience, to break it down into components, perspectives, dimensions, and so forth with the eventual hope of putting it all back together again and reporting it in a linear form appropriate to scholarly conventions, then we mix in the metaphor of the machine to the metaphor of the organism, and render the cultural, social, and semiotic—those symbolic, complex, and meaningful processes and relationships—into a technology of scholarship governed by a technique of writing.

Given these sources of knowledge, it seems reasonable to assert that, if one is accounting for some event in which another was present, considerations of self, other, and context should be included. This, of course, begs a question that cultural anthropologists have already confronted in accounts of their own cultural history (Clifford & Marcus, 1986; Davis, 1986; Geertz, 1988; Marcus & Fisher, 1986; Van Maanen, 1988). To wit: When a researcher goes into a foreign land and imposes his or her own cultural categories and biases upon the "savages," the result is a "homogenization" of cultural understanding toward the dominant (Western, scientific) model which obscures the meanings of the observed reality (or the copresent meanings of multiple realities) and denies to the observed the opportunity to respond. Furthermore, as Edward Said (1978) has argued, the rhetorical devices used within the genre of Western scholarly discourse value the activity (and active voice) of the author over the activities (and passive voice) of the subjects, rendering the discourse little more than further testimony to an exercise in power rooted in neocolonialism.

For discourse that aims at creating knowledge of and about a people and their practices—the essential task of cultural anthropology—meaning is not an aspect of reality to be observed and classified as any other empirical fact (if, indeed, such a statement can be made of any data). Instead, meaning is derived from one's insertion of self into a setting in which knowledge of self, others, and the setting all figure into the calculus of what is made known.

Consider, for example, the following argument made by Robert Paul in a *New York Times Book Review* essay in which he considers the dilemma posed by having an anthropologist (in this case, Wade Davis) produce two accounts of the same experience—one for a scholarly audience and one for a more general reader:

> The purpose of the revision, so it seems, is to present the author's findings in a form more acceptable to science than the lively first-person narrative in "The Serpent and the Rainbow." Consequently, Mr. Davis has omitted from the present volume the story of the human events and encounters that led him to his findings.

> The irony is that this revision not only makes "Passage of Darkness" less interesting to the lay reader, but also reduces its value as anthropology. Anthropologists these days do not imagine themselves to be objective observers of empirical cultural facts, but understand themselves as actors whose research is a complex process involving the construction of meaning, power relations and the placement of oneself and the people one studies within a real continuing social and historical setting. (21 August 1988, p. 14)

These insights are, in my view, equally applicable to communication research. While it seems unnecessary to point out that meaning can occur only within contexts (Carbaugh, 1988; Goodall, 1989a; Mishler, 1979), and that any study of communicative motives, meanings, practices or actions occurs within specific cultural, social, and historical circumstances, these self-evident truths all too often seem absent from scholarly discussions in our literatures. It is as if we still maintain that empirical reality is not socially constructed, power relations among those who do the studying and those who are studied are important as data to that construction of knowledge, or that placement of oneself—and taking account of that placement—is a condition of the knowledge that ultimately will be constructed. As a result, what we claim to believe does not surface in our writing and, therefore, is absent from the tangible corpus of knowledge we produce.

Communication Literature as a Cultural Artifact

Our professional literature is a cultural artifact, the dominant evidence of our scholarly beliefs and values (Calas and Smircich, 1986). In it we find, in addition to testimonies concerning our rituals (presidential addresses, attention to professional conventions, the encouragement of debates between advocates of differing points of view) and rites of passage (tenure, promotions, awards for teaching, research, and service), a curious absence of a common definition for communication.

In fact, for some scholars for a number of years this has been a central, and confounding, concern (Dance, 1970, 1980; Miller, 1966). Like Yah-Way, what gives us life and sustains us seems almost ineffable, so complete a mystery that our scholarly lives are spent contributing to and occasionally revising the sacred texts that we pass on to new generations of worshippers. As new generations prosper, new sects—methods of "proper" worship—develop among spiritual leaders whose noble quests seem destined to lead us to new truths, and for awhile our sacred texts are dominated by displays of prophecy found alternately in various locations. Still, the meaning of what we study eludes us, and communication becomes—again like Yah-Way—sometimes a subject for explanation and inspiration, sometimes an object for critical and scientific scrutiny, and more recently, as a political term that legitimizes our scholarly and teaching endeavors (Mader, Rosenfield, & Mader, 1985).

Common to communication as both subject and object is the need to express knowledge in a language that is always removed from the contexts that generate it. There is a world within the word, too. One world is lived in and everyday, full of the made- up alongside the constructed, dreamy and real, felt, random, fragmented, and maybe well planned. The one used to describe and analyze it hovers in the literature that exists as a copresent but virtually inaccessible reality around and perhaps above life, everydayless as reverie and noetic as police.

Communication, as a term and as a discipline, has no intrinsic meaning. Because meaning is found in contexts, as a source of tensions among self, other, and setting, the study of communication—regardless of method or purpose—must always be context specific. This does not mean that generalizations cannot or should not be made, nor that knowledge derived from one particular set of tensions is not applicable to another. It is to recognize that the experience of meaning in doing research is bound inextricably to (1) the assumptions, beliefs, and attitudes of the self-as-researcher, an actor in a scene that has no set script, (2) the perceived realities that are mutually constructed between self and others, including the researcher, and (3) the understanding that whatever occurs within a specific context may not be experienced nor explained in the same ways by all participants. Only the discursive product—the essay or book—legitimizes the role of researcher as author of the experience, and that occurs primarily because "the literature" is where, as a discipline, "communication" and our professional identities exist (see Goodall, 1989b, for extended discussion).

Perhaps this is why, as the opening quotation from two communication ethnographers rightly points out, when one does "communication" research the experience is more akin to entering a "no-man's-land" than a foreign culture. This is because the border between self and other, between observer and the observed, is seldom clearly articulated. And because it is seldom articulated, there is both an absence of context and a negation of self and other as dominant motifs in our literature. The border disappears, and with it goes a powerful source of human understanding.

Reading a Research Report for Clues to This Dilemma

Consider, for a moment, a typical research report in any of our professional journals. The researcher reveals no self apart from a name, an institutional affiliation, and the references employed to help make the case. The subjects for the research are seldom named or given relational dimensions (for an excellent exception, see Krueger, 1982), and are seldom asked to comment on the report after it is written, despite the fact that it is written about them. The context for the research project is described only by inference—it must have been in a classroom if students were asked to fill out a questionnaire. For the moment I will leave out the long-standing argument about using students to generate conclusions applicable to the rest of the world, and concentrate on what this practice suggests about our research culture.

First, the meanings we attribute to what we observe are derived from our dominant literature, rather than from the subjects we claim to be studying or from our contact with them within particular cultural contexts. Ours is the scholar's license, evident since Plato, to compare what we see and hear to what we believe ought to exist in some perfect elsewhere that is, in our own time, simply referred to as "the literature." Because "the literature" is a sacred text, its legitimacy is seldom questioned, and when questions are raised they are raised in the spirit of revisionary scholarly pluralism that, over the years, dramatizes various political battles that exude at best a hermeneutical zeal for the "proper" interpretation of a literary reference or authority and that seldom have much to do—or interest in—how that interpretation squares with "communication."

Second, researchers are presented in similar *personae*, as if the granting of advanced degrees in speech communication automatically inscribed a particular view of reality and way of seeing it on individual characters. Clearly, this is not the case, for one only has to attend any of our annual conventions to see that we each endorse particular sacred texts, few of which are fairly common while most are appealed to and appealing only to the particular sect to which we belong. Hence, despite the presence of a sacred literature, within the sects we seldom share even a common language for describing our assumptions, methods, or the results of "communication" research. Why then, do we persist in the niggling and self-negating practice of writing our research reports in self-less prose that renders, falsely, a sense of commonality and fully shared beliefs?

What I am after here is not merely the insertion of "personality" or even "style" (because occasionally that occurs despite the limitations of the genre) that marks the individual as person as well as author of the experience, but moreover a fuller sense of immersion in the reasons for, and experience of, conducting the study. Aside from the obvious disclaimers of gaining a reputation, working toward tenure, why are we doing this? What are our motives? What are our goals? When we conducted the research, what were the contextual clues that induced our attention, that led us to believe that we had found something interesting? What were our sources of angst, frustration, or pleasure? What did we not understand about the context, ourself, and the others that is also part—albeit unspoken—of this text? Questions such as these move us closer to the terrain of communication as practiced and experienced than do exclusively distanced inquiries.

Third, there is a bureaucratization of our organization evident from the way research reports are solicited, recognized, and reviewed that values narrow in-group legitimacy over broader cultural values. In a way this is reminescent of Irving Janis's concept of "groupthink" (1982), in which the beliefs of decision makers who use themselves as the only applicable reality often interfere with the quality of their products. This charge can be revealed in two distinct cultural practices: (1) the way in which we are asked to affiliate within the profession, and (2) the way in which research reports are written and reviewed.

When we join our professional associations we are asked to affiliate with no more than two divisions. What if our interests are broader than that? The only real purpose to divisional affiliation has to do with gaining numbers of members to justify program slots (after all, there has to be some method to this decision), but it encourages us, I think, to see our professional lives as participating in separate and often distinct categories. In an era marked by Clifford Geertz's (1980) memorable phrase "blurred genres" for scholarship and the encouragement of interdisciplinary and multidisciplinary research programs, such labeling is often merely a structurally convenient myth that has as a side effect a perpetuation of bureaucracy for its own sake.

More importantly, this local bureaucracy carries over into the politics of journal publication and convention space, the very contexts that we use to define our "literature." As in any culture there is a distinct need for new members to acquire the knowledge and skills and to generally "fit in." Research papers reveal how this is accomplished in three interrelated ways.

First, the research paper must "look like" other writing within this genre. Odd, then, that in a discipline named "communication" that admits to the legitimacy of a variety of expressive outlets—speech, poetry, dance, drama, television, movies, video, cartoons, performances of texts, etc.—we have adopted the already conservative standards for scholarship among the humanities and social sciences. We study these forms, but have yet to use them as productive vehicles for our own scholarly work. For years this has been an active concern of members of our discipline in the dramatic and performance areas, and it seems to me that their experiences foreshadowed the current problem discipline wide. When ideas must conform to arbitrary and narrow forms of expression, we are limiting expression and committing to scholarly exile ideas that may well express precisely the sorts of alternative wisdom that can help us overcome our native "groupthink."

Second, research reports must be read and reviewed by persons "knowledgeable" in the field. Viewed cynically, this can be interpreted as meaning the three other specialists who are within the minority who care about or support this idea. However, as a person who has served on editorial boards for various publications, I am not ready to be quite this cynical.

My concern is what counts as an "authority." If we, as a discipline, grant ourselves sole responsibility for the legitimacy or truth of an idea, we further separate ourselves from those whom we claim to be studying, not to mention those with whom we might profitably interact, and further narrow the concept of context to our own literature and professional identities. Perhaps we should consider letting outsiders, such as the students in the groups we use to generate our studies, or the professionals working the organizations we make claims about, or historians, political scientists, literary critics, and psychologists, from whom we often derive ideas, methods, and good reasons, to join the ranks of our "reviewers." Not only would this be a way to encourage others outside our field to look at what we do and offer criticisms aimed at improving our work, it would also encourage us to improve the quality, readability, diversity, and scope of impact of our scholarly expressions.

These observations are not meant to demean or devalue our scholarship. They are made out of a sense of debt to a tradition of scholarship that has served us well, but, to borrow two terms Kenneth Burke (1969) has taught us, a tradition of scholarship that also offers "terministic screens" that in this case may be leading us toward "occupational psychosis." What we need is a challenge to our perspective. Particularly in this commemorative volume it is not enough to look back fondly over familiar territories; we need to begin to chart our exploration of the future, starting with a commitment not to confine that exploration to more of the same.

The Dialectical Bridge for Understanding Humans Communicating

The late Professor Wayne Brockriede, in an essay aptly entitled "Arguing About Human Understanding" (1982), creates a critical stance consisting of three dimensions—the empirical, personal, and linguistic—that encourages a holistic approach to constructing knowledge about human communication. It is unique to our discipline in that it can be used to create the grounds for interpretive, pluralistic approaches to doing research about human communication that invites active and evident consideration of self, other, and context.

Brockriede's model assumes that "*persons* come to understandings about *things* through *language*" (p. 138) and that "human understanding embraces all of the methods, processes, and products people use when regulating their uncertainties about the empirical, personal, and linguistic aspects of their worlds . . . [while] deemphasizing such terms as analysis, categories, variables, and boundaries" (p. 137). In other words, one does not have to distance oneself from the experience, define it and categorize it according to some preexisting system of critique to arrive at understanding. While such analyses may be performed and may be useful for some purposes, this does not and should not preclude the possibility—nor the utility—of alternative forms of understanding.

One such possiblity, Brockriede suggests, is to use the figure/ground metaphor to emphasize that when one dimension of human understanding (say, the empirical) is brought to the forefront, others do not disappear, they instead become the background against which the dominant figure dances (the personal realm of experience and the words that belong to the situation). The critical products of this pluralistic sense of how the world is apprehended and constructed is different from "monistic" perspectives that "reduce human understanding either to empirical things *or* to personal relations *or* to linguistic experience" (p. 138).[3]

A second feature of Professor Brockriede's essay is his conception of how arguments of and about human understanding may proceed. Working from an earlier framework established by Joseph Wenzel (1979) that distinguishes a vocabulary for three perspectives on argument (logical, rhetorical, dialectical), Brockriede places the dialectical as the figure

---

3. Herbert Blumer (1969, pp. 140–152, 171–182) argued this point prior to Professor Brockriede, although his concern was primarily with social psychology and not within the narrower context of argument theory.

against the ground of logical products of argument and rhetorical processes for arguing. When this is conceptualized two possible outcomes are established: (1) the either/or, or forced choice, useful for making decisions, achieving consensus, or warranting claims; and (2) the both/and, useful for understanding perspectives involved in ongoing, interdependent, symbiotic contexts in which "the continued existence and health of one member of a dialectical pair is needed for the continued existence and health of the other" (p. 144).

The value of building the dialectical bridge to arguments about human understanding is manifested in three ways. First, one can adopt the Burkeian stance toward linguistic transformations that mark "a person [as] *both* a unique substance *and* consubstantial with other persons" (p. 144). Second, this approach has much in common with "the ancient Chinese symbol of yin-yang, which recognizes unity in dualisms and treats such apparent polarities as dark and light, good and evil, not as separate entities dueling to the death with one another, but as indivisible wholes" (p. 144). Third, acceptance of the both/and dialectical schema encourages a broader range of acceptance in matters of arguments about human understanding, following the lead provided by Toulmin, Rieke, and Janik (1979) regarding aesthetic experience: "accepting one interesting and reasonable interpretation of a work of art does not necessitate rejecting others that are also supported by good rationales" (p. 144).

The advantage of this figure/ground, both/and, dialectical bridging of the empirical, personal, and linguistic dimensions of human understanding lies in the complexity and sensitivity of its imagery. Consider again the problem of understanding what—and who—creates and constitutes "communication" and what is being "communicated" in any context. First consider the role of the researcher in this scene—her or his motives, ambitions, purposes, beliefs, values, understanding of the professional literature, understanding of others, sensitivity to context, knowledge of self. Now, if you will, consider the other(s) in the context, both those being studied and those to whom the final product (essay, book, video, film, etc.) will be shown or who are simply imagined as audience for this drama, and try to dig into their individual and collective senses of knowledge of and about self, other (including you, as the researcher), and scene. Finally, consider the elements of the scene itself—its colors, textures, props, lighting, etc.—consider them as partners to the meanings that will be both evoked and ignored by those present, that will be judged or read or interpreted according to other scenes, other places, and other understandings of what it all means.

With all of this going on, and I believe all of this does go on every time we study "communication" within any setting, how can we not appreciate the complexity and sensitivity of an interpretive model that values all perspectives, rationales, and judgments as being potentially useful? As Brockriede has it:

> The critic whose emphasis is on interpreting or explaining an experience need not offer any definitive account. A critic who takes a perspectival view cannot do so. He or she interprets an experience within the context of particular times, places, and cultures. The experience under criticism can be illuminated from the criticism of persons who choose to emphasize different dimensions, see the event or process from different points of view, or use different constructs" (p. 145).

Brockriede's dialectical bridge was intended "to be a useful complement to the traditional approach in such activities as theory, practice, criticism, and research" (p. 147). However, I believe his rationale has two other, perhaps subtler, messages for persons engaged in "communication" research. First, and most important, the humans that are to be understood or interpreted, that provide us with data about their communicative performances, and that serve as the constant ground against which our theories about and criticism about them form the figures (at least in our professional literatures), are *significant* others.

Within a research context we need to pay more attention to how *they* make and manipulate meanings, for as our dialectical partner, the depth and richness of our literature depends as much on their involvement and continued cooperation as it does on ours. This means more than simply observing more carefully and giving closer attention to details, it means encouraging experimental ways of representing the research experience, particularly the ways of writing the research report.

Anthropologists have given us the lead by endorsing a wide variety of genres for reporting research news—dramas, documentaries, dialogues, interviews, and fiction (not in the sense of "untrue," but as perspectival truth rendered within the conventions of this genre of expression). What they have recognized is that there is a genuine and unavoidable connection between how an experience is experienced, and how that experience is rendered in prose. As long as the author is content to work within traditional modes of reporting, the knowledge reported remains exclusively traditional.

The second insight provided by this remarkable essay concerns sensitivity to context. Put simply, if meanings occur only within contexts, then contexts must become part of the description of the research experience. This does not mean, I think, that it is enough simply to state that "subjects for this research were 122 undergraduates enrolled in a basic speech course at a large midwestern university," or to state that "I spent three months observing and interviewing persons at the XYZ Corporation." In either case what is left out is any sense of context as it is lived through by human beings, and what is put into the description is merely a conventional line designed to answer conventional reviewer concerns about *where* or *when* the research was conducted, not what meanings were attributed by the researcher (or others) to the scenes in which the drama was enacted. Context is not a static description of place or time, it is an unfolding of clues, a weaving of a pattern, that at some point becomes part of the articulated presence that is further woven or read into the meaning of the experience.

Brockriede's point about arguments concerning human understanding leaves out nothing that is indigenous to human experience. The beauty of his case rests with its appreciation of human complexity, and its urging of all critics to admit to and account for that complexity. Furthermore, however, his is an argument that lends itself to the interpretive turn in understanding that currently characterizes one of the newest and most promising movements within the discipline. Although no doubt the essay can be read simply as support for the valuing of interpretive critique, I prefer to read it (or perhaps read *into* it) as having a more radical motive. And that motive has to do with how we report on what we experience when we argue about human "communication."

In the culture that is speech communication, that is represented by our professional literature as a dominant artifact, the first seventy-five years have contributed to a great and noble tradition of scholarship, in part derived from other academic cultures and in part created and sustained by the labor of women and men in our discipline who have advanced what we claim to know about humans communicating. It is no coincidence, I think, that these advances and traditions have occurred historically during a literary period marked by the rise of modernism and a broadening of the scope of natural science that transformed the image of the humanities and fostered the birth and spread of social science, and during a period of academic history in which the worth and legitimacy of a discipline was measured by its numbers of scholarly publications, accumulation of dollars in grants, and reputations of researchers.

There have been at least two results of this turn for our place in history. One result has been the devaluing of education to the image of research in how universities and colleges define their mission, a result that has implications beyond the scope of this essay. The other result has been the acceptance of conventionalism and complacency in our chosen method for reporting and judging the value of published research. The dominant artifact of a discipline named "communication" represents a division between what we know and what we do.

All Accounts Are Interpretive Episodes

This is the place in the essay to bring together the two themes that have thus far been developed—the border as metaphor for a context capable of dividing self and other, and the dialectical bridge of both/and that is capable of revealing a necessary relationship between self and other through empirical, personal, and linguistic dimensions—and to use them to transform our ideas about communication, research, and understanding.

Communication, Research, and Understanding

In 1977 Arthur Bochner reviewed the current state of scholarship and scholarly journals dedicated to the scientific advancement of communication theory and research and asked the poignant question "Whither?" This review occurred at a particularly important time within this history of our discipline because new journals such as *Human Communication Research*, *Journal of Applied Communication Research*, and *Communication Research* were adding outlets for researchers interested in revising monistic theories of science and charting new inroads into empirical (mostly quantitative) "middle-range" work.

It was also interesting because the concept of "communication" was described as "so pregnant with meaning, that it stymies our best efforts to circumscribe its boundaries" (p. 325). The "boundaries" were then *de facto* defined as occurring within seven specific professional journals.

Then, as now, "communication" is a territory defined by borders of professional journal space and scholarly volumes, an existence often described as being "at the cutting edge of theory" but nevertheless an existence in sentences spoken at the margins of society. Put simply, our contribution to the commonweal has tended rather heavily toward issues relevant only within the ivory tower. Furthermore, these contributions serve to distance the study of communication from cultures of persons who do the communicating by failing to enter into a dialogue with our subjects about their feelings, experiences, and insights on the topic of communication. Instead, we force college sophomores (who have no real choice), occasional consulting clients (whose names—and often contexts—are changed to mask their identities), and the numerous faceless others whom we have seen and observed within the contexts of our own lives and who become the examples we use to document our own work to accept our definitions of what counts as meaningful when they communicate. Our focus—our concept of other—is ourselves and our professional colleagues who are united by a language code, not the people who "communicate" outside of it.

In 1984 Julia Wood cautioned us to honor the real world connection by "(1) focus[ing] on communication as a substantive, formative activity in its own right, (2) respond[ing] to human issues and problems charactering the world beyond the ivory tower, and (3) develop[ing] research designs and methods that are compatible with the recommended conceptual *foci*" (p. 3). Her recommendations still seem useful and increasingly necessary. Unfortunately, rare is the article that incorporates them.

Earlier in this essay, I argued for a Brockriedeian dialectical bridge for more inclusive treatments of self, other, and context when accounting for knowledge of and about communication. That may sound like fairly fancy language, and a fairly complex method, to carry into the marketplace. But it is not intended to be. To build a dialectical bridge requires talking with those whom you are studying, and being receptive to their interpretations of the context you share. You will exchange ideas, engage in arguments, occasionally reach agreement. Through this give-and-take approach to learning about communication, you will encounter words, phrases, sentences, expressions, gestures, and silences that all contribute to the meaning you will, at some point, walk away from the encounter with. That is one way to conduct real-world research.

The more difficult part will be how to represent the knowledge you gain from the experience. It is intriguing to me that the method I have just advocated corresponds to the way some of the more enduring ideas about communication in Western civilization have been generated—witness the dialogues of Plato, the observations and lectures of Aristotle, the letters of Cicero to Brutus, etc.—yet we have no similar genres available to us for reporting current scholarly research. It is also true that people who do not live within the scholarly community have read, and no doubt will continue to read, these works long after the cutting edge of our work has been dulled by the next most fashionable idea or method.

The issue here is both the way we conduct research and the available means of reporting it. While our forebears saw fit to display their work in multiple formats, and to invent new genres when old ones could not contain the meanings they encountered, we tend at the end of the twentieth century to be far less open-minded. Our research must look like scholarly research, follow the scientific method or its derivative formulas, and provide at least the image of truth to a world that counts on images. The number of publications and the places where they appear in the literature mean more to our culture than what has been discovered about humans communicating.

As one of my colleagues who is also a departmental chair put it, "If you had to make a choice between two faculty members—one of whom publishes regularly in top journals but whose work has little originality or a faculty member who had one really good, truly insightful publication—which one would you tenure?" From his point of view I gave the wrong answer.

If history is our lesson in matters of academic traditions, to transform the current problems of "communication" scholarship will require changes more powerful than arguments can sway. To change the meaning of a cultural artifact means either to change the culture or to change the way the culture itself views the artifact, and that means a societal—more than a paradigmatic—shift. In the history of academic theorizing this sort of change has occurred only when current scholarship could no longer satisfy the demands for knowledge made by its constituents and when the enterprise of teaching became widely suspect as preparation for living in the world. It is no surprise, I think, that these are precisely the conditions of our current endeavors within the academy. What we have to say to the world about its communication is generally ignored and/or belittled, and both the functions and effects of higher education are currently under attack from a variety of internal and external sources. We may be smarter than they are, but we may also outsmart ourselves right out of our jobs when those who pay for our services inquire about the meaning or value of what we are doing and our only response is to point to dusty volumes within which specialists hold an in-group dialogue.

Understanding is the final arbiter of scholarly worth. If a piece of work helps us to understand, it can lay the foundation for intellectual satisfaction and pragmatic improvements. In the world beyond the ivory tower, communication has meaning, very often because it is misunderstood. Helping others understand the hows, wheres, and whys of that misunderstanding is important work, and should be seen as worthy scholarship.

Objections to What I Have Argued So Far

Probably some readers are at this point in the essay both shocked and amazed by these assertions. Trying them out on colleagues prior to this writing, I have encountered rejoinders such as "That's not how science is done!"; "I don't care what motives people have for their research, I only want to see what they came up with!"; and "Do you realize how this would look to my dean, if people starting writing like this?" Assuming these to be representative criticisms, each one characterizing honest and deeply held feelings on the subject, I will now address them in the hope of clarifying some misconceptions and identifying some problems evident in these pleas.

The concern for whether or not we are "doing science" is simply irrelevant. There is no common conception of what "doing science" is, and accounts of how scientists have behaved, what they have read and thought about while they were "doing it" indicate no one dominant pattern. Furthermore, we aren't biologists studying plants in gardens, nor animal scientists studying the behavior of horses in herds (Wyatt and Phillips, 1988). We are studying people communicating with other people within specific contexts, people who have meanings for their talk, and who attribute meanings to the talk of others, and who mostly know where they are—and have feelings about it—when they behave this way. Our task is "scientific" to the extent that we get outside the office more often and observe how this miracle at the intersections of culture and nature takes place. Science, after all, is a term whose meaning derives from our practices. It is as amenable to change as those of us who use it.

The objection based on not wanting to know what a scholar's motives are, just what they found, suggests that there is no connection between motive and outcome. It is true that people do not always articulate their motives, but that does not mean they do not have them, nor does it mean that a close reading of their performance could not reveal them. The fact is that when we admit this to be true for others, but deny its relevance to our own behavior, then we are engaging in little more than cultural elitism (see especially Keller, 1985). To acknowledge ourselves, complete with our motives and performances in the scenes in which our research and writing is conducted, seems a small, ethical request for scholarship that maintains "communication" to be the substance of human relationships.

Finally, concern for how a dean (or department chair or tenure and promotion committee) will view new scholarship is at best a paranoid reaction to an imagined state and at worst a tragic display of cowardice. The scholar's task is to seek truth and explore both the charted and uncharted domains of knowledge—to create as well as to perpetuate. If this task is defined within the politics of publication and as a way to please one's hierarchical superiors, it is profaned as well as prostituted and says at least as much about the character of the person doing the publishing and pleasing as it does about the person judging the results.

There remains one problem. It is relatively easy for those of us who have job security to advocate change; it is quite another for those without job security to act on it. It is not enough to encourage alternative forms of scholarship among those whose professional characters may be judged noble, creative, and brave but whose professional careers may be damaged during the quest. Endorsement of these research and writing practices carries with it an ethical obligation to pursue opportunities for persuasion with teaching and research faculty, department heads, deans, and other organizational members about the merits of these methods of inquiry and discourse.

Within any culture, subcultures and countercultures emerge; the degree to which they are successful in gaining acceptance and creating change depends on two interdependent processes. First, there must be results that are worthy of the order's attention and praise, and second, there must be attempts to alter the ways in which perceptions of what is praiseworthy can be made and articulated. Without the former there is no point to the latter, and without the latter the former may be easily discounted or mistaken. Together these two processes—quality work that reveals a redefinition of communication scholarship capable of broadening our audience *and* arguments presented to others within the academic culture about how such work should be evaluated—provide ways and means of productive change.

Conclusion

As we look back in reverence at the progress of our association in its first seventy-five years, it is easy to be optimistic about our accomplishments and its future. This is a discipline that enjoys a central place in both the humanities and social sciences and has as its subject, according to the late Richard McKeon, that "architectonic art capable of informing all disciplines and subjects." It is also a discipline that holds as one of its central values the freedom of expression, and as one of its principles that the way a message is communicated is as important as its content in judgments of effectiveness and in judgments of meaning. It is also important to examine that progress within the historical, cultural, literary, and social contexts that contributed to its theories and style of reporting research. As we celebrate this time and take account of what we have created as knowledge of and about communication, let us also look ahead to the new frontiers of scholarship *and* to new ways of reporting and displaying our work.

This essay has essentially forwarded a very simple case. It has been a case for examing relationships among self, other, and context in accounts of communication research. I have suggested that we learn from the experience of cultural anthropologists about the power dynamics inherent in studies of persons within cultures both familiar and exotic, and learn to see that relationship as part of the data we use to construct meaningful interpretations. I have shown why family systems theorists have embraced a relational perspective on all accounts of why humans behave in the ways they do, and asked that we consider their ideas within the contexts of our research, again focusing on the meanings we attribute to actions in the name of communication. And I have argued, perhaps too passionately, for opening up reporting methods for our research in ways that can take full advantage of this frontier.

In essence my thoughts are those of a person interested in pursuing—

and in encouraging others to pursue—a *meaning-centered* relational approach to communication. For years this sort of approach has gone under the general label of "ethnomethodology" (Garfinkel, 1967; Hymes, 1962), and it has recognized the need to expand our research techniques and methods of reporting the results to readers who, through the act of reading, become partners in the creation of meanings within our shared text (Hickson, 1983). There have been numerous calls for doing this sort of work in our discipline (see especially Ellis, 1980; Hawes, 1978; Pacanowsky, 1985; Philipsen, 1977), and some published studies accomplished within this general schema (see especially Benson, 1981; Carbaugh, 1988; Goodall, Wilson, & Waagen, 1986; Katriel & Philipsen, 1981; Philipsen, 1975). But as yet the interpretive dimensions of this sort of immersion and critique have not greatly influenced the mainstream understandings of what communication research is or does.

The new frontier of communication studies aims at a more general interpretation of meaning as the core of human experience and ways of accounting for meaning as inherent in *all* communication research. The idea is not to define meaning, but to evoke it; not to claim that it is a source of perfecting discourse, but to admit, outright, that it is imperfect; and not to perpetuate the scientific myth of control, but to advance a post-scientific notion of communication as the process in which and through which self, other, and context make and exchange meanings (see especially Newman, 1984; Tyler, 1988).

This essay, then, is making a decidedly postmodern case for the cultural, relational, and contextual primacy of meaning as the conceptual and methodological bases for *all* interpretations of human experience and behavior. This is a large call and a major challenge to existing wisdom, and one that recognizes its place in a postmodern, post-scientific world that understands textual strategies as embodiments of world views and genres of writing and reporting research as rich with rhetorical implications for viewing those worlds.

I began this essay by evoking a passage from the work of two communication ethnographers, Tamar Katriel and Gerry Philipsen, who observed that ethnography is less a journey into a foreign land or culture than it is a journey into a "no-man's land" belonging neither to the self, nor to the other. I want to return to that passage again, and ask you to read its last sentence again, this time aloud and within the context we have evolved in this essay. Here it is: "The ethnographer, like the careful tourist, pays his or her tribute to the border at designated spots, but the border stretches and winds between these spots as well, and it is in this unmarked territory that the 'person' searches for a sense of personal meaning."

References

Benson, T. W. (1981). Another shootout in cowtown. *The Quarterly Journal of Speech, 67,* 347–406.

Blumer, H. (1969). *Symbolic interactionism: Perspective and method.* Englewood Cliffs, NJ: Prentice-Hall.

Bochner, A. P. (1977). Whither communication theory and research? *The Quarterly Journal of Speech, 63,* 324–332.

Brockriede, W. (1982). Arguing about human understanding. *Communication Monographs, 49,* 137–147.

Burke, K. (1969). *Permanence and change.* Indianapolis, IN.: Bobbs-Merrill.

Calas, M.B., & Smircich, L. (1987). Reading leadership as a form of cultural analysis. In J. L. Hunt, R. Baligia, C. Schriesheim, & P. Dachler (Eds.), *Emerging leadership vistas.* Lexington, MA: Lexington Books.

Carbaugh, D. (1988). Cultural terms and tensions in the speech at a television station. *Western Journal of Speech Communication, 52,* 216–237.

Clifford, J., & Marcus, G. E. (1986). *Writing culture: The poetics and politics of ethnography.* Berkeley, CA: University of California Press.

Dance, F. E. X. (1970). The concept of "communication." *Journal of Communication, 20,* 201–210.

Dance, F. E. X. (1980). Swift, slow, sweet, sour, adazzle, dim: What makes human communication human? *Western Journal of Speech Communication, 44,* 60–63.

Davis, W. (1986). *The serpent and the rainbow.* New York: Simon & Shuster.

Ellis, D. G. (1980). Ethnographic considerations in initial interaction. *Western Journal of Speech Communication, 44,* 104–107.

Garfinkel, H. (1967). *Studies in ethnomethodology.* Englewood Cliffs, NJ: Prentice-Hall.

Geertz, C. (1980). Blurred genres. *American Scholar, 49,* 165–179.

Geertz, C. (1988). *Works and lives: The anthropologist as author.* Palo Alto, CA: Stanford University Press.

Goodall, H. L. (1989a). Interpretive contexts for decision making. In G. M. Phillips (Ed.), *Group skills and group outcomes.* Norwood, NJ: Ablex.

Goodall, H. L. (1989b). *Casing a promised land: The autobiography of an organizational detective as cultural ethnographer.* Carbondale, IL: Southern Illinois University Press.

Goodall, H. L., Wilson, G. L., & Waagen, C. L. (1986). The performance appraisal interview: An interpretive reassessment. *The Quarterly Journal of Speech, 72,* 74–87.

Haley, J. (1976). *Problem-solving therapy.* New York: Basic Books.

Hawes, L. C. (1977). Toward a hermeneutic phenomenology of communication. *Communication Quarterly, 25,* 30–41.

Hickson, M., III. (1983). Ethnomethodology: The promise of applied communication research? *The Southern Speech Communication Journal, 48,* 182–195.

Hymes, D. (1962). The ethnography of speaking. In T. Gladwin & W. Sturtevant (Eds.), *Anthropology and human behavior.* Washington, DC: Anthropological Society of Washington.

Janis, I. L. (1982). *Groupthink* (2nd rev. ed.) Boston: Houghton Mifflin.

Katriel, T., & Philipsen, G. (1981). "What we need is communication": "Communication" as a cultural category in some American speech. *Communication Monographs, 48,* 301- 317.

Keller, E. F. (1985). *Reflections on gender and science.* New Haven, CT: Yale University Press.

Kerr, M., & Bowen, M. (1988). *Family evaluation: An approach based on Bowen Therapy.* New York: W. W. Norton.

Korzybski, A. (1933). *Science and sanity.* Lakeville, CT: International Non-Aristotelian Library Publishing Company.

Krueger, D. L. (1982). Marital decision-making: A language-action analysis. *The Quarterly Journal of Speech, 68,* 273–287.

Mader, T. F., Rosenfield, L. W., and Mader, D. C. (1985). The rise and fall of departments. In T. Benson (Ed.), *Speech Communication in the 20th Century.* Carbondale, IL: Southern Illinois University Press.

Marcus, G. E., and Fischer, M. M. J. (1986). *Anthropology as cultural critique: An experimental moment in the human sciences.* Chicago: University of Chicago Press.

Mead, G. H. (1934). *Mind, self, and society.* Chicago: University of Chicago Press.

Miller, G. R. (1966). On defining communication—another stab. *Journal of Communication, 16,* 88–98.

Mishler, E. (1979). Meaning in context: Is there any other kind? *Harvard Educational Review, 49,* 1–19.

Newman, C. (1984). *The postmodern aura.* Evanston, IL: Northwestern University Press.

Pacanowsky, M. E. (1986, November). Slouching towards Chicago. Paper presented at the annual convention of the Speech Communication Association, Chicago.

Paul, R. (1988, 21 August). The living dead and the puffer fish. *New York Times Book Review,* p. 14.

Philipsen, G. (1975). Speaking "like a man" in Teamsterville: Cultural patterns of role enactment in an urban neighborhood. *The Quarterly Journal of Speech, 61,* 13–22.

Philipsen, G. (1977). Linearity of research design in ethnographic studies of speaking. *Communication Quarterly, 25,* 42–50.

Phillips, G. M., & Wood, J. T. (1983). *Communication and Human Relationships.* New York: Macmillan.

Rawlins, W. K. (1985). Stalking interpersonal communication effectiveness: social, individual, or situational integration? In T. W. Benson (Ed.), *Speech communication in the 20th century*. Carbondale, IL: Southern Illinois University Press.

Sackmann, S. (1987, August). *Beyond cultural artifacts*. Paper presented to the Conference on Interpretive Approaches to Organizational Study, Alta, UT.

Sahlins, M. (1976). *Culture and practical reason*. Chicago: University of Chicago Press.

Said, E. (1978). *Orientalism*. New York: Random House.

Toulmin, S., Rieke, R., & Janik, A. (1979). *An introduction to reasoning*. New York: Macmillian.

Turner, V. W. (1986). Dewey, Dilthey, and drama: An essay in the anthropology of experience. In V. W. Turner & E. M. Bruner, (Eds.), *The anthropology of experience*. Urbana, IL: University of Illinois Press.

Tyler, S. (1988). *The unspoken*. Madison, WI: University of Wisconsin Press.

Van Maanen, J. (1988). *Tales of the field: On writing ethnography*. Chicago: University of Chicago Press.

Wenzel, J. W. (1980). Perspectives on argument. In J. Rhodes & S. Newell (Eds.), *Proceedings of the Summer Conference on Argumentation*. Alta, UT: Speech Communication Association and American Forensic Association.

Wood, J. T. (1984). Research and the social world: Honoring the connections. *Communication Quarterly, 32*, 3–8.

Wyatt, N. J., and Phillips, G. M. (1988). *Studying organizational communication*. Norwood, NJ: Ablex.

• II •

Health Communication and Interpersonal Competence

GARY L. KREPS
JIM L. QUERY, JR.

What We Know

The State of Health Communication Inquiry

Health communication has emerged during the 1970s and 1980s as an active and exciting area of social scientific inquiry concerned with the central role of human interaction in the provision of health care and promotion of health (Arntson, 1985; Kreps, 1981a, 1988a; Thompson, 1984). It is an important area of communication inquiry that demonstrates communication's relevance to satisfactory health care, a concern affecting the lives of virtually all members of society. Health communication inquiry can also serve the communication discipline by applying and testing extant communication theories and principles, helping to refine communication theory and increase the external validity of communication knowledge. Most important, however, health communication inquiry can help increase the effectiveness of health care delivery by generating relevant knowledge that provides health care consumers and providers with direction for enhancing their effectiveness as health communicators (Kreps, 1988b, 1988c).

The central analytic perspective of most health communication inquiry concerns the role of interpersonal communication in health care delivery. Such inquiry has examined the range of communication relationships established between and among health care providers and consumers, demonstrating how these interpersonal relationships exert powerful influences on health and health care delivery (Kreps, 1988b). While the interpersonal relationship has emerged as the contemporary focus of

293

health communication research and education, past health communication research has also examined key aspects of intrapersonal, group, organizational, mediated, and societal communication in health and health care (see Kreps, 1988a, for a review of health communication inquiry at these levels). These hierarchical levels of health communication inquiry are generally framed in terms of their influence upon interpersonal relationships, building into or building upon the interpersonal level of communication (Phillips & Wood, 1983; Wood, 1982). Consistent with the current emphasis, this chapter focuses on the role of interpersonal communication competence in health care, reviewing pertinent literature, identifying significant issues, and suggesting directions for future health communication research and pedagogy.

What We Believe

Central to health communication inquiry is the assumption that effectiveness of health care depends largely on the communication skills and competencies of health care providers and consumers (Arntson, 1985; Cassata, 1980; Cline, 1983; Hill 1978; Kreps, 1981a, 1985, 1988a, 1988b; Kreps & Query, 1986; Kreps & Thornton, 1984; Lane, 1982; Morse & Piland, 1981; Thompson, 1984). This assumption is based on a more general disciplinary assertion that effective communication is based upon the development and expression of communication competencies (Bostrom, 1984; Spitzberg & Cupach, 1984; Wiemann, 1977). Communication competency in health care is conceptualized as the ability to effectively utilize interpersonal relations skills to elicit cooperation from, gather information from, and share health information with relevant individuals within the health care system (Kreps, 1988a, 1988b; Kreps & Query, 1987; Maibach & Kreps, 1986; Ruben, 1976; Ruben & Bowman, 1986). According to this central assumption, development of communication competencies is imperative for effective health care.

Competent Health Communication and the Effectiveness of Health Care

Health communication competence has often been applied to the provider consumer relationship, linking interpersonal communication effectiveness to outcomes such as client satisfaction, compliance with treatment regimens, and enhanced recuperative abilities (Ben-Sira, 1976; DiMatteo, 1979; DiMatteo, Prince, & Taranta, 1979; Hulka, Cassel, Kupper, & Burdette, 1976; Hulka, Kupper, Cassel, & Efird, 1975; Lane 1982, 1983). Communication competencies are important for health care consumers and for health care providers (Jones & Phillips, 1988; Kreps, 1988a, 1988b; Kreps & Query, 1987). Competent communication is seen as enabling health care consumers and providers to gather and interpret pertinent information for accomplishing their health care delivery objectives because it encourages cooperation between providers and consumers and facilitates the sharing of relevant information necessary to accomplish health evaluation and maintenance (Babbie, 1973; Kreps, 1988a).

In addition to describing the need for interpersonal communication competence in provider-patient relationships, several authors have identified the importance of interpersonal competence in the interprofessional relationships established between health care providers (Hill, 1978; Kreps, 1988a; Kreps & Thornton, 1984). Interdependent health care providers use their interpersonal communication skills to share relevant health information and elicit cooperation from one another. The effectiveness of interpersonal communication relationships established between providers influences the abilities of these professionals to coordinate complex health-preserving activities.

This assumption about the importance of interpersonal communication competencies in health care is clearly illustrated in Kreps's (1988b, p. 354) model of Relational Health Communication Competence (see Figure 1). The model is a wheel, the spokes of which represent interdependent health care providers, while the hub represents the health care consumer. This model illustrates the interdependent communication relationships that exist between providers and between providers and consumers in the delivery of health care, as well as demonstrating that the health care system revolves around the consumer.

In the model, communication flows between the different spokes (providers) of the wheel and between the spokes and the hub (consumers) of the wheel to facilitate effective health care delivery. The levels of interpersonal communication competence (including specific communication knowledge and skills) possessed by interdependent health care providers and consumers is depicted by the rings that surround the hub of the wheel and the circumference of the wheel. The terrain upon which the wheel rolls represents the specific health care contexts within which

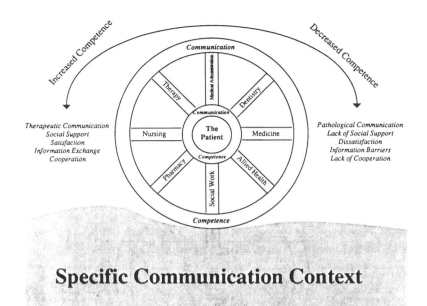

Figure 11-1.   Model of relational health communication competence.

providers and consumers interact. Certain health care contexts may be more difficult (steeper and more difficult to traverse) than other contexts, demanding high levels of interpersonal communication competence between providers and consumers to enable the wheel to roll forward to accomplish health communication goals, such as increased interpersonal satisfaction, therapeutic communication outcomes, cooperation between providers and consumers, social support, and effective information exchange. Insufficient levels of communication competence will prevent the wheel from moving forward or even cause the wheel to roll backwards, failing to fulfill health communication goals.

A consensual belief of health communication inquiry is that human communication is central to all aspects of health care. Clinical knowledge and skills are not enough. Effective communication enables health care providers and consumers to apply clinical knowledge and skills appropriately in health care situations by allowing them to share relevant health information, to make informed health care decisions, and to coordinate efforts in health care treatment. Competent communication in health care situations is believed to be a crucial element of effective health care.

Interpersonal Health Communication Research

Therapeutic communication is an interpersonally based topic of health communication inquiry that has received a great deal of attention from health communication scholars. Past study of therapeutic communication has helped identify specific interpersonal communication characteristics that lead to individual problem solving, enlightenment, and reorientation (Barnlund, 1968; Kreps, in press). Clinical psychologists such as Ruesch (1957, 1961, 1963), Ruesch and Bateson (1951), Rogers (1951, 1957, 1967), and Carkhuff (1967) were pioneers in examining the interpersonal communication behaviors and characteristics of helpers that enable them to be therapeutic. Later studies by communication scholars such as Burleson (1983), Northouse (1977), Pettegrew (1977), Pettegrew and Thomas (1978), and Rossiter (1975) built upon that pioneering work by identifying and exploring specific communication strategies used in therapeutic communication, such as communicating empathetically and comfortingly with others. The approaches taken and conclusions reached in these studies of therapeutic communication have been diverse, yet all support the contention that establishing and maintaining supportive and caring human relationships increase the potential for therapeutic outcome in interpersonal communication.

Another interesting relationally based area of health communication research that is closely related to therapeutic communication is examination of the social support functions of interpersonal communication (Albrecht & Adelman, 1984, 1987; Dickson-Markman & Shern, 1984; Droge, Arntson, & Norton, 1981; Gottlieb, 1981; Query, 1987). Social support appears to be a special form of nonclinical therapeutic communication developing within communication networks, often between family members, friends, and peers. Studies of social support have demonstrated the need for expressive social communication contacts with others to help maintain individual well-being and psychological health (Gottlieb, 1988, Kessler & McLeod, 1985). The social support construct has become increasingly important as Americans have gradually taken more personal responsibility for their own health and health care, depended more on informal relational partners for health information, and begun widespread use of self-help groups for emotional, psychological, and educational health care (Kreps, 1988a).

A great deal of health communication inquiry has centered on planning and directing relationship development in provider-patient interviews (Arntson, Droge, & Fassl, 1978; Carroll & Monroe, 1980; Cassata, Conroe, & Clements, 1977; Foley & Sharf, 1981; Hawes, 1972a, 1972b; Hawes & Foley, 1973). Much of this research has examined interpersonal communication patterns in interviews, identified specific communication characteristics used by health care providers to control interview communication, and developed communication strategies to help health care providers establish rapport and elicit full and accurate information from health care consumers. The research concerning health communication in interviews has been very pragmatic, applied to the realistic concerns of information exchange in health care interviews.

Recent health communication research has highlighted the important role of interpersonal communication in establishing and maintaining effective and satisfying provider-consumer health care relationships (Street & Wiemann, 1987). For example, the groundbreaking research conducted by Greenfield, Kaplan, and Ware (1985) directly relates communication to the physical outcomes of health care treatment, suggesting that the effectiveness of communication relationships established between health care providers and consumers significantly influences the success of health care. In their field study, they demonstrated that the physical conditions of health care consumers who interacted often with their providers about health care treatment decisions improved more than the physical conditions of those consumers who were less involved in interaction with providers (Greenfield, Kaplan, & Ware, 1985). Building upon these studies, future research can help identify the specific characteristics of provider-consumer communication that promotes advantageous patient responses to health care treatment.

Research has also shown that interpersonal communication of accurate and timely information about health and illness is crucial to all individuals involved in health care systems, helping them direct individual and conjoint behaviors toward the accomplishment of health evaluation and maintenance (Feldman, 1976; Maibach & Kreps, 1986; Roter, 1983; Ruben & Bowman, 1986; Smith, 1976). Health care providers, especially physicians, have the potential to strongly promote public health and health risk prevention by providing their clients with relevant health information through interpersonal counseling and health education (Center for Health Education, 1984a; 1984b; Maibach & Kreps, 1986; McIntosh, 1974; Pierce, Watson, Knights, Glidden, Williams, & Watson, 1984; Relman, 1982). For example, a recent national survey of public health beliefs and practices identified primary care physicians as

Americans' most preferred source of health information: 84 percent of the 1,250 persons surveyed identified discussions with their personal physicians as their most useful source of health information (Kreps, Ruben, Baker, & Rosenthal, 1988).

This selective review of relevant literature concerning interpersonal communication in health care has clearly identified potential psychological, physical, and educational benefits of effective interpersonal health communication. Research has shown that supportive and caring interpersonal communication can be therapeutic, helping people cope with and overcome many difficult life problems. It has shown that strategic interpersonal communication between health care providers and consumers can help increase the exchange of relevant health information. Such communication can increase consumer involvement in health care decision making, promoting knowledge and practices consistent with health. Furthermore, cooperative communication relationships between health care providers and consumers can enhance the success of health care treatment.

What Are the Current Issues for Research and Development?

There are several thorny research, theory, and application issues in health communication inquiry, as well as many communication-based health care delivery problems that have been recurrently addressed in the health communication literature. First we will examine several major research, theory, and application controversies in health communication scholarship. Then we will review the role of health communication in seven serious problems that limit the effectiveness of the health care system.

Health Communication Research Issues

Arntson (1985), in an insightful evaluation of health communication research, has identified four major methodological problems:

1. Too much health communication research has utilized conceptually flawed dependent measures such as simplistic operationalizations of patient satisfaction and compliance. For example, health consumers often have a cultural predisposition toward satisfac-

tion with their physicians because of the status afforded to medicine within society. This predisposition skews self-report data on patient satisfaction with their physicians.

2. Most health communication research fails to examine the interactive nature of consumer-provider communication. For example, much research examines only the communication patterns of health care providers, ignoring discursive interaction between providers and consumers.

3. There has been overreliance in health communication research on cross-sectional, rather than longitudinal, research designs. Studies often examine health communication behaviors at one point in time, rather than examining the developing patterns of health communication relationships over time.

4. Researchers have tended to overgeneralize the results of health communication studied to external populations that are not equivalent to the research samples studied (the ecological fallacy). For example, results of studies of doctor-patient communication conducted in university health care clinics or private practice offices are often generalized to all health care delivery systems. Moreover, studies of communication in specialized health care practices, such as pediatric or psychiatric health care settings, are unrealistically generalized to other health care service situations.

Thompson (1984), in a provocative review of the health communication literature, contends that too much health communication research deals oversimplistically with the communication process and, in fact, often does not really focus on communication. "The process of creating meaning or the creation of a relationship through communication are rarely the focus," Thompson argues (1984, p. 148). This lack of communication focus, she explains, is due to a failure to ground many health communication studies on a well-developed base of communication theory.

Kreps (1988a, 1988c), in evaluating health communication inquiry and setting the agenda for future health communication research and development, argues that health communication researchers should apply their work to improving the health care system. He explains that, far too often, health communication researchers have been naively content to report research data without applying these data to help improve health care delivery. Kreps contends that past health communication research has failed to adequately address serious communication-based health care problems and must be extended to help develop and implement relevant policies and programs to help resolve serious health care issues.

Additional issues in health communication research include a provider bias, narrow professional focus on medicine and nursing, and failure to focus on the communication needs and problems of specialized groups of consumers (Kreps, 1988b). The focus of attention in much health communication research has been on the communication needs of health care providers, often ignoring the needs of health care consumers (Thompson, 1984). Consumers, as well as providers, of health care have important and challenging interpersonal communication needs in health care. To help consumers achieve their goals future health communication research must focus on how to increase the effectiveness of both consumer and provider communication in health care. Health communication research has favored examination of communication in the fields of medicine and nursing, neglecting other relevant health service areas (Thompson, 1984). Past health communication research has also tended to neglect important groups of underserved consumers, such as women (Corea, 1977; Lennane & Lennane, 1973, Mendelsohn, 1981), the poor (Kosa & Zola, 1975; LaFargue, 1972), minorities (Hoppe & Heller, 1975; Martiney, 1978; Quesada & Heller, 1977; White, 1974), and the aged (Callahan, 1987; Kreps, 1986a, 1988a; Thompson, 1984). Future research should be designed to examine the health communication needs of these groups of health care consumers.

Pragmatic Communication Issues in Health Care

As well as the issues surrounding health communication research, seven major pragmatic health care delivery problems have been identified in the health communication literature (Kreps, 1988a, 1988b):

1. Low levels of *patient compliance* have been linked to the failure to establish effective provider-patient communication relationships (Charney, 1972; DiMatteo, 1979; Lane, 1982, 1983; Stone, 1979). Past research has focused on patient compliance with health care appointments (Alpert, 1964; Hertz & Stamps, 1977), regimens (Caron, 1968; Davis & Eichorn, 1963; Lane, 1982),

and use of prescribed drugs (Blackwell, 1973; Hulka, Cassel, et al., 1976; Hulka, Kupper, et al. 1975). Most of this literature emphasizes the characteristics of patients that lead to poor compliance, failing to adopt an interactive perspective on the compliance issue that would explore the level of cooperation elicited in the provider-consumer relationship (Kreps, 1988a; Kreps & Thornton, 1984; Lane, 1982, 1983). From a relational perspective, the responsibility for health care cooperation is shared by both the consumer and the provider, and compliance is encouraged by the different interpersonal influence strategies used by communicators (Arntson, 1985; Speedling & Rose, 1985). Research has demonstrated that the quality of interaction between health care providers and consumers strongly influences the level of cooperation engendered between these health communicators (Lane, 1982; Stone, 1979).

2. *Miscommunication and misinformation* in health care has been related to inaccurate interpersonal interpretations, ineffective and manipulative message strategies, and failures to seek and utilize interpersonal feedback between health communicators (Golden & Johnson, 1970; Ley, 1972; Ley, Bradshaw, Eaves, & Walker, 1973; Waitzkin & Stoekle, 1972, 1976). Current data suggest that many physicians' communication practices fail to supply clients with satisfactory levels of health information (Hess, Liepman, & Ruane, 1983; Kreps, Ruben, Baker, & Rosenthal, 1988; Maibach & Kreps, 1986; Newell & Webber, 1983; Relman, 1982; Ruben & Bowman, 1986). The Center for Health Education (1984a) concluded that inadequate interpersonal communication skills, lack of prevention-oriented training, concerns about patient compliance, perceived lack of support services, and administrative constraints are among the key factors that inhibit the success of physicians' health care and health education efforts.

3. *Insensitivity* in health care has been related to low levels of interpersonal respect, attempts at relational control, and inability to accurately interpret nonverbal messages (Daly & Hulka, 1976; Kane & Deuschle, 1967; Korsch, Gozzi, & Francis, 1968; Korsch & Negrete, 1972; Lane, 1982). Both health care providers and health care consumers sometimes communicate insensitively when they are preoccupied with health care problems.

The norm of reciprocity can encourage escalating patterns of insensitivity in response to disrespecting, messages further disrupting the development of satisfying and effective health care relationships.

4. Unrealistic and unfulfilled consumer and provider *expectations* have been linked to cultural stereotypes, misinterpretations of relational needs, and inflexible relational role performances (Blackwell, 1967; Fuller & Quesada, 1973; Mechanic, 1972; Meyerhoff & Larson, 1965; Walker, 1973). Consumers often expect health care providers to be all-knowing and allpowerful. These unrealistic expectations can result in significant disappointment when the outcomes of health care treatments are less than perfect. Provider expectations of dutiful compliance with health care regimens can be equally unrealistic, leading to anger and resentment when orders are not faithfully followed.

5. Lack of *interprofessional understanding and cooperation* in health care has been linked to ineffective health care delivery (Boyer, Lee, & Kirschner, 1977; Frank 1961; Hill, 1978; Kindig, 1975). Competitive, uncooperative interprofessional relationships established between health care providers have become a major problem in health care delivery systems. Power and status discrepancies between practitioners often lead to professional domination and conflict between health care providers (Freidson, 1970). Differences in education, orientation to health care, and evaluation of various health care roles can lead to ethnocentric provider perspectives about the legitimacy of certain professions in comparison to others. This ethnocentrism may result in conflict over domain consensus and authority because of the overlapping responsibilities and interdependent activities of health care providers (Kreps, 1988a; Kreps & Thornton, 1984; Starr, 1982). The broad range of interdependent specialized health care provider roles and functions in health care delivery suggests that health care specialists must elicit cooperation and coordination, collaborate on treatment strategies, share relevant health information, and coordinate professional activities to provide effective health care services, often as members of health care teams (Given & Simmons, 1977; Nagi, 1975; Thornton, 1978). It is difficult to facilitate open sharing of information if any one team member disrespects and attempts to dominate others. The effectiveness

of health care teams is dependent to a large extent on the abilities of the team members to overcome interprofessional status barriers to communication and establish functional interprofessional relationships (Kreps & Thornton, 1984).

6. *Ethical improprieties* in health communication concerning such issues as informed consent about treatment, equal treatment and access to health care, paternalism, confidentiality, and withholding or misrepresenting health information have been identified in the literature (Kreps, 1988a; Kreps & Thornton, 1984; President's Commission for the Study of Ethical Problems in Medicine and Biomedical and Behavioral Research, 1982a, 1982b). Ethical standards for health behaviors are established through information generated by interaction within a given community, and for that reason are largely culturally bound (Kreps & Thornton, 1984). Health behaviors, then, are ethical to the extent they are appropriate to the cultural orientations of health communicators.

Moral dilemmas develop when there are contradictory cultural values guiding the health behaviors individuals choose. For example, if a physician believes it is his or her responsibility to offer medical treatment to a seriously ill child, yet the parents of the child believe that prayer, rather than medical treatment, is the only appropriate way to help their child, the contradictory cultural perspectives of the physician and the parents lead to a moral dilemma. Representatives of different cultures often disagree about what is ethical health behavior. Even within a single culture, health care issues, such as euthanasia, can pose moral dilemmas for individuals. Ethical issues are complex and are not easily resolved, but communication among members of a community of peers and professionals can be used to mediate cultural differences and help individuals gather and examine intersubjective information about health care issues to make mutually satisfactory ethical health care decisions (Kreps & Thornton, 1984).

7. *Dissatisfaction* of both providers and consumers with health care has been tied to many other health communication problems, such as failure to express interpersonal empathy, relational dominance, and dehumanization (Ben-Sira, 1976; Kane & Deuschle, 1967; Korsch, Gozzi, & Francis, 1968; Korsch & Negrete, 1972; Lane, 1983; Street & Wiemann, 1987). Dissatisfied health

care providers are more likely than satisfied providers to experience symptoms of job stress and burnout since they are not receiving sufficient psychological benefits from their work. Such burnout can lead to deterioration of professional performance and increased job turnover (Kreps, 1986b). Dissatisfied health care consumers are less likely to comply with medical advice and more likely to avoid needed treatment (Lane, 1982; 1983).

What Are the Urgencies and Priorities for Future Research?

To address the methodological and pragmatic controversies identified in the previous section of this chapter, we recommend integration of a relevant body of communication literature, namely, interpersonal communication competence, with health communication inquiry. We will begin by providing a critical review and analysis of interpersonal communication competence theory and research, and conclude by offering specific suggestions for applying communication competence to health communication research, development, and pedagogy.

If the central assumption of health communication inquiry (addressed in an earlier section of this chapter)—that competent interpersonal communication is a crucial element in effective health care—is correct, then promotion of competent communication between health providers and consumers addresses many of the pragmatic problems faced by these two groups. For example, each of the seven major pragmatic health communication problems identified in the literature review in the previous section of this chapter should be relieved by increased consumer and provider communication competence.

Conceptualization of Interpersonal Communication Competence

A considerable body of literature addressing the issue of competence in interpersonal communication can be fruitfully applied to the health care system. Past research has examined both the nature of communication competence and the manner in which interpersonal communication competencies are developed in different social contexts, concluding that communication competence is a multidimensional construct based on a wide range of communication abilities that are developed from a combination of communication knowledge and skills (Bochner & Kelly, 1974; Bostrom, 1984; Spitzberg, 1983; 1981; Spitzberg & Cupach, 1984; Wiemann, 1977). Interpersonal communication competence is also situationally bound, dependent on the abilities of communicators to adapt to one another in specific settings (Ruben, 1976).

How to conceptualize interpersonal communication competence is a subject of much debate. Many definitions lack consistency, clarity, or widespread acceptance (Bennett, 1985; Brunner, 1979; Cegala, 1983; Chin & Ringer, 1986; Spitzberg & Cupach, 1984). Exemplifying the pervasive confusion is the wide range of terms employed to describe the competence construct: 1) social skills, 2) communication skills, 3) interpersonal skills, 4) psychosocial competence, 5) social competency, 6) relational competence, 7) rhetorical competence, and 8) environmental competence (Parks, 1977; Spitzberg & Cupach, 1984; Wiemann, 1977). Lack of agreement on a conceptualization hindered theory building and the development of reliable instruments to measure competence (Brunner, 1984; Spitzberg, 1985a). Between fourteen and thirty-two different components of interpersonal communication competence have been identified in previous studies (Duran & Wheeless, 1980; Phelps & Snavely, 1979; Spitzberg & Cupach, 1984). At issue are the validity and reliability of conceptual definitions of the components comprising communication competence, as well as the generalizabiltiy of research based upon these conceptualizations.

Several researchers have linked their definitions to arguments about the nature of competence. For example, Foote and Cottrell (1955) and Spitzberg and Hurt (1985) proposed criteria for determining competent and incompetent individuals, centered on abilities of interactants to attain desired outcomes. According to this perspective, competent individuals are those who consistently control their interactions with others to realize personal goals. Similarly, Argyris (1965) assessed skills of interpersonal communication along the dimension of active versus passive and devised a scale that assigned higher point values to the assertive components than to the passive ones. Thus, competent individuals were judged to be those who engaged in the assertive behaviors, while minimizing occurrence of passive ones. Bennis, Berlew, Schein, and Steele (1968) described competent individuals in terms of their abilities to send and receive information and evoke the expression of feelings in others. Finally, Wiemann (1977), in perhaps the most widely cited work on interpersonal communication competence, defines interpersonal communication competence in terms of selection of interactional choices among available communication behaviors, accomplishment of interpersonal goals, and recognition of the interpersonal and contextual constraints of communication situations.

Different conceptualizations of what comprises interpersonal communication competence can be integrated by recognizing three consistently identified broad categories of skill: cognitive, affective, and behavioral. The cognitive dimension includes abilities to receive, process, and send information in creating, maintaining, and terminating relationships, as well as in communicating task-related information to other persons (Bennis et al., 1968; Cegala, 1981). The affective dimension encompasses psychological characteristics of internal or external locus of control of communication behaviors in interpersonal interactions (Tubbs & Moss, 1977). The behavioral dimension refers to how individuals select strategies to achieve personal goals, while maintaining the integrity of other interactants (Wiemann, 1977).

Beyond this broad level of analysis, conceptualizations differ, largely because of the nature of competence. Each social context constrains opportunities to send, interpret, and act upon communication. Context plays a major role in determining which strategies are used to negotiate the interaction, so that it is not surprising that strategies applicable to one relational encounter will not necessarily be effective in others. Competence, then, is inherently variable—it must be judged in relation to the demands of particular situations (Phillips & Wood, 1983; Wood, 1982). Given this, the hope of formulating a single definition of competence is unrealistic and undesirable.

Operationalization of Interpersonal Communication Competence

Methods to measure interpersonal communication competence are even more diverse than definitions. Spitzberg and Cupach (1984) identified sixty-two different instruments employed to assess interpersonal communication competence and classified these into three broad categories: self report measures; self report of others measures; special context or population measures. The first two categories contained three subgroups of measures: general dispositional, multiple-episodes stimuli, and episode specific. The third category contained four subgroups of measures that assessed children's and adolescents' skills, mental ability, assertiveness, empathy, and role-taking.

In evaluating these instruments, Spitzberg and Cupach (1984) and Spitzberg and Hurt (1985) concluded that their measurement utility was limited. Indeed, only ten of the instruments could be used to identify specific behavioral deficiencies of the interactants. According to Spitzberg and Hurt, the primary reason for the limitations of the instruments was the assumption that a single instrument could assess qualitatively different skills distinguished by their inferential levels and components. For instance, highly inferential skills include subjective impressions of underlying motivation or behavior as smooth versus awkward or cooperative versus uncooperative, while less inferential skills include discrete and objective activities, such as eye contact and vocal variety.

Another problem with most of the measures of interpersonal communication competence is their inflexibility and unstable factor structure. "Virtually all extant measures are self-report only, rating of other only, expert or knowledgeable rater only, trait (dispositional) only, state (event focuses) only, or context bound" (Spitzberg & Hurt, 1985, p. 4). Thus, measures of interpersonal communication competence tend to be limited to the specific sample and preclude generalizations across studies, samples, and contexts. Complicating matters further are the diverse factors thought to undergird each instrument. For example, Chin and Ringer (1986) examined three of the most frequently used interpersonal communication competence instruments, the Wiemann Scale (1977), the Brunner Scale (1984), and the Spitzberg Scale (1985b). Their factor analysis revealed that the strongest factors for each instrument were somewhat similar. Wiemann's (1977) general communication competence factor resembled the other-oriented factor in Brunner's (1984) scale, as well as the "speaking about self and other" factor within the Spitzberg (1985b) scale. All remaining factors for the three scales were dissimilar, supporting Spitzberg's (1985a) contention that no consistent core of components informs current operationalizations of the interpersonal communication competence construct.

As this review suggests, both the conceptualization of communication competence and the appropriate operationalization of competence are matters of dispute. The research to date has identified and explained many alternative definitions and measures. For scholarship to progress further, some agreement must be reached on these two key issues.

Interpersonal Communication Competence and Health Communication

Since competent communication is believed to be extremely important for health care providers and consumers, the merging of communication competence and health communication inquiry seems to be a natural
extension of both areas (Kreps & Query, 1986). Interpersonal communication competence research can be fruitfully applied to health care, providing communication-based theoretical grounding and validated research
instruments. The collaboration of researchers in these two areas can also
benefit communication competence research by helping to test and refine
competence theories and instruments. Furthermore, by conducting communication competence research in different health care contexts, specific,
situationally appropriate interpersonal health communication competencies for consumers and providers can be identified.

We next consider how definitions of measures of communication
competence, discussed in the prior section, have been treated by researchers whose focus is specifically health care communication. Several studies
have already attempted to define competence by identifying various
dimensions of the construct that are relevant to health care contexts, such
as the abilities to communicate with empathy (Carkhuff, 1967; Fine &
Therrien, 1977; Rogers, 1967), to listen nonjudgmentally (Cline, 1983;
Gibb, 1961; Ruben, 1976), to demonstrate interpersonal respect (Rogers, 1967; Ruben, 1976), to display informational congruence between
message intended and message received (Powers & Lowry, 1984), and
to manage interactions (Ruben, 1976; Wiemann, 1977). Wilmington
(1986) reported thirty-seven oral communication behaviors identified by
nursing supervisors as essential to judgments of communication competence and organized these data into seven top health communication
skills: (1) being able to give accurate and sufficient feedback to others,
(2) listening attentively to others, (3) interpreting accurately what others
are saying, (4) giving clear directions, (5) treating others in a professional
manner, (6) communicating information clearly, and &) establishing
one's credibility with others.

Kahn, Cohen, and Jason (1979) surveyed sixty-two medical schools
to determine which interpersonal skills were being taught, identifying:
(1) listening, (2) recognizing verbal and nonverbal cues within interaction, (3) responding, (4) initiating questions while being open to challenges, and (5) information-gathering as the top five communication

skills being taught, with at least 84 percent of the schools indicating they were actively providing instruction in these five skills. Muchmore and Galvin (1983) surveyed practicing professionals serving as members of career advisory boards of community colleges to identify communication competencies of entry-level health care employees. Three broad categories of competencies were identified: speaking skills, listening skills, and human relations skills. Within the area of speaking skills, respondents indicated the importance of using language understood by others; using language, punctuation, and grammar that does not alienate others; and employing appropriate speaking rate, volume, and clarity in diverse situations. Regarding listening skills, respondents emphasized that employees needed to understand directions, obtain necessary information from others, and understand any complaints or relevant needs of others. Concerning human relations skills, respondents stressed the ability to work cooperatively in groups, recognize the feelings of others, and maintain friendly relationships with clients, customers, and co-workers.

DiSalvo, Larsen, and Backus (1986) identified communication skills deemed important to the competence of health care workers by administering a revised version of the Communication Activities Questionnaire (CAQ) (DiSalvo, Larsen, & Seiler, 1976) to 168 supervisors of health care providers, psychologists, rehabilitation counselors, and nurses. They determined that relationship building and listening were the top two skills, while giving and eliciting feedback, exchanging routine information, and motivating others were also seen as essential to effective job performance. Similarly, Morse and Piland (1981) assessed the import of nine communication skills (advising, persuading, instructing, exchanging routine information, speaking before large groups, communicating in small groups, issuing orders, listening, and managing conflict) in three interpersonal communication contexts: nurse-nurse, nurse-physician, and nurse-client interactions. A revised version of the CAQ was administered to 156 nurses from four large midwestern metropolitan hospitals. Five skills were consistently identified as "most essential" for effective job performance across all three interpersonal contexts: (1) listening, (2) exchanging routine information, (3) managing conflict, (4) communicating in small groups, and (5) instructing. Because of its theoretic grounding and multilevel analysis, this study offers perhaps the most useful view of what comprises competent health care communication.

Paralleling efforts to define health communication competencies have been various attempts to measure them. Several techniques for measuring communication competence have been developed specifically for directly and indirectly assessing health care providers. For example, Kahn, Cohen, and Jason (1979) describe indirect assessments such as multiple-choice examinations and patient management simulations, and direct assessments such as staff observation of live medical interviews and review of videotaped provider-client interactions. Direct assessment techniques are exemplified by the verbal profile content analysis method developed by Stiles, Putnam, Wolf, and James (1979), which is used to code and evaluate—in eight mutually exclusive and exhaustive categories—the effectiveness of the verbal utterances of health providers during medical interviews. Additional assessment methods include video examinations where health care providers observe and then respond to realistic health care vignettes, direct observation of health care interactions coupled with global rating scales, and the use of Bales (1950) interaction process analysis to evaluate the use of task and maintenance strategies in health care interactions (Kauss, Robbins, Abrass, & Bakaitis, 1980; Samph & Templeton, 1979; Schoonover, Bassuk, Smith, & Gaskill, 1983; Stillman, 1982; Templeton & MacDonald, 1982). These measurement strategies have relative strengths and weaknesses, suggesting the desirability of correlating multiple measures to validly and reliably assess health communication competence.

In these early studies of communication competence in health care, the most commonly identified interpersonal skills include listening, giving and seeking feedback, giving clear directions, exchanging routine information clearly, gathering information, and building relationships. These studies also reinforce the influence of context in determining situationally appropriate communication competencies. Communication skills that are appropriate to one health care context do not necessarily transfer to another situation.

Communication Competence and Health Communication Education

To facilitate health care providers' and health care consumers' communication knowledge and skills, educational institutions should design curricula to develop both appreciation for the importance of interpersonal communication in health care and enhanced abilities to communicate competently in different health care situations (Barnlund, 1976; Cassata, 1980). Providers and consumers need support in developing knowledge and skills of competent human communication (Association of American Medical Colleges, 1984a; 1984b; Kreps and Query, 1986). Education is the most promising channel for increasing health communication competencies (Kreps, 1988a).

Health communication can and must be taught in several different ways at many different educational levels. For example, in elementary schools, lessons for school children—how to talk about health problems at home and in health care systems, how to utilize communication to help others—can be integrated into basic health courses. In health professional educational programs, such as schools of nursing, pharmacy, dentistry, allied health, social work, and medicine, health communication courses or course sections should be introduced to supplement existing courses for health care providers (Cline & Cardosi, 1983). For practicing health care professionals, continuing education programs can offer programs about current health communication issues and competencies (Kreps, 1984). Undergraduate and graduate college communication programs can also offer courses to groups of students representing different health care consumers and professions to promote the development of interprofessional understanding that can translate into cooperation and teamwork in the effective delivery of health care (Hill, 1978; Kindig, 1975; Kreps, 1985).

Health care delivery organizations can promote effective health communication through policies and in-house training guidelines to increase awareness of the communication demands of health care jobs and the optimal communication skills appropriate to them (Kreps, 1988a; Ruben and Bowman, 1986). Orientation programs in health care institutions should emphasize the importance of trust, cooperation, and other communication qualities established by research and stress the organization's support for good communication. Health care organizations can utilize communication media such as video-tape programs, closed-circuit television systems, and computer systems to educate providers and consumers (Elmore, 1981). Health care organizations can also share their health information resources with the public by implementing health education programs and health fairs to promote public health and good will, as well as to gather information from these audiences about their specific health care concerns, needs, and problems.

Institutions offering program for educating health providers, professional societies for health care providers, and accrediting bodies for both health care organizations and educational programs have the opportunity to establish standards for effective communication by health providers as well as educational programs for helping health care providers and consumers develop effective communication skills (Kreps, 1988a). These organizations can develop criteria for accrediting health care personnel, educational programs, and organizations by assessing the quality of health communication in health care practice. Such assessment and accreditation activities can spur the introduction and dissemination of health communication education and facilitate improvements in health communication practices. For example, a report of a recent national review of medical and premedical education programs conducted by the Association of American Medical Colleges (1984a) indicated that many medical faculties were lagging behind in the development, teaching, and evaluation of the communication skills of physicians and recommended that medical "faculties should teach effective communication with patients (including the medical interview) and must evaluate students' communication with patients with much more care than they do at present" (p. 126). Such institutions can also help stimulate and support health communication research, such as research designed to identify specific communication competencies needed by health care providers and consumers (Kreps, 1988a).

Conclusion

Application of the communication competence construct can provide health communication inquiry with a strong communication-grounded theoretical base as well as help refine the competence construct. Future research on competent communication in health care should develop an interactive perspective for examining the communication skills of both consumers and providers, help identify appropriate communication competencies for health care consumers and providers to use in health communication contexts, and inform relevant health communication educational programs for health care consumers and providers. Future health communication research should also address the related issues of assessment, testing, and promotion of, and education about, communication competencies in health care delivery.

References

Albrecht, T., & Adelman, M. (1984). Social support and life stress: New directions for communication research. *Human Communication Research, 11*, 3–32.

Albrecht, T., & Adelman, M. (1987). *Communicating social support.* Newbury Park, CA: Sage.

Alpert, J. (1964). Broken appointments. *Pediatrics, 34,* 124–132.

Argyris, C. (1965). Explorations in interpersonal competence—I. *Journal of Applied Behavioral Science, 1,* 58–83.

Arntson, P. (1985). Future research in health communication. *Journal of Applied Communication Research, 13,* 118–130.

Arntson, P., Droge, D., & Fassl, H. (1978). Pediatrician-parent communication: Final report. *Communication Yearbook, 2,* 505–522.

Association of American Medical Colleges (1984a). Report of the working group on fundamental skills. *Journal of Medical Education, 59,* 125–134.

Association of American Medical Colleges (1984b). *Physicians for the twenty-first century.* Washington, DC: Author.

Babbie, S. (1973). *Medical communication requirements.* Springfield, VA: U.S. Pacific.

Bales, R. F. (1950). *Interaction process analysis.* Reading, MA: Addison-Wesley.

Barnlund, D. (1968). Therapeutic communication. In D. Barnlund (Ed.), *Interpersonal communication*, pp. 613–645. Boston: Houghton Mifflin, 613–645.

Barnlund, D. (1976). The mystification of meaning: Doctor-patient encounters. *Journal of Medical Education, 51,* 716–725.

Bennett, D. W. (1985). The effect of relationship type, thrust and different perceptual loci on judgements of interpersonal communication competence. (Doctoral dissertation, Ohio University, 1985). *Dissertation Abstracts International, 46,* 2453.

Bennis, W. G., Berlew, D. E., Schein, E. H., & Steele, F. I. (1968). Towards better interpersonal relationships. In W. G. Bennis, D. E. Berlew, E. H. Schein, & F. I. Steele (Eds.), *Interpersonal dynamics: Essays and readings on human interaction* (2nd ed., pp. 647–674). Homewood, IL: Dorsey.

Ben-Sira, Z. (1976). The function of the professional's affective behavior in client satisfaction: A revised approach to social interaction theory. *Journal of Health and Social Behavior, 17,* 3–11.

Blackwell B. (1967). Upper middle class adult expectations about entering the sick role for physical and psychiatric dysfunctions. *Journal of Health and Social Behavior, 8,* 83–95.

Blackwell, B. (1973). Patient compliance. *New England Journal of Medicine, 289,* 249–252.

Bochner, A., & Kelly, C. (1974). Interpersonal competence: Rationale, philosophy, and implementation of a conceptual framework. *Speech Teacher, 23*, 279–301.

Bostrom, R. (Ed.). (1984). *Competence in communication.* Beverly Hills, CA: Sage.

Boyer, L., Lee, D., & Kirschner, C. (1977). A student-run course in interprofessional relations. *Journal of Medical Education, 52*, 183–189.

Brunner, C. C. (1979). *An examination of the relationship between interpersonal communication competence and androgyny.* Unpublished master's thesis, University of Miami, Oxford, OH.

Brunner, C. C. (1984). An investigation of interaction involvement and judgements of interpersonal communication competence. (Doctoral dissertation, Ohio State University, 1984). *Dissertation Abstracts International, 45*, 1571A.

Burleson, B. (1983). Social cognition, empathic motivation, and adults' comforting strategies. *Human Communication Research, 10*, 295–304.

Callahan, D. (1987). *Setting limits: Medical goals in an aging society.* New York: Simon & Schuster.

Carkhuff, R. (1967). Toward a comprehensive model of facilitative interpersonal processes. *Journal of Counseling Psychology, 14*, 67–72.

Caron, H. (1968). Patients' cooperation with a medical regimen. *Journal of the American Medical Association, 203*, 922–926.

Carroll, J., & Monroe, J. (1980). Teaching clinical interviewing in the health professions: A review of empirical research. *Evaluation and the Health Professions, 3*, 21–45.

Cassata, D. (1980). Health communication theory and research: A definitional overview. *Communication Yearbook, 4*, 583–589.

Cassata, D., Conroe, R., & Clements, P. (1977). A program for enhancing medical interviewing using videotape feedback in the family practice residency. *Journal of Family Practice, 4*, 673–677.

Cegala, D. J. (1981). Interaction involvement: A cognitive dimension of communicative competence. *Communication Education, 30*, 109–121.

Cegala, D. J. (1983, November). *Interpersonal communication competence: Recent research and issues.* Paper presented at the annual meeting of the Speech Communication Association, Washington, D.C.

Center for Health Education. (1984a). *Physician involvement in cancer risk reduction education.* Baltimore: Center for Health Education.

Center for Health Education (1984b). *Needs assessment: Physician's role in cancer risk reduction.* Baltimore: Center for Health Education.

Charney, E. (1972). Patient-doctor communication: Implications for the clinician. *Pediatric Clinics of North America, 19*, 263–279.

Chin, J. J., & Ringer, R. J. (1986, April). *What do measures of communication competence measure: A factor analytic study of three competence measures.* Paper presented at the annual meeting of the Central States Speech Association, Cincinnati.

Cline, R. (1983). Interpersonal communication skills for enhancing physician-patient relationships. *Maryland State Medical Journal, 32*, 272–278.

Cline, R., & Cardosi, J. (1983). Interpersonal communication skills for physicians: A rationale for training, *Journal of Communication Therapy, 2*, 137–156.

Corea, G. (1977). *The hidden malpractice: How American medicine treats women as patients and professionals.* New York: William Morrow.

Daly, M. B., & Hulka, B. S. (1976). Talking with the doctor, 2. *Journal of Communication, 25*, 148–152.

Davis, M., & Eichorn, R. (1963). Compliance with medical regimes: A panel study. *Journal of Health and Human Behavior, 4*, 240–249.

Dickson-Markman, F., & Shern, D. (1984, May). *Social support and health: Is quantity as good as quality?* Paper presented to the International Communication Association Convention, San Francisco.

DiMatteo, M. (1979). A social psychological analysis of physician-patient rapport: Toward a science of the art of medicine. *Journal of Social Issues, 35*, 12–33.

DiMatteo, M., Prince, L. M., & Taranta, A. (1979). Patients' perceptions of physicians' behaviour: Determinants of patient commitment to the therapeutic relationship. *Journal of Community Health, 4*, 280–290.

DiSalvo, V. S., Larsen, J. K., & Backus, D. K. (1986). The health care communicator: An identification of skills and problems. *Communication Education, 35*, 231–242.

DiSalvo, V. S., Larsen, J. K., & Seiler, W. (1976). Communication skills needed by persons in business organizations. *Communication Education, 25*, 269–275.

Droge, D., Arntson, P., & Norton, R. (1981, May). *The social support function in epilepsy self help groups.* Paper presented to the International Communication Association Conference, Dallas.

Duran, R. L., & Wheeless, V. E. (1980, November). *Social management: Toward a theory based operationalization of communication competence.* Paper presented at the annual meeting of the Speech Communication Association, New York.

Elmore, G. (1981, October). *Integrating video technology and organizational communication.* Paper presented at the annual meeting of the Indiana Speech Association, Indianapolis.

Feldman, J. (1976). *The dissemination of health information.* Chicago: Aldine Press.

Fine, V., & Therrien, M. (1977). Empathy in doctor-patient relationship: Skill training for medical studies. *Journal of Medical Education, 52*, 752.

Foley, R., & Sharf, B. (1981). The five interviewing techniques most frequently overlooked by primary care physicians. *Behavioral Medicine, 11*, 26–31.

Foote, N. N., & Cottrell, L. S., Jr. (1955). *Identity and Interpersonal Competence.* Chicago: University of Chicago Press.

Frank, L. (1961). Interprofessional Communication. *American Journal of Public Health, 51,* 1798–1804.

Freidson, E. (1970). *Professional dominance: The social structure of medical care.* Chicago: Aldine Press.

Fuller, D., & Quesada, G. (1973). Communication in medical therapeutics. *Journal of Communication, 23,* 361–370.

Gibb, J. (1961). Defensive communication. *Journal of Communication, 3,* 141–148.

Given, B., & Simmons, S. (1977). The interdisciplinary health care team. *Nursing Forum, 16,* 164–184.

Golden, J., & Johnson, G. (1970). Problems of distortion in doctor-patient communication. *Psychiatry in Medicine, 1,* 127–149.

Gottlieb, B. (1981). *Social networks and social support.* Beverly Hills, CA: Sage.

Gottlieb, B. (1988). *Marshaling social support: Formats, processes, and effects.* Newbury Park, CA: Sage.

Greenfield, S., Kaplan, S., & Ware, J. (1985). Expanding patient involvement in care: Effects on patient outcomes. *Annals of Internal Medicine, 102,* 520–528.

Hawes, L. (1972a). Development and application of an interview coding system. *Central States Speech Journal, 23,* 92–99.

Hawes, L. (1972b). The effects of interviewer style on patterns of dyadic communication. *Speech Monographs, 39,* 114–123.

Hawes, L., & Foley, J. (1973). A Markov analysis of interview communication. *Speech Monographs, 40,* 208–219.

Hertz, P., & Stamps, P. (1977). Appointment-keeping behavior re-evaluated. *American Journal of Public Health, 67,* 1033–1036.

Hess, J., Liepman, M., & Ruane, T. (1983). *Family practice and preventive medicine: Health promotion in primary care.* New York: Human Sciences Press.

Hill, S. K. (1978). Health communication: Focus on interprofessional communication. *Communication Administration Bulletin, 25,* 31–36.

Hoppe, S., & Heller, P. (1975). Alienation, familism, and the utilization of health services by Mexican-Americans. *Journal of Health and Social Behavior, 16,* 304–314.

Hulka, B. S., Cassel, J. C., Kupper, L. L., & Burdette, J. A. (1976). Communication compliance, and concordance between physicians and patients with prescribed medications. *American Journal of Public Health, 66,* 847–853.

Hulka, B. S., Kupper, L. L., Cassel, J. C., & Efird, R. L. (1975). Medication use and misuse: Physician-patient discrepancies. *Journal of Chronic Disease,* *28,* 7–21.

Jones, J. A., & Phillips, G. M. (1988). *Communicating with your doctor.* Carbondale, IL: Southern Illinois University Press.

Kahn, G. S., Cohen, B., & Jason, H. (1979). The teaching of interpersonal skills in U.S. medical schools. *Journal of Medical Education, 54,* 29–35.

Kane, R., & Deuschle, K. (1967). Problems in doctor-patient communication. *Medical Care, 5,* 260–271.

Kauss, D. R., Robbins, A. S., Abrass, I., Bakaitis, R. F., & Anderson, L. A. (1980). The long-term effectiveness of interpersonal skills training in medical schools. *Journal of Medical Education, 55,* 595–601.

Kessler, R., & McLeod, J. (1985). Social support and mental health in community samples. In S. Cohen and S. Syme (Eds.), *Social support and health,* (pp. 219–240). New York: Academic Press.

Kindig, D. (1975). Interdisciplinary education for primary health care team delivery. *Journal of Medical Education, 50,* 97–110.

Korsch, B. M., Gozzi, E. K., & Francis, V. (1968). Gaps in doctor-patient communication: Doctor-patient interaction and patient satisfaction. *Pediatrics, 42,* 855–871.

Korsch, B. M. & Negrete, V. F. (1972). Doctor-patient communication. *Scientific American, 227,* 66–74.

Kosa, J., & Zola, I. (Eds.) (1975). *Poverty and health—a sociological analysis.* Cambridge, MA: Harvard University Press.

Kreps, G. L. (1981a). Communication education in the future: The emerging area of health communication. *Indiana Speech Journal, 16,* 30–39.

Kreps, G. L. (1981b, October). *Therapeutic communication in the interview process.* Paper presented to the Indiana Speech Association Conference, Indianapolis.

Kreps, G. L. (1984). Communication training for health care employees: Implications for higher education and the health care industry. *Proceedings of Partnerships for Employee Training: Implications for Education, and Business, and Industry, National issues in Higher Education, 11,* 175–192.

Kreps, G. L. (1985, May). *The development and presentation of an interdisciplinary survey course in health communication.* Paper presented to the Eastern Communication Association Conference, Providence, R.I.

Kreps, G. L. (1986a). Health communication and the elderly. *World Communication, 15,* 55–70.

Kreps, G. L. (1986b). Description and evaluation of a nurse retention organizational development research program. In H. Gueutal & M. Kavanagh (Eds.), *Proceedings of the Eastern Academy of Management* (pp. 18–24), New York: Eastern Academy of Management.

Kreps, G. L. (1988a). The pervasive role of information in health and health care:

Implications for health communication policy. *Communication Yearbook, 11*, 238–276.

Kreps, G. L. (1988b). Relational communication in health care. *Southern Speech Communication Journal, 53*, 344–359.

Kreps, G. L. (1988c). Setting the agenda for health communication research and development: Scholarship that can make a difference. *Health Communication, 1*, 11–15.

Kreps, G. L. (in press). The nature of therapeutic communication. In G. Gumpert & S. Fish (Eds.), *Mediated therapeutic communication.* Norwood, NJ: Ablex.

Kreps, G. L., & Query, J. (1986, November). *Assessment and testing in the health professions.* Paper presented to the Speech Communication Association Conference, Chicago.

Kreps, G. L., Ruben, B., Baker, M., & Rosenthal, S. (1988). A national survey of public knowledge about digestive health and disease: Implications for health education. *Public Health Reports, 102*, 270–277.

Kreps, G. L., & Thornton, B. C. (1984). *Health communication.* New York: Longman.

LaFargue, J. (1972). Role of prejudice in rejection of health care. *Nursing Research, 21*, 53–58.

Lane, S. (1982). Communication and patient compliance. In L. Pettegrew (Ed.), *Straight talk: explorations in provider patient interaction* (pp. 59–69). Louisville, KY: Humana.

Lane, S. (1983). Compliance, satisfaction, and physician-patient communication. *Communication Yearbook, 7*, 772–799.

Lennane, K., & Lennane, R. (1973). Alleged psychogenic disorders in women—a possible manifestation of sexual prejudice. *New England Journal of Medicine, 288*, 288–292.

Ley, P. (1972). Comprehension, memory, and the success of communications with the patient. *Journal for Institutional Health Education, 10*, 23–29.

Ley, P., Bradshaw, P., Eaves, D., & Walker, C. (1973). A method of increasing patients' recall of information presented by doctors. *Psychological Medicine, 3*, 217–220.

Maibach, E. W., & Kreps, G. L. (1986). *Communicating with patients: Primary care physicians; perspectives on cancer prevention, screening, and education.* Paper presented to the International Conference on Doctor-Patient Communication, London, Ontario, Canada.

Martiney, R. (1978). *Hispanic culture and health care—fact, fiction and folklore.* St. Louis: C. V. Mosby.

McIntosh, J. (1974). Process of communication, information seeking control associated with cancer: A selected review of the literature. *Social Science and Medicine, 8*, 167–187.

Mechanic, D. (1972). *Public expectations and health care: Essays on the changing organization of health services.* New York: Wiley.

Mendelsohn, R. (1981). *Male practice: How doctors manipulate women.* Chicago: Contemporary Books.

Meyerhoff, B., & Larson, W. (1965). The doctor as cultural hero: The routinization of charisma. *Human Organization, 24,* 188–191.

Morse, B., & Piland, R. (1981). An assessment of communication competencies needed by intermediate-level health care providers: A study of nurse-patient, nurse-doctor, nurse-nurse communication relationships. *Journal of Applied Communication Research, 9,* 30–41.

Muchmore, J., & Galvin, K. (1983). A report of the task force on career competencies in oral communication skills for community college students seeking immediate entry into the work force. *Communication Education, 32,* 207–220.

Nagi, S. (1975). Teamwork in health care in the United States: A sociological perspective. *The Milbank Quarterly, 53*(1), 75–91.

Newell, G., & Webber, C. (1983). The primary care physician in cancer prevention. *Family and Community Health, 5,* 77–84.

Northouse, P. (1977). Predictors of empathic ability in an organizational setting. *Human Communication Research, 3,* 176–178.

Parks, M. R. (1977, November). *Issues in the explication of communication competence.* Paper presented to the annual meeting of the Western Speech Communication Association, Phoenix, AZ.

Pettegrew, L. (1977). An investigation of therapeutic communicator style. *Communication Yearbook, 1,* 593–604.

Pettegrew, L., & Thomas, R. C. (1978). Communication style differences in formal vs. informal therapeutic relationships. *Communication Yearbook, 2,* 523–538.

Phelps, L. A., & Snavely, W. B. (1979, February). *Development of conceptual and operational definitions of interpersonal communication competence.* Paper presented at the annual meeting of the Midwest Basic Course Directors Conference, Ames, IA.

Phillips, G. M., and Wood, J. T. (1983). *Communication and human relationships: The study of interpersonal communication.* New York: Macmillan.

Pierce, J., Watson, D., Knights, S., Glidden, T., Williams, S., & Watson, R. (1984). A controlled trial of health education in the physician's office. *Preventive Medicine, 13,* 185–192.

Powers, W., & Lowry, D. (1984). Basic communication fidelity: A fundamental approach. In R. Bostrom (Ed.), *Competence in Communication* (pp. 57–71). Beverly Hills, CA: Sage.

President's Commission for the Study of Ethical Problems in Medicine and Biomedical and Behavioral Research (1982a). *Making health care decisions:*

The ethical and legal implications of informed consent in the patient-practitioner relationship (Vols. 1–3). Washington, DC: U.S. Government Printing Office.

President's Commission for the Study of Ethical Problems in Medicine and Biomedical and Behavioral Research (1982b). *Splicing life: The social and ethical issues of genetic engineering with human beings.* Washington, DC: U.S. Government Printing Office.

Query, J. (1987). *A field test of the relationship between interpersonal communication competence, number of social supports, and satisfaction with the social support received by an elderly support group.* Unpublished master's thesis, Ohio University, Athens, Ohio.

Quesada, G., & Heller, R. (1977). Sociocultural barriers to medical care among Mexican-Americans in Texas. *Medical Care, 15,* 93–101.

Relman, A. (1982). Encouraging the practice of preventive medicine in health promotion. *Public Health Reports, 97,* 216–219.

Rogers, C. (1951). *Client-centered therapy.* Boston: Houghton Mifflin.

Rogers, C. (1957). The necessary and sufficient conditions of therapeutic personality change. *Journal of Consulting Psychology, 21,* 95–103.

Rogers, C. (Ed.). (1967). *The therapeutic relationship and its impact.* Madison, WI: University of Wisconsin Press.

Rossiter, C. (1975). Defining therapeutic communication. *Journal of Communication, 25,* 127–130.

Roter, D. (1983). Physician/patient communication: Transmission of information and patient effects. *Maryland State Medical Journal, 32,* 260–265.

Ruben, B. D. (1976). Assessing communication competency for intercultural adaptation. *Group and Organization Studies, 1,* 334–354.

Ruben, B., and Bowman, J. (1986). Patient satisfaction (Part 1): Critical issues in the theory and design of patient relations training. *Journal of Healthcare Education and Training, 1,* 1–5.

Ruesch, J. (1957). *Disturbed communication.* New York: W. W. Norton.

Ruesch, J. (1961). *Therapeutic communication.* New York: W. W. Norton.

Ruesch, J. (1963). The role of communication in therapeutic transactions. *Journal of Communication, 13,* 132–139.

Ruesch, J., & Bateson, G. (1951). *The social matrix of psychiatry.* New York: W. W. Norton.

Samph, T., & Templeton, B. (1979). *The interpersonal skills project: Strategies for the evaluation of competence of physicians who assume responsibilities for patient care in graduate medical education* (Final report to Health Resources Administration, HRA 231–76–0067). Philadelphia: Board of Medical Examiners.

Schoonover, S. C., Bassuk, E. L., Smith, R., & Gaskill, D. (1983). The use of videotape programs to teach interpersonal skills. *Journal of Medical Education, 58,* 804–810.

Smith, R. (1976). *Doctors and patients.* Boise, ID: Syms-York.

Speedling, E., & Rose, D. (1985). Building an effective doctor-patient relationship: From patient satisfaction to patient participation. *Social Science and Medicine, 21*, 115–120.

Spitzberg, B. H (1981, November). *Competence in communicating: A taxonomy, review, critique, and predictive model.* Paper presented at the Speech Communication Association Conference, Anaheim, CA.

Spitzberg, B. H. (1983). Communication competence as knowledge, skill, and impression. *Communication Education, 32*, 323–329.

Spitzberg, B. H. (1985a, May). *Can of worms in the study of communication competence.* Paper presented at the annual meeting of the International Communication Association, Honolulu, HI.

Spitzberg, B. H. (1985b). *Conversational skills rating scale.* Unpublished manuscript, North Texas State University, Denton, TX.

Spitzberg, B. H., & Cupach, W. R. (1984). *Interpersonal communication competence.* Beverly Hills, CA: Sage.

Spitzberg, B. H., & Hurt, H. T. (1985, November). *The measurement of interpersonal skills in instructional contexts.* Paper presented at the annual meeting of the Speech Communication Association, Denver, CO.

Starr, P. (1982). *The social transformation of American medicine.* New York: Basic Books.

Stiles, W. B., Putnam, S. M., Wolf, M. H., & James, S. A. (1979). Verbal response mode profiles of patients and physicians in medical screening interviews. *Journal of Medical Education, 54*, 81–89.

Stillman, P. L. (1982). Arizona clinical interview medical rating scale. *Medical Teacher, 2*, 248–251.

Stone, G. (1979). Patient compliance and the role of the expert. *Journal of Social Issues, 35*, 34–59.

Street, R., & Wiemann, J. (1987). Patients' satisfaction with physicians' interpersonal involvement, expressiveness, and dominance. *Communication Yearbook, 10*, 591–612. Beverly Hills, CA: Sage.

Templeton, B., & MacDonald, M. (1982). Use of interaction analysis in assessing physician trainees interpersonal skills. In J. Lloyd (Ed.), *Evaluation of Noncognitive Skills and Clinical Performance* (pp. 155–167). Chicago: American Board of Medical Specialties.

Thompson, T. (1984). The invisible helping hand: The role of communication in health and social service professions. *Communication Quarterly, 32*, 148–163.

Thornton, B. (1978). Health care teams and multimethodological research. *Communication Yearbook, 2*, 538–553.

Tubbs, S. L., & Moss, S. (1977). *Human Communication* (2nd ed.). New York: Random House.

Waitzkin, H., & Stoekle, J. (1972). The communication of information about illness. *Advances in Psychosomatic Medicine, 8,* 180–215.

Waitzkin, H., & Stoeckle, J. (1976). Information control and the micropolitics of health care: summary of an ongoing research project. *Social Science and Medicine, 10,* 263–276.

Walker, H. (1973). Communication and the American health care problem. *Journal of Communication, 23,* 349–360.

White, E. (1974). Health and the Black person: An annotated bibliography. *American Journal of Nursing, 74,* 1839–1841.

Wiemann, J. M. (1977). Explication and test of a model of communicative competence. *Human Communication Research, 3,* 195–213.

Wilmington, S. C. (1986). Oral communication instruction for a career in nursing. *Journal of Nursing Education, 25,* 291–294.

Wood, J. T. (1982). Communication and relational culture: Bases for the study of human relationships. *Communication Quarterly, 30,* 2.

• 12 •

What Doth the Future Hold?

CARROLL C. ARNOLD

The study of speech communication has its own history and has earned a significant place in the global world of scholarship. Thinking about our history and our status in 1989, I am struck by the parallel between our profession's development and the stages of learning that Ralph Waldo Emerson (1837/1925) outlined in his "The American Scholar" as the growth pattern of "Man Thinking." Emerson said "The Thinker" first learns from direct contact with nature. As he put it: "Classification begins. To the young mind every thing is individual, stands by itself." Now, it was indeed as a specific phenomenon of nature that the founders of our association wanted to focus study on human speech. Speaking and listening were different from writing and reading, they thought. Oral discourse was different from literary address. The features peculiar to adaptive *oral* communication needed the same kind of special attention that biological phenomena, linguistic behavior, history, and literature received. So, the National Association of Academic Teachers of Public Speaking was created to foster attention to speech as a specific phenomenon of nature.

Almost at once, however, our predecessors moved to explore "the mind of the Past," pursuing what Emerson called "the next great influence into the spirit of the scholar." Until about the time of the Second World War, the dominant foci of research in speech communication were historical conceptions of speech and historic practices in speaking. The immediate necessity was to recover and explain what had already been thought about spoken communication. Since the end of World War II, however, we have labored with growing success in the third of Emerson's

---

The early portion of this essay is adapted from the author's Keynote Address at the Awards Luncheon, Speech Communication Association, Seventy-second Annual Meeting, Chicago, IL, November 14, 1986.

stages of "The Thinker's" development—the domain of action, of expanding human knowledge. In this stage, Emerson said: "The world . . . lies wide around. Its attractions are the keys which unlock my thoughts and make me acquainted with myself. I run eagerly into this resounding tumult. I grasp the hands of those next me, and take my place in the ring to suffer and to work, taught by an instinct that so shall the dumb abyss be vocal with speech. I pierce its order. . . ."

As the essays in this volume attest, in rhetorical theory, history of public discourse, rhetorical criticism, and in the humanistic and social scientific study of human communication, we have built a true scholarly literature on human communication, especially oral. Emergence of that mature, scholarly action in the world of intellect necessarily took time. At the outbreak of World War II, a very short shelf could have held all of the book-length, non-textbook studies produced by people associated with the Speech Communication Association. By the end of the 1940s, *Communication Monographs* had achieved only its tenth single-issue volume. *Communication Education* did not yet exist, nor was there any *Southern Speech Communication Journal*. The *Western Journal of Speech Communication* reached Volume 5 in that decade. The *Central States Speech Journal* began in 1949, and what is now *Communication Quarterly*, the journal of the Eastern Communication Association, was still in the offing. Excellent work was being done in our specialties, but we had not yet joined hands with the world of general scholarship, nor had we summoned the courage or the pride to recognize formally our own colleagues' excellence in research. But the time was ripe for richer, more productive intellectual action.

Quantity of output is not a measure of excellence, of course, but I suggest that progressing from a literature of one thin journal in April of 1915 to a professional literature of two national journals, two regional journals, and a short shelf of specifically scholarly books, and doing it in only some thirty years, was a significant intellectual achievement, yet even this was preparatory.

The way for more original and sophisticated inquiry had been opened. Past thinking about practical communication had needed to be rediscovered and digested. New kinds of academic programs had had to be created. Our handful of founders had to train up a cadre of younger scholars who would be ready to take their places in the ring of academic scholarship. In 1940 only 198 doctorates in speech, drama, and the speech sciences had been awarded. That was hardly a magnificent pool of scholars ready to go into action! Still another generation had to be trained to produce a literature that could stand with, and eventually influence, the many other literatures of scholarship.

After a good bit of hard work in the ring of free and active scholarship, our status in 1989 is strikingly good, thanks in considerable part to the facilitation and stimulation of our national association. Five national, refereed journals are published quarterly by this association. There are two annual SCA yearbooks. We have five refereed, regional journals, and, still more impressively for the point I want to make, there has sprung up an array of distinguished, international, interdisciplinary journals founded and edited, in whole or in part, by active SCA members. I mention specifically *Human Communication Research*, the *Journal of Social and Personal Relationships, Philosophy and Rhetoric*, and *Rhetorica*. They are exclusively scholarly publications. They are internationally read and contributed to. SCA members collaborated with scholars from other fields in founding each. Moreover, as this is written, each has an SCA member as editor or as principal associate editor.

Given my limitations as a student of the social scientific study of human communication, I defer on that subject to observations by Gerald R. Miller concerning the scientific side of our work. Miller is immediate past editor of *Communication Monographs*. In the International Communication Association's *Journal of Communication* for Summer, 1983, Miller wrote:

> In the past decade . . . the critical mass of capable communication researchers has grown dramatically. Colleagues in other fields have developed an awareness of our work and are citing it with increasing frequency in their own journals. Some original theorizing has appeared in our books and journals, and communication research has improved markedly, both in terms of the sophistication and importance of particular studies and in respect to the number of concerted programmatic researches that have extensively probed a particular problem area. . . . It does not seem unduly optimistic to express pride in the progress achieved thus far and to look forward to the future with a confident eye.

Miller's audience for those words was the membership of the International Communication Association, but that is an organization spun off from SCA, and, furthermore, a large portion of the work Miller was referring to came from people who identify with both SCA and ICA.

The quality and general recognition of other kinds of research is at least equally gratifying. Do scholars affiliated with other fields of study seek us as audience and our learned journals as vehicles for communication to the world of scholarship? Indeed they do. Of authors contributing to *The Quarterly Journal of Speech* in the year 1979, to the final 1985 issue, and to the first three 1986 issues, one-fourth to one-third of the authors were affiliated with scholarly disciplines other than our own. English, political science, and history were the most numerous outside affiliations, but biology, sociology, and law were also represented. Clearly, other scholars than ourselves think our readership is worth addressing.

As I have said, a short shelf would have held the book-length, non-textbook studies in speech communication in the 1940s, but it would be a major project to assemble the full list of such works existing in the late 1980s. I have not undertaken that project. Rather, I have settled for a little survey of my own private shelves. My books tend to deal with rhetorical theory, history, criticism, and philosophy, and I do not buy absolutely everything published along those lines. My sample is therefore *very* restricted. To make my survey still more severe, I excluded from my count all textbooks, all collections of essays, and all works with more than two authors, no matter how scholarly the works were. Despite all of those restrictions, I find that I possess thirty-five single- or double-authored, book-length, scholarly studies written by dues-paying members of SCA. Only four of these books were published before 1940; thirty-one were published after 1940, and the majority of all the works appeared after 1960. Are these books any good? Indeed they are. At least half are viewed as standards or classics of their kinds and are cited as sources in humanistic studies generally. My accounting excluded such fine, multi-authored, scholarly works as Auer's *Antislavery and Disunion,* Bowers and my *Handbook of Rhetorical and Communication Theory,* Sidney Kraus's *The Great Debates,* and other distinguished volumes. Neither does my accounting include any of the excellent *scientific* studies our members have written or contributed to. In my view, what has been accomplished by SCA scholars in just my little corner of SCA interests is impressive, even when taken by itself. So one judgment of our intellectual maturity is that our general scholarly record, especially in the past two and a half decades, has been qualitatively and quantitatively very much to our credit.

There is another standard by which we can measure our attainments. Are we grasping the hands of those next to us in the global world of scholarly inquiry? Yes indeed. I have mentioned four of the several international, interdisciplinary journals in which our members regularly associate with international scholars of other academic disciplines. Moreover, it was through our literature and our departments that such scholars from other countries as Chaim Perelman, Samuel Ijsseling, and Stephen Toulmin, to name only three, were brought to the general attention of American scholars.

On the same point of our role in international scholarship, a number us are members and leaders in the International Society for the History of Rhetoric, in the World Communication Association, and in the International Communication Association. Another specific instance: At the First International Conference on Argumentation, sponsored by the Faculty of Arts of the University of Amsterdam, more than 300 scholars from twenty-one countries gathered to discuss theory of argument. More than two dozen SCA members appeared on the program of that first conference, and many have continued to contribute to later conferences, now held annually.

These are but instances of the many ways in which our scholars have firmly joined hands with others in the broad world of interdisciplinary, scholarly work. The old complaint that no one knows or cares about what we do simply does not apply any more. To use Emerson's phrase, we individually and collectively "run eagerly into this resounding tumult" of international scholarship. Social scientist, humanist, artist—we have taken our places in the work of the intellectual world. To paraphrase the memorable words of the late John Houseman in his commercials on behalf of the Smith, Barney investment firm: We *earned* it.

The seventy-fifth anniversary of the Speech Communication Association happens to coincide with the fiftieth year of my membership in that order. A thought about the major change I have observed in that half-century will give context to my speculations about the future. Fifty years ago, the term that guided most of our teaching and research was *speech*. Today, *speech* is being changed from a field-defining *noun* to—at most— a field-modifying *adjective*. *Communication* is increasingly the noun that specifies the range of our professional activity. That shift of emphasis does not better enable us to distinguish ourselves from, say, mass media specialists, journalists, specialists in dramatic art, acousticians, speech pathologists, or teachers of writing, but the change is being made, and facts are stubborn things. We might, perhaps, have evolved a discipline of exploring the nature and implications of *oral* communication, but we did not, and it appears that we are unlikely to do so in the near term.

The Speech Communication Association is an umbrella organization within which varied subdisciplines associate for convenience and for promotion of shared professional goals. SCA exists to serve, and I think will continue to serve, any and all persons specially interested in nonprint communication who enjoy each other's professional company. We have been and continue to be an association of teacher-scholars joined together for intellectual and for academically political rather than disciplinary reasons. SCA's continued growth, especially in the most recent decade, suggests that this is reason enough to justify an organization such as ours. Whether this is or is not the most desirable destiny imaginable for the next quarter-century, nothing in the winds at present suggests a significant change of course.

It appears to me that some important challenges lie in the future of virtually all of our subdisciplines. The challenges I have in mind are products of a growing distrust of linear, mechanical conceptions of communication, of Western culture's general abandonment of positivism as philosophy, and of the global nature of our interests as expressed in key terms like *communication* and *rhetoric.*

A growing consensus among scholars is that perhaps the single, most pressing challenge is to find ways of understanding and studying human communication as a highly complex, *interactive* process. Commenting recently on the historical record of empirical research on persuasion, Miller, Burgoon, and Burgoon (1984) concluded that far too little of that research had viewed "all parties to a persuasive transaction as *changeable* and *interactive.*" Instead, they said, most research had been carried out "conceiving of persuasion as a process whereby the persuader(s) *act* and the targets *react*" (p. 456). In a comparable review of empirical research on communication in small groups, Gouran (1985, p. 108) concluded that "until those designing studies begin reflecting more thoughtfully on the ways in which all classes of variables affecting group processes are *interconnected,* the prospects for accumulating integratable knowledge will remain more a hope than a reality" (my emphasis). We face many problems in conceptualizing human communication as *interplay* of forces with *variable* consequences for different, individual, *situated* persons, and those problems call for reexamination of the most basic concepts used in our scholarship, empirical or qualitative.

In a symposium on the conception of *audience* in the September 1988 issue of *Critical Studies in Mass Communication,* James Lull (1988, p. 242) wrote: "Documenting increasingly complex audience activity is one of the major challenges that we have in media studies. . . . Social science long ago abandoned any 'simple causal model,' and we have learned that even the most elegant and sophisticated multivariate statistical assessments are unable to describe well the rich and revealing domain of audiences. In my view, qualitative empirical research and rule-based communication theory hold the greatest promise for understanding audiences better." And Kathleen Newman (1988, p. 243) wrote in the same issue: "It is easy to see that audiences of electronic communications, though an obvious first formulation, can too quickly be considered a unitary mass rather than, to borrow an older term, an ensemble of serial and contradictory subject positions."

How do we meet this challenge of more accurately conceptualizing the phenomena we study? Revisions in how we formulate research questions and engage them will be needed. Such revisions are already under way. As "qualitative empirical research," Lull recommended ethnographic study of audiences. Others have also recommended ethnographical and anthropological inquiries as models for arriving at inclusive descriptions and theories concerning the operations and effects of the multivariate processes that constitute human communication. In his essay "Stalking Interpersonal Communication Effectiveness," William Rawlins (1985) recognized similar conceptual problems. He pointed in a slightly different direction for their solutions. He said, "The emerging formulation [for analyzing interpersonal communication] involves a rhetoric of conversation which blends ancient principles with modern predicaments" (p. 129). Exactly what this rhetoric will be and how it can be stated remains unclear, but struggling toward some such articulation of what *situated* communication is and how it works seems to me the most important item on our profession's general agenda for future inquiry.

Whether we think of studies of media, persuasion, small-group communication, informal interpersonal communication, or formal public communication, our problem is to conceptualize communicative *processes* so that *interplaying* and constantly changing situational and personal forces are included within the concept. The call is for nonlinear descriptions. Descriptions and analyses based on the source-channel-receiver model inherited from S-R psychology and information theory have not yielded sufficiently integrative explanations of naturalistic communication. We are, collectively, uncertain about how an accurate and encompassing conceptualization of those processes is to be built. The problem has been clearly identified; solving it is a concern for all of the subdisciplines in our field. Happily, in a number of our subdisciplines, experiments are being made to collect and interpret data in ways that truly recognize and try to capture the dynamic, situated complexities inherent in any and all symbolic practices.

At its root, our problem seems a philosophical one. Calvin O. Schrag (1985), a phenomenological philosopher, addressed it in discussing what he termed "the contemporary hermeneutical turn in rhetoric." Schrag said:

> In his reading of Aristotle, Heidegger directs our attention to the impor-
> tance of the role of the human affects in their binding of self and other,
> rhetor and interlocutor, in their collaborative being with one another. The
> rhetorical event achieves its directedness to the other through the play of
> affects. Clearly affects here are not data for psychology. They are not
> isolated and objectivised mental states. They are intentional vectors of
> discourse, making manifest the meaning of self and other as they interface
> with the *polis*. Affectivity is a hermeneutical gestalt of concern in which
> the situated affects (pity, fear, trust, sympathy, love, anger, shame, etc.)
> comport a precognitive intentionality that discloses various textures of
> intersubjectivity. Admittedly, these affects can be abstracted from their
> world-engaging operations and rendered into objectified data for scientific
> analysis; however, in the performance of such abstraction and objectifica-
> tion, one should not lose sight of their function and role in the speech and
> action of everyday life. (p. 171)

Schrag continued:

> What is at issue here is a shift from epistemological space as a system of
> beliefs and propositions to the broader and more vibrant hermeneutical
> space of affect-imbued and praxis-oriented engagements. . . . What is
> displaced is the philosophically incoherent pursuit of "knowledge of knowl-
> edge" and the sublation of beliefs and knowledge into a theory of justifica-
> tion and cognitive representation. Beliefs and knowledge are reclaimed as
> inhabitants of the terrain of praxis and take their place among the citizenry
> of affects, habits, skills, and institutional practices, with which they
> commingle in the adventure of making sense together. (pp. 171–172)

Schrag and Lull both recommend that we follow enthnographical/ anthropological patterns of inquiry. In this they echo the general advice of Goodall's essay in this volume. Rawlins' claim that we must construct the *rhetoric* of conversation is compatible with the ethnographic recom- mendations. What is basically urged by all those whom I have cited and that is being attempted in a good deal of current research is that we extract from *naturalistic* data the relational-affective evidence that is there, and begin our theory building from *that* evidence rather than from premises of formal logic, positivistic scientific method, or other a priori assumptions about the nature of the human world. No agenda item for the future could be more basic.

What kind of thinking is being urged by these authors? Eugene E. White (n. d.), a rhetorician-historian, offers an example of assumptions embedded in such thinking when he calls for *configurational* analysis of public persuasion:

> The gestalt of communication is never static. This is the first thing we must recognize about it—hence my use and special meaning for "configuration."
>
> Any persuasive experience is a dynamic, cyclical flow of antecedents-events-consequences that, in the course of developing, encompasses not only the particular piece(s) of persuasion . . . but also all other successful and abortive attempts at modification [that are relevant to the urgency or exigence being dealt with]. The second thing we must understand about the gestalt of communication is that any persuasive experience consists of certain identifiable and regularized forces that, through their configured interplay, produce the relationship of the communication(s) with the rest of the configuration, including the cause for the communication, the context and thrust of the communication as a modifying force, and the consequences of the communication. (White, unpublished ms.)

It is in this general direction that new, encompassing thought about communicative occurrences must continue. In reviewing James Boyd White's *Heracles' Bow: Essays on the Rhetoric and Practice of the Law* , Robert L Scott (1986) wrote, "A major task for post-modern rhetoric may be to reconceptualize the relationships implied in [the concepts] speaker and audience" (p. 475). It appears to me that such reconceptualization is an obligation not just of rhetoricians but of empiricists, media specialists, pedagogues, interpreters of literature, theorists of argumentation, and all others among us.

I turn next to a few more specific but related issues that are on our agenda for the next decade or two. They, too, have largely to do with *conceptions* of communicative processes and with definitions of key terms we seem to require. *Mediation* of communication is, or should be, a matter of the most serious and immediate concern. Kaplan, in this volume, highlights some of the technological-social consequences of variously mediated mass communication. There are pragmatic problems to be addressed. As Kaplan indicates, we now communicate through the various media of mass communication, through computer networks, by means of facsimile messages, and so on. An eminently practical question is: What do these different media *do* to messages, to message makers, and to consumers of messages? More broadly put, the question is: How does a medium alter, block out, intensify, or otherwise affect *such and such* a kind of message, for a particular kind of situated message maker and for a given kind of listener-viewer? Subsidiary questions ask about *whether* and *how,* say, face-to-face, or exclusively auditory, or televised and/or filmic messages are perceived differently by different kinds of situated consumers; about *how* and *to what extent* various types of messages are screened or skewed when mediated through this or that communicative medium; about what happens to communicative *relationships* when this or that medium is used. To illustrate, I recall that in a convention paper a few years ago, Jim Chesbro suggested that it would be useful to probe what happens to human relationships in computer networking, where one communicator cannot interrupt another communicator's message as it appears on the computer screen. The problems of *process* and of *effects* are this detailed. To illustrate further, we have sketchy and largely intuitive notions that some kinds of messages (say, instructions) are more effectively communicated in writing than orally, but we say that face-to-face communication is most persuasive, telephonic communication is next best, and written communication is near or at the bottom of the list of persuasive modes. But just *why* are these things so, if they are true? Such questions are pragmatically very important as we try to work out specific principles of effectiveness that apply in varied circumstances. And we should notice that these questions—especially the more detailed ones—are open to empirical analysis as well as to the sort of philosophical analysis urged by Schrag.

Problems for our intellectual agenda also arise because we have abandoned older ways of thinking. Like other kinds of scholars, we have pretty much put aside belief in "traits" and in such images of influence as are provided by unqualified S-R models of communicative experience. That has by no means simplified our work. Let me cite just a few basic notions that require more detailed analysis than they have yet been given. Our understanding of *communicative competence* has not yet been rounded out, as the controversial issues discussed by Rebecca Rubin clearly show. *Rhetorical sensitivity* seems a very inviting concept, but just what it alludes to *as experience* has not been settled. *Empathy* has returned to our vocabulary after long exile by radical behaviorists, but just what do we now *mean* by "empathy"? In their chapter on interpersonal communication, Hewes, Planalp, Roloff, and Seibold address this question when they focus on understanding and adapting to communicative partners as prerequisites to impact, influence, and consideration.

We shall probably never define *metaphor* in a final way, but the nature and function of metaphoric thinking and other modes of informal reasoning deserve continued attention. Various people, including our colleagues Michael Osborn, William Owen, and Ernest Bormann, have interestingly discussed the suggestive functions of metaphors, analogies, and related informal structures of thought. But how do metaphors *mean* in different *kinds* of *interactions?* So far metaphors have been explored chiefly as recurring linguistic phenomena with *general* suggestive potentialities. Yet, metaphors and other informal forms doubtless persuade differently under different circumstances and with as yet unexplored consequences for the *rest* of interactive thinking.

In his essay "Rhetorical Depiction," Michael Osborn (1986) discusses the still broader concept, *depiction,* which, he suggests, "may eventually prove to be one of those archetectonic concepts that can reorder our conception of rhetoric itself" (p. 99). But let us keep in mind that Miller, Burgoon, and Burgoon (1984) insist that whoever investigates persuasion "should involve themselves more heavily in issues associated with *reciprocal* influence," and not think of persuasion as "linear and unidirectional." They urge "more attention to persuasion as a person-centered rather than an action- or issue-centered activity" (p. 456). If we follow those leads, a major task is to discover how and why metaphorical or depictive or any other informally rational language gets *shared* in various kinds of communicative situations.

I take just one more crucial conception we must further clarify. Rhetoric was defined in the broadest way at the Wingspread and Pheasant Run conferences (Bitzer & Black, 1971), but what we mean and do not mean by *rhetoric* or *rhetorics* will need reinspection if *communication* becomes the defining term of our profession. Is there *any* kind of communication that is *not* rhetorical? If, as Meyer claims (1986, p. 118), "all discourse, from the simple phrase to the great text, can thus assure a priori the double function of language, *viz.,*, to treat the problems posed therein by proposing their solution or by expressing their nature," must we set ourselves up as expert explainers of *all* phrases, clauses, and sentences in the world? I think most of us would prefer some narrower purview and field of endeavor, but what? Defining our boundaries in a way that allows focused scholarship is an urgency of the first order.

As most readers of this volume will know, an excellent series of books on the rhetorics of various academic disciplines/practices is being published by the University of Wisconsin Press. The authors and editors of those books are not communication specialists in our sense of that term; they are recognized scholars in other disciplines: economics, law, sociology, political science, and the like.

Three of these books were reviewed in the November 1986 issue of *The Quarterly Journal of Speech.* They were *The Rhetoric of Economics* by Donald N. McCloskey (reviewed by Arjo Klamer, an economist); *Lying Down Together: Law, Metaphor, and Theology,* by Milner S. Ball (reviewed by Robert Ivie); and *Heracles' Bow: Essays on the Rhetoric and Poetics of the Law,* by James Boyd White (reviewed by Robert L. Scott). Another book in the same series addresses problems we struggle with even more directly. It is *The Rhetoric of the Human Sciences,* edited by John S. Nelson, Allan Megill, and Donald N. McCloskey. Reviewers of all four books found that they suggested pertinent problems that need our sustained attention:

> One noteworthy limitation of McCloskey's treatise is that while he identifies and highlights rhetorical devices in economics, he refrains from exploring what certain figures of speech do, and why they dominate. . . . Rhetorical devices tend to favor one method of argument over another. (Klamer, 1986, p. 471)

> Ball's analysis of law as metaphor is undoubtedly worthy of close inspection by speech communication scholars. . . . The dialogue it initiates across disciplines should prove rewarding for everyone who chooses to become involved. (Ivie, 1986, p. 473)

> White returns repeatedly to the idea that rhetoric is constitutive. We are nothing without culture and in turn we *make* as well as are made by culture. What we are given by culture is our "characters" and the constant task of understanding ourselves and others. Rhetoric is a chief instrument (if not *the* chief instrument) in our reflexive and never completed struggle. (Scott, 1986, p. 475)

I (Arnold, in press) reviewed *The Rhetoric of the Human Sciences* for *Philosophy and Rhetoric,* and I was especially intrigued by John S. Nelson's essay "Seven Rhetorics of Inquiry." In that essay, Nelson confronts the pervasive problem of what is "reasonable" or "logical" in communicating knowledge. Nelson contends that "logic" is "pluralized" in inquiry, and that the "logical" principles of poetics, tropics, dialectics, hermeneutics, ethics, and epistemology *all* operate in rhetoric associated with inquiry— by which he means any professional analysis in any field.

These four contemporary volumes were all motivated in one way or another by perplexities concerning how we should conceptualize logic and style in practical communication and concerning what enables such communication to be at once expressive of points of view, persuasive among interacting *persons,* and thereby *constitutive* of lives, immediate circumstances, and culture. In our recently rather muted debates about whether and how discourse is *epistemic ,* our profession has also addressed these fundamental problems of what discourse *does* and *how,* to *whom, situationally.* The contemporary necessity seems clear. Whether empiricist or humanist, our professionals need to give these fundamental issues high priority in the next decades. Having shed the linear, mechanistic, positivistic, sender-receiver image of human communication, we need further to examine afresh how we ought to conceive of "reasonableness" within our present image of human communication as *situated* interpersonal and even cultural *interaction.*

Beginnings have been made. I cite a few among rhetorical studies familiar to me. Michael Calvin McGee and John R. Lyne have suggested some propositions they say are implicit in "the 'common sense' behind the political practice of American voters" (1987, p. 399). These include such propositions as: "Personal qualities in politics ought to be more important than the technical competence of reasoned discourse," and "Though governments ought to act so as to respect the rights of individual citizens, social order must be maintained." These kinds of implicit propositions, say McGee and Lyne, make up some of the "logic" of political communicative interaction in America, and they

> need to be taken seriously, and their power understood. This power is not adequately depicted, we believe, by the metaphor of conversation, which carries with it an implication that one might simply withdraw from talk that fails to meet one's expectations of it. . . . If academics "image" themselves in such a way as to make it easy freely to select pleasing interlocutors, they will have resigned themselves to the charge that what they do is *merely* talk, and they will have cut themselves off in yet another way from the broader audience that willy-nilly conceives of scholars as "the experts" (p. 400).

What is being said in such studies as I have cited asserts that the informal and implicit "logics" and "figurations" in discourse are always parts of *the argument that all discourse is*—parts of "an ensemble of serial and contradictory subject positions," to borrow Kathleen Newman's phrase. In his *Human Communication as Narration* Walter R. Fisher (1987) contends that *all* human communication is subject to the informal tests of a "narrational logic": to be reasonable, discourse must be consistent with other "stories" that communicatees know, and it must *cohere* as an account of an imaginal or a "real" world. Beyond this "logic," Fisher argues, we later learn and add other formal and informal, situationally relevant, tests.

Parts of the logical ensemble are field-dependent, as McGee and Lyne imply. By the time this book is published, *A Rhetoric of Science* by Lawrence J. Prelli will probably also be available. In that book Prelli asks the question: If we can no longer make scientific claims with the certainty of logical positivists, what *is* the nature of the reasoning that legitimizes claims as "scientific"? His answer is, in part, that the special logic of science is "a topical logic" inculcated by education in "the scientific method." It establishes such informal, communally agreed-upon, logical criteria as that a scientific claim must rest on *accurate* supporting evidence, must be offered by *disinterested* claimants, must be *consistent* with received knowledge and theory, and so on. Like McGee and Lyne, Prelli insists that human discourse is rendered "reasonable" by its conformity to "logical tests," but that diverse logical tests are established and "authorized" by various self-identifying *communities*. In Fisher's terms, these are special logics we *learn* through life, education, and specialization and that we add to the basic "narrational logic" we learned in childhood.

Each of the scholars I have cited is contending that the *logic* that renders communication *reasonable* is largely informal, sometimes merely suggestive as in depiction and metaphor, but sometimes rigorous as in science, and that *what* logic is relevant in a given situation is determined by received and agreed-upon values held by the situated audiences to whom discourse is addressed. Thrusts in this direction are beginning to identify some of the forces and processes that allow human communication to *constitute* interrelated selves, even as those selves at the same time *constitute* colleective experience of and with others.

I have been saying in several different ways that as the twentieth century draws to a close, students of human communication find themselves living in a new intellectual world. Old definitions and old ways of explaining how and why communication affects us have proved inadequate to our needs. Push-pull notions of human affect no longer satisfy empiricists or humanists. Terms that heretofore seemed almost self-explanatory (e.g., communication, competence, audience, empathy) prove more complex than we have supposed, and they must be explored and explained anew if we are to understand ourselves and our communicative experiences. As Stuart Kaplan's essay and others in this volume attest, new technologies, new research strategies, new modes of analyzing isolated bits of communication have already evolved and will continue to evolve. In such evolving circumstances, *what we are talking about when we mouth such terms as "communication," "rhetoric," and "persuasion"* is the most fundamental thing we must clarify in the decade(s) ahead. Our critical question has become: What *is* the nature of an *interactive experiencing* of communication? We ought to rejoice at finding ourselves confronted by such truly intriguing and fundamental questions rather than by merely incidental queries.

References

Arnold, C. C. (in press). [Review of J. S. Nelson, A. Mcgill, and D. N. McCloskey (Eds.), *The rhetoric of the human sciences: Language and argument in scholarship and public affairs.*] *Philosophy and Rhetoric.*

Bitzer, L. F., & Black, E. (Eds.) (1970). *The prospect of rhetoric.* Englewood Cliffs, NJ: Prentice-Hall. See especially the "Report of the committee on the scope of rhetoric and the place of rhetorical studies in higher education," pp. 208–219.

Emerson, R. W. (1925). The American scholar. In N. Foerster & R. M. Lovett (Eds.), *American poetry and prose,* pp. 380–389. Boston: Houghton Mifflin. (Originally delivered as the Phi Beta Kappa oration at Cambridge, MA, 31 August 1837.)

Fisher, W. R. (1987), *Human communication as narration: Toward a philosophy of reason, value, and action.* Columbia, SC: University of South Carolina Press.

Gouran, D. S. (1985). The paradigm of unfulfilled promise: A critical examination of the history of research on small groups in speech communication. In T. W. Benson (Ed.), *Speech communication in the 20th century,* pp. 90–108. Carbondale, IL: Southern Illinois University Press.

Ivie, R. I. (1986, November). [Review of M. S. Ball, *Lying down together: Law, metaphor, and theology.*] *Quarterly Journal of Speech, 72,* 472–473.

Klamer, Arjo. (1986, November). [Review of D. N. McCloskey, *The rhetoric of economics.*] *Quarterly Journal of Speech, 72,* 469–472.

Lull, J. (1988, September). Critical response: The audience as nuisance. *Critical Studies in Mass Communication, 5,* 239–243.

McGee, M. C., & Lyne, J. R. (1987). What are nice folks like you doing in a place like this? Some entailments of treating knowledge claims rhetorically. In J. S. Nelson, A. Megill, & D. N. McCloskey (Eds.), *The rhetoric of the human sciences* (pp. 381–406). Madison, WI: University of Wisconsin Press.

Meyer, M. (1986). *From logic to rhetoric.* Amsterdam: John Benjamins.

Miller, G. R. (1983, Summer). Taking stock of a discipline. *Journal of Communication, 33,* 41.

Miller, G. R., Burgoon, M., & Burgoon, J. K. (1984). The function of human communication in changing attitudes and gaining compliance. In C. C. Arnold & J. W. Bowers (Eds.), *Handbook of rhetorical and communication theory* (pp. 400–474). Boston: Allyn & Bacon.

Nelson, J. S. (1987). Seven rhetorics of inquiry: A provocation. In J. S. Nelson, A. Megill, & D. N. McCloskey (Eds.). *The rhetoric of the human sciences* (pp. 407–434). Madison, WI: University of Wisconsin Press.

Nelson, J. S., A. Megill, & D. N. McCloskey (Eds.). *The rhetoric of the human sciences: Language and argument in scholarship and public affairs.* Madison, WI: University of Wisconsin Press.

Newman, K. (1988, September). Critical response: On openings and closings. *Critical Studies in Mass Communication, 5*, 243–246.

Osborn, M. (1986). Rhetorical depiction. In H. W. Simons & A. A. Aghazarian (Eds.), *Form, genre, and the study of political discourse* (pp. 79–107). Columbia, SC: University of South Carolina Press.

Rawlins, W. K. (1985). Stalking interpersonal communication effectiveness: Social, individual, or situational integration? In T. W. Benson (Ed.), *Speech communication in the 20th century* (pp. 109–129). Carbondale, IL: Southern Illinois University Press.

Schrag, C. O. (1985, May). Rhetoric resituated at the end of philosophy. *Quarterly Journal of Speech, 71*, 164–174.

Scott, R. L. (1986, November). [Review of J. B. White, *Heracles' bow: Essays on the rhetoric and poetics of the law.*] *Quarterly Journal of Speech, 72*, 473–475.

White, E. E. (n.d.). Configurational criticism of rhetorical discourse (unpublished manuscript).

Notes on Contributors

Notes on Contributors

CARROLL C. ARNOLD (Ph.D., University of Iowa, 1942) is Professor Emeritus of Speech Communication at The Pennsylvania State University and is Editor of Rhetoric/Communication, a series published by University of South Carolina Press.

STEPHEN H. BROWNE is Assistant Professor of Speech Communication at The Pennsylvania State University. His research focuses on rhetorical practices in the eighteenth century.

RICHARD A. CHERWITZ is Associate Professor and Director of Graduate Studies in the Department of Speech Communication at the University of Texas at Austin. He specializes in rhetorical theory and argumentation and is co-author of *Communication and Knowledge: An Investigation in Rhetorical Epistemology* and editor of *Philosophical Perspectives on Rhetoric* (in press).

SONJA K. FOSS earned her Ph.D. in communication studies from Northwestern University and is currently Associate Professor of Speech at the University of Oregon. Her work in rhetorical criticism includes *Rhetorical Criticism: Exploration and Practice* and numerous articles on the theory and practice of criticism. Her other research and teaching interests include contemporary rhetorical theory, feminist approaches to communication research, and visual images as rhetoric.

H. L. GOODALL, JR. (Ph.D. The Pennsylvania State University, 1980) is Associate Professor of Communication at The University of Utah. His research focuses on interpretive understandings of groups, organizations, and communities. In addition to articles published in learned journals, he has authored or co-authored eight books, the most recent of which is *Casing a Promised Land: The Autobiography of an Organizational Detective as Cultural Ethnographer*.

DENNIS S. GOURAN is Professor and Head in the Department of Speech Communication at The Pennsylvania State University. He is the author of two books and numerous articles dealing with decision making in groups. In 1988, he was elected Second Vice President of the Speech Communication Association.

DEAN E. HEWES (Ph.D., Florida State University, 1974) is Professor of Speech-Communication at the University of Minnesota. His research interests include interpersonal communication, group decision making, the cognitive bases of communication, rumor and gossip, research methodology, and fishing for bass in heavy moss.

MARY FRANCES HOPKINS, Professor and Chairperson of the Department of Speech Communication, Theatre, and Communication Disorders at Louisiana State University, is former editor of *Literature in Performance* and has served on the editorial boards of *Communication Education, Southern Journal of Speech Communication,* and *Text and Performance Quarterly.* Her articles on the rhetoric of performance and on narrative fiction have appeared in national and regional journals as well as in book-length collections. Her current research focuses on the rhetoric of narrative discourse.

ROBERT S. ILTIS is Assistant Professor of Speech Communication at Texas Tech University. Professor Iltis is interested in public address, past and present, in the South.

PETER E. KANE is Director of Graduate Studies and Professor of Communication at the State University of New York, College at Brockport. He is the chair of the Speech Communication Association's Commission on Freedom of Speech, an associate editor of the SCA's *Free Speech Yearbook,* and has served as the editor of both *Free Speech* and the *Free Speech Yearbook.* He is the author of *Murder, Courts, and the Press: Issues in Free Press/Fair Trial.*

STUART J. KAPLAN is Associate Professor of Communications at Lewis & Clark College. His articles on source credibility, television programming, and new communication technology have appeared in several professional journals. He chaired the Cable Regulatory Commission, Portland, Oregon, from 1985 to 1988.

GARY L. KREPS (Ph.D., University of Southern California, 1979) is Associate Professor, Director of Graduate Studies, and Coordinator of the Corporate Communication Resources Network of the Department of Communication Studies, Northern Illinois University, where he was elected to membership in the Gerontology Program Faculty. His research focuses on the role of information in health care and human organization. He was selected as a Senior Research Fellow at the National Cancer Institute (1985–1986), helping to frame national policy for disseminating cancer information, and as a Fulbright International Colloquium Speaker on "Communication, Health, and the Elderly" at the University of Wales (1988). He is founding chair of the SCA Commission on Health Communication, chair of the SCA Organizational Communication Division, and vice-chair of the ICA Health Communication Division. He also served as chair of both the SCA Commission on Communication and Aging and the ECA Health Communication Interest Group. He is the author of many articles and several books, including *Health Communication* (with Barbara C. Thornton) and *Organizational Communication*.

BEVERLY WHITAKER LONG is Professor and Chairperson of the Department of Speech Communication at the University of North Carolina at Chapel Hill. She has published books and articles about performance theory, criticism, and pedagogy. Her current research focuses on contemporary value theory, on performance criticism, and on the intertextual relations of poetry and painting. She has been a member of the editorial boards of *Speech Monographs, Speech Teacher,* and *Communication Education*. She is the founding editor of *Literature in Performance* (now *Text and Performance Quarterly*), and she served as president of the Southern Speech Communication Association.

GERALD M. PHILLIPS (Ph.D., Case/Western Reserve University, 1956) has been Professor of Speech Communication at The Pennsylvania State University since 1964. He is author of 33 books and more than 100 articles and monographs. His research specialty is shy performance behavior. Currently, he is working on artificial intelligence programs designed to facilitate oral performance by rhetorically deficient communicators.

SALLY PLANALP (Ph.D., University of Wisconsin, 1983) is Assistant Professor of Communication at the University of Colorado-Boulder. Her research interests include personal relationships, discourse processing, social cognition, and emotion.

JIM L. QUERY, JR. (M.A., Ohio University), is a Ph.D. candidate in the School of Interpersonal Communication at Ohio University. His research focuses on the communication of social support, communication in health care, and organizational communication. He received the Outstanding Masters Student Award from the School of Interpersonal Communication at Ohio University in 1986. He also served as a Student Research Fellow at the National Cancer Institute, conducting research on the dissemination of cancer information (Summer, 1986). An article based upon his master's thesis has been accepted for publication in the new journal *Health Communication*.

MICHAEL E. ROLOFF (Ph.D., Michigan State University, 1975) is Professor of Communication Studies at Northwestern University. His research interests include social exchange within intimate relationships, persuasion, interpersonal conflict resolution, and bargaining and negotiation.

REBECCA B. RUBIN is Professor of Speech Communication at Kent State University. She has published articles on communication competence, interpersonal communication, and personal and mediated communication in several journals, and she has written or edited several books, including *The Communication Competency Assesssment Instrument: Rating Book and Technical Manual, Assessing Speaking and Listening Skills, Communication Research: Strategies and Sources,* and *The Road Trip: An Interpersonal Adventure.*

DAVID R. SEIBOLD (Ph.D., Michigan State University, 1975) is Professor of Speech Communication at the University of Illinois, Urbana-Champaign. His research interests include attribution theory, interpersonal influence processes, group decision making, health communication, and program evaluation methods.

MARY S. STRINE, Professor of Communication at the University of Utah, has published widely in the area of interpretive and critical studies. Her recent articles on modern critical theory, the rhetoric of cultural forms, and the relationship between American literature and culture have appeared in various national and regional journals as well as book-length collections. Her current research focuses on the communicative practices of interpretive communities and on the cultural authority of aesthetic forms of communication. She has served or is currently serving on the editorial boards of several professional journals.

JOHN THEOBALD-OSBORNE is a lecturer in media criticism at California State University at Sacramento. He is Ph.D. candidate in rhetoric in the Speech Communication Department of the University of Texas. His research interests include theories of media, rhetorical effects, and the relationship between forms of communication and the outcomes of democratic processes.

JULIA T. WOOD (Ph.D., Pennsylvania State University, 1975) has been a member of the Department of Speech Communication at the University of North Carolina since 1975. She conducts research and teaches graduate and undergraduate courses in interpersonal communication and communication and gender. In the course of her academic career she has co-edited one prior book, authored or co-authored three other books, five chapters of books, and published over thirty articles.